A CULTURAL HISTORY OF THE EMOTIONS

VOLUME 1

A Cultural History of the Emotions
General Editors: Susan Broomhall, Jane W. Davidson, and Andrew Lynch

Volume 1
A Cultural History of the Emotions in Antiquity
Edited by Douglas Cairns

Volume 2
A Cultural History of the Emotions in the Medieval Age
Edited by Juanita Ruys and Clare Monagle

Volume 3
A Cultural History of the Emotions in the Late Medieval, Reformation, and Renaissance Age
Edited by Andrew Lynch and Susan Broomhall

Volume 4
A Cultural History of the Emotions in the Baroque and Enlightenment Age
Edited by Claire Walker, Katie Barclay, and David Lemmings

Volume 5
A Cultural History of the Emotions in the Age of Romanticism, Revolution, and Empire
Edited by Susan J. Matt

Volume 6
A Cultural History of the Emotions in the Modern and Post-Modern Age
Edited by Jane W. Davidson and Joy Damousi

A CULTURAL HISTORY OF THE EMOTIONS
IN ANTIQUITY

Edited by Douglas Cairns

BLOOMSBURY ACADEMIC

Bloomsbury Publishing Plc, 50 Bedford Square, London, WC1B 3DP, UK
Bloomsbury Publishing Inc, 1359 Broadway, New York, NY 10018, USA
Bloomsbury Publishing Ireland, 29 Earlsfort Terrace, Dublin 2, D02 AY28, Ireland

BLOOMSBURY and the Diana logo are trademarks of Bloomsbury Publishing Plc

First published in Great Britain 2019
This edition published in Great Britain, 2022

Copyright © Bloomsbury Publishing, 2019

Douglas Cairns has asserted their right under the Copyright, Designs and Patents Act, 1988, to be identified as Editor of this work.

Cover image: The Sacrifice of Iphigenia, from the House of the Tragic Poet, Pompeii, 4th decorative style, *c.* 30 CE (fresco), Roman, (1st century)/Museo Archeologico Nazionale, Naples, Italy/Bridgeman Images

All rights reserved. No part of this publication may be: i) reproduced or transmitted in any form, electronic or mechanical, including photocopying, recording or by means of any information storage or retrieval system without prior permission in writing from the publishers; or ii) used or reproduced in any way for the training, development or operation of artificial intelligence (AI) technologies, including generative AI technologies. The rights holders expressly reserve this publication from the text and data mining exception as per Article 4(3) of the Digital Single Market Directive (EU) 2019/790.

A catalogue record for this book is available from the British Library.

A catalog record for this book is available from the Library of Congress.

ISBN: HB: 978-1-4725-3580-1
       PB: 978-1-3503-4497-6
       Set 978-1-3503-4769-4

Series: The Cultural Histories Series

Typeset by RefineCatch Limited, Bungay, Suffolk

For product safety related questions contact productsafety@bloomsbury.com.

To find out more about our authors and books visit www.bloomsbury.com and sign up for our newsletters.

CONTENTS

LIST OF ILLUSTRATIONS		vi
GENERAL EDITORS' PREFACE		xi
	Introduction: Emotion History and the Classics Douglas Cairns	1
1	Medical and Scientific Understandings George Kazantzidis	17
2	Religion and Spirituality F. S. Naiden	35
3	Music and Dance Eleonora Rocconi	47
4	Drama David Konstan	63
5	The Visual Arts Viktoria Räuchle	83
6	Literature Ruth Scodel and Ruth R. Caston	109
7	In Private: The Individual and the Domestic Community Lin Foxhall	125
8	In Public: Collectivities and Polities Angelos Chaniotis and Catherine Steel	147
NOTES ON CONTRIBUTORS		163
NOTES		167
REFERENCES		185
INDEX		215

ILLUSTRATIONS

CHAPTER 1

1.1 Portrait of Hippocrates holding his *Apophthegms*. Fourteenth-century Byzantine miniature. Paris, Bibliotheque nationale. Photo by Photo 12/Alamy Stock Photo.   18

1.2 Achilles binds Patroclus' wound. Attic red-figure drinking cup by the Sosias Painter, *c.* 510–490 BCE. Berlin, Antikensammlung, Staatliche Museen zu Berlin F 2278. Photo by Azoor Photo/Alamy Stock Photo.   23

1.3 Attic votive relief for Amphiaraos in Oropos, dedicated by Archinos, 400–350 BCE. Athens NM 3369. Athens, National Archaeological Museum. Photo: Eirini Miari. © Hellenic Ministry of Culture and Sports/Archaeological Receipts Fund.   27

1.4 Red-figure aryballos with depictions of blood-letting. Paris, Louvre. Photo by DEA/G. Dagli Orti.   32

CHAPTER 2

2.1 Marble statuette of Nemesis with portrait resembling the Empress Faustina I. Roman Empire, *c.* 150 CE. In her left hand she holds a wheel of fate. Photo by Artokoloro Quint Lox Limited/Alamy Stock Photo.   42

2.2 Neo-Attic sarcophagus, 50–40 BCE. In the center, Erôs and Anterôs are portrayed as twins, while on both the left and right a centaur appears, one with a satyr on his back and the other with a maenad. Galleria dei Busti, Museo Pio Clementino, Vatican. © Vanni Archive/Art Resource, New York.   42

2.3 A copy of an engraving made of the reverse of a rare gold coin of Commodus, featuring at the bottom the abbreviation *Conc Mil*, for *Concordia Militum*, or "Concordia among the Soldiers." The rest of the legend reads P M TR P XI IMP VIII COS V PP, or "Pontifex Maximus, Tribune of the People for the eleventh time, Imperator for the seventh time, Consul for the fifth, and Father of his Country." From W. Stevenson, C. R. Smith, and F. W. Madden (eds), *The Dictionary of Roman Coins, Republican and Imperial* (London: Seaby, 1889), p. 244.   43

CHAPTER 3

3.1 Women lamenting during a *prothesis*. Attic black-figure funerary plaque, *c.* 520–510 BCE. New York, Metropolitan Museum of Art, 54.11.5. — 49

3.2 Dionysus with satyrs and maenads playing music. Attic red-figure bell krater, *c.* 450 BCE, attributed to the Methyse Painter. New York, Metropolitan Museum of Art, 07.286.85. — 49

3.3 Dancing maenad. Terracotta plaque, Roman, *c.* first century BCE–first century CE. New York, Metropolitan Museum of Art, 12.232.8b — 50

3.4 Orpheus enchanting the Thracians with the lyre. Red-figure krater from Gela, *c.* 450 BCE, detail. Berlin, Antikensammlung, Staatliche Museen zu Berlin. © 2017. Photo Scala, Florence/bpk, Bildagentur für Kunst, Kultur und Geschichte, Berlin. — 51

3.5 Women enchanted by *barbitos* music in a domestic setting. Attic red-figure bell krater, *c.* 460 BCE, attributed to the Danae Painter. New York, Metropolitan Museum of Art, 23.160.80. — 52

CHAPTER 4

4.1 Tragic mask, first century BCE or CE. Oxford, Ashmolean Museum. © C. Raddato via Wikimedia Commons. This file is licensed under the Creative Commons Attribution-Share Alike 2.0 Generic license. — 65

4.2 Glykera (left) after her hair has been shorn in Act 1 of Menander's *Perikeiromene*, with Polemon (seated) and the slave Sosias; from the Antioch mosaics (*c.* third century CE). Photo courtesy of the excavator, Ömer Çelik. See K. Gutzwiller and Ö. Çelik, "New Menander Mosaics from Antioch," *American Journal of Archaeology* 116 (2012): 573–623. — 76

4.3 Comic masks; from the preface to the *Andria* in a manuscript of Terence's comedies. Paris, Bibliothèque nationale de France, MS Latin 7899 (ninth century). See S. Nervegna, "Graphic Comedy: Menandrian Mosaics and Terentian Miniatures," in M. Fontaine and A. C. Scafuro, *The Oxford Handbook of Greek and Roman Comedy* (Oxford: Oxford University Press, 2014), 717–34. Courtesy of Bibliothèque nationale de France. — 77

4.4 Comedy scene depicted in the Roman mosaic from Villa de Cicero (Villa of Cicero) in Pompeii, now on display in the National Archaeological Museum (Museo Archeologico Nazionale di Napoli) in Naples, Campania, Italy. Two women consulting with a witch are depicted in the mosaic. Signature on the top: signed by Dioskourides of Samos. Photo by Azoor Photo/Alamy Stock Photo. — 80

4.5 A moment in Act 2 of Menander's *Phasma* or "The Ghost" when the "ghost" makes its appearance; from the Mytilene mosaics, photo courtesy of Professor Kyriaki Ioannidou (University College, London), © Archaeological Museum, Mytilene. See E. G. Turner, "The *Phasma* of Menander," *Greek, Roman, and Byzantine Studies* (1969) 307-24, esp. p. 320. — 80

CHAPTER 5

5.1 Centaur biting Lapith, western pediment of the temple of Zeus at Olympia, c. 460 BCE. Olympia, Archaeological Museum. © Museum für Abgüsse Klassischer Bildwerke München. Photo: Walter Hege/ Museum für Abgüsse Klassischer Bildwerke München. 85

5.2 "Pasquino Group," Roman copy from Hellenistic original, c. 150–120 BCE. Florence, Loggia dei Lanzi. Photo by Tommaso Di Girolamo/AGF/UIG via Getty Images. 85

5.3 Poseidon chasing Amymone. Athenian lekythos, c. 420 BCE. New York, Metropolitan Museum of Art 17.230.35. © Metropolitan Museum of Art. 87

5.4 Athenian lekythos, c. 430 BCE. Athens, National Museum 1935. © Hellenic Ministry of Culture and Sports/Archaeological Receipts Fund. 91

5.5 Roman sarcophagus, 120–130 CE. Agrigento, Museo Nazionale. Photo by Christophe Boisvieux via Getty Images. 92

5.6 Wall painting from the "House of the Tragic Poet" in Pompeii, 62–79 CE. Naples, National Archaeological Museum 9112. Photo by Mondadori Portfolio via Getty Images. 94

5.7 John F. Kennedy's family at his funeral in Washington, DC, November 1963. Photo by Keystone/Getty Images. 95

5.8 Athenian krater, c. 450 BCE. Paris, Louvre G 424. © bpk/Musé du Louvre, Dist. RMN-Grand Palais/Stéphane Maréchalle. 97

5.9 Wedding ceremony. Athenian loutrophoros, 420 BCE. Oxford, Ashmolean Museum 1966.888. © Ashmolean Museum, University of Oxford. 98

5.10a Fresco from the "House of Punished Love," Pompeii, c. 20 CE. Naples, National Archaeological Museum. Photo by DeAgostini/Getty Images. 99

5.10b Fresco from the "House of Punished Love," Pompeii, c. 20 CE. Naples, National Archaeological Museum. Photo by Leemage/Corbis via Getty Images. 99

5.11 Athenian grave stele of Korallion (drawing), c. 350 BCE. Athens, Kerameikos Museum P688. After Conze 1893: pl. 98. 101

5.12 Roman funerary altar, first century CE. Rome, Museo Nazionale Romano 124514. Photo by DEA/A. Dagli Orti/De Agostini/Getty Images. 102

5.13 "Ludovisi Gaul," Roman marble copy from Hellenistic original, c. 220 BCE. Rome, Museo Nazionale Romano 144. Photo by DEA/A. Dagli Orti/De Agostini/Getty Images. 104

CHAPTER 6

6.1 Jacques Louis David, *Andromache Mourning Hector* (1783). Moscow, Pushkin Museum of Fine Arts. Photo by Fine Art Images/Heritage Images/Getty Images. 115

ILLUSTRATIONS ix

6.2 Roman silver-gilt drinking cup depicting King Priam of Troy appealing to Achilles for the return of his son Hector's body. Found in a chieftain's grave at Hoby, Denmark, first century BCE. Copenhagen, Nationalmuseet. Photo by Roman via Getty Images. 116

6.3 Aphrodite of Knidos, Roman copy from the end of first century BCE of a fourth-century BCE Greek original by Praxiteles. Munich, Glyptothek. © C. Raddato via Wikimedia Commons. This file is licensed under the Creative Commons Attribution-Share Alike 2.0 Generic license. 122

6.4 Trimalchio's dinner, in *Satyricon* by Federico Fellini. © P.E.A. Produzioni Europee Associate S.A.S, 1969. 124

CHAPTER 7

7.1a Fattoria Fabrizio farmhouse in the Metaponto countryside, fourth–third century BCE. From *The Chora of Metaponto 5: A Greek Farmhouse at Ponte Fabrizio*, edited by Elisa Lanza Catti and Keith Swift. © UT Institute of Classical Archaeology/University of Texas Press, 2014. 128

7.1b Pyramidal loom weight inscribed, late sixth–early fifth century BCE. © Lin Foxhall, with thanks to the UT Institute of Classical Archaeology. 129

7.2 Grave stele of Phanostrate, late fourth century BCE. National Museum Athens 993. © Hellenic Ministry of Culture and Sports/Archaeological Receipts Fund. 130

7.3 Model textiles in lead from the Sanctuary of Artemis Orthia, Sparta. Dawkins 1929: pl. 185, 186. Clockwise from top left: 185.20, 185.21, 186.21, 186.22. © Society for the Promotion of Hellenic Studies. 138

7.4 Grave stele of Ampharete holding her grandchild. Kerameikos Museum P695. DSI Negative: D-DAI-Ath Kerameikos 2478. © Deutsches Archäologisches Institut. 139

7.5 Houses in the Athenian Agora (Young 1951: 189, Fig. 7). © American School of Classical Studies at Athens: Agora Excavations. 142

7.6a The Umbro Greek site, a classical rural "farmhouse" near Bova Marina, Calabria. Primary phase with roof tiles lying on floor. © Lin Foxhall. 143

7.6b The Umbro Greek site, a classical rural "farmhouse" near Bova Marina, Calabria. Secondary phase divided into probable animal stalls. © Lin Foxhall. 144

CHAPTER 8

8.1 Funeral games for Patroclus: Attic bf. dinos by Sophilos, 570–560 BCE. Athens, National Museum 15499. Photo: Eirini Miari. © Hellenic Ministry of Culture and Sports/Archaeological Receipts Fund. 148

8.2	Ostrakon inscribed with name of the Athenian politician Themistocles, fifth century BCE. Athens, Agora Museum. Photo by Fine Art Images/Heritage Images/Getty Images.	151
8.3	Marcus Tullius Cicero (106–43 BCE). Portrait from Villa Quintilii, Appian Way. Rome, Vatican Museums. Chiaramonto. Photo by Lanmas/Alamy Stock Photo.	155
8.4	Cicero denounces Catiline. Fresco by Cesare Maccari. Photo by Atlaspix/Alamy Stock Photo.	159

GENERAL EDITORS' PREFACE

The General Editors, volume editors, and individual authors of this series have many organizations to thank for helping to bring it into existence. They gratefully acknowledge assistance from the Arts and Humanities Research Council (UK); the European Research Council Project, the Social and Cultural Construction of Emotions, University of Oxford, and its Director, Professor Angelos Chaniotis; the Leverhulme Trust; and the Wellcome Trust. Above all, the series has depended on support from the Australian Research Council Centre of Excellence for the History of Emotions (CE110001011). The project was conceived as a key part of the Centre's collaborative research work and has benefited greatly from the generous help of its academic and administrative staff.

The General Editors also express their deep gratitude to the volume editors and authors for their time, expertise, and gracious willingness to revise essays in the light of readers' comments. Many other people helped in reading, tracing images, and advising in various ways. Our thanks go to Merridee Bailey, Jacquie Bennett, Sophie Boyd-Hurrell, Frederic Kiernan, Mark Neuendorf, Fiona Sim, and Stephanie Thomson; and to the patient staff at Bloomsbury: Dan Hutchins, Claire Lipscomb, Beatriz Lopez, and Rhodri Mogford. We especially acknowledge Ciara Rawnsley, who as Editorial Assistant for the entire series has tirelessly helped authors and done indispensable and meticulous work on all aspects of the volumes' preparation.

This series is dedicated to the memory of Philippa Maddern (1952–2014) who was an original General Editor, and an inspiring friend, mentor, and colleague to many of the contributors.

Introduction

Emotion History and the Classics

DOUGLAS CAIRNS

The aim of this volume is to provide an overview of some of the salient aspects of emotions and their role in the life and thought of the Greco-Roman world, from the beginnings of Greek literature and history to the height of the Roman Empire. This is a wide remit: we are dealing with a wide range of sources in two ancient languages, and in the full range of contexts that are covered by the format of this series. But our scope is also necessarily restricted. For emotions are everywhere—in everyday transactions, in interpersonal relationships, in religion and politics, in the objects that people use in their daily lives, and in the buildings and spaces they live in. At any period, all we can ever do is scratch the surface. The ancient author of the treatise *On the Sublime*, writing in Greek under the Roman Empire, observes (22.1) that "there is an indefinite multiplicity of emotions [*pathê*] and no one can even say how many they are." Nearly two thousand years later, William James (1890: ii.485) makes a similar point, one that is of considerable relevance to our current project:

> [I]f one should seek to name each particular one [of the emotions] of which the human heart is the seat, it is plain that the limit to their number would lie in the introspective vocabulary of the seeker, each race of men having found names for some shade of feeling which other races have left undiscriminated.

The experiences we pick out and label as emotions or emotional episodes are just the peaks and troughs in a continuous affective landscape; not only individuals, but also cultures will differ in the experiences they label and the categories into which they organize them.

This makes the history of emotions, in any period, a difficult thing to write. In contemporary or recent societies, the data that we might be able to access and evaluate will inevitably be just the tip of the iceberg. In the case of ancient societies, we have access only to the tip of the iceberg's tip, given that the available data have been sifted and vastly reduced by the passage of time and the accidents of survival and transmission. The historical distance that separates us from the Greeks and Romans has imposed substantial limits on the scope of our studies. And yet the range of sociocultural contexts from which the relevant data derive and the variety of theoretical approaches to those data in Classical Studies (and the other disciplines on which emotion researchers in Classics rely) remain impressively wide. By the same token, our source base is in some ways limited not only by the accidents and biases of transmission and reception, but also by the norms and ideologies of the societies in which they originate: the literary, medical, musical, and philosophical sources that provide the material for many of our chapters overwhelmingly reflect the views of an educated and literate elite (even if some of them do derive from forms of popular entertainment or reflect in various other ways the expectations of wider audiences). At the same time, however, this volume is also reflective of recent currents in emotion research in Classics in so far as several of its chapters (Chaniotis and Steel; Foxhall; Naiden; Räuchle) make extensive use of non-elite texts and documents, especially those preserved on stone, papyrus and similar media, as well as of material culture. The combination of these recent approaches with the discourse of a subdiscipline that has been maturing for the past thirty years or more puts Classicists at the forefront of contemporary approaches to the history of emotions.

EMOTIONS, *PATHÊ, MOTUS ANIMI*

Yet there remains room for doubt as to what the history of emotions is a history of. As Geoffrey Lloyd, a leading scholar of ancient Greek (and classical Chinese) thought, has observed, "very considerable confusion still exists including on what emotion is and how it should be defined" (Lloyd 2007: 58). The English-language term "emotion" is itself historically contingent and of comparatively recent currency. Thomas Dixon has lamented the "displacement, in the history of systematic psychological theorising, of more differentiated typologies (which included appetites, passions, affections and sentiments) by a single over-arching category of emotions during the nineteenth century" (Dixon 2003: 2; cf. 2012). The limitations imposed by the dominance of this English-language category, or of English-language categories of particular "emotions," in contemporary emotion research is a regular complaint among those who seek to study the conceptualization of comparable forms of experience in other cultures (e.g. Wierzbicka 1999).

The issue of definition is at the heart of some of the most central disputes in emotion research.[1] For James A. Russell, "Emotion researchers face a scandal. We have no agreed upon definition of the term—*emotion*—that defines our field" (Russell 2012: 237). One approach to this "scandal" is to attempt to move away from vernacular terminology in favor of an allegedly more "scientific" redefinition of "emotion." This is the strategy pursued by those, led by Paul Ekman, who have argued for a category of "basic" emotions based on supposedly universal patterns of facial expression and other (neuro-)physiological changes.[2] Ekman and those who follow his approach deploy everyday English terms for the phenomena that are categorized as "basic emotions," but this category is clearly not coextensive with the English-language category of emotion, nor are its members coextensive with the everyday English-language categories of particular emotions: "An emotion is either basic, or it is another affective phenomenon saturated with but different from the emotions" (Ekman and Cordaro 2011: 365)—basic, facially expressed emotions are the only emotions that there are, even if it just so happens that certain English-language terms accurately label these as distinct categories. For the philosopher of science, Paul Griffiths, basic emotions (or "affect program responses") are related only homonymously to other phenomena that we label as emotions in English, such as the "higher cognitive emotions" of shame and guilt. The category of affect program responses is not a category of emotion as we know it; it offers not a refinement or specification of the category of emotion, but a new and different category (Griffiths 1997: 17, 78–9, 230, 241).

These approaches either redefine the category of emotion or dispense with it altogether. This poses problems in itself and for those who propose to study emotion in the cultures of the past. One problem is that basic level categories of emotion in English (i.e. categories such as "fear") just do span the supposed divide between affect program and higher cognitive responses—not all fear, by any means, is "basic" in Ekman's sense of the word. And yet, semantically and conceptually, the link between my fear of the snake that has just appeared in front of me and my fear that I'm too busy to stop for a chat is not an arbitrary one. A related problem is that a category of basic emotions for which the existence of a characteristic facial expression is the criterion for membership turns out to include items such as "surprise" that not everyone, by any means, would recognize as emotions.[3] Surprise belongs in this list not because it is prototypically an emotion, but because it has, at least in the eyes of some observers in some cultures, a characteristic facial expression. The scientific study of surprise as a member of the category of basic emotions is constructed by the discursive practice, i.e. the culture, of a section of the scientific community in making facial expression a criterion for basicness and for emotion. It is not clear that the study of emotion, even the scientific study of emotion, can so easily dispense with the categories given by particular natural languages and specific societies and cultures in favor of revisionary categories called into being by the practices of the subcultures involved in certain forms of scientific investigation. Though the affect-program response associated with an emotion such as fear may antedate the development of language, every human being who has ever felt, thought about, and labeled this response (using the relevant token in his or her native language) has thereby made it a member of a wider category, an element in an interrelated system. Categories just *are* functions of language, thought, and culture. Emotions are not *only* features of language and culture, but among all the other things they may be, they are features of language and culture *as well*. The inclusion of more and less prototypical members in a given category, the indeterminacy (fuzziness) of category boundaries, and a lack of precision over which items do and do not belong are not special but rather everyday features of category formation.[4] What fear is, as a psychological and social category, is inevitably shaped by how it is represented in language and thought; even as a so-called basic emotion its nature is fundamentally affected by such representations. Representations of fear as a human emotion are inextricably enmeshed in human cognition, language, and culture.

The quest for the one essential feature or set of features that qualifies a phenomenon as an emotion is in practice widespread, and it encompasses the entire spectrum of approaches, from the scientific to the social constructionist. For Jesse Prinz (2004b), though emotion episodes may be multidimensional syndromes of factors, there must be just *one* element among all those that make up the episode that *is* the emotion.[5] For Daniel Gross, on the other hand (2006), emotions are constituted above all by social relationships, their significance in particular cultural and historical contexts conditioned by the specific dynamics of power relations and social hierarchies. But approaches to emotion, whether synchronic, diachronic, or cross-cultural in orientation, need to be as alert as possible to the full range of factors that are or have been associated with the category of emotion, the categories that have preceded it in our culture, and its partial analogues in other cultures. The absence of a single and definitive set of criteria for membership of the category "emotion" is a significant feature of the phenomena under investigation, not something to be eliminated through redefinition of the phenomena and remodeling of the categories to which they belong. All the problems with the definition of "emotion" in English, as well as the problems associated with the difference in extension between modern English "emotion" and the various conceptual categories that preceded it or the categories of other languages in both past and present, are inherent in the enterprise of studying phenomena of this type. It is important that "emotion" cannot be essentialized; the answer is not to redefine it until it can.

These observations about the nature of our own categories have important implications for our project as students of the historical and cross-cultural dimensions of emotion. Even if the revisionist approach were desirable scientifically, it would not be desirable for us as historians of emotion. In dealing with the emotions of the ancient Greeks or Romans, we are dealing with the categories of ordinary Greek and Latin discourse, with folk taxonomies of those categories, and with scientific or philosophical approaches that start, at least to some extent, from those categories. It is salutary to bring the historical and cultural contingency of one's own categories into confrontation with those of other languages. If nothing else, this should prevent our seeking greater precision and conceptual clarity in the languages and cultures that we study than we are able to find in the languages we use and the cultures we inhabit.

If we *were* to replace our folk categories of emotion with others more conducive to scientific understanding, then we should have to give up our work as students of Greek and Roman emotions, for in investigating these cultures we have no unmediated access to raw scientific data. Everything we have—even the data on body language and expression provided by the visual arts—must be interpreted in the light of the categories and representations for which our only evidence is textual and linguistic (cf. below). Equally, we have no access to the felt symptoms of ancient emotions except as they are embedded in language and texts (again, see below). But Classicists proceed as they do not merely because they cannot treat the Greeks and Romans as experimental subjects. The discipline's concentration on linguistic categories and cultural models stands as a reminder to researchers in other fields of the extent to which emotion research would be impoverished if it ignored historical and cultural differences in the conceptualization and categorization of the phenomena that we currently regard, with all the imprecision that the term implies, as emotions. If we can study only genuinely scientific categories then we cannot do emotion history; if we can do emotion history, then complexity of categorization within a culture and divergence of categorization among cultures is not noise to be filtered out, but an integral and important aspect of the phenomena under investigation.[6]

The modern English "emotion" is not by any means coextensive with its nearest equivalents in Greek or Latin. The nearest equivalent in Greek is *pathos* (sometimes *pathêma*; both from *paschô*, to undergo), a term used in fields from logic to medicine, and not restricted to psychological experience. From the fourth century BCE onwards, however, Greek writers refer regularly to the *pathê* of the *psuchê* or soul. The Romans never settled on a single term for what we might call emotion, referring instead to *adfectiones, adfectus, commotiones, motus animi, passiones, perturbationes*, and so on. But if we need constantly to be mindful of the historical and cultural contingency that affects both our own categories and those of our ancient sources, we must also recognize the potential for overlap between those categories. The categories of different languages may not be coextensive, but neither are they necessarily discrete. Anna Wierzbicka (1999: 275–307) lists a number of ways in which the categories of other cultures capture phenomena that are salient in the English-language concept of emotion: all languages (she claims) possess words which describe a combination of thinking and feeling and which link certain evaluations with typical bodily reactions, and though individual emotion terms are culture-specific, the emotion terms of many languages exhibit a substantial degree of semantic overlap. Not many of us will have the linguistic expertise to test these claims in full, and there are aspects of Wierzbicka's arguments that one might wish to challenge.⁷ But this does not matter much for present purposes. If our modern concept of "emotion" in English has a specific history, as Dixon (2003) has emphasized, so too does it have members that previously belonged to the categories of "passion" or "sentiment," even though those three categories are not coextensive. Other cultures have and have had categories that share some or many of the features of these English-language categories: the extensive list of *pathê* given by Aristotle in Book 2 of his *Rhetoric* consists very largely of items which, even if they would not all necessarily occur to us as prototypical examples of emotion, would still fall straightforwardly under that category, and which, even if they do not coincide precisely with their nearest English equivalents in sense, reference, extension, and connotation, all have near-equivalents or analogs in English which would be regarded by the average English-speaker as emotion words. Other inventories of *pathê* and analogous terms in Latin similarly contain items that we have no trouble in recognizing as emotions.

Wierzbicka's formulation in terms of "thinking" and "feeling" captures two features that we might plausibly see as the prototypical aspects of the phenomena that we label as emotions, the Greeks called *pathê* of the soul, and the Romans *motus animi* (etc.). The first is that prototypical cases of emotion have both an intentional and a phenomenal aspect: they are *about* some feature of the world and they involve a sense of what it is to *feel a certain way* about such features. The most persuasive modern theories of emotion are multidimensional, encompassing eliciting conditions, appraisals of those conditions, bodily changes and the feelings they cause, outward expressions, and patterns of behavior.⁸ Though researchers are increasingly skeptical of antitheses between mind and body, reason and passion, cognition and affectivity (Colombetti 2014), there is broad agreement that some element of appraisal or at least intentionality (even if that element is no more than implicit in an embodied organism's sensorimotor interaction with its environment) is typical of the phenomena that we call emotions. But there would be no need for a category of that sort at all if emotions were nothing but judgments; one thing that English "emotion" shares with similar categories in other cultures is an emphasis, at least in prototypical cases, not only on an intensity of arousal but also on a sense that emotions are to some extent things that happen to us rather than things that we do. Though modern research suggests that affectivity is essential to normal psychological processes (Damasio 1994), the Greek and Latin terms listed above resemble English "emotion" and the folk categories of other cultures in picking out events that typically stand out against the background of normative functioning.⁹

EMOTION RESEARCH IN CLASSICS

The history of emotion is a field in which Classicists, among Humanities scholars, have been both pioneers and leaders. It thus seems a particularly opportune moment to step back and consider, in a synthetic overview such as this volume provides, the advances made by Classicists in the study of ancient emotion over the past thirty to forty years. The development of a dialog in which research in Classics and Ancient History slowly began to take account of contemporary research in other fields can be traced to the later years of the twentieth century. A pioneering work here is William Fortenbaugh's 1975 book on Aristotle, which is fully informed by the cognitive–evaluative approach to emotion which achieved prominence in the 1950s and 1960s.¹⁰ The approach outlined in Fortenbaugh's book was a crucial stimulus to Cairns's volume on *aidôs*, which sought to synthesize the perspectives on honor and shame offered by Classical thinkers such as the Sophists, Plato, and Aristotle with the representation of *aidôs* and similar affective phenomena in imaginative literature, especially epic and tragedy (Cairns 1993). The cognitive–evaluative approach to emotion is central also to the spate of monographs and edited collections on emotion and particular emotions that have appeared since the 1990s,[11] works whose central strength has been their focus on the ancient emotional lexicon and the construction, conceptualization, and valorization of emotion in ancient authors, genres, philosophical schools and societies.

A central figure in this upsurge of interest has been David Konstan, who (in several accounts of particular emotions and affective phenomena and in his major study of *The Emotions of the Ancient Greeks*) has contributed in particular to our understanding of ancient theories of emotion (particularly those of Aristotle and the Stoics, which offer particularly fruitful opportunities for dialog with modern cognitive-evaluative approaches),[12] to the semantics and history of ancient emotional concepts,[13] and to the sharpening of our appreciation of salient differences between ancient emotional lexica and our own. One of the central emphases of Konstan's work (and of many of the other studies on ancient emotion produced since the 1990s) has been the interaction between emotion and moral and social norms. This is a phenomenon that needs to be viewed from both angles, in terms not only of the embeddedness of ancient emotions, emotion concepts, and theories of emotion in social interaction and cultural normativity, but also of the fundamentally affective character of ancient moral, social, and legal values. These are features that are emphasized in some of the most important contributions within Classical Studies,[14] but they also constitute major topics in other disciplines.[15]

Literature has loomed large in these discussions, especially because literary sources provide rich evidence for the complex dynamics of emotional episodes in multifaceted depictions of more-or-less realistic forms of social interaction (see the chapters by Konstan and by Scodel and Caston in this volume). Genres such as epic and drama provide manifold perspectives on characters' motivation and substantial information on the eliciting conditions of their emotions, all of which can guide our interpretation both of explicit ascriptions of emotion and of implicit representations of emotional behavior. A wide range of other genres (from elegiac poetry and historiography to forensic oratory and biography) rely similarly on narrative constructions of characteristic affective scenarios as contexts for their representations of and appeals to emotion. In a very real sense, the manifold forms of dramatic enactment and narrative representation of emotion in literature reflect the paradigmatic scenarios of emotion in the wider culture or in particular "emotional communities" within that culture.[16] Drama and narrative have a particular role in developing an audience's inventory of scripts, paradigm scenarios, and the range of affective responses that they evoke.[17] The process can be one of extending and deepening the reader's, auditor's, or spectator's powers of imagination and perspective-taking. The minds of self and other are intricately related in the fundamental cognitive and emotional processes that make us what we are; engaging with others' minds and others' lives in imagination, and perhaps especially in the kinds of imagination possible when we enter into the worlds of narrative fiction, builds capacity.[18] But the same process can also be a matter of codification and normalization: stories recur to typical patterns, serving to crystallize the paradigmatic cases and the norms by which audiences respond emotionally to those cases. The condensation of such complexes of thought and feeling in typical and traditional forms and genres makes a particular ethical or emotional perspective tangible, tractable, and transferable.[19] These forms and genres capture important aspects of a culture's emotional and normative repertoire in a way that allows them to be reconstituted and applied in the mind of each recipient or audience member. The encapsulation of traditional norms, with their associated ways of feeling, in a traditional artistic form encourages a symbiotic replication both of the form and of the response that it evokes; it helps define the repertoire of both artists and audience. In this way, other works of literature constitute a significant aspect of the contextual background against which the emotions portrayed in and elicited by particular literary texts must be read.[20]

If literary representations of agency are successful, then we have good evidence of affectivity in action in the cultures we study—in the agents represented in literary artefacts, in their interaction with other agents and with internal audiences, and in the appeal to the emotions of external audiences (see Scodel and Caston, this volume). This is one reason why Classicists have been right to make such extensive use of literary evidence in their contributions to the historical study of emotion, and why literary sources still provide much of the evidence and subject matter for emotion research in contemporary Classical Studies.[21]

The emotional texture and affective character of literary works also figure prominently in contemporary emotion research.[22] But a further feature of this strand of research is its focus on the emotional responses of readers and audiences.[23] Here, the concerns of modern emotional research and those of ancient poetics, aesthetics, and rhetoric coalesce in seeing emotion as a salient element in readers' and audiences' engagement with texts, performances, and narratives and in the techniques by which those texts (etc.) succeed in fostering that engagement (again, see Scodel and Caston in this volume). The emotion-eliciting power of texts is not just a matter of the depiction of emotion in the text.[24] The mechanisms by which texts exert this power, however, as well as the nature of the responses that these mechanisms elicit, are matters of controversy; this is an area where the centuries' worth of implicit and explicit testimony that classical literature and classical literary theory have to offer on the emotional power of texts and performances can still make a contribution to contemporary debate, not only in applying modern theory to ancient sources or in bringing our literary-theoretical approaches into contact with the cognitive and affective sciences,[25] but also in using the richness of ancient theory to interrogate modern assumptions.[26]

Thus the general approach to emotion that has become established in Classics, based on language and its deployment in (above all) literary and philosophical texts, still has much to offer. But beyond literary, dramatic, and philosophical texts, recent approaches have brought a widening of the field, its focus, and its source base, with greater attention to sources for the expression, performance, and context of emotion, especially in non-literary texts and material culture (in this volume cf. Chaniotis and Steel, Räuchle, Naiden, and Foxhall).[27] In one respect, this represents a move away from elite and culturally authoritative texts to other forms of textual evidence—for example, letters, wills, and petitions;[28] inscriptions set up by private individuals;[29] and inscriptions, both religious and secular, commissioned by communities of various kinds.[30] But the broadening of the source base also encompasses a shift of focus on to non-textual forms of evidence—to visual and material culture. Visual culture, in particular, is an area in which great opportunities exist, but also considerable obstacles. In principle, sources such as vase-painting and sculpture might be thought to afford direct access to the physical expression of emotion in gesture and body language (see Räuchle in this volume). But we have no unmediated access to the non-verbal expression of ancient emotions; as Glenys Davies points out, "although some aspects of body language are universal and found across cultures many behaviors are culture-specific, and it should not be assumed that an interpretation that seems natural or obvious to us would have been so for the Roman [or Greek] viewer" (Davies 2017: 159). Modern scientific accounts can help, especially if they can offer strong grounds, with robust cross-cultural evidence, that a given expression or gesture genuinely is found in a range of cultures; but even so it would be unsafe merely to assimilate representations of emotion in the visual arts of the ancient Greeks and Romans to our own understanding (even if scientifically informed) of what appears to be depicted. To link the depiction of non-verbal behavior in ancient art to ancient concepts of emotion, we typically require warrant from linguistic (and especially narrative) sources,[31] together with as much contextual information (e.g. about the identity and status of the individuals depicted, the relation between their depiction and ancient norms of self-presentation, proxemics and emotional display, and so on) as can reasonably be obtained, as well as a thorough understanding of the iconography of the wider corpus to which the depiction belongs. Though progress is being made,[32] works which in the past attempted to survey this field systematically are now outdated and inadequate,[33] and coverage remains in many respects sporadic.[34]

Chaniotis' work (e.g. Chaniotis 2017) indicates another fruitful approach in this connection, insofar as it represents a growing tendency to consider the products of the visual arts not just in their own right, as evidence for the depiction of emotion, but (as far as possible) in their wider original context, as functional objects in specific physical and cultural settings: statues not only represent emotional experience, but also express emotional commitment and elicit emotional responses. Chaniotis' 2017 study of the multiple ways in which the dedication of a statue provides evidence for aspects of ancient affectivity complements earlier work on the emotional dimensions of sanctuaries and other locations for ritual performance.[35] Epigraphic texts, dedications, religious architecture, and the configuration of the site more generally all contribute to the creation of a shared space for emotional experience and emotional performance, a locus for the enactment of the emotions—awe, fear, wonder, respect, hope, gratitude, and so on—on which religious experience depends.[36] Such an orientation reflects the turn towards materiality in archaeology and ancient history more broadly, a concern that is also manifest in studies that focus more generally on the affective implications of human beings' interaction with objects and artifacts.[37]

Yet this is not an approach that needs to restrict itself to material evidence. The literary texts that have dominated the study of ancient emotions to date also have a great deal to offer those who wish to investigate the concrete physicality of ancient emotions as aspects of the ways in which embodied human beings interact with the world and the objects that it contains. This is partly a consequence of the fact that literary sources are rich in representations of the objects, artifacts, spaces, symptoms, movements, postures, and gestures through which emotions can be expressed, symbolized, constructed, and elicited.[38] But there is also a very real sense in which there is no absolute gulf between the material and the linguistic, the physical and the mental, in the study of emotion. Metonymies and metaphors drawn from the experience of emotion itself (especially from its symptoms and physical expressions) and from other aspects of embodied experience and from our interaction with the physical and social environments more generally not only play a fundamental role in the formation and extension of emotion concepts, but also afford us at least a degree of access to a linguistic community's shared representations of the phenomenology of emotion. As Angelos Chaniotis has pointed out (2012b: 94), "the ancient historian cannot study what people really felt." But the ancient experience of emotion is not completely inaccessible to us, at least insofar as we can study shared cultural models of emotion phenomenology through their representation in the intersubjective medium of language, especially as they are represented in the use of metaphor. Almost always, these metaphors will be conventional, or at least not unique to individuals; very often, they will reflect not subjective experience as such, but shared models of the forms that subjective experience was expected to take. In this way, metaphor gets us from what cannot be studied historically—the totality of living human beings' actual subjective experience of affective events and states (that "indefinite multiplicity of *pathê*" mentioned in *On the Sublime* 22.1 and quoted at the head of this chapter)—to what can, the representation of subjective experience in language. Scholars are beginning to explore what metaphor can tell us about the conceptualization of emotion in ancient Greek and Roman societies.[39] To say "I shudder" rather than merely "I am afraid" is to give a more vivid and immediate sense of the emotion as a holistic, embodied experience; to present the onset of grief as the feeling of being suddenly enveloped in a cloud or a garment presents an individual's emotion in terms of a shared cultural model of what that emotion is supposed to feel like to a subject (and links it to the visible expression of the emotion in body language and dress).[40] When Achilles wishes that anger (*cholos*) would disappear from the world, that anger that is sweeter than liquid honey and expands like smoke in a man's chest (*Iliad* 18.107–10), he is, to be sure, telling us what anger has felt like to him, but he does so in a way that draws on his culture's metaphorical models of emotional experience (e.g. as the movement of gases and fluids in a container), so that his description is meaningful also in terms of the conceptual schemas that the poem's audiences use to articulate their own subjective experiences. The similarity between these schemas and those that are found in other (including modern) societies will at least partly reflect the constraints that actual physiology, symptomatology, and other features of human embodiment place on metaphors and metonymies that depend on embodiment.

ANCIENT THEORIES OF EMOTION

Just as Classicists have been pioneers in the study of emotion and emotions in history and historical sources, so Classics has a special place in the history of emotion theory: because this is a discipline that, in terms of Western culture, at least, begins in ancient Greece.

Ancient theorizing about emotion begins in earnest with Aristotle, but earlier thinkers had also shown an interest in affective phenomena. The *Encomium of Helen* by the fifth-century Sicilian Sophist Gorgias, for example, reflects an interest in the emotional effects of poetic speech that is rooted in the implicit aesthetics of earlier Greek (especially epic) poetry and anticipates later discussions in works such as Plato's *Ion* and Aristotle's *Poetics* (see Scodel and Caston, and Konstan, this volume). Plato never attempts to develop a systematic category of emotional *pathê*, but what we should call emotions do feature prominently in his work. A notable feature for Plato is their ambivalence: in the *Philebus* they are introduced as mixtures of pleasure and pain in the soul (*Philebus* 47e–50e). In the *Republic* and in *Phaedrus*, emotions such as anger and shame are crucial to the account of the "middle" element of the tripartite soul, the *thumoeides* or "spirited" part. The potential of the *thumoeides* both to support and to conflict with reason suggests a combination of cognition and affectivity in the emotions with which it is associated. Though the *Republic* recognizes educable, morally useful emotions, at the same time public emotional display, and in particular the effects that representations of emotion in epic and tragic poetry have on the emotional character of audiences, are also central to the dialog's case (in Book 10) against the performance of those genres (again, see Caston and Scodel, and Konstan, this volume). In later dialogs, such as *Timaeus* (69c–d) and *Laws* (644c–d), fear, anger, confidence, hope, and so on are typically represented as unreliable motives.

Aristotle's two main discussions of what we call emotions are to be found in the *Rhetoric* and in the treatise *On the Soul* (*De anima*). In the *Rhetoric*, he defines the *pathê* as the things that cause people to change and differ in respect of their judgments (2.1, 1378a19–22), and specifies these as "anger, pity, fear, and all other things of that kind, as well as their opposites" (cf. *Nicomachean Ethics* 2.5, 1105b21–3, *Eudemian Ethics* 2.2, 1220b12–14). In the discussion that follows (*Rhetoric* 2.2–2.17), Aristotle discusses twelve emotions in terms of the dispositions of their patients, their targets, and the conditions and circumstances in which they are elicited, concluding with a series of character sketches outlining the differences in people's emotional dispositions according to age and circumstance. As befits its emphasis on persuasion, the *Rhetoric*'s emphasis is on emotions as evaluative responses.[41] Similarly, the primary focus is on the emotions of the audiences to whom speeches (e.g. in law courts) are addressed. This focus on audience emotion becomes a general orientation of ancient rhetorical theory (cf., e.g., Cicero, *On the Ideal Orator* (*De oratore*) 2.185–216; Quintilian 6.1–2). But the scenarios discussed also provide material for narratives of the emotional behavior of others (e.g. one's opponents), and the speaker's representation of his own emotions is also important (e.g. 3.7, 1408a9–23). Throughout, the social aspect of emotion is to the fore: the emotional scripts that Aristotle adumbrates reflect his chosen emotions' role in social and political interaction, the dynamic interplay between emotion and social norms, especially in terms of the relation between emotion and social status.

But the *Rhetoric* also specifies that emotions are accompanied by pleasure and pain (2.1, 1378a20–1). The occasional addition of the term "disturbance" (*tarachê*) in the ensuing discussion suggests that pleasure and pain, as aspects of emotion, encompass not only what modern psychologists call "valence" (i.e. the intrinsic appraisal of a state of affairs as good or bad for the agent), but also the subjective phenomenology of physiological arousal.

In the *De anima* discussion the physical aspect comes much more to the fore. In the opening chapter, Aristotle includes examples of what we might call emotions (anger, confidence, wanting, 403a7; *thumos*, mildness, fear, pity, courage, joy, loving, hating, 403a17–18) alongside processes such as "perceiving in general" (403a7) in discussing whether all *pathê* of the *psuchê* are shared by the body. These *pathê* encompass all that the *psuchê* undergoes, all its "affections" in the most general sense. For the purposes of this argument, the emotions are chosen as prototypical cases of the *pathê* of the soul mainly because they best illustrate the point that all or almost all of these *pathê* are "with body." The overall position of the *De anima* is that soul and body may be distinct in definition, but are inextricable as aspects of the living organism (1.1, 403a10–16, 2.1, 412a1–413a10). But the emotions and the other *pathê* of the soul are even more deeply enmattered than that:[42] the *pathê* (both as emotions and in general as affections of the soul) are "enmattered accounts" (*logoi enuloi*). A dialectician and a natural scientist may offer different (formal *versus* material) definitions of (e.g.) anger (as "desire to cause pain in retaliation" and as "boiling of the blood and hot stuff around the heart"), but neither of these is correct in itself. The true natural scientist's definition, that is, the proper definition of an emotion (or rather of all "affections of the soul")—as "a certain movement of a body of a given kind or a part of it or a capacity of it produced by such and such and for the sake of such and such" (403a16–b19)—requires both. Aristotle thus distinguishes the true natural scientist from the doctor (403b13–14), who might be concerned only with the affections of the body *qua* matter (see Kazantzidis, this volume). For Aristotle, emotion is embodied not only in the sense that all experiences of embodied individuals are embodied but also in the sense that an emotion requires a specific and occurrent physiological process (403a18–19, 403a31–403b1). Both conditions, formal and material, are necessary, but neither is sufficient: one can be faced with powerful reasons for anger or fear, but not feel the emotion because one is not in the requisite physical state, but equally, if one is in that state, the emotion may result even when the external circumstances do not warrant the appraisal that normally elicits it (403a19–24; cf. *Rhetoric* 2.2, 1379a10–22). This does not mean that physical conditions can determine the occurrence of an emotion without any appraisal at all (for the physical state is not in itself the emotion), but that an appraisal of external circumstances which would not otherwise elicit the emotion can result from the physical condition of the patient. Though the physiological aspects of emotion are not highlighted in the *Rhetoric*, they are given a prominent role in the *De anima*, and this emphasis recurs in Aristotle's other works.[43]

Emotions are prominent factors elsewhere in the Aristotelian corpus. In the *Nicomachean* and *Eudemian Ethics*, the proper development of emotional capacities forms the basis of the virtues, which involve feeling emotion as reason prescribes in a given situation (*EN* 2.6, 1106b18–23). Emotion is thus essential for the developed forms of disposition and judgment that enable one to practice the virtues and to live a good life. This is not a matter either of repressing emotion or of moderating it in all circumstances, but of the development of states of character that allow one to feel emotion whenever and however it is appropriate to do so (*EN* 2.6, 1106b18–23). The utility of emotion and its alignment with moral judgment also emerge in the *Poetics*, where pity (*eleos*) and fear (*phobos*) are the means by which tragedy effects the famous yet enigmatic *katharsis* (purification) of such emotions (*Po*. 6, 1449b27–8; see Konstan, and Scodel and Caston, this volume). In one kind of tragic plot (the best, one of the two best, or the second best, depending on one's interpretation),[44] Aristotle goes on (*Po*. 13, 1452b28–1453a12), pity and fear are elicited by the change of fortune (from good to bad) of a high-status individual who is neither outstandingly virtuous nor thoroughly wicked, but who fails because of some error (*hamartia*). Though there is a passage in the *De anima* (3.3, 427b17–24) which suggests that we are unaffected when we contemplate emotion-eliciting scenarios in works of art (and indeed even when we conjure up such scenarios in imagination), the position of the *Poetics* is much more in keeping with ancient aesthetic and rhetorical theory in general in emphasizing that we experience real emotion, as we would do in comparable real-life situations, in response to representations in art, narrative, and drama.

The approach to emotion in the main Hellenistic philosophical schools bears comparison with Aristotle's account to the extent that both Stoics and Epicureans would agree on the indivisible unity of emotions as cognitive and physiological experiences: for both, all mental events are at the same time experiences of the body, including its no less material *psuchê*, mind and body affect each other mutually, and both judgments and physiological changes are necessary for emotion. But for Aristotle, the ordinary emotions of everyday life can be integrated into a life that fulfills human potential for virtue and flourishing; for the Stoics and Epicureans, on the other hand, though the virtuous life is by no means affect-free, common-or-garden emotions are by and large regarded as material for therapy (Nussbaum 1994). In Hellenistic and Roman sources, this is caricatured as a distinction between the allegedly Aristotelian pursuit of moderation in emotion (*metriopatheia*) and a Hellenistic therapeutic approach which takes emotion, at least as commonly understood, to be a bad thing (e.g. Cicero, *Tusculan Disputations* 4.38–57; Seneca, *On Anger (De ira)* 1.6–21).

Of the two schools, the Epicureans make more concessions to the empirical phenomena of everyday experience, but the Epicurean approach can also involve a critical attitude towards many ordinary emotions, as factors which will detract from the goal of psychological stability (*ataraxia*). Substantial reflections of Epicurean approaches to emotion survive in two first-century BCE discussions, namely the fragments of Philodemus' *On Anger* and Lucretius' influential *On the Nature of Things (De rerum natura* 3.258– 322). From Philodemus, it appears that Epicureans classified emotions similarly to the way they classified desires—as natural and necessary; natural but not necessary; or neither ("empty").[45] The tendency to anger is natural (*On Anger*, columns XXXVII.16–XLIV.35 Indelli),[46] but not necessary (fragments 10.14–15, 12 Indelli). It is found even in the wise (XXXVI.17–20, XLVI.40–XLVII.18, XLVII.41–L.8), who may experience its pain when friends are wronged or when a friend does wrong (XLI.17–25); but such anger will be brief and mild (XXXIV.16–XXXV.5, XLII.4–14, 21–40, XLIV.26–8, XLVII.29–41), stopping far short of anything that could be described as "rage" or "fury" (*thumos*, XLIII.41–XLVI.14). The error of treating anger as necessary, on the other hand, and taking pleasure in revenge or punishment (XLII.21–34, XLIV.28–35), makes it "empty" (XXXVIII.1–6, XXXIX.7–8). For Lucretius, anger is a matter of an individual's physical constitution: the degree to which a person is disposed to anger will depend on the element of heat in that person's soul (3.288–306). Reason cannot completely remodel such dispositions—there will be residual traces (3.310–22); but it would in any case not be right to eradicate anger, as it is sometimes called for (3.312–13).

The Epicurean approach can, as noted above, involve a critical attitude towards emotions, but the Stoics go further in arguing that all *pathê* involve mistaken judgments and therefore have no place in the virtuous life (Graver 2007; key texts in Long and Sedley 1987, §65). For them, *pathê* are in one way rational and in another not. They involve an impression (*phantasia*) that leads to arousal, but also an assessment that a stimulus of a certain type is present, an assent to that assessment, and a judgment that it is appropriate to be moved on that basis (see, e.g., Long and Sedley 1987, §65 B (Andronicus); Cicero, *Tusculan Disputations* 3.25, 3.61, etc.; Seneca, *On Anger* 2.4 = Long and Sedley 1987, §65 X; Graver 2007: 44–5). They are functionally rational but normatively irrational (Gill 1998; Graver 2007: 37–8). Though they depend on rational assent, they are irrational not only in being mistaken about the good, but also in being the product of defective psychological states and insofar as they are, after assent, compulsive, overwhelming and difficult to stop.

The Stoics distinguish four general categories of *pathê*: two that focus on one's present situation (pleasure and pain) and two concerning the future (desire and fear).[47] But Stoic definitions also typically make summary reference to physical changes (e.g. "contraction" in the case of pain and "elation" in that of pleasure: Long and Sedley 1987, §65 D (Galen); Stobaeus 2.7.10b). Emotions are not only judgments but also alterations in the *pneuma* (a mixture of fire and air) that is concentrated in the control center or *hêgemonikon* in the heart (Chrysippus in Galen, *On the Doctrines of Hippocrates and Plato* 3.7.2–4 = von Arnim 1903, 2.900). But *pneuma* also suffuses the entire body, and the Stoics are also attentive to a wide variety of physical symptoms beyond the changes that occur in the *hêgemonikon*: soul and body affect each other mutually (i.e. they exhibit *sumpatheia*). All these processes entail physical changes of an ensouled body (Graver 2007: 33–4). Thus, though the Stoics are famous for their claim that emotions are judgments, they are judgments of a particular sort: both the judgment (with its own physiological underpinnings) and the accompanying feelings and symptoms are necessary for an experience to count as an emotion.

Since emotions are not simply "cool" judgments, and since, once the subject has given assent, they are difficult to control,[48] it appears that motivational conflict is a possibility in Stoic theory at all stages of its development (Graver 2007: 69, 75–81; Gill 1998, 2010: 152). For the Stoics, however, this is a matter not of the conflict of rational *versus* irrational desires, but of temporal vacillation between successive judgments of value.[49] The fact that, in adult human beings, they involve assent makes all adults responsible for them: it is up to us to be the kind of people who do not get carried away; if we're not, we are the ones to blame (Graver 2007: 64).

The Stoic ideal is the eradication of all such *pathê*; but this is not a demand that human beings should be immune to all forms of affective experience. Seneca (*On Anger* 2.2.5) writes of "preliminary beginnings of emotion" (*principia proludentia adfectibus*), and from other sources it appears that earlier Stoics also had a category of "pre-emotions" (*propatheiai*: Graver 2007, 85–108).[50] These are described in terms (such as "bites" or "pangs") very like those used of the *pathê* in ordinary language. Even the Stoic sage will experience pre-emotions,[51] though she will not assent to them. The sage will also experience what are sometimes called "good emotions" (*eupatheiai*). To the four categories of *pathê* there correspond three of *eupatheiai*, emotions informed by virtue (see Long and Sedley 1987: § 65 F, from Diogenes Laertius). These are joy (at being virtuous), wish (to be virtuous), and caution (against anything that detracts from virtue). There is no virtuous analog to pain (*lupê*), because nothing bad is present to the sage (Graver 2007: 53–4).[52]

Both Stoics and Epicureans see emotions as misguided beliefs about the goals of life, be it virtue or freedom from disturbance (*ataraxia*). For the ancient Skeptics, an avoidance of commitment to beliefs also avoids the distraction of emotions, and they too believe that people are better off without them (Betts 1998). In this respect, all the Hellenistic schools contrast markedly with Aristotle: Seneca (*Moral Epistles* 116.1; cf. 85.3–5) sees the Peripatetics as advocating moderation in forms of behavior and experience that the Stoics seek to eradicate altogether. But even for the Stoics the good life remains one that is rich in affective experience.

EMOTIONS AND THE ANCIENT HISTORIAN

Ancient philosophical and psychological theories of emotion clearly have a history. And since the main ancient theories are cognitive-evaluative in their orientation, this is inevitably a history that is bound up with the norms and values of specific ancient societies and the psychological and ethical theories of the major ancient thinkers and schools. It is therefore also a history that will inform the histories that we write of the periods in which these theories developed and mutated.

For the ancient historian, emotion history involves not only the history of emotion concepts or philosophical theories, but also the role that emotions play as historical causes. It may be the case that hope and fear, as diametrically opposed attitudes towards imagined futures, are the quintessential political emotions (and thus loom large as historical motives and causes),[53] just as, for Thucydides, the "truest cause" of the Peloponnesian War is Sparta's fear (*phobos*) of Athenian expansion (1.23.6). But an ancient historian would surely insist that anger and the desire for revenge should figure just as prominently in analysis—Western historiography begins with Herodotus' narrative of offence and retaliation between Greeks and non-Greeks; the motif of vengeance structures his work on several levels (de Romilly 1971). Greek and Roman historians recognized the importance of emotions in history in ways that are only now coming back into focus.

Emotions pervade ancient historiography in other ways too. Tacitus claims to write *sine ira et studio* ("without anger or favor," *Annals* 1.1), but few believe him. Authorial judgments, often emotional in character, are by no means absent from the pages of the ancient historians. When Thucydides writes that Nicias, of all his contemporaries, least deserved his fate (7.86.5), he not only pays tribute to Nicias' virtue (*aretê*), but also classes him as worthy of pity. In invoking that emotional script, Thucydides may be expressing his own feelings; but he is also addressing his readers' emotions. Direct authorial intervention is just one of the many ways in which historical texts do this. Historiography is thoroughly influenced by the emotion-eliciting practices of other literary genres (especially epic and tragedy) and by the theorization of those practices, especially in rhetoric. Though there could be controversy over how a historian might seek to move his audiences, as in the Hellenistic historian Polybius' criticism of his predecessor, Phylarchus, for using sensationalist and dishonest methods to elicit sympathy for people who allegedly did not deserve it (2.56–63; Marincola 2003, 2013; cf. Scodel and Caston, this volume), Polybius is fully in step with his fellow historians in regarding readers' emotions (specifically pity and anger, 2.56.13) as essential elements in their understanding of historical processes. As the author of *On the Sublime* observes (38.3–5), this need not involve the use of especially emotive vocabulary. But in a case such as Tacitus' account of the death of Vitellius (in Book 3 of his *Histories*), a complex set of emotional responses is steered by the portrayal of Vitellius' own actions and feelings, the deployment of typically emotion-inducing scenarios (such as the dramatic reversal in Vitellius' fortunes, 3.68.1), authorial spin, and the reactions of internal audiences (Levene 1997). As a victim of the mutability of fortune, Vitellius is a potential candidate for sympathy (*misericordia*), until the abject terror in which he attempts to escape his fate and the unseemliness of his end make him "a disgusting spectacle," object of the mob's abuse rather than their tears (3.84). The emotional texture of the narrative itself is in such cases considerable.

In such passages, we see the techniques of literary narrative, elements of theatricality, and the vividness (*enargeia*) so prized by literary and rhetorical theory (Levene 1997; cf. Chaniotis 2013c; Damon 2017; on *enargeia* in general, see Webb 2009). These are the techniques by which the emotionality of the work itself engages the emotions of readers and audiences, the primary aim of literary and rhetorical *enargeia* (*On the Sublime* 15; Quintilian 6.2.29–32). Large among the emotions thus elicited looms pity (Webb 1997; cf. Scodel and Caston, this volume). A typical scenario for pity, from the final book of Homer's *Iliad* onwards, is the mutability of fortune, a fact of human existence that permits the recognition that others are as vulnerable as we are and a persistently recurring theme in ancient historiography (Hau 2016). Already in Homer, the manner in which one bears vicissitude may be as much a source of consolation and admiration as of fellow-feeling (Cairns 2014a): Polybius (1.1.2) regards the use of others' reversals to instruct people how to bear their own misfortunes as fundamental to the historian's craft (Marincola 2003: 303–6). Polybius uses the Aristotelian term *peripateiai*, but evidently disagrees with Aristotle (*Po.* 9, 1451a36–b7) that history, unlike poetry, deals only with particulars. The presentation of exemplary figures as worthy of emulation (Sallust, *Jugurtha* 4.5) is as central to ancient historiography as it is to ancient biography.

But though the historians do return repeatedly to a particular range of core emotions and emotional scenarios, the emotional texture of the genre is variegated and diverse. Readers may feel sympathy or antipathy, pity or horror, anger or disgust; but they may also experience the sense of wonder that impelled Herodotus to ensure that the great deeds of Greeks and non-Greeks should not go unrecorded (Book 1 *init.*): Herodotean *historiê*, and thus European historiography, just like the love of wisdom (*philosophia*) in general (Plato, *Theaetetus* 155d; Aristotle, *Metaphysics* 1.2, 982b12–13), begins in wonder (cf. Scodel and Caston, this volume). Ancient historiography itself at once enacts and furnishes material for the cultural history of emotions. Historians of ancient culture have done well so far to follow its lead; but there is also much to hope for as the cultural history of emotions moves even more firmly to the forefront of our discipline.

CHAPTER ONE

Medical and Scientific Understandings

GEORGE KAZANTZIDIS

INTRODUCTION

Hippocrates' *Epidemics* 1.9 (2.650–2 L.) describes a deadly outbreak of fever on the island of Thasos with the following symptoms:

> Now, those suffering from ardent fever, when fatal symptoms attended, showed signs from the beginning. For right from the beginning there was acute fever with slight rigors, sleeplessness, thirst, nausea, slight sweats about the head and collar-bones, but in no case all over the body, much delirium, *phoboi*, *dusthumiai*, very cold extremities, toes and hands, especially the latter. The exacerbation occurred on the even days; but in most cases the pains were the greatest on the fourth day, with sweat for the most part chilly, while the extremities could not now be warmed again, remaining livid and cold.
>
> —trans. Jones 1923a: 173, modified

The list of symptoms cited above is characteristic of the way in which emotions are evaluated clinically in the Hippocratic corpus (see Fig. 1.1), the earliest collection of medical writings (fifth to fourth centuries BCE) to have survived from Greek antiquity, which will be the focus of this chapter. *Phobos*, "fear," and *dusthumiê*, "despondency," follow upon the observation that some of the patients show signs of mental disturbance. Indeed, when the suspicion is raised in medical texts that a patient's mind has been affected, along with his or her body, emotions become increasingly significant as symptoms. At the same time, there is no indication that either fear or sadness is highlighted as if they were qualitatively different from the physical symptoms, for example cold extremities, sweat in the forehead, or nausea; in fact, the text shows no awareness of what we would today call patient "psychology." In Hippocratic medicine, emotions are most often treated as an extension of the body, rather than independently. In this context, it is highly likely that *phobos* and *dusthumiê* have been adduced by the author as additional symptoms—confirming simply the presence of excessive coldness in the patients' bodies.[1] On the whole, even though early medical writers are keen on observing—and indeed develop a rich and refined vocabulary for—emotional anomalies, the overall tendency is to frame "affective" symptoms in a context which is predominantly concerned with what is happening inside the (material) body: "the body," as Peter Singer puts it, "can be used," in the medicine of this period, "to give an account of total experience."[2]

FIGURE 1.1: Portrait of Hippocrates holding his *Apophthegms*. Fourteenth-century Byzantine miniature.

The question of how Greek medical science understands the emotions necessarily implicates their relation to the body. In *De anima* 403a3–20, Aristotle seeks to identify whether the soul exists independently of the body by asking precisely whether the so-called *pathê* of the *psychê* (a generic term indicating everything that the soul undergoes, including the emotions) belong only to the soul;[3] for if it could be proved that such emotions as anger and courage are not shared by the body, it would then follow that the soul can maintain an independent existence (403a10–12). As it happens, the hypothesis is soon dismissed—emotions cannot be experienced unless through the body (403a17–20)—but Aristotle, as is well known, places emphasis (both in *De anima* and in the *Rhetoric*) also on how they are formed mentally by complicated thoughts, evaluations, and judgments:[4] thus, for instance, while both anger and fear are accompanied by an unpleasant sensation of pain (*lupê*), anger is specifically qualified by the belief that we have been wrongfully mistreated (*Rhetoric* 1378a31–3) whereas fear is experienced as a mental picture of some destructive or painful evil in the future (*Rhetoric* 1382a21–2).[5]

Hippocratics assume a more radical position: while they are certainly familiar with the fact that "feeling" involves "thinking," for the most part they deliberately ignore the fact that emotions can be shaped cognitively by a separate mental faculty, and they prefer to analyze an emotion into its bodily and material coordinates. Aristotle is familiar with this tendency: the issue of what anger is, as we are told in *De anima* 403a29–b2, can be addressed differently, depending on the perspective we adopt; thus, the "dialectician" would try to understand its formal cause, describing it as "a desire for retaliation" which arises from one's judgment that one has been wronged;[6] the "natural scientist" (*phusikos*),[7] on the other hand, would seek to define it materially, concluding that anger is "the boiling of blood and hot stuff around the heart." As we look further into the Hippocratic corpus, we realize that the doctors' profoundly "physical" understanding of emotions is not simply a matter of emphasis; on the contrary, it is a calculated attempt to sidestep the idea of a ruling mental faculty and to propose instead that appraisal in affective experience should be viewed as an organismic activity that is distributed across the body and in which the body operates as the prime sense-making mechanism. This is not to say that medical emotions lack "intelligence," but that intelligence has been subsumed by a feeling and perceiving body which functions as the primary seat of emotion.[8] As Michael Frede observes, one of the usual mistakes we make in our approach to ancient philosophical and medical texts is that we "underrate the physical to the extent that we tend to think of it as being determined by certain ultimate material constituents and a few basic properties of these material constituents";[9] yet, when we consider that the distinction between mind or soul and the body is not always evident in ancient sources and that in some of them psychic activity is conceived as a certain disposition of the body (see especially the Hippocratic *On Regimen*),[10] it then follows that thinking or feeling is "something that a living body does in virtue of the soul, rather than something which the soul or the mind does for it."[11] In this context, the emphasis placed by the Hippocratics on the raw physicality of emotions will be discussed as a means of assigning to the body an enhanced role as a sense-making, appraising mechanism. The main underlying notion is that there is no need to discuss affect by presupposing a superimposing mental process; rather, it is the body that does the "feeling" and incorporates, in all its material dimensions, what we call "emotion."

EMOTIONS IN HEALTH

Emotions are of interest to medical authors mainly as symptoms of disease—as an index of erratic behavior showing that the patient's body is out of balance. This means that we lack a comprehensive medical account explaining how emotions arise under normal circumstances and how they are related to body and mind in a state of health. The most detailed attempt to speak about emotions in their natural state is found in *On the Sacred Disease* 14 (6.386 L.)—in a treatise which sets out to explain epilepsy by attributing its origin to the brain,[12] the most important of all organs in the human body according to the author:

> Men ought to know that from the brain, and from the brain only, arise our pleasures, joys, laughter, and amusement, as well as our sorrows, pains, griefs, and tears. It is especially through this organ that we think, see, hear, and distinguish the ugly from the beautiful, the bad from the good, the pleasant from the unpleasant. Sometimes we judge according to convention; at other times according to what we sense to be in the best for our interests.
>
> —trans. Jones 1923b: 175, modified

Modern lists of "basic affects" or "basic emotions" typically include anger, disgust, fear, happiness, sadness, and surprise.[13] In the Greek passage cited above we can easily recognize the equivalents of happiness/pleasure and sadness/distress.[14] Furthermore, although disgust is not explicitly mentioned in the text, we can trace it behind the author's remark that the brain helps us distinguish between "pleasant" and "unpleasant" things,[15] in the same way that it allows us to make aesthetic judgments or ethical decisions. On that reading, disgust would be more directly linked to an appraising process—than, say, happiness or sadness—thus approximating to a "higher cognitive" emotion.[16] Indeed, it is worth remembering that while disgust is seen by some as a basic affect, assumed to be triggered and executed on a largely automatic basis of instinctive reactions, there are those who argue that "the word is merely a rough generalizing label that captures the sensation of judging something to have polluting and defiling powers."[17] But with the exception of disgust, the relationship between affects and mental functions in the Hippocratic text—the latter including *phronêsis* ("intelligence"), *sunesis* ("understanding"), and *diagnôsis* ("discerning thinking")[18]—remains for the most part obscure: while the brain is identified as the ultimate source for every psychic power in the body, there is no attempt by the author to discuss in detail the kind of thoughts and judgments that shape our feelings. In fact, when later in the treatise "fear" (*phobos*) is added to the list of emotions, its link to the brain is explained strictly in materialist terms: when too much bile enters the cavity of the head and raises the brain's temperature, a person is seized by *phobos*, which subsides only after the humour has moved down to the body and back into the veins (*On the Sacred Disease* 15, 6.388 L.). In the same spirit, it is stated that the heart and the diaphragm—an area of the body that is best endowed with feeling (*aisthanesthai*) and the location in which strong emotions reach their culmination—are actually "void of intelligence" (*phronêsis*').[19] This seems to create a sort of calculated contrast between affect and mental activity, and invites closer consideration of the extent to which a ruling cognitive faculty is intrinsic to emotional experience in Hippocratic medicine.

Throughout the corpus there are many examples which indicate that for an emotion to be experienced there is no need for a separate cognitive process to have taken place; rather, appraisal appears to be something that is distributed and executed across the body.[20] As we read in *On Humours* 9 (5.490 L.), in a section of the text devoted to "things happening to the body" when we experience an emotion:

> How the body behaves: when a mill grinds the teeth are set on edge; the legs shake when one walks beside a precipice; *the hands shake when one lifts a heavy load*; the *sudden* sight of a snake causes pallor. Fear, shame, pain, pleasure, passion, and so forth; to each of these the appropriate member of the body responds by its action. Instances are sweat, palpitations of the heart, and so forth.
>
> —trans. Jones 1931: 81, modified

Scholars have long been troubled by the close connection drawn in this passage between bodily sensations which accompany an emotion (e.g. trembling with fear when walking by a precipice or turning pale at the sight of a snake) and the image of one's hands "shaking under the burden of a heavy load."[21] It is tempting to speculate that the reason why a purely somatic reaction is introduced at this point as analogous to instances of embodied emotion has precisely to do with the fact that, even during an affective experience, the body is thought to act, more or less, autonomously, without being necessarily shaped by prior thoughts and judgments—when the hands tremble with pain, this happens not because we have evaluated the situation as physically exhausting but simply because our body gets tired and reacts instinctively. The emphasis placed on the autonomy of the affective body, and the implicit attempt to reduce the mind's ruling function, would also seem to explain the author's decision to discuss fear by invoking the example of a snake which is "seen suddenly": the external stimulus in this case leaves little time for conscious thought and processing, causing the body to "turn pale" before one has the opportunity to assess fully what he or she has seen as well as the specific threat posed by it. Thus, while the list of affects in *On Humours* 9 includes also "higher cognitive emotions," such as shame (*aischunê*) and anger (*orgê*), the text is mostly preoccupied with emotional experience in the form of a series of instinctive reactions (for instance, grinding one's teeth at the sound of a mill) which lack a distinctly cognitive component. In this context, the main priority is given to the body, which assumes the role of an agent.[22] This does not mean, of course, that the author ignores the fact that external triggers are perceived mentally, either through vision or hearing; as his examples illustrate, however, the focus remains on how affective experience is mediated through the body (rather than the mind) without which emotions cannot exist.[23]

Whether or not we take such automatic reactions to qualify as fully formed emotions,[24] the case remains that Hippocratic writers display the tendency to discuss the relationship between emotions and the body without assuming—or, at least, without stating explicitly—that the mind's prior intervention is necessary. This is often explained by the fact that emotions are said to occur "unexpectedly"[25]—in this sense, all affective responses share a common "startle reflex" quality which inscribes them within a realm of instinctual experience. In *On the Sacred Disease* 10 (6.378–80 L.) the connection between *phobos* ("fear"), phlegm, and the chilling of the body is made in the following way:

> In other cases the cause is that the south wind, *suddenly* coming on after north winds, loosens and relaxes the brain when it is braced and strong, so that the phlegm overflows, and thus it produces the flux. The same thing is also caused *by sudden fear*, if the patient be afraid at a shout . . . Whichever of them occur, the body is *immediately* chilled.
>
> —trans. Jones 1923b: 167

Phobos is discussed exclusively at the level of its physical manifestation, its internal cause (*phlegma*), and its consequent effects on the body (*phrikê*, chill or shivering). The reason why we find no reference to the thoughts that give rise to emotion is clearly that the stimulus occurs "all of a sudden," at a time when no one is expecting it—this is intensified by the observation that the cause is a shout, not a sight, which makes the person's reaction even more instinctive, considering that among the five modes of sense-perception, hearing is considered to be inferior to vision[26] Accordingly, while the brain is said to play an integral part in the process, it is approached strictly as a material cause, and not as the seat of cognition: by entering into a state of "looseness," the brain discharges increased amounts of phlegm and induces "immediately" a state of coldness in the body, which is necessary for the emotion of fear to be felt. Exactly the same thing can happen to the brain when there is a "sudden" change from north to south winds: the idea that an emotion forms itself by following the same principles that apply also to our bodies' reaction to external environmental changes is suggestive, and underscores the raw physicality of affective experience in a medical context. Finally, it is worth noting that the notion of fear being caused "suddenly" is paralleled by the similar use of "unexpectedly" at a later point in the text, where the author is explaining that the diaphragm is most sensitive to emotion, but has no capacity to think: "I do not know what power the diaphragm [*phrenes*] has for thought [*noein*] and intelligence [*phronein*]. It can only be said that, if a man is unexpectedly over-joyed or grieved, the diaphragm jumps and causes him to start" (ch. 17 = 6.392 L.). The idea of an emotion flooding the body "in excess" is highlighted at the expense of the thinking faculty (contrary to what is commonly believed, as the author explains, the *phrenes* have nothing to do with *phronêsis*, "intelligence"),[27] and it should not be seen as a coincidence that once more it is implied that the cause of the emotion enters our perception without any prior warning.

Aristotle, as we saw, insists that emotions are intimately linked to the body but also places special emphasis on the thoughts that shape and direct our feelings. What remains ambiguous is whether the body should be given priority over the mind, or vice versa. In his discussion of anger, *orgê*, for instance, Aristotle distinguishes between a "material" and a "formal" cause for the emotion, but it is not made clear whether we get angry because we believe that we have been wronged by someone or, alternatively, because our blood's temperature has increased (or whether these two things happen simultaneously).[28] The question can be phrased as follows: is the appraisal of an annoying external stimulus primarily a matter of an embodied reaction which consequently conditions the way we think, or is it necessary for thinking to take place first before our blood temperature increases? Although we find no such explicit statement, the medical evidence indicates that for the Hippocratics the body comes first: this is not simply to say that they choose to focus on the material aspects of the emotion—at the expense of exploring its formal cause—but, more importantly, that they are keen to establish the body's priority as an agent during an affective experience.

As Jesse Prinz points out, "in developing a theory of emotion, we should not feel compelled to supplement embodied states with meaningful thoughts: we should instead put meaning into our bodies and let perceptions of the heart reveal our situation in the world."[29] This observation has two important implications: on the one hand, it helps to show that "perception," in the context of an affective experience, is distributed across the body; on the other hand, it suggests that the body defines the way in which we engage emotionally with our external environment. The bodily feelings assigned to a specific emotion do not always require an intervening judgment nor do they necessarily arise as responses to such a judgment; rather, to the extent that they occur instinctively and automatically, they provide a bodily disposition through which any subsequent evaluation is being formed and acted upon. According to this model, an increased heart rate—when we suddenly encounter a snake, for instance—is not the result of a perceived threat but assists us in identifying an external object as threatening; the emotion is first being enacted as a bodily state characteristic of fear, and it consequently alters our cognitive processing in a manner that fits the state of fear.[30]

Modern scholarship on "distributed cognition" provides a good parallel to this thought. In Giovanna Colombetti's words:

> Acknowledging [that] all our affective life is bound up with ... evaluations ... need not lead to the further claim that appraisal exists as a separate process or mechanism that triggers emotional responses. Indeed ... neuroscientific considerations as well as phenomenological ones suggest otherwise and indicate rather that evaluating the world and responding emotionally to it are not distinct processes. From an enactive perspective, the process of appraising is best characterized as an organismic activity, not separate but overlapping with what are usually seen as noncognitive, bodily components of emotion.[31]

Similarly, what makes the Hippocratics' account of emotions distinctive is the way in which affective experience is decentralized—which means that it is not linked, nor is it considered subject, to a central appraising faculty—and is dispersed throughout the body. This should explain, for instance, why in some cases emotions are experienced on a micro-level, by being attributed not to the person as a whole but to individual bodily parts, as in for example *On Breaths* 8 (6.100 L.), where blood is said to "fear for itself"[32] when too much "cold air" has entered into the veins and "moves" to warmer places. In this context, the body emerges as a prime operative factor—a material entity which not only reflects emotional experience but also defines it in an essential way. Emotions are consistently discussed by the Hippocratics in connection with their underlying physiological circumstances; so much so that their status as "psychological" entities seems sometimes contestable. It is worth noting, for instance, that words such as *lupê* and *tromos*, which in contemporary non-medical literature are used to convey also a psychological state, occur in the Hippocratic corpus almost exclusively with a literal meaning; that is, they are primarily conceived as conditions of the body: *lupê* (see Fig. 1.2) is more often employed to describe bodily pain and discomfort[33] (rather than "sorrow" or "mental distress"),[34] while *tromos* (a word associated with "terror")[35] refers exclusively to the "trembling" of a feverish patient, without the slightest hint that it can also indicate some kind of psychological distress.[36]

Medical writers maintain that emotions cannot be abstracted from their physical symptoms or causes, usually by narrowing down a word's range of metaphorical meaning(s) to the level of primary, material qualities.[37] This is a process that often requires imaginative thinking and even involves the invention of humoral substances whose existence in the body cannot be confirmed: as Brooke Holmes argues, in its attempt to dismiss the notion of divine agency and to naturalize the cause of disease by containing it

FIGURE 1.2: Achilles binds Patroclus' wound. Attic red-figure drinking cup by the Sosias Painter, *c.* 510–490 BCE.

within the physical body, Hippocratic medicine often transforms that same body into a highly figurative realm of hidden and unseen forces.[38] The case of anger is fairly characteristic: *cholos*, a word that is widely attested in early Greek in the sense of "anger," increasingly gives its place in the Hippocratic corpus to the medical term *cholê*, "bile," whose "black" (*melaina*) variety—believed by some to be a medical fabrication, in the sense that it did not correspond to an actual fluid[39]—is thought to make a person angry, or drive him insane. *Cholos*, in the Homeric texts and in Greek tragedy, is broadly conceived as an emotional state, and its physiology remains elusive at best; what we witness in the medical texts is a shift towards its concrete, humoral cause.[40] Such a shift requires a process of inversion: *cholos* is rich in metaphorical associations (it "holds" a person "in its grip"; it "enters" the body; it "makes one's heart swell," and so forth)[41] and it is figuratively compared to liquids which "burn," "boil," or can even be "digested."[42] By contrast, *cholê* is primarily a fluid which can cause damage to the body (when it is found in excess) and, incidentally, it can also affect a patient psychologically. What lies behind this change of meaning and shift of focus is a strong commitment to physicality—the notion that emotional states exist primarily in the form of material substances.

The limits between body and emotion in Hippocratic medicine are so hard to determine that sometimes it is difficult to tell whether a medical term refers to an emotional state or to its underlying physiological condition—or to both. One word whose meaning remains elusive in medical texts is *asê* (from *aân*, "to satiate"), which is variably translated as "dizziness," "nausea" or—in a more affective sense—as "disgust" and "distress." One medical author mentions *asê* side-by-side with "sweat" (*hidrôtion*): while sweat, in that particular instance, is said to run "almost through the entire of the patient's body," *asê* is specifically located around the heart and—from what we can tell from the description—it refers predominantly to some sort of physical discomfort.[43] In another text, we read that *asê* stops once the patient drinks milk mixed with honey, and vomits (*Epid.* 7.94, 5.450 L.); considering that the word is etymologically linked to "surfeit," one assumes that vomiting (i.e. getting rid of a *material* excess in the body) is enough to relieve the person affected from it. And yet, there are other passages which show that the word implies more than a physical feeling: a patient whose heart and insides are in pain, as we read in *Internal Affections* 35 (7.254 L.), is gloomy and avoids contact with people; every time someone speaks to him, "he becomes distressed, and displays *asê* and he cannot stand to even listen" to those around him. Similarly, in *On the Sacred Disease* 15 (6.388 L.), excessive coldness in the head causes "unexpected fits of distress and anxiety (*asê*)." Overall, what we seem to have here is a semi-physical, semi-psychological state whose semantics are thinly balanced between body and emotion. Its exact meaning remains obscure precisely because the line between affect and its constitutive material elements is hard, almost impossible, to determine.

In many of the instances where emotions come to the fore in the Hippocratic corpus, reference is made to the heart (*kardiê*). In *Epidemics* 6.6.5 (6.316 L.) it is stated that "anger" (*oxuthumiê*) contracts the heart and the lungs, and draws the hot and the moist substances into the head; conversely, a state of contentment—which we may loosely translate as "happiness" (*euthumiê*)—is exclusively associated with the heart's relaxation. The passage is characteristic of the medical tendency to speak of emotions simply by referring to the physical states to which they correspond. More importantly, while the implication is raised that the body reacts to an emotion which has been processed mentally (one feels happy and as a result the heart relaxes), it seems equally likely that *euthumiê* cannot be experienced unless the heart has been previously dilated.[44] In this context, it is worth adding that while the heart is often mentioned as the location of emotion, some Hippocratic passages describe it as being, at the same time, completely void of intelligence. In fact, one is tempted to speculate that the reason why the heart is singled out as the affective space par excellence is related to the implication that it does not have the capacity to "think." According to *On the Sacred Disease* 16–17 (6.390–4 L.), the area of the body that is best endowed with "feeling" (*aisthanesthai*), and where an emotion becomes physically manifest, is the heart (*kardiê*) and the diaphragm (*phrenes*). Every part of the body participates in intelligence in direct proportion to the air received from the brain; the best quality of air stays in the head, and what is left for the rest of the body is, by definition, inferior. At this point, the author makes a striking claim: the heart and the diaphragm, because of their thin and solid structure, receive no air at all—they are literally devoid of the material which distributes "intelligence" across the body.[45] As a result, their special link to emotions is explained in purely mechanical terms: due to the fact that veins extend from all over the body to the area of the chest, the latter becomes extremely sensitive and it "convulses" every time someone experiences physical "pain [*ponos*], tension [*tasis*] or excessive joy." Once more, we see how an emotion registers in the body as a reflex-like type of reaction, similar to the instinctive reaction we have when we receive a blow in the stomach or when we shudder in the cold. What allows for this association of ideas to take place is the fact that in medical writings there is no expressed commitment to the notion that emotions have to be shaped by clearly formulated judgments: just as the body is instinctively strained (*sunteinesthai*) when responding to pain (*aniômenon*), in the same way the heart is especially receptive to emotion because it happens to be located in an area of the body that is more sensitive than the others. This area has the special power to move and "feel" (*aisthanesthai*) but has no capacity whatsoever to think. *Aisthanesthai* has been used earlier in the text (*On the Sacred Disease* 13, 6.384–6 L.) to describe the sensing and reacting of inanimate substances: everything, including ceramic pots and the tissues of the human body, senses and reacts to the south wind.[46] Similarly, in our text the heart's sensation of distress or happiness is seen to be executed at the level of movement: while the heart has no intelligence, it can still enjoy a privileged relationship with emotion precisely because of its capacity to "convulse."

Emotions are occasionally addressed also in the context of treatment; this, however, is not meant to have a psychological effect but simply to regulate a patient's humoral chemistry. While in modern medicine the notion prevails that doctors should try to support their patients psychologically,[47] the Hippocratics seem to be mostly interested in the body. In one striking passage we read that "it is appropriate to induce anger for the sake of restoring color and humors, as well as fear, happiness and the like" (*Epidemics* 2.4.4 = 5.126 L.). It is hard to understand how making a patient angry or fearful would have actually helped him feel better. The reasoning here seems to be that each one of these emotions corresponds to a specific bodily state and, once it has been invoked, it can contribute to restoring physical balance (e.g. inducing fear, a "cold" emotion, would have helped counteract and reduce a patient's high temperature; conversely, if a patient is freezing, making him angry would have raised his temperature). Emotional therapy, in this context, is strictly conceived as a way of affecting a person's body and does not involve any attempt to address his or her state of mind independently.

EMOTIONS AS SYMPTOMS

When and how does an emotion turn into a symptom? The Hippocratics have an easy and obvious answer to this question: when a person displays emotional behavior that is not in sync with or cannot be explained by external circumstances, this is taken as an indication that the body's chemistry (its temperature, humoral balance, etc.) has changed because of illness. Such lack of correspondence is typically highlighted in medical texts by the adjectives *alogos/akairos* ("unreasonable," "untimely")[48] or the phrase *para kairon*, "at the wrong time." When too much phlegm, for instance, enters the cavity of the head and affects it with excessive coldness, the patient is seized by sudden fits of "causeless distress and anxiety" because the brain has been contracted "contrary to custom" (*On the Sacred Disease* 15, 6.388 L.). The cause that is missing, of course, is not a physiological one (this is explained in the text in meticulous detail) but refers to the absence of an appropriate psychological trigger in the patient's external environment. Similarly, in *On Regimen* 1. 35 (6.518–20 L.)—a text which maintains that the soul is a mixture of fire and water—we read that when moistness takes over the hot and dry elements in the body, "people start crying without an (apparent) cause, they fear what is not frightening and grieve for reasons that are not appropriate." All in all, "they do not feel [*aisthanesthai*], either in part or entirely, as is appropriate for the sane people."[49] It is interesting to see how different models of the body are invoked by different medical writers to account for what are essentially the same emotional abnormalities: be it the phlegm that affects the brain or the watery moisture that extinguishes the soul's fire, they are both assumed to lead, through excessive coldness, to "inexplicable" sadness and dejection.[50] The vocabulary that is employed to describe affective abnormality can thus be seen to create a shared medical discourse, and to impose a sense of common agenda among doctors who hold irreconcilably different beliefs regarding the inside of the body and the location of the mind.[51]

More importantly, the implicit distinction between "timely" and "untimely" emotions requires an integrated reading of a patient's psychology and does not rely simply on random medical observation. In *Epidemics* 7.10 (5.382 L.), we read of a patient who "spoke more aggressively and greeted people more warmly than the occasion warranted." The text should be read in connection with other clinical instances in which a "strange mood" essentially helps to establish that someone is acting "out of character." *Prorrhetic* 1.44 (5.522 L.) posits that "an insolent answer from a polite person is a bad sign"; and in *Epidemics* 4.15 (5.152 L.) the patient uses foul language (*aischromuthein*) and behaves in an unruly fashion. This kind of behavior, as the author observes, is "not of his type." These and other passages illustrate how emotional symptomatology allows the patient to emerge as an "individual": while the Hippocratic patient is notoriously elusive, being most of the times present only as body and subject to the doctor's complete authority, the discourse linked to affective disorders opens a window to behavioral patterns which confirm that behind a patient's silenced voice there lies a concrete identity (see Fig. 1.3).[52]

In pathological contexts, emotions are mentioned regularly side-by-side with signs of mental disturbance. Patients are described as shouting, singing, weeping, and laughing; they are distressed, dejected, in anguish, and then again optimistic. They jump suddenly out of bed, become aggressive, and are not to be managed. This symptomatology is usually framed by the vocabulary of insanity, by words such as *maniê*, *paraphrosunê*, and so on.[53] However, we should be careful to avoid identifying mental and emotional disorders. In fact, in at least two major accounts found in the corpus, regarding issues of intelligence, feeling, and perception, mental and affective pathology are explained with a view to a different causation. In *On the Sacred Disease* 15 (6.388 L.), as we saw before, "causeless distress and anxiety" are due to the fact that the brain is "contracted" because of excessive quantities of cold phlegm. What is meant here is an actual, qualitative change in the brain's constitution, hence the author's use of "corruption" (*diaphthorê*) when it comes

FIGURE 1.3: Attic votive relief for Amphiaraos in Oropos, dedicated by Archinos, 400–350 BCE.

to indicating the phlegm's corrosive effects. Phlegm is responsible also for insanity (*maniê* and *paraphrosunê*), but the explanation in this case is different: we turn mad because of an excess of "moisture"; the brain floats in the liquid that had been concentrating in the head and, as a result, it moves up and down, right and left, without allowing our senses of sight and hearing to remain still. Consequently, perception is disturbed, and the person sees and hears things that do not correspond with external reality; even more worryingly, he speaks in strange ways, thinking his hallucinations to be true. Thus, while emotional disturbance results from corruption, insanity is primarily a matter of irregular, pathological movement.[54] What lies behind this imaginative thinking, and the different aetiology proposed for each case, is an attempt to distinguish between purely mental pathologies and affective disorders. To be sure, the two are closely linked to each other, but they do not always overlap. Being depressed, for example, does not necessarily require (nor does it always entail) a radically changed perception of reality—and this is something that a Hippocratic doctor was in a position to recognize, hence the need to come up with two discreet aetiologies.

The same attempt to maintain a line of distinction between the mental and the emotional can be traced in *On Regimen* 1.35–6:[55] both mood and intelligence are dependent on the state of the soul, conceived as a mixture of fire and water; while the soul's intelligence (and sanity), however, is a matter of proportion between dry and moist elements in the body, its disposition—which determines, for instance, whether a person will be "irascible," "quarrelsome," or "easy going"—is linked to the state of the "passages through which the soul traverses in the body" (*On Regimen* 1.36, 6.522–24 L.). Once again, qualitative change and motion (as in the case of the brain, being corrupted by phlegm or, alternatively, floating in it) provide two different explanatory models on the basis of which a line of distinction between (disturbed) cognition and (pathological) affect is drawn.

Even so, the link between abnormal emotions and insanity persists and invites closer consideration. One may argue that while "healthy" emotions are discussed primarily on a physiological basis, when it comes to evaluating an emotion as a symptom of illness there is a tendency to implicate the mind more directly—as a separate, autonomously acting entity. In *Diseases of Women* 2.174 (8.356 L.), a female patient with inflammation in the womb is first affected with swellings in the feet, which then expand to the upper parts of her body. When they reach the area of the chest, the patient is seized by fever, has difficulty in breathing, and is overcome by weakness and fainting fits. At this point, the author observes, "while she felt pain all over her body, her mind grew restless and dejected." This is an intriguing passage in many respects: on the one hand, it becomes clear that psychological discomfort (resembling a state of depression) is attributed to a biological cause. Fear and sadness, melancholy's hallmark symptoms, are normally linked to an excess of cold elements in the body, and it is no coincidence that when the swellings reach the chest, the patient is said to be "freezing." On the other hand, we cannot fail to notice that dejection is specifically said to affect the patient's mind (*gnômê*)—the implication here being that, however it has been originally induced, an emotional state can be increasingly felt on a mental level. Although linked to a bodily condition, pathological affects can thus be occasionally experienced in a way that makes them different—if not categorically, at least diagnostically—from other physical symptoms.

Gnômê, like *nous* and *dianoia*, typically indicates in the corpus mental and intellectual activity. In *On the Sacred Disease* 16 (6.390 L.), the air, the carrier of intelligence, is said to leave its best part in the brain, "everything in it that has the capacity of *phronêsis* and *gnômê*," before moving down to the lower parts of the body. More importantly, *gnômê* can sometimes serve as the locus of emotion without (apparently) requiring the body's interference: in *Epidemics* 6.8.10 (5.348 L.) we read that the "mind's consciousness" can develop the capacity to experience emotion "by itself," independently of the body and regardless of the external circumstances: "it feels distress and pleasure, it becomes afraid and confident; it hopes and loses hope." One way of interpreting this exceptional passage is by connecting it with instances of recollection, imagination, anticipation, and so on, in which case mental activity suffices to activate a whole array of emotions.[56]

As it is, *gnômê*, when occurring in a pathological context, marks a tendency to stress the distinction between body and mind. A telling example is provided by the adjective *melancholikos* ("black-bilious"), which is regularly used in the corpus either with reference to patients whose bile turns black during an illness or, on a more tentative reading, to describe a constitutional state characterized by a permanent excess of black bile in the body.[57] Even when the implication of a melancholic constitution is raised—which would seem to allow some space for the development of a "type" of person in the psychological sense—the idea is pursued exclusively on a physiological level: in *Epidemics* 3.14 (3.98 L.), for instance, "melancholics" are simply mentioned in connection to the fact that their bodies make them sensitive to "high fever, phrenetic conditions, and dysenteria." In one instance, however, things are different. A female patient in *Epidemics* 3.17(2) (3.112 L.), originally suffering from acute fever following a difficult birth, displays a set of symptoms including loss of appetite, insomnia, and depression; she is aggressive and becomes easily distressed. As the author concludes, "concerning her state of mind [*gnômê*], she seemed to be melancholic." Of all its occurrences in the corpus, this is one of the most straightforward cases where "melancholic" refers to a psychological state. There is no doubt that *gnômê* helps, once more, to turn a word of predominantly biological associations (melancholic = black-bilious) into a designating term for a set of symptoms which are identified as a group on the basis of their common psycho-pathology.

But one can go further than that. In the passages discussed above, emotions occur as symptoms of illness; they emerge as side effects whose meaning is determined by the bodily condition to which they are linked. Emotions, however, can also function as causes—in which case an analogy could be drawn with what modern medicine identifies as a "psychogenic" condition. In *Aphorisms* 6.23 (9.568 L.), we read that "if fear or despondency persists for a long time, such a condition is melancholic." The medical author's diagnosis relies on the tendency to speak of pathological (that is, "inexplicable") emotions in terms of time: not every kind of fear or sadness is a sign of illness, but only those which persist "for so long" that they end up being disproportionate, unrelated even, to external circumstances in a person's life.[58] The exact amount of time required before an emotion becomes pathological is not specified, but this is hardly due to a lack of precision on the author's part. It is worth remembering that the marking line between temporary sadness and a fit of depression remains still a highly contestable issue in modern medicine. What renders the Hippocratic passage even more elusive is its syntax, which makes it hard to identify the relationship between cause and effect in the text: thus, while there has been a tendency in scholarship to read fear and sadness as "symptomatic" of an underlying melancholic pathology (literally, an excess of black bile in the body causing psychological distress), other readings raise the possibility that the two emotions appear as causes of the illness, and not as its results.[59] In that case, we should assume that the melancholy which is produced is essentially psychological in nature. The text is exceptional in other respects too: as Jacques Jouanna notes, "explicit descriptions," such as this one, "of the disturbances of the mind associated with melancholy are extremely rare in the Hippocratic Corpus."[60] One may add that *Aphorisms* 6.23 is also unique in the sense that it describes a disease (*to melancholikon*) which can apparently be diagnosed exclusively on psychological grounds: that is to say, fear or sadness or both, provided that they persist for uncommonly long periods of time, suffice by themselves to indicate a medical condition, and no bodily symptoms have to be considered in the process.

Although we have no concrete evidence to establish that the Hippocratics recognized a special form of illness caused by emotional distress, there are significant examples of patients throughout the corpus which show that, occasionally, emotional disturbance is all that there is to speak about, without any (explicit) reference to the body as the ultimate cause. In *Epidemics* 5.81 (5.250 L.), we read of a certain Nicanor who visits the doctor with the following complaint: every time he went to a drinking party he was terrified by the sound of the flute girl. "He said that he could hardly bear it when it was night, but if he heard it in the daytime he was not affected." Such symptoms, the author concludes, "persisted over a long period of time." Nothing else is added to the account, and although scholars have tried to connect Nicanor's "drinking" with some sort of humoral imbalance (too much wine could, in theory, extinguish the body's internal heat and cause depression),[61] this remains only an assumption. In the clinical case following immediately after (*Epidemics* 5.82, 5.252 L.), Democles displays symptoms which similarly resist a straightforward, physiological explanation. Democles becomes paralyzed and suffers from temporary loss of sight every time he is about to set foot on a bridge or when he happens to walk by a cliff; as with Nicanor, the doctor simply observes that this peculiar affection persisted "for some time," without venturing a hypothesis regarding its cause.

Even when phobias of this kind are explicitly described to result from physical illness, they can occasionally acquire a life of their own. In *Epidemics* 7.45 (5.414 L.), Mnesianax suffers from a serious eye disease, and one day "as he was walking about in the marketplace he started seeing sparks before his eyes and could not see the sunlight well." The patient is taken home in a hurry and spends some time bedridden, suffering from spasms and excessive coldness while also displaying symptoms of insanity; "and when he regained control of himself and stood up he did not want to go out, but said that he was afraid; and if someone mentioned to him something about a serious illness, he was taken by fear." Mnesianax's "hypochondriac" obsession is not causally linked to *ophthalmia*, at least not directly; in fact, it makes its appearance at precisely the point when his body starts showing signs of recovery. What we have here is some sort of anxiety disorder which evolves as a psychological response to the traumatic experience of physical illness, and continues to affect the patient on an emotional level.[62]

In light of these observations, let me conclude by examining what is perhaps one of the most intriguing cases of emotional pathology in the Hippocratic corpus. The text in question comes from *Epidemics* 3.17.11 (3.134 L.) and is worth citing extensively:

> In Thasos a woman of gloomy temperament [*dusanios gunê*], after a grief [*lupê*] with a reason for it, without taking to bed lost her sleep and appetite, and suffered from thirst and nausea... On the first day, as night began there were fears, much rambling, depression [*dusthumiê*] and slight feverishness. Early in the morning, frequent convulsions; whenever these frequent convulsions intermitted, she raved and uttered obscenities. On the third day, the convulsions ceased but they were succeeded by coma and lethargy, followed in turn by wakefulness. She would jump up; could not restrain herself; said a lot of things that made no sense; fever acute; on this night a copious, hot sweating all over the body; no fever; slept; was perfectly rational and had a crisis. About the third day urine black and thin, with particles mostly round floating in it, which did not settle. Near the crisis, copious menstruation.
>
> —trans. Jones 1923a: 27, modified

Dusanios ("hard to please," "easily annoyed," "grumpy")—the adjective translated "gloomy"—occurs only once in the Hippocratic corpus and remains an extremely rare word in Greek literature. As Galen (17a 778 K.) explains it, the word combines two meanings: it can either refer (a) to a person who becomes easily distressed even when the cause is not that important, or (b) when that cause is present and cannot be ignored, to someone who reacts by displaying feelings of sadness more intensely and for a longer period of time than other people. The idea that someone's temperament—approximating what we would call "character"—is dependent on bodily constitution is by no means uncommon in the Hippocratic corpus.[63] Concerning specifically women, the medical preconception that the female body is by nature moist and cold,[64] combined with the assumption that coldness functions as a material substrate for fear and sadness, seems to explain why "depression"-related feelings are highlighted more often in medical accounts of female patients rather than male ones. *Dusthumiê*, which makes its appearance in *Epidemics* 3.17(11), occurs six more times in the corpus.[65] It is no coincidence that in all cases where the patient's gender is explicitly stated in the text, the person affected is always a woman: in *Diseases of Women* 2.182, *asê* and *dusthumiê* are said to result from an excess of black bile in the womb; in *Epidemics* 3.2.6, *dusthumiê* is coupled with the woman's silence; and in *Epidemics* 3.2.11 the "wife of Hicetas" becomes delirious on the fourth day of her illness and suffers from *phoboi* and *dusthumiai*. In its single occurrence as a verb in the corpus, *dusthumeein*, "to be despondent," appears likewise in a gynaecological treatise (*Mul. affect.* 2.174). Finally, considering *dusthumiê*'s close association with "melancholia," it is worth noting that the phrase "she was melancholic in mind"—discussed above as an exceptional instance of psychological vocabulary applied to black bile—is used in *Epidemics* 3.17(2) in connection with a female patient. This is not to say, of course, that *dusthumiê* was not believed to affect men too: *Aphorisms* 6.23 states that the condition should be counted as one of melancholy's significant symptoms, without linking it specifically to a certain gender or age. Still, as we go through individual medical cases in the corpus, it transpires that depression is especially relevant when it comes to women; this may have resulted not so much from actual observation as from the doctors' expectation that the "cold" female body was likelier to produce feelings of sadness and fear under the extenuating circumstances of disease.[66]

Epidemics 3.17(11) is a typical example, in this respect, of the tendency to deal with female patients as being predisposed to episodes of excessive sadness. However, we should note that, in this particular instance, the body's role is downplayed and emphasis is placed instead on a psychological cause. This is the clearest occurrence in the corpus where someone is said to become ill because of mental and emotional pain (*lupê*). More importantly, the author's qualifying remark that *lupê* in that case happened to have "a reason"—which means essentially that "an external cause" could be identified—allows us to assume that the opposite can also be true, namely that people of a gloomy temperament do not always need a manifest cause to keep being sad:[67] depression and discontent can be perpetuated without being linked to external circumstances, and Hippocratic doctors, as we have seen, are careful in recognizing certain emotions as "unreasonable," *aloga*.

The passage did not escape the attention of Galen, the prominent Greek physician who lived and practiced medicine in Rome during the second century CE. While the text clearly gives priority to a psychological event, Galen insists on reading it as yet another case of humoral imbalance. Drawing on parallels from other gynaecological passages where *phobos* and *dusthumiê* are caused by the presence of black bile in the womb (e.g. *On the Diseases of Women* 2.182, 8.364 L.), he proceeds to explain *dusanios* not as a word that indicates a character trait but as a state of mind which is incidentally and temporarily induced because too much "melancholic menstrual blood" has been trapped in the woman's body (17a 778 K): "I am astonished by the fact," Galen writes, "that the author did not add that the woman suffered either from complete or partial retention of the menses . . . For clearly this is a case of melancholic menstrual blood being trapped in the body, and because of that it was natural that the woman would have become gloomy." Galen's reading is consistent with the way in which emotions are usually discussed in the Hippocratic corpus: it sidesteps the implication that affects can occasionally derive from a psychological cause and highlights the need to understand them as direct consequences of things happening inside the body. *Epidemics* 3.17(11), however, shows that, in some cases at least, emotions are more open to a psychological reading. While in the case of the woman in Thasos, body and mind interact closely, priority is given to temperament; the bodily ailments that follow are attributed to a permanent emotional disposition which takes an aggressive form because the patient has been affected psychologically, by *lupê*. The fact that we can find other instances in the corpus where a disease is identified by what seems to be a psychological label,[68] combined with the observation that some medical records consist primarily of a patient's affective disorders,[69] confirm that some of the Hippocratic emotions, though ultimately linked to the body, can be discussed as psychological phenomena in their own right.

CONCLUSION

What is missing from the story of the "gloomy woman" from Thasos is the suggestion that the patient might have benefited from some sort of "psychological" treatment. In fact, although we find numerous occasions of patients experiencing intense emotional pain, there is only one occurrence in the sixty-odd treatises contained in the Hippocratic corpus where the proposition is made explicitly that a patient should be treated psychologically.[70] As we read in *On Regimen* 4.89 (6.648–50 L.), if in one's dreams the heavenly bodies seem to wander about without a reason, this points to "a disturbance of the soul due to mental preoccupation": the person should relax and watch spectacles, preferably comedies, or whatever else he most enjoys; if one follows this treatment, recovery will take place "within two or three days."

This is the only occasion in which a Hippocratic author advises something that is meant to be beneficial "for the soul," that is, one's state of mind, without taking into account the state of the body. This line of treatment becomes increasingly significant during the first and second centuries CE. Celsus, the Roman encyclopaedist of the first century CE, proposes that those who suffer from "melancholia" should be subjected to physical as well as psychological therapy: apart from bloodletting and pharmaceutical treatment (see Fig. 1.4), the doctor should try to remove the causes of the patient's

FIGURE 1.4: Red-figure aryballos with depictions of blood-letting.

phobias and entertain him though storytelling and games; in addition, "his depression should be gently reproved as being without cause; he should have it pointed out to him now and again how in the very things which trouble him there may be a cause of rejoicing rather than of solicitude" (*On Medicine* 3.18.17–8). Similarly, Rufus of Ephesus (late first century CE), whose work on "melancholia" is praised by Galen as the best on the subject,[71] tells the story of a patient who was saved from drowning and was consequently affected by depression. Help is offered by two doctors: the first is said to administer strong drugs and black hellebore; the second prescribes a fitting diet but he also takes care of "cheering up" the patient.[72] In the early medical writings of the Hippocratic corpus this mode of therapy is virtually absent: considering that emotional disturbance is believed in this period to be simply an extension of an anomaly that is taking place inside the patient's body (e.g. in the case of melancholia, lasting sadness is a manifestation of an excess of black bile), treatment is exclusively concerned with restoring balance in that body; "psychotherapy," in the modern sense of the word, has not yet been invented.

As Brooke Holmes points out, "even when the Hippocratic writers are implicating the springs of our actions in physical conditions, they are doing so as part of a larger project to account for all of human nature within a limited set of causal terms, rather than addressing patients as agents with a critical role to play in health and disease."[73] While it would be a mistake to say that early medical scientists are uninterested in the *psuchê* as an object of medical enquiry, they are nonetheless reluctant to address their therapies to expressions of the patients' own agency, preferring instead to correlate the capacities of the soul (mental, emotional, etc.) to a material substrate. In this context, the medical analogy used by the philosophers of the fifth and fourth centuries BCE—according to which philosophy is to the soul what medicine is to the body[74]—could be seen as insinuating a critical attitude: it "lays bare the limits of the physician's expertise" by declaring that traditional medicine is solely concerned with the body, while establishing at the same time "both the space and the need for another kind of therapy, a therapy of the soul."[75] As we have seen, when emotions appear as symptoms in medical accounts of disease, they are occasionally linked with the implication that behind a patient's body there also lies a character—for example *Epidemics* 3.17(11); *Epidemics* 4.15 (5.152 L.); *Prorrhetic* 1.44 (5.522 L.)—a concrete identity with distinct behavioral patterns and temperamental traits. The fact that in the majority of the cases emotions are reduced to something little more than side effects of a bodily condition may have been the result of an overbearing medical authority,[76] exerted at the expense of the patient's suppressed (emotional) agency.[77]

CHAPTER TWO

Religion and Spirituality

F. S. NAIDEN

What can you say, Cordelia? Speak!
Nothing, my lord.
Nothing will come of this nothing. Speak again.
Unhappy as I am, I cannot heave my heart into my mouth.

King Lear (Act 1, Scene 1)

Centuries before Shakespeare wrote these lines about thwarted emotions, several Greek poets described how an altogether different heroine, Althaea, expressed her feelings. Homer says that Althaea cursed her son Meleager for slaying her brother. These two men had taken part in the Calydonian boar hunt and then quarreled over the spoils. As she knelt and beat the earth, she invoked Hades and Persephone. Although the two gods did not answer Althaea's call, an Erinys or Fury did (*Iliad* 9.565–72). Hesiod briefly says that Meleager died at the hands of Apollo while fighting the Curetes, who also took part in the boar hunt. He does not mention Althaea's feelings (Hesiod fragment 25.10–13, ed. Merkelbach-West). Bacchylides restores Althaea to the story. His Meleager accidentally killed not one but two of her brothers during the war between the Curetes and his own people. As Althaea grieved for them, she set fire to a brand that an oracle connected to Meleager's survival, and so she caused his death (Bacchylides 5.127–35).[1]

The first of these three versions describes an angry mother who channels her feeling through a curse and through a spirit resembling a personification. The second describes an evidently angry god. The third describes a grieving mother, and links her to an object rather than a spirit (cf. Hyginus, *Fabula* 171). In spite of these differences, each of these versions features some fundamental religious act: first, a ritual; second, an act of divine intervention; and third, an oracle. Each features a supernatural element: a spirit or personification, a god, and a magical object. Each also correlates emotion and religion. In the first case, human emotion informs a ritual invigorated by the supernatural. An expressive Althaea dominates the story. In the second case, the anger is mythic and not ritualistic. Divine retribution dominates the story. In the third case, grief has severe but symbolic consequences. The fatal brand dominates the story.

Homer, Hesiod, and Bacchylides suggest several definitions of ancient religious emotions. Homer suggests a popular, current definition in which religious emotions inform religious rituals, such as curses. Rituals, in turn, channel emotions. To this body of ideas, dating back to Robertson, Smith, and Durkheim, recent scholars add an appraisal theory of emotions. This theory says that emotions mark a response to dangers or other features of the environment. Individuals or groups appraise the danger or phenomenon and then express fear or some other reaction.² A ritual then harnesses the emotion. They have a preceptor in Aristotle, who anticipated appraisal theory in his treatment of ritual-related emotions such as pity and shame.³ If epic poetry is one valuable source for this sort of study, inscriptions are another. So are Roman antiquarian writers.

The Hesiodic story of Apollo's anger at Meleager suggests a second, neglected definition: religious emotions are those that arise during intercourse between gods and worshippers. In this definition, divine epiphanies—meaning all manifestations of a divine presence—are more important than rituals. By the same token, the emotions inspired by gods are more important than the emotions channeled by worship. Emotions such as joy and awe may outweigh the Aristotelian emotions of fear and shame. Epic poetry may be less valuable than more-or-less autobiographical sources, many of them of Roman imperial date, such as Aelius Aristides.

Bacchylides' flaming brand suggests yet another definition. Rather than be ritualistic or epiphanic, religious emotions may be objectified, as if by magic. More commonly, religious emotions are personified, as Althaea's anger is personified, more or less, by the Fury (Erinys) of Homer. Both Greeks and Romans worshiped personified emotions, such as Greek Aidôs, or Shame, and Roman Concordia, or Harmony. In these cults, Greeks and Romans addressed their feelings rather than channeling them, as with rituals, or succumbing to them, as with epiphanies. In no other respect do Greek and Roman religion depart so far from modern monotheism. In that kind of religion, any kind of self-worship would be misplaced or idolatrous. The sources for this, the most distinctive ancient mode of religious feeling, are diverse—Hesiod and other poets, but mostly antiquarians. Douglas Cairns's monograph on *aidôs* (Cairns 1993) gives the only extensive recent treatment of any of these emotions and the related cults.

This chapter will briefly essay all three of these definitions. Each proves to be valuable, but the subject of religious emotions is both complex and tenuous. It is complex because of cultural differences. Greek religion was the religion of the Greek people, and so Greek sources extensively report both rituals and regulations, including regulations by private persons and groups. "Roman religion" was not the religion of the Roman people alone, and it was not the only religion of the Romans, so Latin sources do not describe rituals as thoroughly. As for regulations, Roman law controlled public cult, but it did not affect private cult, save for practices deemed to be *prava religio*, so private cult went unregulated. The pontiffs had some control over it, but otherwise it went unnoticed. In the Greek case, we know more about less, and in the Roman case, less about more.

With regard to the religions of the eastern half of the Roman Empire, another difficulty arises. Greek rituals have many Semitic and Anatolian parallels, if not sources. Joy at sacrificial feasts, for example, appears commonly in the Old Testament.⁴ Roman ritual, however, owes much to the Etruscans and early Italic peoples, and for these cultures there is no text comparable to Scripture. Because of this background, Greek rituals—and emotions—may seem typical, or even prototypical, whereas Roman rituals and emotions may seem historically limited. This contrast has affected scholarship: Greek instances are theorized, whereas Roman instances are contextualized.

The subject of ancient religious feelings is tenuous because Greek and Roman literature seldom describes religious feeling at any length. The most important source for curses, the *defixiones*, speaks of physical impairment, but not of the suffering that results.⁵ Even the famed records of cures performed at Epidaurus, the fourth-century BCE *iamata*, are little better. These texts speak only of occasional disparaging laughter and of naiveté, grief, and shame.⁶ Fear, sorrow, and despair never appear. In contrast, a later source for cures performed by Asclepius, Aelius Aristides, speaks at length about fear, sorrow, and despair. This chapter concludes by asking whether religious feelings changed over time.

RITUAL EMOTIONS

In our first definition, emotions accompany rituals. Most prominent is the emotion of fear. Often, a fear of the gods inspired ritual. The fear of heavenly anger noticed by Angelos Chaniotis (2012a) led to the establishment of cults. Worshippers feared the anger not only of gods, but also of other beings. The hero's wrongful death might cause the anger, which would take the form of *nemesis*, or rightful indignation, or a heroine's curse might express anger. Similarly, her indignation at being put to shame might express it, or even her grief at being wronged—as in the case of Althaea.[7] The answer to this kind of anger was hero cult.

A similar sense of respect for divine power, combined with a sense of shame, supported the Greek custom of *xenia*, or guest-friendship, and the Greek and Roman custom of supplication. Here the worshiper's sense of *aidôs* or his fear of divine *invidia* or ill-will induced him to honor these divinely sanctioned customs. In Greek, one of the two Homeric epics, the *Odyssey*, hinges on *aidôs* as a sense of respect due to the greatest of all superiors—Zeus *xenios*. A subgenre amounting to about a quarter of complete extant tragedies turned on the same sense of *aidôs* due to Zeus *hikêsios*.[8] This feeling could spill over into a sense of respect for the altar of supplication or into a sense of respect for the suppliant as opposed to the god—in the second case, a social and not religious sort of *aidôs*.[9] In the background lay fear of divine anger. Zeus did not require that all suppliants be shown pity—the undeserving might be subjected to *nemesis*—but he punished those who received suppliants and mistreated them, so did Jupiter together with Fides or good faith. Under the empire, Roman suppliants invoked not Jupiter or Fides, but the emperor, at whose statues they could supplicate. Those who mistreated them would face his quasi-divine *invidia*.[10] A would-be suppliant might even carry an image of the emperor about his person, and thus claim protection in advance—and broadcast imperial *invidia* towards any who would mistreat him.[11]

Although fear and related feelings inspired rituals, the roles played by ritual and emotion might be reversed. Then rituals created emotions—positive emotions such as fellowship and joy. These emotions are the keynotes of the well-known interpretation of sacrifice by Vernant and Detienne.[12] For Plutarch, this was "the joyful thing about a festival."[13] Several writers call this elation *terpsis*, or delight, Thucydides' description of *thusia*. Plato calls *thusia* one of the pleasures, or *hêdonai*.[14] This delight or pleasure was not epiphanic in the narrow sense. It nonetheless was intense—as intense, perhaps, as the fear that preceded it while the worshipers strove to meet divine expectations.

On occasions like sacrifice, Greek worshippers sometimes asked gods to give them joy.[15] The same was true of the Romans, and the same root, *gau*, yielded terms for this feeling. In Greek, this root produced not only *gêtheô* but also *ganos*, meaning both joy and brightness, and thus a term that linked this feeling to the landscape and climate. In Latin, it yielded *gaudeo*.[16] *Laetitia publica* was the common Latin expression for the joy experienced at religious festivals.

Yet not all festivals were joyous. Mommsen divided the *tristes*, like the Lupercalia and Feralia, from the *hilariores*, like the Vestalia.[17] The Greeks did not divide festivals according to emotions, but knew the difference between those that brought joy and those that did not, such as apotropaic rites, graveside rites, and rites of purification. In the former case, the ritual brought an emotion into being. In that latter case, it served the common purpose of dealing with divine displeasure.

Neither society regarded the balance between the two kinds as stable. In Roman terms, the *pax deorum* might break down, and then renascent divine anger would create many more occasions that were *tristes*. This "peace" or stability might break down even as a ritual was underway. Greek ritual, including highly regulated rituals such as sacrifice, required that worshipers maintain *euphêmia*, or good conduct. Otherwise they would face divine displeasure. To express displeasure, the god would withdraw, a possibility that explains the common Greek and Roman prayer that a god be present and active during a sacrifice or other ritual.[18] This scenario allowed for fear of misconduct after the ritual was over. At the start of every Athenian assembly meeting, for example, a proper sacrifice secured the blessing of the gods, but before the meeting got underway, the herald called down curses on anyone present who was going to give the Athenians bad advice. The curse would mobilize divine anger, as it had for Althaea.[19]

By the same token, the emotions expressed during rituals were not always acceptable. A funerary law at Gambreion (in Asia Minor) offers a strikingly severe example. After ordering men to stop mourning after four months, this law orders women to stop after five, and to form processions according to regulations. The force of law, though, might not suffice to restrain the women, so the magistrate in charge of women, the *gunaikonomos*, should harangue them:

> On the occasion of the acts of purification before the Thesmophoria, let the magistrate address the women who obey . . . the law and say that this is good, and that it supports the good things they already have, but let him say the opposite to those who disobey. Since they are impious, it is not proper for them to sacrifice to any god for ten years.[20]

This punishment does not mainly serve to harm the women: the anger of the gods will harm them regardless. It serves to protect the community from the adverse consequences of associating with the women during acts of sacrifice. The community fears being guilty by association, and thus being subject to the gods' wrath. The community may be compared to a full lifeboat where the skipper must throw someone overboard. He knows who to pick and does not flinch.

Fear and joy, expression and repression: the relation between ritual and emotion was diverse. There were also two other variables. First, it is difficult to distinguish religious emotions from other emotions more or less affected by rituals. One Hellenistic inscription describes the joy felt by mimes who danced in the orchestra of a theatre. The word for "orchestra" is *thumelê*, which means "altar," and in particular the altar that always stood front and center. Was this joy religious? Perhaps the dancers would not have understood this question. The Greek language had a word that sometimes meant emotion, *pathos*, but it did not have an adjective meaning "religious." It had the word *hieros*, "belonging to the gods." The altar belonged to Dionysus; in another way, so did the theatre, as did the emotions of the spectators and performers. In that sense, aesthetic emotions were religious.

Second, rituals involved not just particular feelings, but emotional dispositions—for example, the disposition of being kind-hearted as well as the feeling of pity. The practice of rituals might even encourage a shift from the one to the other. As Pascal observed, if a worshipper kneels and moves his lips often enough, he will come to believe in the words he is uttering.[21] Similarly, a worshipper who experienced camaraderie during communal sacrifices (as in Vernant's account) might develop a sense of habitual communal solidarity. This sense of solidarity is crucial for contemporary explanations of the Greek democratic polis.

EPIPHANIC EMOTIONS

In describing "the joyful thing about a festival," Plutarch spoke of "good hope and impression that the divine is present and kindly." This sense of the divine might be as weak as some vague manifestation or as strong as an epiphany.[22] Greek religion ran the gamut from the one to the other, but early Roman religion centered on numinousness that was strong yet impersonal. For worshipers, the climactic emotion was no longer fear or joy, but awe—a sense of fear complicated by shock and disorientation, yet often by a sense of beauty.[23] A divinized ruler could inspire it as well as a god. On the god's part, the characteristic emotion was beneficence, no longer anger.

These occasions could overlap with rituals. Plutarch says as much, and so does one of the lesser *Homeric Hymns*. In this scene, sailors in trouble at sea sacrifice to the Dioscuri, and then see "beautiful signs" of the twin gods in the rigging. Knowing they will be safe, they rejoice. Divine presence and ritual overlap, and awe gives way to joy, but the miracle tips the balance towards epiphany.[24] Rather than be beautiful, the divine presence may be terrible, as in another *Hymn* in which Dionysus appears first as a handsome youth. Then, when pirates kidnap him, he turns into a lion and sets a bear loose among the crew (*Homeric Hymn* 33.16–17, 7.44–6).

Whereas the god of ritual was distant, impassive, and exempt from suffering, the god of epiphany was all too human. Homer set the precedent for this aspect of the gods in the *Iliad*, in which just one god, Apollo, feels most of the chief emotions described by Aristotle in the *Rhetoric*: anger, shame, indignation, pity, confidence and graciousness or gratitude (*charis*). Aphrodite alone feels fearful, but Zeus is among several feeling both friendly and hateful.[25] These were human feelings in the sense that one person might feel them for another: Thetis, for example, wore a veil to express her *aidôs*, just as a mortal might (*Iliad* 24.90–4). In this human mood, gods in later literature would feel anger not at human violations of ceremonial or moral norms, but at human success—*phthonos*, not *nemesis*.[26] They would expected to be placated, not merely honored.

Just as sacrifice was the paradigmatic ritual encounter between god and worshiper, initiation was the paradigmatic encounter that, in spite of the rituals that preceded it, centered on a revelation. Plutarch's description of the experience of the soul after death, a passage patterned on initiation at Eleusis, contrasts with his portrayal of joy and hope during acts of sacrifice:

> Before the initiation there is every fearful thing—shivering, trembling, sweating and amazement. After that, some wonderful light appears, and pure places and meadows receive the initiates—places where there are sound and dancing and solemnities that result from hearing holy and beholding sacred things.
>
> —Plutarch, *On the Soul*, fragment 178, ed. Sandbach

Apuleius' description of the initiation of priests of Isis adds cosmological touches:

> I drew near to hell, to the gates of Persephone, and after that, I was utterly ravished. I returned to my place, but about midnight I saw the sun shine, I saw the gods of heaven and hell, I presented myself to them, and I worshipped them.

He adds, "So—now I have told you. Although you have heard it, you must pretend not to know. I have spoken without giving offence so that the profane might understand."[27] This warning points to another difference between revelation and awe, on the one hand, and sacrifice and fellowship on the other: revelation and awe might be difficult or dangerous to transmit. Like Cordelia's dutifulness, they go too deep for words.

In battle, however, Greeks and Romans experienced epiphanies that were dangerous yet unavoidable. The oldest Greek report, from Marathon, describes the heroes Theseus or Echetlaeus fighting alongside the Athenians.[28] One Athenian soldier, Epizelus, went blind after seeing some unidentified hero kill the man alongside him (Herodotus 6.117). The oldest Roman report, about the dictator of the year 499 BCE, Aulus Postumius, says the Dioscuri fought on the Roman side against the Latins at Lake Regillis.[29] The phenomenon lasted for centuries. A student of Callimachus compiled a book of military epiphanies by Apollo; Jupiter attacked the Dacians for Trajan's sake, as shown on Trajan's column.[30]

Recent scholars have speculated that combat trauma deranged these soldiers. Temporary blindness, such as Epizelus suffered, may be regarded a symptom of conversion disorder, in which the victim, rather than evaluate a threat, displaces and then ignores it.[31] Yet the ancient religious spectrum of "peak experiences"—to use Maslow's phrase— suggests an explanation that does not depend on contemporary medical analysis.[32] Like a magnet, the gods attracted the strongest emotions, and then deflected these emotions through the rituals described in the previous section of this chapter and the epiphanies described in this one. Ritual and epiphany said to the worshipper, "You are not alienated. Like it or not, you are included."

Epiphanies also appear in less dangerous circumstances than those at Marathon or in the campaigns of Trajan. When Iris, a mere messenger, appears in the *Iliad*, she strikes awe into mortals, but peaceably delivers her messages (*Iliad* 24.170) and when Telemachus realizes that Athena has come near him, he looks away but continues to respond (*Odyssey* 16.178–80). Provided the jolt was not too strong, worshippers would even seek out epiphanies. Asclepius provides the obvious example, but not always in the form of a dream in which the god and the worshipper encounter one another and the worshipper would awake cured and overjoyed. In one instance in the *Sacred Tales* of Aelius Aristides, two complications arise. The worshipper has his dream, but in it sees a statue of the god and then the god himself. That is one complication. Then comes another:

> We worshipers stood by [the statue], as we do when singing the paean ... As the god nodded for us to depart, he struck the very same pose as is usual for a statue. All the others were leaving ... yet the god waved for me to stay. This honor delighted me ... and I exclaimed, "The one!" meaning the god. He replied, "*You* are the one."[33]

The statue-like god has come alive, the worshipper is "delighted," and the two beings momentarily merge as the power of the god's presence envelops Aristides.

Statues could excite or distress worshippers not only by appearing in dreams or traveling to a battlefield, but, more simply, by sweating, wailing, or even turning. For the last, no miracle was required; priests would carry the statue in a procession, and bring good or bad tidings to the worshippers.[34] In that case, the epiphany was more or less a routine aspect of a ritual. Inevitably, generals learned to manipulate soldiers' belief in these encounters. One military commander sent fake Dioscuri among the enemy, who ran in fright (Polyaenus 11.31). Herodotus reports that the ex-general Pisistratus used an Athenian girl to impersonate Athena by standing, statue-like, in a cart (1.60). The Romans contributed to this kind of play-acting by institutionalizing it: the *triumphator* dressed like Jupiter partly to frighten the republic's enemies.

Attenuated encounters with a god might involve soothing him, as with Greek *hilaskesthai* and Latin *placare*.[35] These common terms implied that the worshipper succeeded in reducing divine hostility by acknowledging divine superiority.[36] *Sebas* was a term for reverence that might be due either to gods or to the most important mortals. As elsewhere, Latin usage was only subtly different. *Verecundia* designated reverence due to fellow mortals, who should plainly and promptly respond, but *reverentia* designated reverence due to gods, who would also respond, but not always plainly or promptly.[37] *Verecundia*, in short, was asymmetrical and reciprocal, whereas *reverentia* was asymmetrical and not reciprocal.

EMOTIONS, OBJECTS, AND PERSONIFICATIONS

The third kind of ancient religious emotion, linked to an object or a personification, stands farthest from religious experience as represented by the Abrahamic faiths. In these religions, emotions such as shame or modesty, indignation, love and fear, or concord, hope, and dutifulness may count as virtues, but they do not receive worship. For a Christian to worship his own love of god, or anyone or anything else, would be impious, whereas to worship god's love for him would be supererogatory.

The Greeks and Romans chose to worship all the emotions just named—*aidôs, nemesis, erôs,* and *phobos* (or shame, indignation, desire, and fear), and *concordia, spes, pietas,* and *pudicitia* (or harmony, hope, devotion, and modesty).[38] The reason for this brief, but coherent list of cults lay in the public and personal impact of these emotions. They ranked as the feelings most able to strengthen or weaken courts, armies, governments, and families. As the Greek and Latin lists overlap, the difference between the two cultures was significant without being absolute.

Of the Greek emotions, the pair of *aidôs* and *nemesis* were perhaps the first to be deified. Hesiod described them as a pair of goddesses sitting next to Zeus, anticipating Aristotle's pairing them in the *Rhetoric*.[39] Aidôs had altars at Athens, Sparta, and no doubt elsewhere.[40] Nemesis was a local goddess worshiped at Rhamnous and Smyrna in the Classical and Hellenistic periods. Roman soldiers in the Danube region later worshiped Nemesis as a protectress of the campground. Meanwhile, Greeks had come to associate her with Tyche and Fortuna, and Pliny the Elder knew of an image of this sort of Nemesis in Rome.[41] Aidôs and Nemesis were beings with the long, quirky histories characteristic of Olympians. As shown by an imperial-era image, Nemesis looks like a typical goddess (see Fig. 2.1).

Although he does not mention *aidôs*, Phoenix explained the notion of cult for beings of this kind in *Iliad* 9. The apologetic and repentant, he says, will have their prayers granted. Or worshippers might reason that if Aidôs kept watch over them, she would prevent other people from having shameless, harmful thoughts. That made it wise to tell Aidôs be vigilant. The worst part of Aidôs being off-duty, Medea says, is that people will break their oaths. Only her presence will keep them honest.[42] Yet an author like Euripides was not satisfied by this elementary, selfish reasoning. Why honor Aidôs? Hippolytus asks. This goddess gives her blessings of her garden only to those who are naturally prudent.[43] Asking her for guidance would seem to be superfluous. The audience might think, we know what will happen to *him*. He should have known better, and sought more guidance. Then he would not have scanted Aphrodite.

The same reasoning would apply to Nemesis, the goddess who wrecked lives when they deserved to be wrecked. Would prayers to her be useless? No, custom said.[44] Prayers to belay *nemesis* abound in Greek authors.[45]

The deified nemesis of personal life, Erôs, apparently began as an attendant of Aphrodite, just as Aidôs began beside Zeus, and began to receive worship in Athens as

FIGURE 2.1: Marble statuette of Nemesis with portrait resembling the Empress Faustina I. Roman Empire, c. 150 CE. In her left hand she holds a wheel of fate.

FIGURE 2.2: Neo-Attic sarcophagus, 50–40 BCE. In the center, Erôs and Anterôs are portrayed as twins, while on both the left and right a centaur appears, one with a satyr on his back and the other with a maenad.

early as the Classical period.⁴⁶ Since Erôs was so closely associated with Aphrodite, the development of a separate cult is hard to explain, but a related cult, to Anterôs, or "Requited Love," suggests that the worship of Erôs developed to deal with one aspect of erotic love, bonding.⁴⁷ Hence in Fig. 2.2, Erôs and Anterôs are portrayed as though they were identical twins. Just as Aidôs frequented places where oaths were taken, and where Zeus oversaw public business, Erôs received worship mainly in gymnasia and military camps.⁴⁸ Deified Erôs was decidedly male.

Why worship Erôs rather than emotions such as friendship (*philia*)? The power of Erôs. As any ancient Greek (or Roman) would say, any being that can make even gods lose self-control must be a god himself. To deify Erôs acknowledges the power of sexual attraction in both fact and myth.

If the cult of Erôs reflects Greek male homosexuality, the cult of Phobos, known mainly in Sparta, reflects that community's military values. Phobos was the fear that makes men run in battle; the Spartan worshipers asked Phobos to visit others, and not themselves, an exclusively apotropaic cult. In peacetime, the god's shrine was closed.⁴⁹ As with Nemesis, the cult developed from both epic roots and local observances.⁵⁰ Phobos also resembled a ghost, or demon, as when painted on a warrior's shield.⁵¹ The demonization of Phobos allowed him, like Erôs, to cause even gods to lose their self-control, so, when Apollo saw him after killing the Python at Delphi, the god fled in terror (Pausanias 2.7.7).

The theme of a loss of self-control appears in the Roman cults of Concordia and Spes (Hope), but inversely, for these cults helped the community maintain self-control and cohesion. Both were old. The temple of Concordia dated back to 367 BCE, when Furius Camillus founded it to foster social reconciliation. Renewed after the Gracchan agitation, it remained important down through the Imperial Period (Wissowa 1912: 272–3). Eventually the theme of concord within the army, *Concordia militum*, came to supplant Concordia among the people, *Concordia civium*, as on the reverse of the imperial coin shown in Fig. 2.3.

FIGURE 2.3: A copy of an engraving made of the reverse of a rare gold coin of Commodus, featuring at the bottom the abbreviation *Conc Mil*, for *Concordia Militum*, or "Concordia among the Soldiers." The rest of the legend reads P M TR P XI IMP VIII COS V PP, or "Pontifex Maximus, Tribune of the People for the eleventh time, Imperator for the seventh time, Consul for the fifth, and Father of his Country."

The first temple of Spes dated from before the First Punic War, and the god also received a private cult before this date.[52] The cult of Spes was, for the worshippers, a mental operation in which they prayed for good luck not to a god who would decide to give it, but to an incarnation of their own hope of getting it; in effect, they asked Spes for *spes*. Farmers and emperors both did so.[53]

These two cults reflected Roman political and psychological priorities. The Greek counterpart of Concordia, Harmonia, received no cult of political importance, and the Greek counterpart of Spes, Elpis, received none at all.[54] The lesser cults of Pietas and Pudicitia also illustrated differences between the two cultures, for Pietas was a minor cult, less important than Aidôs, and Pudicitia was a cult of female modesty only, and also less important than Aidôs.[55] The Greek and Roman cults operated in distinct spheres of life: the agora, the gymnasium, and the hoplite battlefield, as opposed to Roman government and agriculture.

Bigger than any differences was the structural similarity. Confronted with vital but hazardous emotions, Greeks and Romans chose to deify the problem of keeping these emotions in check. Sometimes this conceptual maneuver caused worshippers to be encouraged, and sometimes it let them be consoled. Since personified emotions were not epiphanic, deification did not put worshipers at any risk, and since these emotions were not gods of the first rank, adding them did not upset the shape or balance of religion as a whole. Aidōs and Erōs were servants. Most of these gods were female, and only one, Phobos, was an adult male. Phobos was the son of Aphrodite as well as Ares, and thus was a child of contradiction.[56]

CONCLUSIONS

Did feelings about worship change over time? In Greece, a new desire to make offerings "as handsome (and thus as costly) as possible" (as described by Naiden 2015: 210–17) sometimes replaced an old desire to make them as frequent as practicable. The new desire apparently began in Athens; the old desire survived in Sparta. To reassure old-fashioned worshipers, the Delphic oracle declared that Apollo would always recommend frequent but plain offerings (Theopompus *FGrH* 115 F 344). The Romans had reservations about fancy offerings, too. As Pliny the Elder put it, the Romans' ancestors made offerings of clay, not gold. Should their descendants regret it? Answering in the same spirit as the Delphic oracle, he said no.[57]

These two passages show that the ancients worried about departing from the practices of their forebears. Did they also worry about having different experiences from their forebears? Did their conceptions of their own experience change?

The cult of Asclepius, with its centuries of evidence, and its broad clientele, especially prompts this question. The Classical *iamata* say nothing of sorrow, fear, and the like—nothing whatever that we would associate with the hazards of illness or medical treatment. About 400 years later, Aelius Aristides waxes eloquent on these feelings. In his *Sacred Tales*, he stresses his own distress and the occasional lack of it, and less often his joy, contentment, or gratitude.[58] The contentment comes when he is "wholly with the god" (*Hieros Logos* 4.30, i.e. *Oration* 50).

As these words suggest, this author immersed himself in self-consciousness. At the start of the *Tales*, he justifies his attitude:

> Every one of our days and nights has a story to tell. Someone simply needs to be there and choose to record the events. That means telling the story of god's foresight, and of

his plan. The god revealed some things while he was present himself, and he revealed others by sending dreams, so long as the patient was able to sleep.

—*Hieros Logos* 1

Provided that emotions somehow involve the god and the cure, all of them count. Fear and awe thus make room for emotions incidental to daily life. Emotions related to the epiphany of the god remain crucial, but the epiphany itself is not so much actual as intellectual. It occurs in the patient's mind. These shifts bring to fruition a religious concept in which the worshipper and the god's "plan" for him have partly displaced public cult. In the *iamata*, in contrast, this cult was the main subject.[59]

The self-consciousness displayed by this author finds an echo in one feature of the sources for the Hellenistic period and the Roman Empire. This feature is that later sources are elaborate and sometimes histrionic. Some older studies of the history of religious emotions concluded that Hellenistic and Roman worshipers, especially those beholding epiphanies, became increasingly irrational, a view still found among scholars of epiphanies on the battlefield.[60]

For recent studies, the question of irrationality is misleading. Religious beliefs, such as those underlying reports of epiphanies, are irrational or rational within some cultural matrix. In the ancient matrix, the anthropomorphic quality of the gods was axiomatic, and this quality had obvious consequences—fear, joy, awe. The value and dangers of ritual were also axiomatic, and so were those of more or less intense epiphanies. The most important emotions were naturally deified, and naturally grouped with the most important gods. No worshiper, *qua* worshiper, was irrational, nor was society permanently and generally irrational. Conclusions like these say more about the intellectual limits of those who draw them than about the limits of those whom they study. The way to explain elaborate descriptions of emotion in the Hellenistic period may be stylistic or psychological, but it should not be judgmental.

If we subject ancient religion to the test of complexity, and not rationality, we will not find it wanting. The palette of religious emotions was large, and changed over time, and the same was true of the pantheons, Olympian and otherwise, that policed rituals and affected their outcome. Beyond the confines of this chapter lies the role of religiously inflected emotions in the development of art and literature. Suffice to say that this role was large. Take all emotions related to religion out of Homer and little would remain; take them out of Herodotus or Livy or the speeches of Cicero and much would be lost.

The category of "religious emotion" is a modern one, born of the recent decline of religion in Western Europe and North America. Like any etic category, it has the advantage of revealing and setting off a subject, but it also has the disadvantage of presenting obstacles to profound understanding.[61] When Lear got a glimpse of the inner world of his daughter, he struck an obstacle like this, and so he was amazed at what he did not find: "So young and so untender?" he asked. "So young," she replied, "and true."

CHAPTER THREE

Music and Dance

ELEONORA ROCCONI

The capacity of music and dance to induce and convey emotions is a phenomenon which crosses all borders of educational and cultural environment. All human beings seem to be particularly affected by music, and modern neuroscience has developed various experimental methods by which this particular relationship can be assessed and evaluated.[1] Music may be investigated as a source of emotions from many different perspectives, according to the scientific disciplines involved: if the experimentally oriented affective sciences focus their attention on the *elicitation* of emotions by music, the main area of interest for aesthetics, philosophy, and musicology, by contrast, has been musical *expressiveness*, that is, the capacity of musical arts to represent or to express human emotions.

Evidence for both these approaches may be found in ancient Greek and Roman sources. There are, however, obvious difficulties in researching this topic so far back in the past. Not only do ancient emotion categories, if we adopt a cognitive approach to them (as in Konstan 2006b), only partially overlap with ours; it has also to be said that the aural aspects of ancient performances are almost completely lost, but for a very few fragments of music recorded on papyrus and inscriptions, or scraps of material remains of musical instruments in the archaeological record, which may make us only remotely aware of how music sounded and was performed in the past. This does not do justice to the remarkable pervasiveness of music and dance in Greek and Roman societies and to the wide range of performative phenomena labeled in antiquity with the term *mousikê technê* (or *ars musica*). Hence any investigation of the relationship between music and emotions in Classical antiquity has to first circumscribe the performative events that ancient Greek and Roman people considered to be part of this phenomenon, and then necessarily focus on the description of its emotional power in ancient texts (especially poetry and philosophy), that may give us only a partial view of an experience that originally belonged in the perceptual domain.

MUSIC AND EMOTIONS IN GREEK ANTIQUITY

The concept of music is culturally variable throughout history. In ancient Greece, the notion of *mousikê* was much broader than what we nowadays call music, embracing the entire field of poetic performance to which the Muses gave their name. *Mousikê* (sc. *technê*) included song, poetry, bodily movement, and instrumental music, all or partially integrated within various performative events that served the purpose of strengthening social bonds (according to gender, age, ethnicity, etc.). Music was in fact a core element of many religious and socially relevant activities, within which it acted as the most effective means of arousing deep emotions in both listeners and performers. The mostly public aspect of musical events, always shared by a more or less extensive community of people and never experienced alone, certainly enhanced their emotional intensity, thanks to what we now call emotional contagion, according to which individuals in communal situations have the tendency to converge emotionally (Hatfield, Cacioppo, and Rapson 1994; Scherer and Coutinho 2013).

In these contexts, the elicitation of emotions through music was not an end in itself, but served to convey and reinforce the values and beliefs shared by the community in question. For instance, the performances of epic singers, such as those described in the Homeric poems, served as an extraordinary tool for sharing past memories and for transmitting knowledge and values to their audiences over centuries (Havelock 1963: 83 and *passim*); the choral hymns sung by male or female groups during various religious rites, while arousing a range of emotions from the solemn to the hilarious, conveyed important religious messages and reinforced the beliefs of the participants in the ritual (Lonsdale 1993; Kowalzig 2007); victory celebrations at the Panhellenic games (Athanassaki 2012) or theatrical performances at the Athenian Dionysia (Visvardi 2015), actively managing emotional engagement in public spaces, expanded the collective emotions of the citizens and channeled them into socially desirable ends; and so on. Therefore it is not surprising that, at some point, ancient philosophers tried to theorize audiences' emotional responses to musical performances, giving them an intellectual basis, and to assess their value and potential benefits for the society of the time.

The exploration of emotional responses to *mousikê* in ancient texts may be very fruitful, especially in archaic and classical poetry, where many different feelings and emotions associated with musical performances are mentioned, such as pleasure and joy (*hêdonê* and *chara*), mourning and grief (*odunê* and *lupê*; see Fig. 3.1), anger and mildness (*orgê* and *praotês*), frenzy and excitement (*lussa* and *enthousiasmos*; see Figs 3.2 and 3.3), and so on. The attempt to superimpose modern classifications on this emotional vocabulary is a difficult, and probably unnecessary, task:[2] we should consider most of these emotional responses to music as reactions caused by precognitive affective appraisals of specific events, confirmed only at a subsequent stage by cognitive evaluations (modern psychological literature has amply demonstrated that not all musical emotions are aroused through a cognitive assessment: cf. Robinson 2005 and Davies 2010).

The most emblematic account of an exceptionally strong reaction to music is given in a famous tale told by many literary sources (both Greek and Latin) in connection with Pythagoras.[3] According to the most famous version of this story, narrated by Iamblichus, Pythagoras managed to calm the frenzy (*lussa*) of a youth from Tauromenium (modern Taormina, in Sicily), who had previously been inflamed and excited by a Phrygian melody played by a pipe player, simply by asking the musician to switch to the "libation tune" (i.e., the *spondeion*, a melody for solo *aulos*, the double reed wind instrument typical of ancient Hellenic culture), which was rhythmically slower and used a Dorian, instead of a Phrygian, melody.[4] Besides these generic references to the psychagogic power of music (i.e. its capacity to move the soul; see Figs 3.4 and 3.5) based on some commonly accepted correspondences between specific musical forms and emotions, it is worth investigating whether there is any ancient literary evidence which describes the underlying mechanisms responsible for the elicitation of emotions by music.

Some hints of theoretical reflections on these topics may be found by taking a look into Greek philosophical sources. Plato is the first to describe emotional reactions to music as a process which relies on both physiological and cognitive components. In different passages of his dialogs, he points out that, although all living beings—including animals—

FIGURE 3.1: Women lamenting during a *prothesis*. Attic black-figure funerary plaque, *c.* 520–510 BCE.

FIGURE 3.2: Dionysus with satyrs and maenads playing music. Attic red-figure bell krater, *c.* 450 BCE, attributed to the Methyse Painter.

FIGURE 3.3: Dancing maenad. Terracotta plaque, Roman, *c.* first century BCE–first century CE.

are by nature emotionally affected by music and have a physical reaction to it, humans alone can really understand it, since they are the only ones truly able to perceive and appreciate the beautiful order of motions and sounds that they call *rhythm* and *harmony*:

> Almost without exception, every young creature is able of keeping [sic] either its body or its tongue quiet, and is always striving to move and to cry, leaping and skipping and delighting in dances and games, and uttering, also, noises of every description. Now, whereas all other creatures are devoid of any perception of the various kinds of order and disorder in movement (which we term rhythm and harmony), to men the very gods, who were given, as we said, to be our fellows in the dance, have granted the pleasurable perception of rhythm and harmony, whereby they cause us to move and lead our choirs, linking us one with another by means of songs and dances; and to the choir they have given its name from the "cheer" [*chara*] implanted therein.
> —Plato, *Laws* 653d–654a, trans. Bury 1926

Since all young creatures are by nature fiery, they are unable to keep still either body or voice, but are always crying and leaping in disorderly fashion; we said also that none of the other creatures attains a sense of order, bodily and vocal, and that this is possessed by man alone; and that the order of motion is called "rhythm" while the order of voice (in which acute and grave are blended together) is termed "harmony", and to the combination of these two the name "choristry" [*choreia*] is given. We stated also that the gods, in pity for us, have granted to us as fellow-choristers and choir-leaders Apollo and the Muses, besides whom we mentioned, if we recollect, a third, Dionysus.

—Plato, *Laws* 664e–665a, trans. Bury 1926[5]

Plato's interest in the emotional power of *mousikê*, however, remained limited to its exploitation (and containment) for merely educational purposes. It is in connection with the Peripatetics, who conceded that music may have other purposes besides education, that we find more detailed remarks on the mechanisms through which music could induce a wider range of emotions.

Before turning our attention to Aristotle and other Peripatetic evidence, we need to make one preliminary observation. It is widely known that, for the ancient Greeks, *mousikê* (like any other *technê*) was a mimetic art: that is, it could imitate, represent or express—according to the meaning we assign to the word *mimêsis*[6]—specific characters, emotions, or even actions. Aristotle, in the *Poetics* (1447a21–8), lists these three among the elements reproduced by any musical art: "all the poetic arts mentioned produce mimesis in rhythm, language, and melody, whether separately or in combinations . . . rhythm on its own, without melody, is used by the art of dancers, since they too, through rhythms translated into movements, create mimesis of characters, emotions, and actions"

FIGURE 3.4: Orpheus enchanting the Thracians with the lyre. Red-figure krater from Gela, *c.* 450 BCE, detail.

FIGURE 3.5: Women enchanted by *barbitos* music in a domestic setting. Attic red-figure bell krater, *c.* 460 BCE, attributed to the Danae Painter.

(trans. Halliwell 1998).[7] The widespread belief that music could influence the character (*êthos*) of those who were exposed to it was hence based on the commonly shared assumption that music had always a representational and narrative content, even when there was no text. Plato, for instance, in a passage of his *Laws* (669e), though criticizing instrumental music, does not dismiss it as pure nonsense, but justifies his disapproval in terms of the difficulty of identifying its object of *mimêsis* (Pelosi 2010: 60–2; Rocconi 2014: 705). A key example of the mimetic capacity of ancient instrumental music is the *Pythikos nomos*, a solo instrumental piece played by the *aulos* whose content was a representation (*dêlôma*, lit. "showing," "display") of the battle of Apollo against the serpent, each part being mimetically connected with a different stage of the contest (Rocconi 2015: 87).

In this view, any specific genre of music could induce the same emotion and instill the character it represented. Indeed different musical items, like the Phrygian, Lydian, or Dorian scales (that is to say, scales named after the geographical regions in which they originated), described as if they imitated distinct characteristics (i.e. frenzy, softness, or courage), were also credited with the associated emotional (and moral) effects: the *locus classicus* on these correspondences is Plato, *Republic* 398c–400d, where musical scales and rhythms are selected according to the goodness of their mimetic content and their consequent value in education (on the peculiarity of Plato's interpretation of the Phrygian scale, see Gostoli 1995 and Pagliara 2000). It can therefore be inferred that, for the Greeks, music and dance could not express emotions in themselves, but only represent them by way of their mimetic contents, that is, by reference to their relationship with something *outside* music.

But the Greeks conceived musical expressiveness not only as purely associative: Peripatetic sources seem to describe it as dependent also on some intrinsically musical features. The Aristotelian work in which we may find the most interesting remarks on the expressiveness of music is the *Politics*. Within the treatment of political issues, in fact, Aristotle devotes great attention to the musical education of the citizens, believed to be essential in forming good members of society; at the same time, he admits that music may also have other purposes besides education, such as amusement (*paidia*) or purification (*katharsis*).[8] Let us have a closer look at the text.

The reason why music may elicit so many different reactions when heard or performed, Aristotle explains, is because it has a recognized effect on the human character and soul (*Politics* 1340a5–6; on the capacity of music to "affect" [*metaballein*] the soul, see also Aristotle, *Prior Analytics* 70b9–10). This happens when people become *sumpatheis* when they listen to *mimêseis*, that is, artistic representations of real actions and events, being thrown in the corresponding mood even when there are no words in the music:

> We would have proof of that [sc. that music has the tendency to improve the character and the soul], if we are caused by music to acquire specific qualities in our characters. And indeed we do acquire specific qualities, as is shown by many things, and especially by the melodies of Olympus: for it is generally agreed that they inspire our souls with ecstasy, and ecstasy [*enthousiasmos*] is a qualification of the character of the soul. Again, when people listen to imitations, their feelings are always changed in sympathy with them [*sumpatheis*], even when they are no words, owing to the rhythms and melodies themselves.[9]
>
> —*Politics* 1340a7–13; all translations from
> *Politics* are from Barker 1984

The implication of these remarks is that music itself is not only a mode of *mimêsis*, but the most powerful way of imitating (or representing) something. In fact, rhythms and melodies—Aristotle explicitly states some lines later—contain *homoiômata*, that is, "likenesses, most closely approximating to the realities, of anger and mildness, of courage and moderation, and their opposites, and of all other dispositions, as the facts make clear; for our souls are altered when we hear such things" (1340a18–23). The emotional reactions we may have (thanks to habituation, *ethismos*, cf. Angier 2010: 105–25) to such likenesses are similar to the reactions we have to the realities themselves. This effect is peculiar to musical *mimêmata*, since in other objects of perception, such as those of touch and taste, there are no likenesses of moral characteristics, but rather "signs" (*sêmeia*) of them, as it sometimes happens with the objects of sight, which at the most serve as a mark (*episêma*) to distinguish emotions (1340a23–35).

It is quite evident that, for Aristotle, musical patterns have a special status among the other objects of perception, since they have the capability both to contain—not only "be signs of"—and to arouse in the listeners *pathê* and *êthê*. After declaring that pure musical elements have this inherent capacity to resemble emotions ("there exist *in rhythms and melodies* likenesses of anger and mildness," 1340a18–20), a few lines later Aristotle reasserts that it is in melodies themselves that there are *mimêmata* of characters, and that the same is true of rhythms (1340a38–9 and 1340b7–8), again without mentioning the songs' texts. In this discussion, in fact, he seems to be restricting the sense of the word *mousikê* to its technical aspects: learning music is about learning to play an instrument and to sing the most appropriate pitches and rhythms for any given context, without making any explicit reference to the ingredient which, at least in Platonic writings, was regarded as primary and crucial for mimetic theory and its ethical implications: the text (*logos*).

It is clear, then, that Aristotle is here openly admitting that music may express contents even through a purely musical argument, without the need for words, and that such an expressiveness involves not only the emotions contained and displayed by the musical composition, but also the corresponding emotions that the performance may induce in the performers and their audience (cf. Halliwell 2002, especially 161).[10] One wonders, however, how a melody or a rhythm can possibly resemble emotions so closely and why this sympathetic mechanism works so well with music in particular.

Aristotle says nothing about this, either in the *Politics* or anywhere else. But such a question, not clearly explored in his surviving writings, seems to have been discussed in his cultural environment, since two passages of the pseudo-Aristotelian *Problems*, a work that certainly originated within the Peripatetic school, appear to be connected with the passages of the *Politics* that have been discussed so far:

> Why is it that what is heard [*to akouston*], alone among perceptibles, has *êthos*? For even if there is a melody [*melos*] without words [*logos*], it has *êthos* none the less, but neither colour nor smell nor flavour have it. Is it because it alone has movement [*kinêsis*], though not the movement that the sound stirs up in us, since that kind of movement exists in the other perceptibles too (thus colour moves the vision)? But we perceive the movement that follows upon a sound of this kind (i.e., a sound that is part of a melodic sequence). This movement has likeness [*homoiotês*] both in rhythms and in the ordering of high and low notes, though not in their mixture: a concord [*sumphônia*] has no *êthos*. This *êthos* does not exist in any other perceptibles. But the movements themselves are related to action [*praktikai*], and actions are indications [*sêmasia*] of character.
>
> —Ps.-Aristotle, *Problems* 19.27, trans. Barker 1984, slightly modified

> Why do rhythms and melodies, which are sound [*phônê*], resemble ethical characters, while flavours do not, nor colours and odours? Is it because they are movements [*kinêseis*], as actions [*praxeis*] also are? Now activity [*energeia*] is ethical and produces ethical character, but flavours and colours do not act in this way.
>
> —Ps.-Aristotle, *Problems* 19.29, trans. Mayhew 2011

Both these passages explicitly refer to the ethical properties of strictly musical components of music, excluding any reference to verbal contents (*Problem* 27: "even if there is a melody *without words*"; *Problem* 29: "rhythms and melodies, *which are pure sound*"). Moreover, as is plainly stated in the first of them, the movement we perceive when we listen to music (a movement which has "in itself," the author says, a likeness to *êthos*) is not the same movement that is generally produced by any sensory stimulus, as happens when we perceive objects of any other sense. It is a movement that "follows" (*hepomenê*) a melodic or rhythmic element which is part of a melodic sequence or a rhythmic pattern: as if to say, it has to do with dynamic, not static elements. What happens when we hear a melodic or rhythmic sequence is very different—the author clarifies—from the reaction we may have when hearing a *sumphônia*, that is, a musical concord (like the octave, the most perfect among the consonances for the Greeks), which is perceived as a motionless mixture of elements (i.e. sounds), not as a sequence of events flowing along through time. This is the reason why melodies and rhythms have similarities with human actions and activities: because both are *energeia*, that is, "activity."[11]

Interestingly enough, at approximately the same period another Peripatetic writer was discussing similar topics. In a passage of the *Harmonic Elements* (p. 48.13–14 Da Rios), Aristoxenus of Tarentum describes musical melody (*melos*) as a process of "coming to be" (*genesis*), since the "movement [*kinêsis*] of the voice" presents itself to our perception as if the voice travels in a quasi-spatial dimension proceeding by intervals or gaps, so that we can follow its course remembering each stop of its journey in sequence (cf. *Harmonic Elements* p. 13.15–23 Da Rios). It follows that, according to Aristoxenus, memory is a very important tool for any theoretical inquiry on melody, since it is only through it that we may assess the role of specific melodic elements within their reference musical scale: "comprehension of music comes from two things, perception and memory: for we have to perceive what is coming to be and remember what has come to be. There is no other way of following the contents of music" (*Harmonic Elements* p. 48.14–18 Da Rios, trans. Barker 1989).

The main point raised by these different Peripatetic sources is basically the same: in melodies—and the same may be said of rhythms too—we hear sounds as a sequence of elements which literally *move* through time, and this movement is something clearly perceptible to us.[12] Such a movement, the author of the *Problems* adds, underpins similarities of rhythms and melodies with human actions because both are, in a sense, *actions*. Since it is mainly through this activity (*energeia*) that a moral character is produced in human beings, this is the reason why music has such a strong psychagogic power. The same mechanism is involved in artistic simulation of actions in drama: this might be the reason why this artistic medium was believed to have such an outstanding power on its audience (cf. Halliwell 2002: 162).

But this dynamism attributed to musical compositions could also be something more. Music moves through time not only because it is temporally dynamic, but also because its structure and sonic patterns tend to develop *formally* in such a way that the listener expects, measure after measure, some specific melodic design or resolution. In modern tonal music, for instance, chords containing a dissonance must be resolved into other (and more stable) chords that provide resting points, either temporary or permanent, like cadences or half-cadences. Similar remarks are made by the same author of the *Problems* about the expectations of ancient audiences, when consonant or dissonant instrumental accompaniments were used in the performance, "as in the case of people who play an accompaniment under a song. Though elsewhere these people do not play the same notes as the melody, still, if they finish on the same note, the pleasure they give with the ending is greater than the pain they give with the differences before the ending, because the common note, that arising from the octave, comes most pleasingly after differences" (*Problems* 19.39, trans. Barker 1984). This is precisely how modern formalists describe the functioning of instrumental music: according to them, pure music does not contain events which are narrated or represented by sounds (since formalism takes the view that absolute music has neither representational nor semantic content), nor is it even related to emotional episodes in the biography of the hearer aroused by his or her listening experience. Rather, instrumental music has a sound structure made of technical passages, melodic as well as rhythmical, that happen *in* the music.[13]

This post-Aristotelian evidence seems, then, to attest a noticeable shift of interest from the (desired) goodness of mimetic content of musical compositions (still typical, for example, of the Platonic attitude) to the mechanisms through which music was thought to operate emotionally on human beings. These mechanisms are identified in the dynamic features of music performance, according to which isolated events (sounds and time values) are transformed into *processes* (melodies and rhythms) that develop and are perceived through time. We have no way of knowing whether this insight should be attributed to Aristotle himself or to one of his pupils, but—from our perspective—it appears very modern, in line with the most recent trends, which attribute to music's processual character and to the ongoing interaction between its elements its ability to induce and express emotions (Davies 2010; Gabrielsson 2010).

The sophistication of these reflections on the role of the dynamic structure of music is clearly remarkable. Aristotle's attention, however, remains (at least in the *Politics*) focused on those emotions that may lead the youth to acquire virtuous habits. Music's psychagogic effect, he says, produces a further benefit if it is actively experienced at a young age, that is, if music is sung and played by the youth, since the repeated performance of "likenesses" of morally estimable characters, emotions, and actions may activate a process of assimilation of the virtues experienced through music (helping also in the process of recognizing and judging them in later life, because "participation in practice should be the development of judgment so that people ought to engage in practice when they are young" 1340b35–7).[14] Despite the various purposes attributed to music and the consequent variety of emotions which it can induce and express, then, the only significant digression within Aristotle's argument is devoted to *katharsis*:

> For a passion [*pathos*] that strongly affects certain souls occurs in all, varying only in that it may be greater or less: this is the case, for instance, with pity [*eleos*] and fear [*phobos*], and with inspired ecstasy too [*enthousiasmos*]. Some people are capable of being entirely possessed by this last disturbance, but we observe that when these people make use of melodies that greatly excite [*exorgiazein*] the soul, out of the resources of sacred melody, they are put right again, just as if they had been given medication [*iatreia*] and purgation [*katharsis*]. This must also happen to those who are particularly prone to pity or fear or emotion of any kind, and to others to the extent to which such things affect them: *katharsis* and alleviation [*kouphizesthai*] come to all, and pleasure with them. In the same way invigorating melodies also provides harmless delight for people; and this is why we should allow the contestants who perform the music of the theatre to employ *harmoniai* and melodies of these sorts.
>
> —*Politics* 1342a4–18

Three *pathē* are here used by Aristotle to stand for a wider range of possible passions: pity (*eleos*), fear (*phobos*), and ecstasy (*enthousiasmos*), probably selected in order to prepare for the definition of tragedy which will be developed in the *Poetics* (1449b27–8).[15] This brief description of musical *katharsis*, besides helping us to understand the mechanisms underlying its tragic counterpart, is interesting especially because it emphasizes Aristotle's interest in the physiological changes induced by emotions. The term *kouphizesthai*, borrowed—as is *katharsis*—from medicine (see *Problems* 2.22, describing the discharge [*kouphizesthai*] of superfluous humors in the human body), indicates the discharge operated by music through a process that cleanses the excitement created by orgiastic melodies by further exposure to the same kind of music. This mechanism is similar to the mechanism operating in homeopathic medicine, based on the famous doctrine that "like cures like."

This use of therapy to modify or extirpate dangerous emotions, as well as physical pathologies, seems to have been a subject widely disseminated in philosophical reflections on music's psychagogic power. Aristoxenus, for instance, not only ascribes the term *katharsis* to the Pythagoreans (who, he says, used medical means for the therapy of the body and musical means for the therapy of the soul, cf. Aristoxenus, fragment 26 Wehrli, probably part of a work titled *On the Pythagorean Life*), but also seems to have himself used music for psychotherapy, as Theophrastus suggests in a treatise titled *On Enthusiasm* (which relates that Aristoxenus cured the madness of a Theban man—induced by the sound of a *salpinx*, that is, a trumpet—by gradually introducing him to the sound of the *aulos*: Aristoxenus fragment 6 Wehrli, on which see Fortenbaugh 2012), and as confirmed by later sources (fragment 122 Wehrli, *apud* Ps.-Plutarch, *On Music* 43, 1147a: "Aristoxenus says somewhere that . . . music, through its own order and proportion, calms bodies and minds and leads them into the contrary condition," trans. Barker 1984). In addition, Theophrastus seems to have investigated the therapeutic effect of music on psychic disorders and physical diseases (fragment 726a Fortenbaugh: "Theophrastus . . . says that music cures many of the ills that affect the soul and the body, such as fainting, fright, and prolonged disturbances of mind"), and he is credited with having connected the origin of music to the purification of evil emotions (fragment 716 Fortenbaugh: "The nature of music is one. It is the movement of the soul that occurs in correspondence with its release from the evils due to the emotions; and if it were not this, neither would it be the nature of music," trans. Barker 1989).[16]

The subject of music therapy remained popular for many centuries, especially in Pythagorean circles: two late Neoplatonic works, *The Life of Pythagoras* by Porphyry of Tyre and *On the Pythagorean Life* by Iamblichus of Chalcis (third–fourth century CE, probably on the authority of Aristoxenus, see Provenza 2012), attest a long tradition concerning the Pythagorean usage of music as a means of therapy (*iatreia*). Their approach to the elicitation of emotions, however, seems to have been quite different from the Aristotelian one. Indeed, the Pythagoreans developed a system that functioned in an allopathic way, that is to say, a system that contrasted diseases by a music producing effects opposite to those aroused, as in the aforementioned story on the Tauromenian reported by Iamblichus, *On the Pythagorean Life* 110–12. According to what we are told in that passage, in fact, Pythagoreans used distinct *melê* for each specific *pathos*: faintheartedness and pain (*athumia* and *dêgmos*), anger and wrath (*orgê* and *thumos*), and any other serious disturbance in the soul.

The existence of two different systems of therapeutic processes, one allopathic and one homeopathic, is also attested in a fourth-century CE musical treatise, Aristides Quintilianus' *On Music*, a work that relies on many different earlier sources (often difficult to identify, because the author has elaborated on them so extensively), aspiring to collect in a single treatise everything relevant to the study of music. This treatise splits the parts of music into two categories, the theoretical and the practical: the value of music in education and in psychiatric therapy—the two main empirical applications of musical structures—is the subject of Book 2, where there is a brief but rather technical explanation of the means through which music therapy operates on human soul. In chapter 14 we are told that, if we apply *harmoniai* (i.e. scales) to each soul on the basis either of their similarity (*homoiotês*) or of their opposition (*enantiotês*) to it, we may "disclose the bad character that lurks within it, and cure it, and replace it with a better" (trans. Barker 1989). If dispositions, by contrast, are obscure or harder to disclose, we should try an experimental approach, beginning to apply whatever melody comes to hand and then evaluating the emotional reaction to it, since "the usefulness of a *harmonia* depends on the character of each individual soul" (*On Music* 2.14, p. 81.2–3 W.-I., trans. Barker 1989). In addition to this, some comments are then devoted to the emotional power of rhythms. Using unspecified medical authorities (who evidently discussed such matters), Aristides describes the physiological reaction of the human pulse to different rhythmical patterns:

> Of the rhythms, those that give an initial calm to the mind by beginning from the thesis are more peaceful ... of the rhythms in equal ratio, those composed only of short syllables are most swift and more passionate ... in the movements of the pulse too, the healthiest people are those in whom contraction and dilatation answer to one another through movements of these kinds.
>
> —*On Music* 2.15, p. 82.4–28 W.-I., trans. Barker 1989

We can thus assert that, starting from Aristotle and the Peripatetics, some Greek philosophers not only attempted a detailed picture of correspondences between specific technical elements in music and different emotions, but they also investigated the underlying mechanisms responsible for emotional arousal through music. The firmly rooted assumption that music was *mimêsis* of something external to it served to justify, on a wider level, the emotional power of music on the human soul, but it did not prevent some of these writers from recognizing in music's dynamic movement and in its processional character the most significant resemblance to the human expression of emotions. This view, however, was soon challenged by opponents such as the Epicurean Philodemus (first century BCE), who—while accepting the mimetic status of poetry—rejected any mimetic model of music, as well as any related idea of music's emotional and ethical power (Halliwell 2002: 281–6).[17]

MUSIC AND EMOTIONS IN ROMAN ANTIQUITY

In Roman culture, we miss similar remarks regarding how music emotionally operates on the human soul. This does not mean that the Romans were not interested in the capacity of music to arouse and to express various *adfectus*. In his work *On the Ideal Orator*, Cicero explicitly states that each emotion finds its vocal and physical expression in different facial expressions, tones of voice, and bodily attitudes:

> For by nature, every emotion [*motus animi*] has its own peculiar facial expression [*voltus*], tone of voice [*sonus*], and gesture [*gestus*]. The entire body of a human being, all the facial expressions, and all the utterances of the voice,[18] like the strings on a lyre, "sound" exactly in the way they are struck by each emotion. The voice is stretched out like the strings of an instrument, to respond to each and every touch, to sound high, low, fast, slow, loud, and soft. And apart from each of these extremes, there is also, in each category, a middle between the extremes. Moreover, from these kinds of sounds are also derived others: smooth and rough, restrained and wide ranging, sustained and staccato, hoarse and cracked, and with crescendo and diminuendo and a changing of pitch. The employment of each of these kinds falls under the regulation of art.
>
> —*On the Ideal Orator*, 3.216–17, trans. May-Wisse 2001

The two contexts that recur most frequently in Roman literary sources within which emotions were conveyed through musical elements of some kind were the courtroom and the theater. In the former, emotions were expressed and aroused through the vocal inflections and body language of the orator; in the latter the process was realized by the corporeal gestures, postures, and movements of the pantomime dancer. This should not come as a surprise since, in ancient times, both language and bodily movements were conceived as parts of the *ars musica*:

> Music has two modes of expression in the voice and in the body; for both voice and body require to be controlled by appropriate rules. Aristoxenus divides music, in so far as it concerns the voice, into rhythm and melody, the one consisting in measure, the latter in sound and song. Now I ask you whether it is not absolutely necessary for the orator to be acquainted with all these methods of expression which are concerned firstly with gesture, secondly with the arrangement of words and thirdly with the inflexions of the voice, of which a great variety are required in pleading.
>
> —Quintilian, *Institutes of Oratory* 1.10.22–3;
> all translations of this text from Butler 1920

Both oratory (especially judicial oratory) and pantomime were very important arts in Rome, especially during the imperial period. Within these genres, however, the emotions aroused by music were not associated with educational purposes, as in Greece, but had mainly the function of amazing and amusing the audience.

An interest in the aural aspects of language was already attested in Classical Greece starting at least from Aristotle's *Rhetoric*, where we find the first definition and classification of emotions in ancient literature.[19] In Book 3, Aristotle explicitly points out the means through which the voice—in rhetoric as well as in poetry, cf. *Poetics* 1447a22—may express the emotions more or less appropriate to a given context, that is, volume (*megethos*), melodic intonation (*harmonia*), and rhythm (*rhuthmos*):

> It is clear, therefore, that there is something of the sort in rhetoric as well as in poetry ... delivery is a matter of voice, as to the mode in which it should be used for each particular emotion [*pathos*]; when it should be loud [*megalē*], when low [*mikra*], when intermediate [*mesē*]; and how the tones, that is, shrill [*oxeia*], deep [*bareia*], and intermediate [*mesē*], should be used; and what rhythms are adapted to each subject. For there are three qualities that are considered, volume [*megethos*], harmony [*harmonia*], rhythm [*rhuthmos*]. Those who use these properly nearly always carry off the prizes in dramatic contests, and as at the present day actors have greater influence on the stage than the poets, it is the same in political contests, owing to the corruptness of our forms of government.
>
> —Aristotle, *Rhetoric* 1403b24–35, trans. Freese 1926

It is important to clarify that, in Hellenic culture, the expression of emotions through the voice was not only concerned with what we would call "affective prosody": nowadays this expression relates to the prosodic cues and features of speech (including pitch, loudness, and articulatory rates; see Bostanov and Kotchoubey 2004), but it can in no way be compared with the highly musical features of ancient Greek prosody. In antiquity, the tone and rhythm of spoken language were in fact perceived as highly distinguishing marks of the language itself: thanks to the pitch accent and the quantitative length of the syllables, melody and rhythm were deeply embodied in ancient *logos* even when no music was attached to it.

The same appears to be true of the Latin language, whose prosody probably displayed a perceptible rise and fall of pitch, at least in classical times (although this hypothesis, held mainly by French scholars, remains open to controversy).[20] The orator—we are told by the Roman rhetorician Quintilian—must always tune his voice to the right pitch, as in the example of Gaius Gracchus, behind whom a musician used to play a pitch-pipe, called *tonarion*, that gave him the tones he had to follow with the voice (*Institutes of Oratory* 1.10.27). It is, in fact, "by the raising [*intentio*], lowering [*remissio*] or inflexion [*flexus*] of the voice that the orator stirs the emotions of his hearers, and the measure, if I may repeat the term, of voice or phrase differs according as we wish to rouse the indignation or the pity of the judge" (*Institutes of Oratory* 1.10.25).[21] In addition to this, his gestures have to conform to the voice, since there are many things, Quintilian says, that can be expressed by him without the assistance of words (*Institutes of Oratory* 11.3.65). The motion of the orator's body, then, "must be suitable and becoming, or as the Greeks call it *eurythmic*, and this can only be secured by the study of music" (*Institutes of Oratory* 1.10.25–6).

But Quintilian is also keen to point out that great theatricality and excessive mimicry are inappropriate in an orator. He condemns the excessive use, in contemporary oratory, of modulations that recall the stage (*modulatio scaenica*) and of gestures that resembled too closely those of a pantomime dancer:

> But any of these faults are tolerable compared with the practice of chanting instead of speaking, which is the worst feature of our modern oratory, whether in the courts or in the schools, and of which I can only say that I do not know whether it is more useless or more repugnant to good taste. For what can be less becoming to an orator than modulations that recall the stage [*modulatio scaenica*] and a sing-song utterance which at times resembles the maudlin utterance of drunken revelers?
>
> —*Institutes of Oratory* 11.3.57–8[22]

> For the orator should be as unlike a dancer [*saltator*] as possible, and his gesture should be adapted rather to his thought than to his actual words, a practice which was indeed once upon a time even adopted by the more dignified performers on the stage.
>
> —*Institutes of Oratory* 11.3.89

The influence of pantomime on imperial performance culture was very substantial indeed (Zanobi 2014): known as *fabula saltica*, the pantomime was the most emotive theatrical medium of the Roman age. It consisted in a performance in which a silent solo dancer (called *orchêstês*), wearing a graceful silk costume and a closed-mouth mask, impersonated in close succession a series of characters and illustrated them with his dance, playing *all* the parts himself, while a chorus sang. The musical accompaniment included both wind instruments (essentially *aulos* and panpipes) and percussion, such as *kumbala* (small brass cymbals), *sistra* (Egyptian musical instruments consisting of a handle and a U-shaped metal frame), and the *kroupezion* (from *krouô*, "to strike"), a sandal with an iron sole, used to mark time for the dance.

The pantomime's origin can be traced back to the mimetic dance of tragic actors, the mythical themes of the two genres being basically the same,[23] even if this dance exponentially enhanced the dramatization of emotions through bodily postures. According to what we know from Lucian, who around the middle of the second century CE wrote a strong defense of the genre (titled *On Dance*), tracing its origins back to the tradition of ancient *choreia*,[24] the *mimêsis* realized by the practitioners of this art relied on a well-established affective vocabulary of steps and gestures, mainly consisting of movements of the hands. The dancers, he reports, were called *cheirosophoi*, that is, "skilled with the hands" (*On Dance* 69), since any dancer "undertakes to present and enact characters and emotions" (*On Dance* 35 and 67, trans. Harmon 1936, clearly echoing Aristotle, *Poetics* 1447a26–8, quoted above). The aim of dancing was in fact "impersonating" (*hupokrisis*), a practice that is cultivated—Lucian goes on to say—in the same way by the rhetoricians, "for in their case also there is nothing which we commend more highly than their accommodating themselves to the roles which they assume" (*On Dance* 65, trans. Harmon 1936, cf. *On Dance* 35 and 62).[25]

The mimetic potential of ancient Greek dance was clearly pushed to the very limit by these exhibitions, whose meanings and values were all based on the abilities of a single performer. Such a performer had to come "as close to the real thing as possible," we are told by Libanius (*Orations* 64.62), and his abilities were deemed to be essential for a successful exhibition, as also Seneca points out (*Letters* 121.6): "We are apt to wonder at skilled dancers because their gestures are perfectly adapted to the meaning of the piece and its accompanying emotions, and their movements match the speed of the dialogue" (trans. Gummere 1925). Moreover, the frequency with which Roman sources compare the mimetic skills of the dancers to those of the orators shows that these two figures had by then become paradigmatic examples of the possibility, for a bodily performance, to portray and express emotions in a particularly effective way. Indeed the transformation of emotions into spectacle, overcoming moral concerns of any sort, became a specific trend of the Roman imperial culture which, by reinforcing the mimetic power of the "body" in different performative contexts, started an unstoppable process of *aestheticization* of emotions.

CHAPTER FOUR

Drama

DAVID KONSTAN

INTRODUCTION

Classical drama, as we know it, arose in Athens at the beginning of the fifth century BCE, when first tragedy, and a couple of decades later comedy, were institutionalized as parts of public festivals, and their production was supported by the state. Other cities too had dramatic performances, but they survive only in fragments too slender to allow for interpretation. All the Greek tragedies that we can read today (with one possible exception) were first staged in the fifth century. Tragedies continued to be produced in Athens in the fourth century (*Rhesus*, ascribed to Euripides, may date to this period), and some scholars have maintained that these may have exhibited heightened emotional effects, for instance by representing little babies on stage, as in Euripides' *Iphigenia in Aulis* (this claim depends on identifying later interpolations in fifth-century tragedies), but such arguments remain speculative. In the case of comedy, on the contrary, we can trace a development from the fifth century, represented by the works of Aristophanes and his contemporaries (the latter surviving only in fragments) to the late fourth and third centuries. Ancient critics distinguished between Old Comedy, of the Aristophanic sort, and New Comedy, a vigorous genre which traveled beyond the borders of Athens and is represented today by Menander, a few of whose works have been recovered whole (*Grouch*, Greek *Dyskolos*) or in part over the past century or so. The two types are quite distinct, and require separate consideration (there are references too to Middle Comedy, but it is not possible today to distinguish its characteristics with any confidence, if indeed it deserves to be identified as a distinct form).

New Comedy achieved a new life in the form of Roman adaptations, of which twenty-six survive today, by Plautus and Terence, who in turn transmitted the form to the Renaissance and beyond. Although Terence—the later of the two—is thought of as being relatively faithful to his Greek models, he nevertheless was happy to combine elements from two different comedies (a practice he defends in the prologues to his plays); Plautus, for his part, introduced musical numbers and other high jinks that gave greater animation to his productions. We cannot assume, therefore, that the Latin versions were identical to the Greek in terms of their emotional register, even apart from differences in the Greek and Latin emotional lexicons. Still, the plots were broadly speaking similar, and in many respects we can think of the Roman plays as continuous with Greek New Comedy.

The Romans also produced tragedies, often based on Greek models. Of these, the only ones that survive intact today are by Seneca, composed in the first century CE. These are inspired by Greek tragedy, but freely alter the plots, and the tone of Senecan tragedy is markedly different from that of his predecessors—it is Seneca who had the greatest influence on the revival of tragedy in the Renaissance and in Elizabethan England.

There were other comic genres in classical antiquity. At one of the two annual Athenian dramatic festivals (the Greater Dionysia), the last of the set of four plays that each poet in the tragedy competition staged was a satyr play, which was a mythological burlesque that lightened the tone after the first three entries (an ancient critic defines the satyr drama as "tragedy at play"); one of these survives complete (Euripides' *Cyclops*), along with substantial portions of a couple of others. Yet another form was the mime, which was a short skit staged in public theaters, though it may also have been put on in the homes of the wealthy (there were also pantomimes, which lacked a proper script and were in the main performed by means of gestures and movement); a few highly literary versions survive, by a certain Herodas or Herondas, along with fragments of more popular types. What sentiments these genres elicited or represented must be deduced from the surviving evidence. In what follows, I discuss first Greek tragedy, then Old Comedy, then New Comedy (both Greek and Roman), and finally Senecan tragedy.

GREEK TRAGEDY

When it comes to tragedy, it is natural to begin with Aristotle's affirmation in the *Poetics* that the emotions proper to tragedy are pity and fear (1452a2–3, 1452b32–3, etc.), a view shared by other classical writers such as the orators Gorgias (*Helen* 9) and Isocrates (*Panegyricus* 112, 168; cf. Plato *Republic* 606b–c; cf. Munteanu 2012). Aristotle's view of the tragic emotions is prescriptive—pity and fear are what tragedy ought primarily to arouse—and he recognized that tragedy stimulated other responses as well. What is more, Aristotle confined his account of the tragic emotions to audience response; he did not choose, in the *Poetics*, to examine the emotions experienced by the characters on stage. The distinction is significant in two respects. First, it is clear that Aristotle is thinking of the audience reaction to the tragedy as a whole rather than to specific scenes or dramatic moments, such as the emergence of Oedipus, now blinded, from the palace toward the end of *Oedipus the King*, or the sudden appearance of the Furies in Aeschylus' *Libation Bearers*, which was said by later writers (on poor authority) to be so startling as to cause pregnant women to give birth prematurely (it is uncertain whether women attended dramatic performances in this period). Aristotle condemns such special effects, as we may call them, reminiscent of modern action films, as producing shock (*to deinon*) rather than fear in the true sense. It is the entire trajectory of Oedipus' life, or that of Hippolytus, say, in Euripides' drama, that elicits the relevant emotions (cf. Konstan 2008).

The second point is that the fear and pity experienced while watching a play would seem to differ from those same emotions as experienced in real life: we know, for example, that there is no genuine danger to ourselves, comparable to that which menaces the characters on stage, and we are not moved to help them, which we would if we felt pity. Some scholars have concluded, accordingly, that by "fear" (at all events) Aristotle in this context means "fear for another" (e.g., Halliwell 2002: 217). Aristotle, however, gives no indication of such a significance, and there are reasons to think he means ordinary fear and also pity. Just as listening to a report about the defeat of an allied state in a debate in the assembly might instil fear about engaging in a war with the victorious power, so too the dramatization of the catastrophe suffered by a legendary hero might generate a certain anxiety about the dangers all mortals face, even those who are innocent of evil motives (as Aristotle stipulates for the protagonists of tragedy), and so inspire, if not precisely

FIGURE 4.1: Tragic mask, first century BCE or CE.

caution, at least a kind of existential apprehension that we (though not Aristotle) might think of as humility. We shall return to the question of audience emotion in connection with comedy and Senecan tragedy.

Turning now to the emotions of characters within tragedies, we may note that pity is relatively rare: whatever pity the audience may feel, the characters do not in general pity one another, although the chorus, which is often a spectator of the action rather than an active participant, sometimes acts as a kind of surrogate audience. In order to see why this should be the case, the best guide is Aristotle's *Rhetoric*, the earliest systematic discussion of the emotions we possess from classical antiquity. Indeed, there is reason to believe that Aristotle was the first to gather the affects that we today think of specifically as emotions under a single heading, namely *pathos*, a term that had a wide range of meanings in classical Greek (Konstan 2006a). Aristotle defines pity as "pain arising from a perceived evil ... in a person who does not deserve to meet with it—an evil that one may expect either to suffer oneself, or that someone of one's own [dear ones] may" (*Rhetoric* 2.8, 1385b13–16). Several features of Aristotle's definition stand out. We may note first the moral dimension: pity is aroused by unmerited suffering, not by misfortune as such. Second, Aristotle makes it clear that the pitier is not in the same situation as the pitied—we must be aware that we are vulnerable to a comparable adversity in the future rather than be victims of it at the moment. Finally, that susceptibility pertains to us and those nearest to us: the implication, which Aristotle spells out explicitly, is that when close kin or friends are afflicted by disaster, we feel, not pity, but rather the same sense of immediate pain or horror that we would had it happened to ourselves. In this regard, pity is different from what used to be called sympathy and is now more often called empathy, in which one puts oneself in the place of the sufferer (Edmund Burke defines sympathy "as a sort of substitution, by which we are put into the place of another man, and affected in many respects as he is affected"; cf. Hume, *A Treatise of Human Nature* 1906 (orig. 1739–40): 317; Schopenhauer 1995: 132–44). Pity requires distance, not identification—which makes sense, since the characters who are suffering are not themselves feeling pity, after all. In interpreting classical drama, we must always bear in mind that ancient Greek and Latin conceptions of the emotions may not map neatly onto our own conventional taxonomies.

Pity, as it is exhibited in tragedy, conforms well to Aristotle's description. At the beginning of Sophocles' *Ajax*, the maddened Ajax slaughters a flock of sheep which he mistakes, in god-inflicted madness, for the Greek leaders who denied him the prize of Achilles' armor and gave it instead to Odysseus. As Odysseus approaches Ajax's tent, Athena appears and offers to expose the miserable hero to his view: "Isn't the sweetest laughter," she asks, "to laugh at enemies?" But Odysseus' reaction is different: "I pity him in his misfortune, though he is my foe, because he has been yoked by evil ruin. And in this I have regard for my condition no less than his: for I see that we who live are nothing but figments, or a frail shadow." Odysseus' vulnerability elicits his pity; as a goddess, Athena is immune and so can safely gloat.

In Euripides' *Hecuba*, Hecuba, seeking to justify her blinding of Polymestor and slaughter of his children, says to Agamemnon, "Consider all these acts of his as shameful, and have respect for me, pity us—step back like a painter and look at me and observe the evils I endure; I was once a monarch but am now your slave" (806–9). Agamemnon is to assume the proper distance for pity (like Odysseus, he becomes a spectator), and is also reminded that he is not invulnerable. When the chorus in Sophocles' *Philoctetes* see Philoctetes' miserable cave, where he has lived since the Greek forces abandoned him on the way to conquer Troy, they exclaim, "I pity him: no human being to care for him, with no companion in sight, wretched, forever alone, he is afflicted by a savage disease and wanders at the mercy of every need that arises" (169–75). But when Philoctetes stubbornly (if understandably) refuses to go to Troy, though his wound can be cured only there, Neoptolemus, who has come to feel a bond with the wretched hero, declares, "it is not just to pardon or to pity those who are involved in self-willed harm, like you" (1318–20)—misfortune does not deserve pity if it is deliberately incurred. Pity may also, however, seem like condescension. In *Prometheus Bound* (attributed to Aeschylus but perhaps by a later fifth-century playwright), the chorus of Oceanids is dismayed by Prometheus' anguish, to which he indignantly replies, "So then, I am pitiable for my friends to look upon!" (242–6; cf. 140).

In the *Poetics* (13, 1453a2–6), Aristotle states that pity and fear are not excited when one witnesses the ruin of thoroughly bad men, "for such a plot may involve kindness [*to philanthrôpon*, literally a philanthropic feeling], but neither pity nor fear, for . . . pity concerns a man who is undeserving, whereas fear concerns one who is similar to us." This third sentiment, alongside pity and fear, would appear to be something like sympathy, a response to suffering as such, irrespective of desert; if so, it is a response that Aristotle deems marginal to tragedy, and it is not among the passions or *pathê* that he discusses in the *Rhetoric*.

We have observed that the fear that tragedy rouses in the spectators, according to Aristotle, is not like the shock effects of horror movies, with their lurking sense of threat, or of high-speed action films with their exploding vehicles, but derives rather from the sense that we are susceptible to the kind of misfortune that befalls the characters in the play, since we are sufficiently like them to suffer a similar fate. Aristotle affirms, indeed, that fear renders people deliberative (*Rhetoric* 2.5, 1382a5): we are more likely, when afraid, to avoid antagonizing those in a stronger position than we are. The protagonists of Greek tragedy are in general powerful and self-confident figures, and they rarely exhibit fear: they resist and struggle, even when the odds are against them (cf. Knox 1964 on the intransigence of the Sophoclean hero, but Aeschylus and Euripides feature equally bold figures). Weaker characters, however, such as women, non-Greeks (or barbarians, as the Greeks called them), or Greek men if they are ill, may be represented as fearful. The women who form the chorus of Aeschylus' *Seven against Thebes*, for example, are panic-stricken at the thought that the Argive army, which is besieging their city, will raze it if victorious; however, even their anxiety is rationally motivated and is allayed when they are assured that the defenses of the city are secure (Konstan 2006b: 144–7). In Euripides' *Orestes*, the main characters, Orestes and his sister Electra, are alarmed that they will be condemned to death for matricide by a vote of the Argive assembly, but as Orestes recovers his health and soundness of mind (he had been maddened by the Furies after the murder), and his friend Pylades arrives to offer support, the three conceive a bold plan to defend themselves, despite the risk to their lives. By contrast, a Phrygian slave, who was witness to Orestes' attempt to slay Helen inside the palace, frankly acknowledges his terror when Orestes threatens to put him to the sword: the scene has a burlesque quality that contributes all the more to the slave's humiliation. In Euripides' *Iphigenia in Aulis*, the young Iphigenia is frightened at the prospect of being sacrificed at the altar by her father, Agamemnon, so that the Greek fleet may sail to Troy, and yet, quite suddenly (as Aristotle noted, with some disapproval), she turns round and courageously proclaims her wish to die so that the Greeks may avenge the abduction of Helen. When the chorus of women fleeing their Egyptian cousins in Aeschylus' *Suppliants* is beset by fear, the Greek king reproaches them for their excessive anxiety (514). The Bacchants (in Euripides' play of that name) are afraid when their leader (in fact, the god Dionysus in disguise) is temporarily imprisoned; when he miraculously breaks down the walls with a thunderclap, the women tremble and Dionysus addresses them: "Barbarian women, have you fallen to the ground, so struck with fear?" (604–5). For the most part, nevertheless, they are confident in the protection of their god. Strong women, however, like Clytemnestra in Aeschylus' *Agamemnon*, Antigone, or Medea, are undaunted.

Aristotle defines anger as "a desire, accompanied by pain, for a perceived revenge, on account of a perceived slight on the part of people who are not fit to slight one or one's own" (*Rhetoric* 2.2, 1378a31–3). The close association between anger and status explains why Aristotle can affirm that "it is impossible to be afraid of and angry with someone at the same time" (*Rhetoric* 2.2, 1380a33), and again that we cannot be angry at someone who is in fear of us (1380a34–5). These claims may strike us as counter-intuitive, but they follow from Aristotle's conception of anger or *orgê*. If you are afraid, you cannot avenge a slight and must passively swallow your resentment (this is the case, Aristotle observes, with slaves); those who fear us, in turn, are in no position to put us down and hence arouse our ire. This is why Aristotle speaks of those who are not "fit" to belittle others: those who are far more powerful than we, for example kings, can slight us with impunity. Contrariwise, it is dangerous to insult one's superiors in strength or status. Thus, the nurse in Euripides' *Medea* declares, "fierce is the temper of tyrants, and though they start small, because their power is great they curtail their anger with difficulty" (119–21; cf. 176–7); Medea's anger—and this is her principal passion in the play—is a sign of her willingness and ability to exact revenge (compare Alcmene's rage at the end of Euripides' *Children of Heracles*, when she is at last in a position to take vengeance on Eurystheus after his defeat and capture by the Athenians). On the contrary, when Deianira, in Sophocles' *Women of Trachis*, declares that "it is not decent for a sensible woman to be angry" (552–3), she may be expressing a view of wifely duty but at the same time she is acknowledging the necessity of submitting to Heracles, her husband, even if he intends to introduce another woman into her home, since she is powerless to prevent it. In the end, Deianira is responsible for Heracles' death, albeit unwittingly, when she sends him a garment steeped in a lethal poison (she had mistaken it for a love potion). It is as though the tragedy, and the myth that lies behind it, fulfilled a repressed fantasy of vengeance analogous to Medea's (Deianira's desire for revenge emerges clearly in Seneca's adaptation of the Sophoclean play, *Hercules on Mount Oeta*). In general, anger is more characteristic of male heroes, such as Ajax, when he feels slighted by his failure to be awarded Achilles' arms, or Oedipus, when he is accused of incest and parricide by Tiresias or believes that Creon is plotting against him. In Sophocles' *Antigone*, Cleon's own ire is aroused by what he regards as the insubordination of his young niece; as he puts it, "While I'm alive a woman will never rule over me" (525). Tragedy continually testifies to the association between anger, power, and status.

There is no word in classical Greek that corresponds precisely to the English "jealousy," and we must be careful about ascribing it as a motive to characters in tragedy. There seem to have been no Greek tragedies in which the plot was based on male jealousy, like Shakespeare's *Othello*. Some have seen jealousy at work in Medea's antagonism to Jason's proposed marriage to the young princess of Corinth, although Medea herself insists that she is furious because Jason betrayed his oaths and dishonoured her; Jason alludes to sexual jealousy (555–6, 568–75), but he fails to recognize the slight to her honor and her royal pride, of which her nurse, as we have seen, was well aware.

Envy too (Greek *phthonos*), which is sometimes hard to distinguish from jealousy, plays a smaller role in tragedy than we might expect. Envy is usually treated as a mean-spirited passion, a kind of spite motivated not by self-interest but by pure ill will; Aristotle declares it wholly unworthy of a decent person. Perhaps it was too petty a sentiment for Greek tragedy, which did not typically depict out-and-out villains like Richard III. In Euripides' *Andromache*, Hermione's inability to give Neoptolemus a child causes her to behave brutally to Hector's widow, whom Neoptolemus received as his war prize. As Ed Sanders notes, "The emotion that most dominates the play, if (typically) rarely named, is *phthonos*" (2014: 153). There is a similar motif in Euripides *Ion*, of which Daniel Ogden writes, "The (supposedly) childless Creusa becomes crazed with envy towards Ion, whom she supposes to be her husband's bastard" (1996: 197; cf. especially *Ion* 1025). The chorus in Sophocles' *Ajax* opine that envy seeks out the great (157; cf. *Oedipus the King* 382). This kind of envy again seems to be ascribed chiefly to women or else to the humble classes. But envy in Greek might also signify the justifiable indignation that people are getting above themselves—a sentiment sometimes ascribed to the gods, who are wont to strike down overweening greatness (Aeschylus, *Persians* 362, *Agamemnon* 947; Euripides, *Alcestis* 1135). The same idea might also be expressed by the term *nemesis* (Sophocles, *Philoctetes* 518, 602), which Aristotle treats as a moral sentiment and the opposite of pity: just as pity is a painful feeling arising from the perception of undeserved misfortune, so *nemesis* or indignation is a painful feeling arising from the perception of undeserved prosperity. (Aristotle employs the verbal form, *nemesan*, which does not appear in tragedy.) Aristotle also distinguishes envy from rivalry or justifiable ambition, which he calls *zêlos* (the root of both English "zealous" and "jealous"). These subtleties are difficult to discriminate in tragedy, which in any case tends rather to illustrate ambition in the sense of a passion for power. Thus Eteocles, in Euripides' *Phoenician Women*, brazenly proclaims his desire to reign as tyrant, to the exclusion of his brother Polynices, with whom he was to share the throne: "Mother, I will speak out and conceal nothing. I would travel to where the stars and sun rise and beneath the earth if I could accomplish this one thing, possess Tyranny, the greatest of the gods. I do not wish to yield this advantage to anyone else, but to preserve it for myself: for it is cowardice to settle for less and lose the greater portion" (503–10). Polynices, in turn, is possessed by resentment at Eteocles' unjust usurpation, though his decision to raise a foreign army against his own city undercuts his pose of righteous indignation (in Sophocles' *Oedipus at Colonus*, the aged Oedipus will furiously condemn him for his unholy ambition).

When it comes to love, ancient Greek distinguished between *philia*, which represents affection in the broadest sense, including friendship, and *erôs* or passionate love, which comes close to the modern idea of infatuation or being in love (in Latin the word *amor* covered both concepts). Friendship plays a significant role in tragedy. In Euripides' *Orestes*, Orestes exclaims to his faithful companion, Pylades, that "it is better to have an outsider as a friend, if he bound to you by character, than ten thousand blood relations" (805–6). In Euripides' *Heracles*, after Heracles has slain his wife and children in a fit of madness, his friend Theseus enters and persuades the suicidal hero to choose life and come to Athens. Sophocles' *Philoctetes* illustrates the formation of a friendship between the young Neoptolemus, who has been sent to inveigle the abandoned hero into giving up his fateful bow so that the Greeks may conquer Troy, and Philoctetes, whom he comes to admire for his grit and integrity. And yet, although Aristotle states that pity and fear are best aroused by crises that occur within relationships of *philia*, such as when a brother slays a brother, a son his father, a mother her son, a son his mother, and the like (*Poetics* 14, 1453b19–23), betrayals of friendship are absent from tragedy and indeed from Greek and Roman drama of every genre. As Aristotle's examples indicate, it is violence within the family that he has in mind, and disruptions of familial bonds are indeed the primary plot motif of tragedy, as illustrated by the many plays centering on Thebes (Oedipus and his kin) and Argos (the house of Atreus). When Electra, in Euripides' play named for her, gazes upon the corpse of her mother, and exclaims, "*philê* and not *philê*" (1230–1), that is, "dear yet not dear," she is contrasting the natural affection that should exist between mother and daughter with the fact that they have been mortal enemies, since Clytemnestra murdered her husband Agamemnon. So, too, Eteocles says of his brother Polynices, in Euripides' *Phoenician Women*, "He was *philos*, became my enemy, but is still *philos*" (1446), because of the natural affective bond between kin. Sisters are less likely to become rivals of their brothers, and their love remains steadfast in tragedy (for example, in Euripides' *Electra* and Sophocles' *Oedipus at Colonus* 1414–16).

Erotic passion, by contrast, is not celebrated in Greek tragedy—there is nothing resembling Shakespeare's *Romeo and Juliet* (the affection between husband and wife, illustrated touchingly in Euripides' *Alcestis*, is rather *philia*). Phaedra's desire for her stepson Hippolytus in Euripides' tragedy leads to catastrophe, and it is no accident that it is a woman who succumbs to *erôs*. Aristophanes, in the *Frogs*, has Aeschylus assert that he never composed plays about whorish Phaedras or Stheneboeas, as Euripides did (the latter is again a Potiphar's wife story), nor, he adds, can anyone point to a single example of a woman in love in his tragedies (1043–4); even if such things actually happen, as Euripides alleges, tragic poets, says Aeschylus, should not represent them on stage (1052–4).

Aeschylus does not think to mention male *erôs*, and in fact it is not a central motive in extant tragedy. Heracles' passion for Iole in Sophocles' *Trachiniae* triggers the crisis, but the plot revolves around Deianira's effort to win back her husband's affection; the chorus indeed sing an ode to *erôs* in Sophocles' *Antigone*, noting its dangers as well as its power, but Haemon has already been betrothed to the young heroine by his father, Creon, and he has other motives for his loyalty to her. Nor does *erôs* figure importantly in Aristophanic comedy; it is only with New Comedy, as we shall see, that it comes to play a major role in classical drama.

It is rare that characters in Greek tragedy have a change of heart, and remorse and shame play a limited role in the genre. Creon in Sophocles' *Antigone* learns that he was wrong to prevent the burial of Polynices and to punish Antigone by immuring her in a tomb, a point driven home by the self-inflicted deaths of his son and wife. In Sophocles' *Philoctetes*, the young Neoptolemus realizes that he ought not to have betrayed his principles and consented to strip Philoctetes of his bow by treachery; pity and shame combine to make him repent of his lapse. Orestes is briefly smitten by shame when confronted by Tyndareus, his maternal grandfather, over his matricide in Euripides' *Orestes* (459–69), but he soon recovers his composure and confidence. However, Electra and Orestes seem stunned, at the end of Euripides' *Electra*, by the matricide they had so confidently embarked upon. Heracles, after he has slain his family, is beset by shame and covers his head (Euripides, *Heracles* 1146–60) until Theseus extends his hand and persuades him that he is not polluted. Helen, usually the example of a shameless woman, is mortified, in the play by Euripides that bears her name, by her evil reputation, which is due, according to this version of her story, to her simulacrum who ran off to Troy with Paris; she is determined, however, not to incur a further shame by submitting to the passion of the king of Egypt (63–7). Clytemnestra, however, in Aeschylus' *Agamemnon*, boldly proclaims her lack of shame when her prior false claims about her loyalty to Agamemnon are exposed ("I shall feel no *aischunê*," 1373), since then it was opportune, and in general tragic protagonists act in the conviction that they are in the right.

Tragedy is largely about suffering, which may be expressed in formal lamentations (most often by women) or as anguished outcries or exclamations; the Greek term *lupê* can signify either physical pain (which is not precisely an emotion) or mental distress, and the two ideas overlap in tragedy. Examples of grief are too abundant to cite, ranging from the laments of captive women after the fall of Troy (Euripides' *Hecuba* and *Trojan Women*) and the queen Atossa's despair in Aeschylus' *Persians* (cf. Dué 2006) to Antigone's sorrow as she is led off to her tomb, Prometheus' or Philoctetes' cries of agony, Oedipus' horror at discovering the truth of his upbringing or Jason's as he is forced to watch as his children are slain, or again the mourning of Heracles when he realizes that he has slain his wife and children in Euripides' *Heracles*. Tragic grief is no respecter of gender (Suter 2008b), and Plato was indignant that audiences, including even the best among them, who hear the tragic poets imitating (as he puts it) heroes grieving openly and beating their breasts, would feel licensed to suffer in the same way themselves. They thereby undermine their commitment to reason's control over the lower passions, even though they pride themselves on their ability to endure adversity calmly, and regard this as proper to men, whereas the complaints we witness and admire in tragedy are rather typical of women (*Republic* 10, 605c–e). Indeed, by Plato's time, Greeks had long since come to frown on histrionic weeping, such as that of Achilles in the *Iliad*, as being unmanly, and perhaps Aristotle, with his mysterious doctrine of catharsis, thought that tragedy could not just elicit but somehow also purge or at least clarify such emotions (see the essays by Jonathan Lear and Richard Janko in Rorty 1992).

OLD COMEDY

Aristotle maintained that the characters in comedy, as opposed to tragedy, are immune to real pain (*Poetics* 1449a34–5; contrast 1452b11–12 of tragedy). He may have been thinking primarily of Old Comedy, but the premise of comedy generally is that the characters do not suffer any real harm—misfortune is transient and conflict is resolved happily in the end; what is more, even the ostensible harm suffered along the way is not taken seriously by the audience, any more than the pratfalls of comedians are today, or the contusions suffered by cartoon characters who plummet off cliffs and leave a hole in the ground below in the shape of their bodies. Even when the bad guys in comedy, the "blocking characters," as Northrop Frye dubbed them, or the humorless "agelasts," in Rabelais' coinage, get their comeuppance, like the pompous general Lamachus in Aristophanes' *Acharnians* or the misanthropic Cnemon in Menander's *Dyskolos*, they are not really hurt and most often are brought back into the social fold at the end.

The second book of the *Poetics*, in which Aristotle discussed comedy, is lost, and it is perhaps idle to speculate what emotions, if any, he would have deemed specific to that genre. One possibility is that they would have been those which, in the *Rhetoric*, he identified as the opposites of pity and fear, namely indignation and confidence. Other emotions have been suggested, for example envy, which was conventionally contrasted with pity as pain at other people's good fortune, without the moral dimension of desert, as Aristotle observes (*Rhetoric* 2.10, 1387b23–5). Ed Sanders (2014: 106) has proposed that Old Comedy appealed to the audience's envy of politically prominent figures. Political envy or antagonism is the theme of Aristophanes' *Knights*, but Aristophanes also staged his own rivalry with other comic poets such as Eupolis and Cratinus, claiming for his own productions a more elevated tone and edifying purpose, in contrast to the way his opponents pandered to the vulgar tastes of the majority. Whether we describe Aristophanes' sentiment as *phthonos* or the more positive notion of *zêlos*, healthy competition, his comedies testify to the agonistic spirit of the theatrical festival, which in the medium of comedy could find expression in direct appeals for the favor of the audience and judges (see Biles 2011; Telò 2016).

Still others have proposed laughter as the response that Aristotle would have deemed proper to comedy. Laughter is not precisely an emotion, any more than tears are, but we need not suppose that Aristotle sought a perfect symmetry with tragedy in this regard. Laughter is a response to the risible or laughable, and we have it on the authority of a curious treatise on comedy, or rather a bare bones epitome of such a treatise, called the *Tractatus Coislianus*, that the laughable is what marks comedy as a genre. What is more, some scholars maintain that the *Tractatus* derives precisely from the second book of Aristotle's *Poetics* (Janko 1984; cf. Watson 2012). It defines comedy as "a representation of an absurd, complete action . . . through pleasure and laughter achieving the purgation of the like emotions" (trans. Janko, 1984: 93). The tractate continues by observing that laughter arises from various devices of speech, such as puns, repetition, or parody, and also from actions involving deception, impossibility or spectacles such as vulgar dancing. These qualities lead to a catharsis of "the human propensity to excessive buffoonery and impropriety" (trans. Janko). There can be no doubt that this sounds like a take, or perhaps a take-off, on Aristotle's definition of tragedy, but even apart from the fact that laughter and pleasure are not strictly emotions, at least as Aristotle seems to treat them in the *Rhetoric* (pain and pleasure are said to be constituents of *pathē*), the tragic emotions of pity and fear arise, according to Aristotle, not from turns of speech or discrete events on stage but from the entire action or plot. Laughter is more punctual, and though it may be elicited by the entire storyline, the tractate treats it as a response to jokes and clowning. This may not be wrong, but it is different from the account of tragic emotion.

There is a sense in which Old Comedy is thin on emotion: it is the more intellectual genre in comparison with tragedy or New Comedy. This may seem paradoxical, given Old Comedy's tendency to slapstick and burlesque, and yet Aristophanic comedy may be said to stand to Menander in much the way Marx Brothers movies do to those of Charlie Chaplin: the humor resides in absurd situations and reactions, and in a good deal of wordplay (just as the *Tractatus Coislinianus* prescribes). Like the Marx Brothers, Aristophanes does not seek to tug at the heartstrings of the audience or to exhibit characters with realistic emotions.[1] The awareness that the characters on stage are fictional, or rather are actors, playing a part, intervenes in the audience's experience of the drama. Richard Green has observed that "Although Sifakis' view [Sifakis 1971: 7–14] that there is no dramatic illusion in Old Comedy has not met with general acceptance, he has a strong point, and there is in any case no doubt that it was part of the convention of Old Comedy that the audience remained aware of the artificiality of what took place ... Old Comedy was always playing a game and the audience saw it for what it was" (Green 1991: 26). Green points out that representations of tragic scenes on vases give no indication that the characters are wearing masks, and might well be taken not as images of a theatrical performance but as illustrations of the myths themselves (save for when a façade in the form of columns and backdrop seems to indicate the theater). When it comes to comedy, and more specifically Old Comedy, however, the characters are shown wearing padded costumes and grotesque masks.[2] Sometimes a comic actor is portrayed as peeping out from behind the mask, further accentuating the distinction between the actor and the character he was impersonating. This is of a piece with the feature in Old Comedy known as the parabasis, in which a character shed his stage identity and spoke directly to the spectators in the voice of the poet himself.

The consequence of this rupture of illusion is that the emotional response of the audience to Old Comedy was mediated through what we might today call an aesthetic distance. Although Aristotle speaks of the pity and fear that tragedy ought to arouse in the audience as genuine emotions (and we have seen that he has good reason to do so), the Stoic philosopher Seneca (first century CE) affirmed that what the audience in a theater, like readers of a book, experience is not emotion at all but, as it calls it, the mere preliminary to emotion, since we know that the action on stage is not real (*On Anger* 2.2). We will return to Seneca's theory of emotion in connection with Senecan tragedy. Here, we may note that the characters themselves in Old Comedy seem to know that they are in a play, and they too feel only a simulation of emotion. We are not alarmed for them and do not pity them not just because there is no threat to ourselves (we know it is a fiction), but also because no one even within the world of the play is really frightened or angry. We know they are acting—and they know it too.

In Aristophanes' *Frogs*, the god Dionysus descends into Hades in order to bring Euripides, his favorite tragedian, back to life (though he decides, after a contest between Euripides and Aeschylus, in fact to rescue the latter). For all his bravado, Dionysus is so terrified by the spookiness of the underworld that he soils himself (308, 479–93). But no one in the audience will have believed that this is authentic fear, any more than that

Dionysus feels more pain than his slave Xanthus, when the two are beaten precisely in order to reveal which is the god and which the mortal (they have been exchanging identities at this point): Dionysus is the god, and though he was traditionally represented as cowardly in comedy, this is caricature, not portraiture. In the *Acharnians*, the protagonist, Dicaeopolis, voluntarily places his head on a chopping block as a sign of his integrity while he instructs the chorus on reasons for ending the war with Sparta. The chorus members are an irascible lot—they make a living as charcoal burners and are among the poorest of the citizen class—and patriotic as well, and are likely to take umbrage at Dicaeopolis' proposal (compare the chorus of wasps in Aristophanes' play of that name, who pride themselves on their quick temper). But their anger is no more serious than Dicaeopolis' ostensible fear, which is like that of Euripides' kinsman when he is threatened by a gang of women in Aristophanes' *Thesmophoriazusae*, and whose self-defense takes the form of lines and actions cribbed from Euripides' own tragedies. He knows as well as we do that he is in a play.

If there is one emotion that Aristophanes seeks to display as authentic, it is anger, in the sense not so much of irritation as a hot-tempered indignation triggered by injustice and exploitation. It is the driving emotion of most of his protagonists, whether they seek to end war (*Acharnians*, *Peace*, *Lysistrata*), expose demagogy and sophistical hanky-panky (*Knights*, *Wasps*, *Clouds*), establish a pie-in-the-sky utopia (*Birds*), or achieve a fair distribution of resources (*Assemblywomen*, *Wealth*). The chorus of poor farmers who depend on jury duty to supplement their livelihood and for their sense of dignity proudly assert their sharp temper or *orgê* (like the English "temper," *orgê* signified temperament as well as "anger"). An irascible disposition was regarded as a moral flaw, and the old men do seem excessively harsh as jurors. But a capacity for anger was also the mark of a free citizen—Aristotle characterizes a total lack of anger as servile (*Nicomachean Ethics* 4.5, 1126a4–8)—and Aristophanes himself boasts (1030) that his anger is like Heracles', thanks to which he has been able to stand up to populist bullies like Cleon (with whom he may have tussled in real life), a claim that he repeated a year later in the *parabasis* (that is, the poet's direct address to the audience) of the *Peace* (752) and again, in different words, in *Lysistrata* (550 and 1113). It is this spirited temper that inspired the chorus in *Wasps* to drive the Persians out of Attica (1082–90), and it is the basis of their fearlessness (1091). Slaves and demagogues are fearful (*Wasps* 427, 715), and the best thing about being a juror is that everyone is afraid of you. Aristophanes would give us to understand that he is just like the heroes of his plays.[3]

Old Comedy is relatively short on emotions such as pity and shame—its villains are mocked as shameless, although this in itself can be seen as a strategy for shaming them. The very frankness or free speech (*parrhêsia* in Greek) of the comic protagonists might also be regarded as a kind of shamelessness, since they were outspoken about matters that were socially taboo and called a spade a spade (so too Socrates appeared shameless when he probed his interlocutors on indelicate topics; see Tarnopolsky 2010). Friendship plays a small role as well: Aristophanic heroes are basically loners, like Odysseus in the *Odyssey* (in the *Birds*, Peisetaerus has a sidekick named Euelpis, but he drops out of sight at the end). The festive joy with which the comedies often conclude is fundamentally collective and expresses a communal bond. This kind of triumphal finale is especially characteristic of the utopian comedies such as *Acharnians*, *Peace*, *Birds*, *Lysistrata*, *Assemblywomen*, and *Wealth*, which culminate in a procession, dance or other celebratory frolic, but there are hints of it even in the more satirical plays like *Knights*, *Wasps*, and *Clouds*. We might label the emotion *khara* or delight, but it is perhaps something more like elation or euphoria, a carnivalesque jubilation associated with the satisfaction of bodily desires, whether for food or sex, and a prosperity in which all citizens, rich and poor alike, can share.[4]

NEW COMEDY

Although we typically associate tragedy with gloom and doom, many Greek tragedies had something of a romantic or melodramatic quality and ended on an upbeat tone (e.g. Euripides' *Alcestis*, *Iphigenia among the Taurians*, and *Helen*), and scholars have argued that these plays were the inspiration for the new style of comedy that would become popular in the fourth century BCE. The plots of New Comedy revolved almost exclusively around love, commonly the erotic passion or *erôs* of a young man for a woman, either a citizen girl or an expensive courtesan (homoerotic desire was almost entirely absent from all theatrical genres). The enamored youth, callow and in need of advice and support from friends or loyal slaves, has to overcome various obstacles, such as stingy misanthropes who refuse to grant their daughter to anyone, brothel keepers whose fees are beyond the means of a young man still dependent on his father, or wealthy rivals such as captains of mercenary troops and even the boy's own father, who, if not actively competing with the lad (three such plays survive from the pen of Plautus), might nevertheless object to a union with a poor girl or to the expenditure involved in purchasing the services of a high-class *hetaera* (this theme seems to have attracted Roman playwrights, perhaps because of the rule of *patria potestas*, whereby a son was legally under the authority of his father until he was formally manumitted or the father died). The principal emotions of the young protagonists in New Comedy are erotic love (to the extent that this is properly conceived of as an emotion) and friendship, along with anxiety and frustration, and sometimes shame at their behavior or jealousy of their rivals. Fathers, on the other hand, are more prone to anger, which was characteristic of them to such an extent that, according to Quintilian, a father who played the major role wore a special mask which "has one eyebrow raised and the other calm, since he is sometimes incensed and sometimes gentle" (*Institutes of Oratory* 11.3.74).

It is thus of particular interest when a young man expresses anger. In the *Samia*, while the neighbors, Demeas and Niceratus, were abroad, Demeas' adopted son, Moschio, raped Niceratus' daughter, as a result of which she gave birth to a child. Fearing their parents' reaction, Demeas' concubine, Chrysis, comes to the rescue and pretends that the baby is hers and Demeas is its father. Moschio is ashamed of what he has done and afraid to face his father when he returns to Athens. Demeas is furious with Chrysis for keeping the child (as a foreigner—she is the Samian woman who gives the play its title—any child of hers will be illegitimate), but truly flies off the handle when he begins to suspect that Moschio is the father and has had an affair with Chrysis during his absence. At first, he directs his anger at Chrysis alone, but when Moschio tries to defend her Demeas no longer seeks to excuse him. When the truth finally emerges, it is Niceratus' turn to be incensed at the rape of his daughter, but in the end, he too is pacified and agrees to the marriage. Then suddenly, in the fifth act, Moschio enters, furious that his father should have suspected him of an affair with Chrysis, and to avenge the insult he pretends that he is planning to enlist in a foreign campaign. Demeas humbly apologizes, reminding Moschio of how well he has always treated him, Moschio relents, the wedding resumes, and the play ends happily. Moschio's anger comes as something of a surprise, since the major complication of the plot has by now been resolved. But if anger at a slight is the hallmark of a citizen, then it may be that Moschio's sense of offended dignity, even if it involves a bit of adolescent posturing, is a sign that he is now indeed prepared to wed and assume the responsibilities of an adult head of a household.

By contrast, the slave Parmeno is never permitted to express anger. At first, he tries to encourage Moschio to come clean with his father, adopting the part of the mature counselor. Then Demeas berates him for failing to inform him about Moschio's doings, which sends Parmeno scurrying off in terror. When Parmeno enters again, in the final act, Moschio demands that he fetch his cloak and sword (he is pretending to become a mercenary soldier), and when Parmeno wonders why, Moschio erupts: "If I get my hands on a whip . . ." (662–3), just as Demeas had threatened earlier (321). When Parmeno learns that the wedding preparations are in full swing and tries to reason with Moschio, the boy punches the poor slave in the mouth (679). We might be tempted to pity Parmeno, but it is well to remember Aristotle's observation that slaves "who contradict us and deny their offence we punish all the more, but we cease to be incensed against those who agree that they deserved their punishment. The reason is that it is shameless to deny what is obvious, and those who are shameless towards us slight us and show contempt for us" (*Rhetoric* 2.3, 1380a16–21). A slave is expected to be abject, and any back-talk, even an attempt to explain, only provokes the master further. As Aristotle goes on to say, we give over our anger at those who "humble themselves before us and do not gainsay us; we feel that they thus admit themselves our inferiors, and inferiors feel fear, and nobody can slight any one so long as he feels afraid of him" (2.3, 1380a22–4). The image of the uppity slave who is unafraid of punishment, favored especially by Plautus (cf. the conclusion to his *Trinummus*), lies in the province of burlesque and may have its roots not so much in Greek New Comedy as in the so-called Atellan farces, a native Italian genre which was something like the Punch and Judy skits. Such behavior is of a piece with the representation of slaves as shameless. In Plautus' *Casina*, a slave has been pretending to marry a girl so that his master may possess her in spite of his wife's interference; when the ruse is exposed and he is given his comeuppance, the slave exclaims, "Like a fool, I'm now doing something new—I am ashamed, I who have never been till now" (858).[5] Shame, like anger, is a free citizen's sentiment.

We may note that, in spite of his anger, Demeas harbors tender and loving feelings toward Moschio, and this is broadly true of parents in New Comedy. In Terence's *Self-Tormentor*, for example, a father who has been excessively stern towards his son on account of the boy's infatuation with a poor girl castigates himself severely after the boy joins the military, and Terence's *Brothers* illustrates the fine line between the need for paternal discipline and a kindly indulgence toward a young man's love affairs (both of these are based on Menandrean originals). Some parental attitudes may shock us, however. A neighbor of the "self-tormentor" berates his wife for not having made sure that their new-born daughter was dead, after he'd ordered her to expose the infant, and he chalks her behavior up to female sentimentality (the child survives to wed the self-tormentor's son—a common comic motif, as in Menander's *Shorn Girl*). We may be less likely to condemn the ancients for want of feeling if we reflect that women today have sometimes insisted on their right to abort a fetus, even without the consent of the potential father.

Where there is love, there is the potential for jealousy, or so we suppose today. In fact, jealousy is sometimes difficult to distinguish from anger, envy, and sadness, of which it is sometimes regarded as a compound. A case in point is the behavior of the mercenary soldier Polemo in Menander's *Shorn Girl*. Upon seeing Glycera, his live-in girlfriend, kiss a young neighbor, he cuts her hair off in a fit of pique, unaware that the boy is in fact the girl's brother (the brother too is ignorant of the fact). As an independent woman (she was raised by a foster-mother after her father exposed his two children), she ups and leaves the soldier and takes up residence next door. The soldier is racked with sorrow, and exclaims, "I don't know what to say, by Demeter, except that I'll hang myself. Glycera has left me, Glycera, she's left me!" (504–7). When he finally learns the truth, the soldier berates himself: "Fiend that I am and jealous [*zêlotupos*] creature . . . I immediately went crazy" (986–8). The Greek term, which includes the root *zêlos*, may mean something like "possessive" here. In the opening scene of Terence's *Eunuch*, again based on a Menandrean original, the young Phaedria is furious that the courtesan Thais has rejected him in favor of a rich soldier (her motive is to liberate a girl in the soldier's possession). When Phaedria protests that Thais is in fact in love with the soldier, she agrees to yield to his wishes (the young man may appear jealous, but we do well to bear in mind that in the finale he will consent to sharing Thais with his rival, precisely on the grounds that he is something of a buffoon, and so hardly a threat to Phaedria; besides, he will pay the bills). Phaedria is finally persuaded to grant Thais three days with the soldier, but he begs "that when you are with that soldier of yours, you not be with him; that day and night you love me, miss me, dream of me, wait for me, think of me, hope for me, rejoice in me, be totally with me—to sum it up, become my soul, since I am yours" (191–6). This is among the most intense expressions of romantic passion in New Comedy (compare the touching affection between a young courtesan and her lover in Plautus' *Cistellaria*, based on Menander), and it offers an insight into the nature of *erôs* or *amor*, as is figured in New Comedy.

The Latin word *amor* covered the range of sentiments expressed in Greek by *erôs*, or "passionate love," and *philia* in the sense of affection generally, although the Romans distinguished between *amor*, "love," and *amicitia*, "friendship." New Comedy, as we have seen, centered on romantic passion, which was represented as indifferent to barriers of class or status, for example the difference between free and slave, or Greek and foreigner. The complex turns of the plot, often involving a recognition scene, served to domesticate

FIGURE 4.2: Glykera (left) after her hair has been short in Act 1 of Menander's *Perikeiromene*, with Polemon (seated) and the slave Sosias; from the Antioch mosaics (*c*. third century CE).

FIGURE 4.3: Comic masks; from the preface to the *Andria* in a manuscript of Terence's comedies.

the outsider, as it were, revealing her (sometimes him) to be a native-born citizen after all. But the passion retained a subversive potential, allowing the audience to identify with the young lover's rebellion against the constraints of traditional mores and parental authority, which might also stand in, in the spectators' imagination, for the power of the aristocracy, which had increased significantly in the period between Aristophanes' comedies and those of Menander, and was especially dominant in Rome (cf. McCarthy 2000). Given the disagreement among scholars over Menander's political allegiances, no less than those of Aristophanes (some render them sympathizers of the democracy, others of the aristocracy), it is unwise to infer the intended, never mind actual, emotional response of the audience, and the passage of the genre to Rome adds further uncertainties. But given the relative naturalism of New Comedy, at least as compared with Old, we might expect a greater degree of emotional identification, whether with the fathers or the sons, or perhaps with both: poets could elicit conflicting sympathies in the public, and even go so far as to affirm, as Terence does at the end of the *Mother-in-Law*, that what has transpired on the stage does not turn out "the way things happen in comedies."

ROMAN TRAGEDY

As mentioned above, the Stoic philosopher Seneca had a two-tiered conception of the emotions. Emotions in the strict sense involve assent: wincing when something flashes before your eyes is not fear; for there to be genuine fear, you must assent to the idea that whatever it was represents a danger. Such a judgment requires reason, and since non-human animals, according to the Stoics, do not possess reason (nor do human infants, for that matter), they do not have emotions, strictly speaking, but only something resembling emotions. In his treatise *On Anger*, Seneca mentions various such instinctive or involuntary responses, such as shivering when sprinkled with cold water, drawing back from things revolting to the touch, hair rising upon hearing bad news, blushing, and dizziness when looking down from heights—none of these requiring a judgment, and so none of them emotions. Seneca also mentions in this context comic stage shows, histories of terrible events, horrible paintings, and the sight of punishments, even when deserved (this latter clause differentiates the feeling from Aristotle's idea of pity), as well as contagious laughter and sadness, which, Seneca says, is not real grief any more than our response to seeing a shipwreck in a mime or reading about a famous military defeat causes genuine fear. Since we know that the events portrayed in mimes and comedies are mere play-acting, we do not run away in terror or try to help the victims on stage. Our involuntary reflexes are rather what Seneca calls "the initial preliminaries to emotions" (*On Anger* 2.2.6), for which the Greek term was *propatheiai* or "pre-emotions" (see Graver 2007: 91–9).

The ten tragedies attributed to Seneca (of which one is certainly by an imitator, and questions have been raised about another) differ markedly from their classical Greek prototypes, to the extent that some critics have doubted that they were ever intended for the stage (they might simply have been declaimed or read aloud). They have also come under suspicion for their vivid depictions of horrors and outsized passions, given that the Stoics sought to eradicate the passions, which they understood as produced by false judgments—that, for example, a threat to life is an evil, and hence something to be feared, whereas the only evil they recognized was the absence of virtue. But what if Seneca conceived of his tragedies as designed to produce, not emotions in the full sense of the term, but rather those involuntary reflexes or pre-emotions to which everyone, even the sage, is subject? This might explain why he exploited the kind of shocking effects that Aristotle had condemned as inappropriate to tragedy: his goal was not to elicit pity and fear, of which the Stoics would have disapproved, but rather to trigger instinctive sympathy or revulsion. Drama as such, Seneca seems to have argued, can only produce such pseudo-emotions, since we know that whatever we see on stage (or read in books) is unreal: aesthetic distance is built into our experience of a work as art (or imitation, to use the classical term).[6] What is more, the effect of the plays evidently resides in the over-the-top rhetorical intensity of individual scenes and speeches, rather than in the narrative trajectory of the plot as a whole, in accord with Aristotle's conception of the source of tragic emotion. It is as though Seneca were deliberately constructing, whether out of Stoic conviction or simply the taste of his times, the literary equivalent of an action film, which is all shock and shudders, with no genuine emotion at all.[7]

Within Seneca's tragedies, characters experience a variety of emotions, for the most part violently. These emotions have intelligible causes: like Aristotle and ancient writers generally, the Stoics understood emotions as cognitive events rather than as mere feelings.

Anger, as we have seen, is a response to an insult; if animals do not experience anger in the true sense, but only something like aggressivity, as Seneca asserts, it is because they do not give their assent to the judgments that they have been belittled and that it is right to take revenge. Like Euripides' Medea, Seneca's heroine too deems that she has been unjustly abandoned, and this is the motive for her wrath.

But Seneca offers a further reason for the extreme reactions of his characters. In his play *Hercules Mad*, which draws in part on Euripides' *Heracles*, Juno launches the action in the prologue by apostrophizing the Furies: "so that Hercules may be driven, his mind controlled, stricken by vast madness, you [i.e., the Furies] must first become insane," and addressing herself in turn she asks, "Juno, why are you not yet raging?" She begs the Furies to drive her out of her own mind, precisely so that she may avenge herself on Hercules, for the hatred she bears toward him as son of Jupiter by Alcmena (107–11). The action of the play is thus motivated by sheer insanity. The *Thyestes* begins with a dialog between a Fury and the ghost of Tantalus, who has been granted a momentary remission from his punishment in Hades, whereby he is driven by hunger and thirst to reach out for the fruit and water that lie before him, only to find each time that they retreat from his grasp. The Fury intends to use Tantalus to bring about the abominable feast that Atreus will serve to his brother Thyestes—namely, Thyestes' own children. Tantalus is unwilling to carry out such a dreadful assignment, but the Fury assails him. "Why," Tantalus exclaims, "do you terrify my eyes with whips and threaten writhing snakes in your savagery? Why do you rouse the hunger fixed in my deepest marrow? A fire burns my heart, seared with thirst, and flares in my scorched entrails. I follow" (96–100); to which the Fury replies: "Spread this, this rage throughout the house." It is Thyestes' own ghost that returns from Hades in the *Agamemnon*, and inspires his surviving son Aegisthus to slay Agamemnon, Atreus' son (48–52). In Seneca's *Oedipus*, Creon reports a hellish rite by which the ghost of Laius, Oedipus' father, is summoned from the underworld. Laius intones, "You, you, who hold the scepter in your bloody hand, I, your unavenged father, will pursue you and your whole city, and I will bring with me a Fury as attendant of your marriage, I'll bring her resounding with lashes, I'll overturn your incestuous house and wipe out your household gods with an impious warfare" (642–6). In the *Phoenician Women*, based on Euripides' play of that name, Oedipus himself, accursed as he is, urges that his sons do something worthy of their father (333). Great passions lead to great crimes, but they are stirred and overdetermined by supernatural interventions.

The effect of these impulses from without is to render the agents insensitive to reason. A wise attendant attempts to dissuade Atreus, in the *Thyestes*, from exacting so horrible a revenge, but Atreus is unmoved. Later, Thyestes argues with his own son, also called Tantalus, against the lure of power, yet as he approaches Atreus' palace, where the trap is laid, he yields to the boy, with the excuse "I follow you, I do not lead" (489); he is following as well his instinctive impulse, his better judgment overwhelmed, like that of the elder Tantalus, by the hunger for comfort and power. Similarly, Medea's nurse is helpless to calm her mistress's passion, as Medea proclaims that she will only be soothed when she sees everything collapse in ruin around her (426–8; cf. the role of the nurse in Seneca's *Phaedra* and *Hercules on Mount Oeta*). In the *Phoenician Women*, Jocasta tries, and fails, to persuade her son Polynices not to attack Thebes (as she does also in Euripides' version). Seneca repeatedly stages the conflict between impulse or *impetus*, which results directly from perception and so gives rise to a pre-emotion, and reason, which argues and resists but is finally forced to yield. The drama in Senecan theater resides not so much in

FIGURE 4.4: Comedy scene depicted in the Roman mosaic from Villa de Cicero (Villa of Cicero) in Pompeii, now on display in the National Archaeological Museum (Museo Archeologico Nazionale di Napoli) in Naples, Campania, Italy. Two women consulting with a witch are depicted in the mosaic. Signature on the top: signed by Dioskourides of Samos.

FIGURE 4.5: A moment in Act 2 of Menander's *Phasma* or "The Ghost" when the "ghost" makes its appearance; from the Mytilene mosaics.

the trajectory of the plot or action as in the workings of emotion itself, and how it is that pre-emotions can cozen our assent despite our best efforts to behave rationally. If the audience is left feeling fear at the end of such tragedies, it is not for the dangers that may beset the life of even an innocent human being, such as Oedipus, but for forces in the self that overwhelm our better judgment.

CHAPTER FIVE

The Visual Arts

VIKTORIA RÄUCHLE

Ancient emotions are *en vogue*: within the last decade, classical studies have brought forth a large corpus of research on the representation and elicitation of emotions in ancient literature, philosophy and politics. In classical archaeology and the history of ancient art, however, the subject is still underrepresented: most studies concentrate on single emotions (especially grief and mourning), or treat them within the wider field of body language and gestural communication.[1] Another field concerns the representation of violence and its (emotional) effect on the recipient.[2] But a comprehensive survey on the manifold "languages of emotion" in ancient art remains a desideratum. Also, while classicists have eagerly applied theoretical and methodological approaches developed in other disciplines and contributed substantially to the science of emotions, most studies on emotions in ancient imagery have not yet drawn upon the full potential of interdisciplinary research.[3]

This is all the more surprising in that, in modern Western culture, visual media are commonly regarded as particularly suited to convey emotional content and, more importantly, to enable an emotional reaction in the beholder (cf. Frevert and Schmidt 2011). Visual language is always highly suggestive; it creates the illusion that it is intuitively comprehensible and does not require any previous knowledge to be read and understood. This is especially the case for ancient Greek and Roman art whose naturalistic style "encouraged (and still does encourage) the imagination to believe that the visual world of a painting or a sculpture is just like our world" (Elsner 2007: 1). This twofold susceptibility to subjectivity might be precisely the reason why classical archaeologists did not jump on the bandwagon but remained skeptical towards the study of emotions (cf. Mylonopoulos 2017: 73).

Naturally, the present chapter can tackle only a small selection of the manifold aspects of the representation and elicitation of emotions in visual media. The first section opens the debate and presents the dominant strategies for conveying emotions in ancient Greek and Roman art: besides gestures and facial expressions, we shall look at personifications of emotional states and the role of context in representing and eliciting emotions. The second section deals with gender- and status-typical emotion expressions, based on a close reading of the iconography of grief and mourning. Thirdly, I elaborate on the differentiation between acute emotional episodes and long-lasting emotional dispositions, taking lust and love as a starting point. In the final section, we turn towards the emotive power of visual media concentrating on the visual representation of violence as a means of eliciting emotions in the recipient.

EMBODIED EMOTIONS: MAKING INNER STATES VISIBLE

In interpersonal communication, we rely on verbal and non-verbal expressions (i.e. words, tone of voice, gestures, postures, facial features) to convey and read internal emotional states. These "emotion codes" are not universal but shaped by display rules, that is, culture-specific prescriptions about who can show which emotions to whom, when, and, most importantly, how. In the representation of emotions in the arts, these "emotion codes" are again modified in accordance with the possibilities and limits of the respective artistic genre and its iconographic or literary conventions. Thus, when we deal with the representation of emotions in literature and art, we deal with a "double coding of emotions."[4]

Maria Luisa Catoni has systematically developed the ancient term *schêma* (lit. "form," "shape," but also "appearance," "fashion," "manner," etc.) as a tool for the analysis of images. Starting from the Platonic dialog *Cratylus*, she describes how all mimetic techniques—terms, images, music, dance, and so forth—use *schêmata* to represent the nature of things in the most exact way. Since every technique has its specific representational limits, it is always a selective imitation (Catoni 2008: 73). In the case of visual media, *schêmata* operate as external properties that transmit information about inner states and characteristics. They imitate not only a figure's outer appearance but also their *êthos* ("character") and *pathos* ("emotion").

Ancient Greek art, especially of the Archaic and Classical era, relies primarily on gestures and postures to display feelings and other inner states, while the faces are quite often relatively calm. Outright manifestations of emotions through features, such as broad smiles, open mouths, angry scowls, disgusted grimaces, or sad frowns, are extremely rare and tend to be restricted to non-Greek figures or members of the lower classes. The western pediment of the Zeus temple in Olympia, which shows the battle between the centaurs and the Lapiths, a legendary people from Thessaly, is an (often-cited) prime example for this phenomenon (see Fig. 5.1).[5] While the coarse, distorted features of the rampant centaurs reflect rage, strain, and agony, their human opponents maintain a relatively calm appearance: although the Lapith is being bitten by his beastly enemy, he is only slightly frowning his forehead instead of displaying his physical pain outwardly.

Starting in the fourth century and catching on in the Hellenistic era, a new style in the visual arts seeks to exploit the full potential of emotional expression. Animated facial features and agitated gestures enter the realm of large-scale sculpture that was hitherto dominated by the vocabulary of idealism and restraint. Even heroes can now be characterized in their physical and psychological struggles as the famous Farnese Herakles impressively shows: "Gone are the days in which Herakles fought monsters, wild animals, and antiheroes with an emotionless face revealing no effort . . . Lysippos' Herakles is a tired hero who challenges and questions his quest" (Mylonopoulos 2017: 82). The "Pasquino Group" aptly portrays Menelaus frowning in agony and pathetically gazing into the distance as he retrieves the lifeless body of Patroclus, draped over his arms in a mannered, hyperextended pose (see Fig. 5.2).[6] Nevertheless, the most excessive forms of affect continue to characterize figures who fall outside the "good order" of Greek culture (Maderna 2009: esp. 31–2). In the Roman imperial period, artists are in the comfortable position of being able to cherry-pick from the century-old pool of different styles and strategies: they prefer to depict their gods and heroes in the sublime style of the fifth century but rely on the effervescent corporality and *pathos* of the Hellenistic era to represent giants, satyrs, and centaurs (cf. Prioux 2011: 136–7).

THE VISUAL ARTS 85

FIGURE 5.1: Centaur biting Lapith, western pediment of the temple of Zeus at Olympia, *c.* 460 BCE.

FIGURE 5.2: "Pasquino Group," Roman copy from Hellenistic original, *c.* 150–120 BCE.

The general reluctance towards the depiction of facial expressions can be explained in terms of the ideal of *sôphrosunê* (lit. "soundness of mind," but also "self-control," "moderation," etc.) that from the fifth century onwards forms an essential element in the conception of good character.[7] Throughout antiquity, the ability of (emotional) self-control is a key concern in the upbringing and education of both male and female children and therefore also constitutes a decisive means of status distinction. The calm features in the visual arts hence have to be understood as idealized manifestations of actual behavioral norms and display rules—a textbook example of the "double coding of emotion."

So, except in the Hellenistic period, which tests the boundaries of artistic expression in all directions, distorted features are, if at all, applied primarily to denote the "other." Instead of manifesting affect through the face, as emphasized in Darwin's *Expression of the Emotions in Man and Animals*, ancient images operate mainly with gestures and postures to convey a figure's internal characteristics. In his extensive study on body language in ancient Greek art, Gerhard Neumann differentiates between two types of gestures and postures: sudden and extensive movements are subsumed under the term "Momentangebärden" and associated with affective reactions to concrete situations. "Zustandsgebärden" are characterized by quiet, contemplative movements and, in his reading, illustrate a figure's mental state, a permanent internal condition.[8] With regard to their different functions and meanings, he also refers to them as "pathetic" versus "noetic" gestures (Neumann 1965: 107–8). Claudio Franzoni offers a slightly different model: starting from Aby Warburg's famous classification of certain "emotionally charged visual tropes" as "*pathos* formulas," he proposes a second category called "*êthos* formulas" that translate a figure's character and attitude into bodily *schêmata* (Franzoni 2006: 245).

While it seems justified to interpret sudden gestures and agitated postures as visual codes for acute emotions, it is in most cases impossible to discern the exact emotion without taking into account the context. The notorious ambiguity of bodily *schêmata* can be demonstrated by the gesture of raised arms. A famous, albeit only fragmentary, dinos by Sophilos features the funerary games for Patroclus, identified as such by an inscription, with spectators sitting on pyramidal terraces and watching a chariot race (see Fig. 8.1). Two of them are stretching their arms out forwards as if they were commenting on the events taking place before them (modern football fans may come to mind). In *prothesis* scenes and other images of the funerary context, however, the raised arms can be interpreted as part of the traditional mourning ritual that also included tearing one's hair and beating one's chest (see Figs 3.1, 5.4–5). And finally, on a wall painting in Pompeii portraying the sacrifice of Iphigenia, the protagonist raises her arms to the sky in fear and supplication (see Fig. 5.6).

There is no clear-cut formula to link a certain way of raising the arms with a certain emotion. If it were not for composition and context, it would be difficult to differentiate between the excitement of the chariot race enthusiasts, the ritualized grief of the mourners, or the desperate plea of Iphigenia. As Évelyne Prioux notes, one and the same *schêma* "can be used to render different emotions and its interpretation will depend on the context in which it appears" (Prioux 2011: 142). Most of the "loud gestures," then, do not necessarily denote a distinct emotion but rather a very basic and in itself neutral bodily reaction, a purely physiological "arousal"—be it negative or positive (see Scherer 2005: e.g. 718). They denote a vague state of commotion, an undefined affect that needs further information to be fully understood.

Another problem concerns the distinction between pathetic and noetic gestures or, respectively, between *pathos* formulas and *êthos* formulas. A red-figure lekythos in New York shows Poseidon pursuing the heroine Amymone with his trident at the spring of Lerna (see Fig. 5.3).⁹ The subject of "erotic pursuit" was very popular in early fifth-century Athenian vase painting and usually shows a male figure (divine or mortal) running after a young woman or boy. In most instances, the "sexual prey" raises both arms in fear and alarm (another meaning of this gesture). But instead of expressing panic, Poseidon's love interest elegantly raises her veil or mantle—a gesture you wouldn't expect in this moment of threat. In archaeological scholarship, this gesture is traditionally associated with the unveiling of the bride during a stage of the Greek wedding ceremony called *anakaluptêria* and interpreted as an iconographic marker to denote brides in particular and married women in general (see Llewellyn-Jones 2003: 85–120, esp. 99–104). In this reading, Amymone would hence be characterized as the, albeit only short-term, "bride" of the sea god. In our case, as in most other "erotic pursuits," however, the woman's hand position suggests that she is rather covering than uncovering herself, which points to another interpretation.

In ancient Greece and Rome, women were generally expected to cover themselves in the presence of men other than their kin in order to demonstrate their modesty: *aidôs* in Greek, *pudicitia/pudor* in Latin (cf. Cairns 2002: 75–6). Written sources even suggest a connection between *aidôs* and the veil that goes far beyond mere behavioral norms: "The veil . . . is a typical symbol of *aidôs*, used both as a concrete physical expression of the emotion and as a metonymy for the emotion itself" (Cairns 2016a: 36). Transferred to ancient iconography, the gesture of pulling one's veil must be understood primarily as a sign of modesty; only in certain contexts may it also refer to the bridal or married status of the figure. But there is more to it: the Greek term *aidôs* oscillates between *pathos* and

FIGURE 5.3: Poseidon chasing Amymone. Athenian lekythos, *c.* 420 BCE.

êthos, as it can refer to both the acute emotion of shame and the character trait of modesty—and so does the act of veiling (cf. Cairns 2002: 75). This ambiguity is also inherent in the visual accounts. Amymone might be pulling her veil in this exact moment because she feels ashamed as a result of a man (or god) appearing on the stage and advancing upon her in a most compromising way. Nevertheless, she is not succumbing to the acute affect of panic but maintains her general disposition of modesty. We shall return to the differentiation between emotional and dispositional phenomena later in this chapter, when dealing with visual representations of desire and love; at this point, it is sufficient to say that most gestures are (deliberately) ambiguous and can have various levels of meaning.

In addition to the translation of *pathê* into bodily *schêmata*, emotional states can be rendered by means of personifications. In a first concrete sense, personifications of emotions have to be taken seriously as real agents that may be invoked, channeled, or controlled by worship (cf. Naiden, Chapter 2 in this volume). In a more abstract sense, however, they also represent the idea of *pathos* as an external force or, as Franzoni puts it (2006: 59), "la provenienza 'da fuori' del *pathos*," a concept already inherent to the ancient emotion terms *pathos* ("suffering" or "experience") and *affectus* ("being affected"), but also formulated in various philosophical treatises and literary accounts (cf. Cairns 2016b). So, without denying the real existence of personifications for (at least some) ancient minds, they can also be understood (and studied) as a "metaphor of emotion as an antagonist or external force—as an entity that 'seizes' or 'holds' a person, or as something that 'comes over' or 'comes upon' us from outside."[10]

Visual representations of personified emotions are sometimes quite unspecific in their iconography and can only be identified by context and/or inscriptions. In many cases, however, there is a visible effort to translate the pivotal aspects of their mode of action into bodily *schêmata* and attributes (cf. Korte 1874). Nemesis, the goddess of indignation and retribution, for example, is often depicted as a winged figure with a wheel that will punish the arrogant and "roll out" wickedness (see Fig. 2.1; cf. Faraone 1999: 64, n. 105). The wings are a common feature of personifications and hint at their status as *daimones* "mid-way between god and men" (Seltman 1923–5: 90). Eros/Amor too appears as a young boy or youth with wings, which in his case may also refer to the fleeting character of erotic desire. When Eros enters Greek art in the late sixth century BCE, he is represented in the iconography of the ideal *erômenos*, the younger party in pederastic relationships, and thus as the object of his own power (see Stafford 2013: 179–90). In a number of vase paintings of this early period, he is chasing a young boy and a woman and thus paradoxically assumes the active role usually ascribed to adult men—in these images, Eros manifests "a pure form of embodied desire" (Lewis 2002: 143). In the course of the fifth century, the adolescent *erômenos* type is by and large replaced by a childlike figure that often serves "as a caption for the desire of others" (Lewis 2002: 144; cf. Figs 5.8–9). This iconography of Eros as a young boy with wings will persist in the centuries to come (cf. Figs 5.10a–b). Childhood and adolescence are traditionally associated with playfulness, foolishness, and self-indulgence—characteristics that one would easily ascribe to passionate love as well. A poem by Alcman articulates this notion in a parable of *êros* as a negligent child:

> Aphrodite it is not, but wild Eros playing like the boy he is,
> coming down over the flower-tips—do not touch them, I beg
> you!—of the galingale.[11]

As we shall see, the image of the "wild boy" (*margos*) bringing ruin to his victims (i.e. lovers) is a persistent *topos* in Greek and Roman art and literature that can be enriched *ad libitum* with various additional elements and anecdotes. At this point, it is important to note that the personification of emotions conveys a core aspect of emotional perception. While the ancient concept of *pathê* as external powers differs from certain modern scientific definitions of emotions as internal processes, we can trace striking similarities from a phenomenological perspective: then and now, the image of romantic love as an autonomous entity (apparent in English expressions such as "hit by love" or "love-struck") emulates its affective, ambush-like character. Then and now, the externalization of emotions in language and art has a metaphorical meaning that reflects the subjective experience of being at the mercy of one's own feelings.

With facial features, body language, and personifications we have discussed the most important strategies of making emotions visible within an image. As emerges from the previous considerations, however, the context of a visual code also plays a decisive role in deciphering its emotional content. On an initial level, the image itself provides a good deal of information by means of composition, figure types, and further pictorial elements. Beyond this, the function of the medium, the context of reception, and the general cultural background can also be crucial indicators in the assessment of the emotional content of an image.

These broader contexts are particularly important when it comes to the elicitation of emotions through visual media: the emotive quality of an image is not necessarily dependent upon the representation of emotions (and vice versa), but can also be generated through the context of use and reception. A funerary monument within its original setting, for instance, can trigger a feeling of sorrow or melancholy in the viewer without making use of an overtly emotional iconography. In the famous fourth-century BCE Attic grave relief of Ampharete, the deceased woman elegantly reclines on a chair and gazes at a small infant on her lap, who is reaching for the little bird she is holding in her raised hand (see Fig. 7.4). The scene is not characterized by vigorous *pathos* but portrays a rather restrained form of mother–child interaction. At first sight, Ampharete's moderate composure is in line with the ideal of emotional self-control that was so crucial in classical society. Yet the emotions are there, subtly conveyed by the dyadic composition of the figures, the longing gesture of the child, and the maternal gaze, filtered through the "double coding of emotion," that is, the display rules and artistic conventions of the time.

The ancient viewer must have perceived this image as the epitome of ideal motherhood— and must have been surprised by the epigram that identifies Ampharete as the grandmother of the infant: "It is my daughter's child that I hold here with love, the one whom I held on my lap while in life we looked on the light of the sun and now (still) hold, dead, like me."[12] Far from mitigating the affective power of the relief, the epigram serves as an emotion catalyst: not only does the text explicitly refer to the affection of Ampharete towards her grandchild (τέκνον φίλον); it also characterizes her as an attentive mother supporting her daughter in early childcare. And thirdly, by deliberately disappointing the viewers' expectations, the epigram commands their attention and consequently heightens the emotive effect of the monument. Within the framework of classical Athens, the calm and restrained habitus of Ampharete is more than enough to elicit an emotional reaction in the beholder. Of course, the desired emotive effect follows the same feeling-rules we see in the image itself: the beholder is expected to develop a feeling of melancholic sympathy rather than excessive grief.

GENDER AND STATUS: THE CASE OF GRIEF AND MOURNING

As pointed out above, both the expression of emotion in interpersonal communication and the artistic representation thereof are culture specific. Some emotion codes apply to all members of a given culture while others pertain only to subgroups or social communities and thus help to identify someone as belonging to a certain age group, gender, or status. In the visual arts, too, the particular modes of depicting emotions are a crucial means of differentiating between members of different social groups. Images not only reflect the various "emotional communities" of their time but also contribute to their formation and consolidation (on the concept of "emotional communities," see Rosenwein 2006).

The function of emotion codes as an element of social distinction can be well demonstrated with the "emotion family" of sorrow, grief, and mourning. Both in Greek and in Roman culture, grief and mourning were governed by numerous restrictions and regulations and thus had a strong ritualized aspect that not only affected the display of emotion, but also its subjective dimension. In other words, "the imposition of limitations regarding the period of mourning, attire, and other facets reflects an understanding of grief as a social function, not merely a private sentiment" (on the ancient Greek concept of "grief," see Konstan 2006b: 244–58, here 252).

From Geometric to Classical times, the most significant image subject for the study of grief and mourning is the *prothesis*, the laying out of the corpse amidst a group of male and female mourners. Already in the earliest *prothesis* scenes we find gender-typical mourning habits: female figures are shown raising both arms and beating their heads, while male figures stretch out only one hand, thus paying their respects in a more controlled way. This basic iconographic pattern reflects the different social roles ascribed to men and women within the funerary ritual, which in turn enshrines in visual discourse the culturally constructed dichotomy between male rationality and female emotionality. It will prove extremely effective and is maintained in later periods, sometimes refined by additional pictorial elements which allow for further differentiation regarding the role and status of the depicted figures and their affiliation to the deceased.

A black-figure pinax (votive or funerary tablet) in New York shows a typical archaic *prothesis* scene for a young, beardless man mourned by female and male relatives (see Fig. 3.1). Two men approach the bier from the right in the traditional greeting gesture; one of them is characterized as being old by his white hair and beard. Although their heads are thrown back to indicate that they are singing the *thrênos* (ritual lament), their behavior is relatively calm. Next to the bier, three women gesticulate wildly, tearing their disheveled hair, while a fourth woman is singled out as she gently touches the head of the deceased. Textual evidence suggests that the last physical contact with the deceased person—albeit automatically accompanied by ritual contamination (*miasma*) that necessitated subsequent purification rites—was perceived as both an emotional need and a privilege of the closest relatives and dependants. In Euripides' *Suppliants*, for instance, the Chorus of Argive mothers demand to touch their sons' "blood-dripping corpses" (σώμαθ' αἱματοσταγῆ, 812): "Let me embrace and hold my children to my bosom in my enfolding arms."[13] As Angelos Chaniotis has shown on the basis of Greek epigrams of the imperial period, for instance, the touching of the dead body was not just a literary *topos* but formed an essential element both in ancient Greek and Roman funerary ritual and was considered an essential means of attesting and perpetuating an affective bond beyond the grave (Chaniotis 2006a: esp. 206–7): In the visual record, too, the physical contact between the dead and the living clearly signals emotional intimacy and seems to be, as far as we can identify the figures and their relationship to one another, restricted to the parents, spouses, and the old nurse of the deceased.[14]

Returning once again to the pinax in New York, there is a fifth female figure squeezed into the right edge of the scene: significantly smaller in size and thus clearly identified as a servant, she is squatting on the floor, lowering her head in despair. Unlike the highly ritualized mourning gestures of the standing figures, her body language indicates that, as a slave, she is neither able nor expected to maintain her composure. The woman touching the deceased and the servant crouching on the floor display emotional reactions that are not included in the standard scheme and only apply to certain members of the community.

A white lekythos, used in the funerary ritual, pushes the stereotype of the hyper-emotional slave woman to the extreme (see Fig. 5.4):[15] an old nurse, characterized by wrinkled, distorted features, sparse hair, a simple dark garment, and tattoos covering her arms, crouches on the ground in front of a tumulus and wails excessively for her deceased foster daughter, who is visible on the left side of the grave as a "shadow image," quietly contemplating her own untimely death (the hydria-loutrophoros crowning the grave mound denotes the deceased as an unmarried, childless woman).[16] With her ideal features, her elegant dress and her calm composure, the young woman forms a sharp contrast to the nurse who is marked as her social inferior not only by her non-ideal appearance but also by her frantic behavior.

FIGURE 5.4: Athenian lekythos, *c.* 430 BCE.

The "outsourcing" of extreme emotion expressions to members of the lower classes can be observed in Roman art too. In the so-called *conclamatio* scenes on sarcophagi, for instance, the family members, that is, free Romans, are usually shown in rather introverted forms of sorrow while the (female) servants play out the entire gamut of mourning gestures, from raising their arms to beating their bare breasts (cf. Dimas 1998: 21). The central image of a child sarcophagus in Agrigento (see Fig. 5.5) shows the deceased boy on his funeral bed flanked by his parents, who bow down with sorrow, fully wrapped in their cloaks, hiding their desolation under their veils.[17] The domestics behind the bier compensate for this rather reticent emotionality with intense gestures and loud lamentation. An aged nurse, identified by her characteristic bonnet, caresses the corpse and thus demonstrates her strong affection and close bond to the little boy, while an agitated pedagogue and another servant raise their arms in distress. Their more excessive forms of mourning help further to heighten the emotive power of the scene while maintaining the norm of passionate restraint for individuals of higher status.

These gender- and status-distinctive mourning habits are not exclusively pictorial phenomena but are based on real display rules well attested in various literary and visual genres (cf. Toynbee 1971: 45). In Plutarch's famous *Consolation to his Wife*, the author tries to calm and comfort her on the death of their youngest daughter by stressing the importance of renouncing the "never-sated passion for lamentation" (θρήνων ἄπληστος ἐπιθυμία, 609b):

> For not only "in Bacchic riot" must the virtuous woman remain uncorrupted; but she must hold that the tempest and tumult of her emotion in grief requires continence no less, a continence that does not resist maternal affection, as the multitude believe, but the licentiousness of the mind.[18]

FIGURE 5.5: Roman sarcophagus, 120–130 CE.

Whether in Dionysian ecstasy or in mourning, a virtuous woman ought never to let herself be carried away by her feelings, but should rather perform a "controlled loss of control" that helps to channel individual emotions in socially acceptable directions. The mourning gestures in the images are not necessarily intended to convey the "real" sentiments of the depicted figures, but rather the appropriate forms of conduct in the face of loss. Or as Beate Wagner-Hasel puts it, "[Es ist] verfehlt, exzessive Trauer mit unkontrollierter Emotionalität gleichzusetzen" – "[It is a] mistake to equate excessive grief with uncontrolled emotionality" (Wagner-Hasel 2006: 84).

It is essential to emphasize that the intensity of emotion expression cannot be equated with the intensity of the emotion (either in interpersonal communication or in its visual representation). Some pictorial elements may appear at first sight to conceal the depicted figure's inner state but turn out to be powerful emotion codes when read against their cultural background. This can be well demonstrated by the act of veiling, which in the Graeco-Roman world was "both a spontaneous expression of grief and an element in mourning ritual" (Cairns 2016a: 35). On a first, phenomenological level, the veil can be understood as a metaphor for the subjective emotional experience of grief and sorrow, as something that "covers" a person like darkness.[19] As demonstrated above, covering with a veil or mantle is also a sign of shame or modesty (*aidôs* in Greek and *pudicitia/pudor* in Roman culture); it was also regarded as the appropriate reaction in various "emotional scenarios in which honour and propriety are in question, for example to express grief or anger" (Cairns 2002: 75; on the veil as an expression of shame, see also above). Returning to the Agrigento sarcophagus, the veiling of the parents thus symbolizes both their physical experience of being "shrouded with grief" and their need to maintain, at least on the surface, their composure (which in turn establishes a hierarchy between them and their servants in terms of emotional restraint and appropriate mourning). As an emotion code in the arts, the veil can be used as a visual symbol for grief as such and thus reveals more than it hides without risking infringing the cultural rules of propriety.

The "aesthetic of *decorum*" also resonates in a number of ancient descriptions of a now lost painting by the Greek painter Timanthes that showed the sacrifice of Iphigenia (cf. Perry 2002: 154–6). The artist displayed varying degrees of grief and sorrow among the Greek spectators (commensurate with their relationship to the victim), but concealed the despair of her father Agamemnon by covering his face with a veil. This pictorial solution can be traced to Euripides, who has a messenger describe Agamemnon's immediate reaction to the horrifying spectacle: "When king Agamemnon saw the girl entering the grove to be sacrificed, he groaned aloud, and bending his head backward he wept, holding his garment before his face."[20] Notwithstanding this literary model, a narrative description of offstage (i.e. non-visible) action, all ancient commentators praise the painter for his artistic ingenuity in rendering the scene visually, yet they differ slightly in their explanation as to why exactly Timanthes chose to shroud the father's grief: Pliny seems to imply that the veil reflected the sheer inability of the painter (or the visual arts in general) to represent Agamemnon's suffering ("cum ... tristitiae omnem imaginem consumpsisset, patris ipsius voltum velavit, quem digne non poterat ostendere"; *Natural History* 35.73); Cicero discusses the painting in the context of rhetoric and praises its *decorum* (Cicero, *Orator* 74); and Valerius Maximus stresses the emotive power of omission when he brings up the viewer's compassion to imagine the father's weeping ("patris fletum spectantis adfectu aestumandum reliquit"; Valerius Maximus 8.11.6). The most comprehensive account is given by Quintilian, who combines the earlier interpretations:

Are not certain things likewise to be covered up in a speech, either because they ought not to be disclosed or because they cannot be expressed adequately? This is what Timanthes of Cythnus (I think it was he) did in the picture with which he won the prize over Colotes of Teos. Having depicted, in his Sacrifice of Iphigenia, Calchas sad, Ulysses even sadder, and given Menelaus the most complete expression of grief that his art could produce, he found he had used up all his means of representing emotion and could discover no way of adequately portraying her father's face; so he covered his head in a veil, and left it to the imagination of the spectators.[21]

A visual reference to the painting, or maybe rather to the rhetorical tradition that developed from it, can be found in the "House of the Tragic Poet" in Pompeii (see Fig. 5.6):[22] covered in a cloak and concealing his face with his right hand, Agamemnon stands to the far left and turns away from the scene in the center, where his daughter is being dragged to the altar.[23] But unlike in the work by Timanthes, the expressions of the other Greek men do not resemble anything like grief: their faces are filled with

FIGURE 5.6: Wall painting from the "House of the Tragic Poet" in Pompeii, 62–79 CE.

astonishment and surprise as they turn their eyes on Artemis and her companion approaching from above with the redeeming sacrifice. In combination with Artemis' intervention, Agamemnon's veiling not only serves as a powerful tool to express his insuperable suffering, but also creates an interesting twist for connoisseurs (a "Pompeian pun," as it were) as he ipso facto misses the miracle of Iphigenia's salvation.

Illuminating as these aesthetic discourses may be with regard to ancient (Roman) art production and reception, we must keep in mind that the act of veiling as an expression of grief was not just a stylistic device but had its roots in real experience: it drew upon collectively shared emotional concepts, reflected actual display rules in mourning, and could thus be intuitively understood by members of Graeco-Roman culture.[24] Some things never change: in the perfectly orchestrated funeral of John F. Kennedy, his wife Jackie became an icon of grief (see Fig. 5.7). Covering her face with a lace veil, she "did not compromise the ritual with outbursts of personal emotion [but] presented a calm demeanour of silent dignity" (Mulvaney and De Angelis 2010: 19) that affected the American public far more than excessive wailing and unrestrained mourning would have.

As we have seen, ancient Greek and Roman imagery developed numerous codes to express grief and mourning, from spontaneous manifestations of sorrow to highly

FIGURE 5.7: John F. Kennedy's family at his funeral in Washington, DC, November 1963.

ritualized gestures of lamentation. While the idiosyncratic possibilities and limits of different visual media certainly contributed to the concrete formation of emotion codes, it must be reiterated that most of them were grounded in everyday experience. The case studies presented also show that emotion codes not only are culturally specific but also vary between different social groups within one and the same culture (e.g. defined by status or gender). Naturally, the visual strategies we identified do not apply solely to the representation of grief, sorrow, and mourning, nor are they implemented only to differentiate between individuals of different status and gender: the same logic of distinction by means of emotional expression comes into effect in the representation of fearful barbarians, pain-stricken monsters, laughing hetaeras, or salacious satyrs.

AFFECTS AND ATTITUDES: THE MANY FACES OF LOVE

The English term "love" (like most of its equivalents in Western languages) comprises a huge spectrum of different emotional phenomena: while some forms of love are experienced as the sudden and uncontrollable onset of intense psycho-physiological changes, others appear to be long-term affective dispositions that are relatively stable and can be formed and modified by deliberate choice (cf. Scherer 2005). The following section will elaborate on the pictorial possibilities of distinguishing between these different affective experiences, taking representations of erotic desire and conjugal love as case studies.

The ancient Greek term *erôs* is multilayered and ambiguous (one need only think of the tributes to Eros in Plato's *Symposium*), but at this point a basic definition as "sexual longing" or "erotic desire" will suffice. The episode of the Trojan saga where Menelaus encounters Helen for the first time after her momentous adventure with Paris may serve as our first example.[25] In Athenian vase paintings of the first half of the fifth century BCE, the story is often rendered using the scheme of "erotic pursuit" that we have already discussed. However, Menelaus' initial intentions are diametrically opposed to those of Poseidon and other philanderers chasing young girls or boys: driven by the bitterness and the fury of the cuckold, he is pursuing his adulterous wife with a drawn sword, ready to take vengeance (see Fig. 5.8).[26] The minute he sees her, however, he is struck by her beauty and falls in love again. The Athenian vase painters found a truly striking formula to emphasize both the instantaneous and emotion-driven nature of Menelaus' change of mind: the suddenness and vehemence of his reaction to the sight of Helen finds its pictorial expression in the sword slipping out of his hand—he has literally dropped his deadly plan—while the initiating sensation is made visible by a little Eros, the personification of erotic desire, fluttering between the two. In a couple of vase paintings, Eros confronts the avenger with a *phiale* in his outstretched arm; a red-figure lekythos in St Petersburg even depicts a mysterious fluid streaming from the bowl directly into Menelaus' eyes.[27] The closest textual parallel to this visual code can be found in Euripides' *Hippolytus*, where the Chorus, consisting of young married women of Troezen, call on "Eros, god of love" and describe him as "distilling liquid desire down upon the eyes, bringing sweet pleasure to the souls of those against whom you make war . . ."[28] Numerous written sources convey the notion of *erôs* as an experience mainly induced by visual stimuli. In Plato's *Phaedrus*, for instance, we find the idea that "the lover's desire is the result of the effluence [*aporrhoê*] of particles from the beautiful body that enter the lover's soul via his eyes" (Cairns 2011a: 43). Both in literature and art, the image of Eros instilling passion through the eyes not only underlines the importance of vision in the ancient concept of erotic desire but also stresses the passive nature of the sensation: as *erôs* invades the body, the lover becomes a helpless victim of passion.

FIGURE 5.8: Athenian krater, c. 450 BCE.

There are other instances, however, where Eros conveys a different notion of erotic love, which is more in line with the ideal of mutual attraction as a long-lasting disposition arising from marriage. In many wedding images on Athenian vases, one or more Erotes are present to symbolize the (desired) desire between the bridal couple. On a loutrophoros fragment in Oxford, the bride is being led to her new home by the groom in the "hand on wrist" gesture, a code closely associated with legitimate marriage (see Fig. 5.9).[29] A winged Eros accompanies the two and carries along two vessels for the nuptial rites, thus supporting the union in the most tangible way by engaging in the wedding ceremony. In these scenes, the concept of *erôs* as an external power does not necessarily signify its uncontrollable nature; on the contrary, by deifying *erôs*, it is possible to address him directly, bribe him with worship, and thus, at least to some extent, also activate and control him (cf. Naiden, Chapter 2 in this volume). And so, immediately following the invocation of Eros "distilling liquid desire down upon the eyes," the Chorus in *Hippolytus* continue: "never to me may you show yourself to my hurt nor ever come but in due measure and harmony."[30] While the married women of Troezen are begging to be spared from the burden of uncontrolled desire, the newly weds have every reason to hope for the support of Eros "in due measure and harmony." In the context of bridal imagery, Eros is not perceived as a warlike spirit but as a benevolent power that reinforces the matrimonial

FIGURE 5.9: Wedding ceremony. Athenian loutrophoros, 420 BCE.

bond and thus leads to a fulfilled life according to the norms and ideals of society—the two poles of *erôs*, condensed in the image of a little boy.

Roman art, too, deploys the ambiguous figure of little Eros/Amor to create complex and sometimes witty statements on the capricious nature of erotic love. The "House of Punished Love" features Amor twice on opposite walls of the *tablinum*, both times in a family environment (see Fig. 5.10a–b).[31] The southern wall shows Mars and Venus in open nature, accompanied by a winged cupid and a female servant stooping over a small box on the floor. The fully-armed god of war approaches his sitting lover from behind and ardently touches her breast, to which she responds with a gesture of "affirmative consent." Mars and Venus embody the paradigmatic couple, the man showing an active and acute interest in the woman who in turn reacts to his intentions with mild control (cf. Lorenz 2008: 155). Amor floats by from the right, charming the divine couple with a *iunx* in his hands, a magical device used in love spells.

While this image sets Amor in the context of mutual attraction and thus stresses his benevolent power (only Hephaestus/Vulcan may object), the northern wall of the *tablinum* shows his unfortunate tendency to cross the line: Venus sits on a rock surrounded by an idyllic landscape and watches her son being "brought to justice" by another female figure

THE VISUAL ARTS 99

FIGURE 5.10a: Fresco from the "House of Punished Love" in Pompeii, c. 20 CE.

FIGURE 5.10b: Fresco from the "House of Punished Love" in Pompeii, c. 20 CE.

(perhaps Nemesis). Presented in back view and tied in bonds, little Cupid is wiping his bitter tears with his right hand, standing before his mother, who has taken his quiver into custody. The scene has been convincingly interpreted as Amor's punishment for torturing lovers, a popular subject in Graeco-Roman art.³² The Hellenistic *Anthologia Graeca* contains a number of epigrams on a statue of Eros in bonds (alas, we cannot tell for certain whether the statue ever existed or was only imagined by the poets); the poet Crinagoras, for example, directly addresses the sinner, leaving no doubt that the punishment is well deserved:

> Weep and groan, schemer, the sinews of your arms bound fast; such are your deserts. There is no one to untie you. Let us have no more piteous glances up. You, Eros, were the one to squeeze tears from others' eyes; you fixed your bitter arrows in the heart, and instilled the poison of passion incapable. The agonies of mortals are your mirth. What is done to you is what you did; justice did an excellent thing.³³

Another epigram from the *Anthologia Graeca* (16.195) draws an analogy between the specific nature of Eros' penalty and his typical mode of action, wondering whether, "perhaps, this prisoner himself did once enchain the mind of the artist" (μή ποτ' ἐκείνου οὗτος ὁ δεσμώτης αὐτὸς ἔδησε φρένα), thereby referring to another *topos* well known in the Graeco-Roman culture, that of the "chained lover," incapacitated by desire.

On an initial level, the image of little Amor being punished for "squeezing tears from others' eyes" can be enjoyed as a delightful story about the notoriously naughty child who "crushes the tops of the flowers" (Alcman fr. 58) and now finally gets his comeuppance. But against the background of erotic metaphor, it unfolds its true potential and opens an entire field of poetic images and ideas revolving around psychological bonding and constraint—they are all grounded in the physical experiences of desire. So again, the visual arts draw upon the same emotion concepts as the written sources: in this case, that erotic desire has to be restrained in order to not restrain you. Returning to our *tablinum* in the "House of Punished Love," the two opposite walls present quite different concepts of erotic love that we have already encountered in earlier descriptions: a desirable state when enjoyed in "due measure and harmony," it tends to exceed the acceptable boundaries and therefore must be chastened.

Against this background, then, it is no wonder that fickle *erôs* was not perceived as the ideal emotional condition in married life. Sexual attraction and amorous love between spouses did not take high priority in Greek and Roman societies and were even eyed with suspicion due to their destructive potential. Ordinary mortals, as opposed to gods, were well advised to establish a long-term relationship that was not susceptible to the turmoils of violent passion, "an emotional tie stronger than pure sexual fascination" (Salvo 2016: 266). In ancient Greece, the ideal relationship between spouses is covered by the umbrella term *philia*, a multifaceted concept that applies to a variety of non-hierarchical relations and encompasses notions of mutual obligation, respect, *and* affection (cf. Hartmann 2002: 126–30; on the manifold notions of *philia*, see also Konstan 1997; Konstan 2006b: 169–84). There is no Roman concept of emotion that covers the whole range of Greek *philia*, but with regard to the relationship between spouses, the closest equivalent might be *concordia* (Larsson Lovén 2010: 204). Unlike the violent passions *erôs* and *amor*, these emotion concepts are characterized by longevity and moderation as they involve a strong rational element that is informed by cultural ideals and social necessities.

On Greek grave reliefs of the classical era, the ideal of a well-tempered and long-lasting emotional disposition towards one another finds its visual expression in the so-called *dexiôsis* (handshake). On classical grave reliefs, it is by far the most common motif to depict the bond between the dead and the living. In most cases, it is performed between husband and wife, but also parents and children or other relatives may be joined by the *dexiôsis*. These images are not necessarily intended to portray concrete situations (e.g. farewell or reunion), but rather they work on an abstract level, as witnesses of a connection beyond death (cf. Meyer 1999: 116–17). The fine grave stele of "Korallion, wife of Agathon" shows the deceased sitting on a stool and shaking hands with her husband, a bearded man slightly past his prime (see Fig. 5.11).[34] The sincerity of their handshake is strengthened by their intense eye contact and Korallion touching her husband's forearm, a gesture mainly performed by female figures to further emphasize the attachment to their partner.[35]

Many scholars have questioned the emotional significance of the *dexiôsis* because of its range of functions within Greek imagery: while it certainly conveys the ideal of family cohesion in funerary art, it also appears on contemporaneous document reliefs where it denotes the contractual obligation between the parties.[36] By interpreting the *dexiôsis* as a

FIGURE 5.11: Athenian grave stele of Korallion (drawing), *c.* 350 BCE.

visual code for the equally versatile concept of *philia*, the putative contradiction disappears: both *philia* and the handshake are based on mutual agreement and reciprocity and thus include, to varying degrees depending on the context, both formal and emotional elements (cf. Räuchle 2017: 235–7).

The Roman equivalent of the *dexiôsis* is the so-called *dextrarum iunctio*, which often features in Roman imperial art to display the *concordia* between two parties (e.g. the emperor and a representative of the army). On private funerary monuments, it refers to the *matrimonium iustum*; thus it responds to legal concerns, but also symbolizes "a union in harmony."[37] So again, the gesture does not allow for a clear decision whether it is supposed to express emotional or formal aspects of marriage—rather, these two dimensions seem to be inextricably linked.

While the handshake on Greek grave stelae is almost always combined with eye-contact and often reinforced by explicitly emotional gestures, the Roman *dextrarum iunctio* appears rather formal and rigid: it "involved a certain degree of touch, but it was usually only the right hands of husband and wife that made contact . . . The couple were often placed side by side, both looking out of the relief at the viewer, rather than at each other" (Davies 2017: 172).[38] Only in rare cases is the impression of aloofness sometimes softened by the woman turning towards her husband and gently touching his shoulder, as can be seen on a funerary altar from Rome (see Fig. 5.12).[39] As in Greek funerary art,

FIGURE 5.12: Roman funerary altar, first century CE.

these more direct displays of affection are usually restricted to women, while men tend to maintain their representative habitus (Davies 2017: 172–3).

The gender differences we can observe in the display of erotic desire and marital love in visual media are in accordance with the emotion concepts formulated in written sources: Aristotle (*Nicomachean Ethics* 1158b20–5) holds that affection should be proportionate, that is, that men would generally receive more love than they return since they are superior (cf. Hartmann 2002: 126). In Roman culture, too, "spousal devotion and loyalty were virtues more commonly attributed to women" (McCullough 2011: 175). Needless to say, these feeling norms played a decisive role in shaping the emotional experiences of the members of the respective community: Greek curse tablets dealing with love matters, for example, show that women were primarily interested in affirming and increasing affection (*philia*), while men primarily wished to arouse passionate love (*erôs*) in their love interests (Salvo 2016: 264).

As could be demonstrated, Greek and Roman art provides manifold strategies of distinguishing between different forms of love—from acute passion to lifelong affection. The first explicit classification of these different emotional phenomena is provided in the *Nicomachean Ethics*, where Aristotle elaborates on the nature of *philia* and defines it as a "fixed disposition," comparable to *êthos* (character)—and opposed to *pathos*: "Liking [*philêsis*] seems to be an emotion [*pathos*], friendship [*philia*] a fixed disposition [*hexis*], for liking can be felt even for inanimate things, but reciprocal liking involves deliberate choice, and this springs from a fixed disposition [*hexis*]."[40] Of course, there is no sharp distinction between these different emotional phenomena: an emotional disposition can encourage the experience of acute emotions, while the repeated experience of certain emotions can lead to the formation of a fixed disposition.[41] The same logic applies to the visual expressions of emotions: many of the codes that appear to be spontaneous emotional reactions can at the same time point to a character trait. By skillfully playing with the ambiguous and multivalent nature of their visual codes, Greek and Roman art has managed to convey the fascinating world of emotions in all its complexity.

THE EMOTIVE POWER OF IMAGES: THE SUFFERING "OTHER"

Having tackled in previous sections various aspects of the representation of emotions in Greek and Roman iconography, we shall now address the emotive qualities of visual media, that is, their ability to elicit emotional reactions in the recipient. There are countless visual strategies for affecting the beholder and innumerable possibilities to emotionally engage with a work of art. The emotive power of an image is not coextensive with the use of explicit *pathos* formulas, but to a large extent also depends upon other factors such as cultural background and context of reception. As the grave relief of Ampharete with her grandchild has shown, even extremely restrained representations can have a strong emotional effect on the viewer.

In what follows, we shall look at the other side of the spectrum and turn to a work of art that combines the subject of violent death and total defeat with the excessive use of emotion expression and *pathos* formulas: the "Greater Attalid Dedication." Also known as the "Greater Barbarians," this famous victory monument was commissioned by King Attalos I on the occasion of his battles against the Gauls between 238 and 223 BCE, and (most likely) erected in the sanctuary of Athena in Pergamum.[42] The original bronze monument is gone, but two figures are preserved in Roman marble copies, namely the "Dying Gaul" and the "Ludovisi Gaul." Both statues can be regarded as epitomes of Hellenistic *pathos* as they are characterized by expressive gestures and postures, exaggerated facial features, and a sophisticated composition that actively involves the onlooker (Kunze 2002: 40–3, 47–51).

The "Dying Gaul," identified by the torques around the neck, the shaggy hair and moustache, has sunk to the ground, severely injured on the back by an absent enemy. The "closed" composition of the figure ingeniously captures the solitude of death: he has withdrawn into himself, suffering in silence and waiting for the "black cloud of death" to enfold him (θανάτου δὲ μέλαν νέφος ἀμφεκάλυψεν, Homer, *Iliad* 16.350; cf. Cairns 2016a: 31, n. 29). The more dynamic "Ludovisi Gaul" represents a Galatian chief who, finding himself in the hopeless situation of being besieged by invisible opponents, has killed his wife and is now turning to suicide as the last resort (see Fig. 5.13).[43] Presenting his muscular body in a dramatic vertical torsion that culminates in a vehement head rotation, he is vigorously driving the sword into his breast while holding the lifeless body of his wife, who has just collapsed under his fatal blow. It is generally accepted that the original dedication did not represent the Greek victors, but focused on the defeated parties (cf. Kunze 2002: 40, n. 148; Winkler-Horaçek 2011: 141). This deliberate omission can be interpreted as a means of actively involving the viewers as they are invited to fill the gap in their mind's eye or even to assume the role of the vanquisher (Pirson 2000: 72–5; Kunze 2002: 51). The

FIGURE 5.13: "Ludovisi Gaul," Roman marble copy from Hellenistic original, *c.* 220 BCE.

radical, unabashed focus on the Gauls' suffering yields an extreme emotive power; yet it is strongly contested what kind of emotions were elicited in the ancient onlooker.

Earlier scholarship held that these images of total defeat portrayed the Gauls in their heroic willingness to self-sacrifice and thus served as a means of glorifying them as worthy opponents. In this rationale, the suicide of the Celtic chief was placed in the tradition of Stoic philosophy and hence interpreted as an admirable act to escape dishonor at the hands of the enemy (e.g. Wenning 1978: 50). Others argued that the close view on the barbarians' misery aimed at the sympathy (*eleos*) of the beholder (Schober 1936: 123). Critics object that both the glorification of the defeated and the elicitation of pity for their lot would be rather counterproductive for a victory monument (Hölscher 1985: 129–30; Winkler-Horaçek 2011: 141). Tonio Hölscher takes a slightly different view and suggests that the strategy of portraying the defeated with "pathetic empathy" (Hölscher 1985: 134) serves as a means of reflecting the vulnerability of human existence, the harsh and merciless nature of fortune—a perspective that is also adopted by the "tragic historians" of the Hellenistic era (cf. Cairns, introduction to this volume). At the same time, Hölscher emphasizes that this "emotional absolutization of defeat" by no means reduces the effect of the monument, but even contributes to the glory and splendor of the victors: their triumph is just as absolute as their opponent's ruin (Hölscher 1985: 128–30).

Luca Giuliani argues against these interpretations that a sympathetic, other-regarding stance towards the enemy was not compatible with the ancient concept of pity (*eleos*), but rather influenced by the Christian ideal of compassion as an unconditional and altruistic sympathy for all mankind (Giuliani 2004: 18). He bases his claim on Aristotle, who at some point in the *Rhetoric* defines *eleos* as "a kind of pain in the case of a destructive or painful harm in one not deserving to encounter it."[44] In this reading of *eleos* as depending "on the judgement of whether the other's suffering [is] deserved or not" (Konstan 2006b: 201; cf. Konstan 2001: 34–43), the wretched barbarians of the "Greater Attalid Dedication" would indeed not qualify for the pity of the beholder. However, numerous sources suggest that even the woe of the villain could elicit sympathy (Cairns 2004: esp. 65, n. 3).[45] Especially in the Hellenistic era, both literature and visual art did not so much aim at a moral valuation of their accounts but rather at their vividness (*enargeia*) that stimulated the imagination (*phantasia*) and thus created an emotional effect of its own. So, on the ground of the extant sources, we cannot dismiss the possibility that ancient beholders felt sympathy at the sight of the suffering Celts.

A diametrically opposed interpretation is offered by Andrew Stewart, who claims that any Greek would "enjoy a put-down of barbarians, especially the hated Gauls" (Stewart 2004: 229), and characterizes the monument in highly suggestive prose:

> So in the statues, the Celts' heads are indeed satyrlike and their physiques are absolutely un-Greek, extremes of either defect or excess. For their skin is either so thick that it obscures the bodies' rational construction, or so thin that the muscles pop out like tumors all over the surface. Their nakedness too is insane, a nightmarish example of Greek artistic convention come to life, but now in the person of the barbarian berserker ... Even the Suicidal Celt's "heroically" poised head is a perversion and parody ... his questing glance is not a sign of strength but an index for weakness and the ultimate, irremediable lack.
>
> —Stewart 1997: 220

This vivid account says much more about Stewart's powers of imagination than about the actual compositional and stylistic properties of the statues in question. While the expressive facial features are indeed rooted in the long tradition of the "barbarian berserker," other *pathos* formulas such as the contortion of the bodies or the exaggeratedly protruding muscles have to be understood as general stylistic devices of the time that could be used for representations of Greek heroes as well (cf. Fig. 5.2). Certainly, it cannot be ruled out that some ancient beholders reacted to the view of the dying barbarians with sadistic satisfaction, but the monument's composition and the rendition of the figures by no means predetermine this particular reaction.

The interpretations just cited differ radically with regard to conjectured emotive effect but nonetheless assume a highly affective reaction in ancient viewers. Luca Giuliani rejects such an emotionalized reading entirely and reconstructs a "curious but cool" recipient who appreciates the precise and concrete description of violence from a purely aesthetical perspective.[46] His concept of an attentive and critical audience is supported by ancient authors such as Plutarch, who states that "a successful imitation manifests a cunning and authority of its own, so that we take a natural delight in the performance but are distressed by the reality" (Plutarch, *Moralia* 673 F–674 A, trans. Clement and Hoffleit 1969: 381). However, as a professed Platonist and a member of a highly educated elite, Plutarch's statement does not necessarily reflect the perspective of common folk.

In short, the ancient sources do not allow for a single interpretation of the "Greater Barbarians" (and other works of art), but rather suggest a diversity of possible perspectives: the commander of a victorious campaign against the Gauls would recognize their relentless fighting spirit in these statues and reactivate the pride of his triumph over such worthy opponents. A veteran who had seen his comrade being brutally slaughtered by a ferocious Celt perhaps experienced flaring hatred at the sight of the barbarians but also a sense of satisfaction at their demise. A woman beholding the statue of the Gaul who just murdered his wife, however, may have reacted with a certain sympathy for the predicament of the female as the perpetual victim of male power games. And finally, a rhetorically trained intellectual may have contemplated the monument primarily on the basis of aesthetic criteria such as successful imitation, artistic ingenuity, and craftsmanship. Of course, the possible reactions are not completely arbitrary but develop within the range of collectively shared values and build upon a common understanding of justice and desert—the "Greater Attalid Dedication" is a victory monument after all. Yet our fictitious recipients open up the possibility that the precise cognitive-affective reaction to an artwork not only depends on the cultural background but also on status and gender, as well as personal experiences and dispositions.

And yet, there seems to be a common core of aesthetic reception, an instinctive response to the sight of human suffering, or to the "vividness" of its representation in visual art, that is shared among all these different reactions. For even the cool eye of the distanced observer needs to be affected in some way in order to appreciate "successful imitation." We may be able to distance ourselves from the misery represented in art—but the full aesthetic experience nevertheless requires an emotional engagement, a basic physiological response to the artwork. We have arrived at the fundamental mystery of aesthetic emotions.

The ancient term *phrikê* may contribute to our understanding of the complex processes at work here (see Cairns 2016b: 3–15; Cairns 2017a). Literally translated as "shivering" or "shuddering," it can also be the name of an (aesthetic) emotion "that responds to the misfortunes of others" (Cairns 2017a: 71). It is this peculiar shiver of excitement at the view of another human being's suffering, a shiver "that springs from a fascination with the spectacle ... and yet also entails an instinctive revulsion towards that spectacle" (cf. Cairns 2017a: 55). The nature of *phrikê* as an "involuntary, instinctive response especially to immediate sensory stimuli" (Cairns 2016b: 14) does not predetermine the appraisal of an artwork, but allows for various emotional reactions. *Phrikê*, then, might be interpreted as an instinctive somatic experience, that enables us "to put some phenomenological flesh on the bare bones" of aesthetic reception (Cairns 2017a: 73).

CONCLUSION

There are various ways in which social and cultural structures stipulate the representation and elicitation of emotions through visual media: the reluctance of ancient artists to manifest emotional states through facial features is in line with the ideal of self-control and respective behavioral norms in everyday interactions. The status- and gender-typical emotion codes in images of grief and mourning are connected to real display rules and different roles in funerary ritual, but at the same time hint at the culturally constructed dichotomies between male rationality and female emotionality, between the self-restraint of the free and the uncontrollable nature of slaves; likewise, the visual distinction between female and male desire and affection in the images can be linked to cultural ideals about gender-conforming behavior and experience. These distinctive patterns in emotion expressions reach beyond the emotional communities of Greece and Rome when barbarians and mythical figures enter the stage: even in the vigorous *pathos* of Hellenistic sculptures one can detect a fine differentiation between the ordered passions of the Greeks and the dangerous passions of barbarians. In short, visual codes of emotion establish a relatively strict hierarchy in emotion management that reproduces and at the same time substantiates the social and cultural structures of the community in which they originated.

In classical antiquity, as in other periods, the spheres of emotion and cognition are inextricably linked and cannot be considered separately. In the ancient Greek (and Roman) thinking, "emotions necessarily involve judgements and beliefs, and without these, one can hardly speak of emotions as [sic] all. In a word, emotions are profoundly rational" (Konstan 2017a: 39). It is no surprise, then, that the distinction between acute emotions and long-lasting dispositions or character traits in the images is anything but clear-cut. As could be demonstrated, this fuzziness is not due to the limits and restrictions of visual media alone, but deeply rooted in ancient perceptions of emotion and cognition: the ambivalence of the visual code of veiling is related to the ambiguity of *aidôs/pudor* as both an acute feeling of shame and a long-lasting, moral disposition towards modesty. The versatile use of the handshake (*dexiôsis* and *dextrarum iunctio*) in Greek and Roman art aptly conveys the equally multifaceted concepts of *philia* and *concordia* that comprise rational and affective aspects. For the ancient mind, the boundaries between emotion and character are fluent.

Thus, the visual languages of emotion are first and foremost cultural phenomena that have to be analyzed in their context(s): the pictorial (and literary) traditions of single codes, figure-types, and compositions; the function and intended message of the image; the conditions of use and reception; the underlying beliefs, norms, and values of the respective community; and finally, the broader context of ancient "mentality."

And then, sometimes, something happens: when we look at the image of Agamemnon covering his face at the sacrifice of his daughter, when we think of the peculiar display rules in grief and mourning at that time, when we then recollect the manifold metaphorical layers of the veil in ancient culture, we can relate to his need to withdraw from the outer world and identify with his experience of being shrouded with sorrow. Ancient literature and art are replete with metaphors that draw on the experiential, embodied nature of emotions; they enable us to glimpse behind the curtain of contextual and cultural specificity and understand, in Dilthey's sense, the emotional and cognitive experiences of the past. There is no cultural history without the emotions.

CHAPTER SIX

Literature

RUTH SCODEL AND RUTH R. CASTON

A fearful shuddering and tear-filled pity and a longing that loves grief enter its [poetry's] audiences; the soul feels through the words its own particular emotion at the good and bad fortunes of the business and bodies of others.

—Gorgias, *Helen* 9

Ion: For when I say something pathetic, my eyes fill with tears, and when I say something frightening or terrible, my hair stands up with fear and my heart pounds . . .
Socrates: Do you know that you [rhapsodes] cause exactly these responses in most of your audience?
Ion: I know it very well. For each time I see them from above on the platform, crying and with fierce looks in their eyes and joining in amazement at what is being said. I have to pay very close attention to them, since if I sit them down crying, I will laugh because I will make money, but if they are laughing, I myself will cry at losing the money.

—Plato, *Ion* 535c–e

This discussion will explore emotions as they appear both in classical literature and in theorizing about literature. Although Greek and Latin are quite different languages, and Greek and Roman cultures were very different in ways that directly affected how emotions were conceived and expressed, with distinct legal, educational, political, and social structures, they can usefully be examined together. Greek literature was central to elite Roman education and to Roman literary culture, and Romans seem to have assumed that the emotional world of Greek literature was entirely transparent to them.

Similarly, in later reception, readers have generally assumed that they could recognize the emotions described in classical literature. Of course, emotions arise in accordance with cultural expectations and norms: what provokes pity or causes anger depends in part on what constitutes misfortune or injustice for the Greeks or Romans.[1] But if the specific conditions that cause emotion differ across cultures, we share much else about emotional experience with the ancients. For us, too, emotions seem to tug and pull on us in opposite directions. They often feel like they attack us from outside, then take hold without our control. And while the struggle with emotion can often make us feel alone, classical literary treatments tend to describe an individual's emotional experience in conjunction with the perspective of other characters, illustrating the way that emotion is deeply embedded in social life and experience. Nor do emotions occur in isolation: a woman's grief arouses someone else's pity, a filthy or aging body brings shame to the self but disgust to the observer. While philosophical and rhetorical treatments of emotion often treat emotions individually and in a formal context between teacher and student, or speaker and audience, literary treatments bring out the dynamics of emotion in a way that provides us with a richer understanding of emotion within the culture.

Most ancient theorizing about literature was the work of philosophers or rhetoricians, and even practical criticism was philosophically or rhetorically inflected. Philosophical ethics wanted to regulate emotions, rhetoric to direct them. The quotation from Gorgias' *Helen* at the head of this chapter celebrates the power of mere speech to provoke intense emotional responses to the fortunes of people with whom the audience has no real connection, and he evidently believes that this emotional power, though most evident in poetry, is available for the persuasive purposes of prose speech. Other authors of the fifth century BCE, however, show deep suspicion of the persuasive powers of speech, but clever arguments rather than direct emotional appeals were usually the main concern. Thucydides praises Pericles for his ability to calm the excessive emotions of the Athenian crowd (2.65.9), while he has the politician Cleon, whom he obviously dislikes, urge the Athenians to act directly on their anger (3.81.1; see Harris 2001: 178–80; Balot 2014: 121–3).

Plato thought of literary response as channeled from poet to performer to audience (*Ion* 533d–536d). The *Ion* presents a dialogue between Socrates and a rhapsode, a professional performer of Homeric epic. Attempting to convince Ion that his ability to interpret Homer depends on divine inspiration, Socrates has Ion (in the passage used as an epigraph for this chapter) describe both his own and his audience's emotional response to his performance of Homeric texts. The passage manifests some pervasive themes in classical thinking about literature and emotion: the performer is so affected by the emotions roused by the text that he responds physiologically, and if the performance is successful, most of the audience will have similar reactions. These are peculiarly mixed responses, since the satisfied audience weeps (Peponi 2012: 51–65).

Plato worried that inappropriate emotional behaviors by characters within poems would lead to inappropriate emotional self-indulgence by members of their audience (*Republic* 10, 606a–b). Aristotle's famous and difficult concept of catharsis is evidently an attempt to respond to this criticism. However we understand catharsis, Aristotle proposes that the powerful emotions literature can arouse have positive effects.[2] But Aristotle's concept, despite its modern influence, did not enter the mainstream of ancient critical thought.[3] Instead, for ancient literary thought the question is usually whether an author prompts appropriate emotions at the right level, as we shall see in Polybius. In "How to Study Poetry" (26D), the Platonist Plutarch criticizes Achilles for his excessive anger, but then praises him for controlling it. The young reader is not to be emotionally engaged, but to be taught to look for positive and negative moral examples of emotional control.

Criticism was regularly concerned with decorum and restraint. Different genres, with different subject matter and linguistic register, had different norms of decorum, and their emotional effects could change over time and could be areas of contention and polemic. Old Comedy could seek to arouse primal disgust, but New Comedy did not. History in the Hellenistic period was sometimes less restrained in arousing emotion than the classical historians. The Greek novel was not a canonical genre at all, and was not even cited in literary discussions.

Rhetoric, like philosophy, required that the orator carefully inspire the right emotions to the right extent. Not surprisingly, the first extended discussion of emotion occupies the second book of Aristotle's *Rhetoric* (1380b–1388b). Aristotle defines each of the emotions he considers—anger and calmness, friendliness and enmity, fear and confidence, shame and shamelessness, kindness, unkindness, pity and indignation, envy and emulation—by providing a basic cognitive script. Anger, for example, is a painful impulse towards revenge for a slight to oneself or one's friends. Orators, but also poets, historians, and novelists, could assume that if they presented the correct prompts, audiences would react accordingly.

Perhaps the most significant difference between the presentation of emotions in classical Greek and in most Latin literature lies in the rhetorical self-consciousness of both authors and readers of Latin. Elite Roman education included extensive rhetorical training and practice, and authors could both apply rhetorical scripts and expect their audiences to recognize them.

Because the norms of decorum were widely shared, poets could deliberately manipulate their own emotional displays. *Votum, timor, ira, uoluptas, gaudia*—wishes, fear, anger, pleasure, joy—says the speaker of Juvenal's first Satire (1.85–6), using a list of emotions as a snapshot of his subject matter, a critique of contemporary Roman society in the second century CE. It is not only *other* people's emotion that Juvenal reveals in his *Satires*, however: the speaker himself is overcome by emotion as he rants and raves from his high pedestal.[4] The speaker's pose of superiority is thus complicated by the exposure of his own vulnerabilities. Becoming a character in his own text, he reveals how unaware we can be of our own emotional state and in the process forces the reader to question his reliability as any kind of guide or moral authority.

The pattern of Juvenal's list also points to the way that literary emotions often involve extremes, from optimism to despair, from anger to joy (and so defy philosophical demands for moderation). Conflicting emotions can even occur at the very same time. Plato's *Phaedo* describes an "unusual" feeling of pleasure and pain at once at the death of Socrates (*Phaedo* 53e–59a). Both emotions, however, are appropriate to the situation. Phaedo is sad at the death of his friend, but the calm and cheerful demeanor of Socrates makes true grief impossible. Neither feeling is excessive. The dialog prompts the reader to share in this mixed, but controlled emotion, and when Socrates sends away the women because they are emotionally uncontrolled, the reader is directed to emotional self-control (60a–b).

Most mixed emotions, however, are not open to such immediate analysis. Homer's Andromache takes her baby "with a tearful laugh" (*Iliad* 6.483). She is amused by the baby's fear of the plume on his father's helmet, but deeply anxious because Hector insists on fighting in the front line. The Roman Republican poet Catullus concisely describes his opposing feelings (poem 85):

> I hate and I love. Why do I do this, perhaps you ask?
> I don't know, but I feel it happen and am tortured.

Although the vicissitudes of the emotional life were part of what seemed so problematic about emotions to ancient philosophers, for poets and other authors, the contradictory and puzzling quality of emotions was precisely what made them so fascinating and fertile for exploration.[5] How *can* one hate and love simultaneously? It is a familiar fact, yet the speaker himself cannot explain it. The hypothetical interlocutor is confused as well, though in choosing the active verb "do" instead of the passive "happen," he seems to suggest the speaker's role in causing his own distress. In a more general way, the question posed by the unnamed interlocutor again invites readers to ask questions of their own, whether about the speaker's emotional extremes or their own experiences.

This chapter will focus on a representative three emotions: pity, wonder, and disgust. Ancient literary and philosophical analysis concerned itself extensively with pity; disgust is not theorized at all, although it is hardly absent from literary texts; wonder is especially interesting because while it is usually viewed positively, sometimes it features in polemic as a sort of cheap trick. First, however, we shall look briefly at how literary emotion works in ancient thought.

Most of the core assumptions of later literary/rhetorical theory about the emotions are already implicit in the Homeric epics. The epics present a wide variety of typically intense emotions and indicate them both explicitly, through narratorial intervention, and through the speech, behavior, and physiological reactions of characters. Of course, there is no theory of emotion in Homer. Early Greek does not have a word even roughly synonymous with "emotion," and epic language does not clearly distinguish emotive from cognitive states. That does not mean, however, that Homer did not understand the emotions as related to each other. The emotions of epic characters are located mostly in the *thumos*, which is both a physical entity or substance in the chest and something less material and precise. Although the *thumos* also does cognitive work, the expression "arouse the *thumos*" always indicates a strong emotional reaction, whether anger, pity, or grief, and points to a unity among the emotions.

The range of emotion in the epics is wide. Besides anger, the theme of the *Iliad*, we see *nemesis*, the special form of anger felt at a violation of social norms; fear; confidence; desire; joy; pity; grief; pride; surprise; regret; *aidôs* (inhibitory shame); impatience; amazement; and *pothos*, longing for something absent.

Homer frequently describes the physiological correlates of emotions, both those visible to others and those not (*Iliad* 15.101–2 is an unusually precise case). Both Hector and Andromache laugh when their baby is frightened by the plume of his father's helmet at *Iliad* 6.471. Then, after Hector's prayer for his son, Andromache takes the baby while "laughing through tears" at *Iliad* 6.483. Hector evidently interprets her tears as a sign that she is afraid for him (she has already begged him not to fight so aggressively). Hector, who pities her (484), tries to reassure her that he will not be killed unless he is fated to die. The narrator, as often, does not signal whether Hector's interpretation of Andromache's feeling is entirely complete, but her feelings are basically legible.

Powerful emotions, and their physical correlates, often operate as outside forces. Pity seizes assemblies in the *Odyssey* (2.81, 24.428), and wonder "holds" Circe when Odysseus resists her drug. Gods occasionally cause emotions: so Iris puts longing for her former husband, town, and parents in Helen's *thumos* (*Iliad* 3.139–40). They can inspire panic in battle, or a longing to lament. The gods, however, do not intervene with characters' emotions as often as they put ideas in their minds (though it is occasionally hard to draw a distinction, as at *Odyssey* 18.158–68).

A normative emotional response depends on a proper evaluation of the cause, so that cognition and emotion are linked. Helen has a drug that can stop someone from crying over the death of a parent, or even if he witnessed the violent death of his brother or son (*Odyssey* 4.220–6). Grief, and related anger over a violent death, has a very clear scale. Ajax can rebuke Achilles by comparing his anger to that of a man whose son or brother has been killed (9.6326), and Apollo also refers to a brother or son (24.47). There is a traditional scale of affection, which is also a scale of appropriate emotion.[6] Achilles in the *Iliad* is an outlier; his anger seems disproportionate. Odysseus in the *Odyssey* is an outlier in his ability to regulate emotion, suppressing the visible manifestations of his anger. The poet can portray emotional regulation simply by stating that the character did not display the expected responses, but characters can urge others to "tame" or "hold back" the *thumos*. These norms are critical in Greek thought about the emotions aroused by literature. In *Republic* 10, 605c10–606b, Socrates argues that Homer and tragedy are dangerous because the desire to cry and lament is an unsatisfied appetite, and the pleasure of such performances lies precisely in indulging this appetite, an indulgence that makes it more difficult to control in everyday life (*Republic* 604b–606c1). Aristotle, in contrast, seems to believe that some literary emotions actually help in regulation, while others are harmless to adults (Heath 2013: 93–5).

Emotion is regularly roused by speech. A speaker can provoke *aidôs* by opening a speech with the bare word itself (Cairns 1993: 68). At *Iliad* 9.590–5, Phoenix narrates how the wife of Meleager, who had in anger retreated to her bedroom, persuaded him to fight by lamenting and enumerating the sufferings of a captured city. Meleager of course must know what these are: the success of the appeal is emotional. Phoenix says that "his *thumos* was stirred" and he saves the city "yielding to his *thumos*." Indeed, the formulaic expression "small children," νήπια τέκνα, often paired with "wives," always carries an affective charge, and is mainly confined to character speech, since the external narrator tends to avoid openly manipulating the audience's responses. At *Iliad* 2.136–7, Odysseus refers to the wives and children left at home; at *Iliad* 4.238–9, Agamemnon refers to Trojan wives and children who will be enslaved when Troy falls; at *Iliad* 6.310, the Trojans pray to Athena to pity their wives and children. Affect is almost automatic with the phrase.

Behind classical treatment of the emotions in literature lie basic assumptions such as that emotions are universal and there is a normative emotional response to a given situation and that certain individuals react or control their reactions more than others; these differences are important generators of narrative, but the response of a large audience is unified enough that a poet or orator does not need to give much consideration to individual variation. Emotion, though often complex, is usually legible and a description of its physiological correlates often enables an audience to recognize it. Although emotions may be inspired by a god or seem to come from outside the person, everyone assumes that individuals can control the expression of emotion.

Pity is among the emotions Greeks analyze and identify most in literature (both passages quoted at the opening of this chapter include it). It may be more useful, however, to consider first how pity works in Homer, especially since it became a characteristically epic emotion. It is ubiquitous, felt by both mortals and gods, and it is one of the predominant responses sought from the audience. There are two word-families for "pity."[7] The deaths of fellow warriors inspire pity, but so do the sufferings of strangers: in one of Odysseus' lying tales, an Egyptian king pities the narrator when he supplicates, even though he has raided Egypt without provocation (*Odyssey* 14.279); Ino/Leucothea pities Odysseus (*Odyssey* 5.336), as Proteus' daughter pities Menelaus (*Odyssey* 4.364). Pity is in fact the default response for a character, mortal or god, who notices another's pain.

Later Greek theorizing stresses that (only) undeserved misfortune is pitied (cf. Konstan, this volume), but in Homer it is hostility, not a judgment that the suffering is deserved, that blocks pity. Apollo comments sarcastically to Athena that she does not pity Trojans who are killed (*Iliad* 7.27), but he himself does not pity Achaeans. A character who is in a position to kill or spare a victim responds to a request for pity by evaluating the potential victim in relation to himself. When Lycaon on the battlefield asks Achilles to pity him, he does not argue that he does not deserve to die, but calls on their earlier relationship and reminds Achilles that he is not a full brother of Hector (*Iliad* 21.74–96). When Odysseus decides not to spare the suitor Leodes, he does not argue about whether Leodes tried to restrain the other suitors, but insists that as the suitors' priest he must have prayed that

Odysseus not return (*Odyssey* 22.321–5). Circe, in contrast, even pities the men she has just released from enchantment (*Odyssey* 10.399). It is wrong to refuse pity where it is appropriate. Achilles is repeatedly rebuked as "pitiless" (*Iliad* 9.632, 16.33, 16.204). The narrator, who does not usually overtly direct the audience's emotional response, uses adjectives from both pity-stems to describe actions like Priam's plea to Hector at *Iliad* 22.37 or Penelope's lament when she hears that Telemachus has sailed to Pylos (*Odyssey* 4.719), as well as the deaths of the maids at *Odyssey* 22.472.

Is pity so dependent on the absence of enmity for the external audience? They are certainly to be expected to feel sympathy for the lonely wives and children of the Achaeans. There can be little doubt that at *Iliad* 6.310 the external audience will pity the Trojans' wives and children, even though Athena does not, and even though the hearer is unlikely to share their wish for Diomedes' death. When Achilles kills Hector, the *Iliad* devotes considerable narrative resources to generating pity for Andromache and her son (22.477–514). The *Odyssey* presents two "good" suitors, the already-mentioned Leodes, and Amphinomus. The disguised Odysseus warns Amphinomus to leave, since Odysseus will soon return (*Odyssey* 18.125–50), but despite bad premonitions, he remains (*Odyssey* 22.153–6). This presentation focuses audience pity on them and deflects it from the rest.

The philosophical tradition, however, links pity to moral evaluation rather than personal hostility: Aristotle, at *Rhetoric* 2.8, states that we pity those who are like ourselves and those whose suffering is undeserved, and he connects pity to the ability to believe that such a misfortune could befall us or our friends. This emphasis on evaluation reflects considerable anxiety about being tricked into misplaced pity. Demosthenes complains that Athenian juries are often misled by pity, resentment, or anger (19.226–8). Other sources also link pity to undeserved suffering (Konstan 2001: 45–8). Aristotle opposes pity to both indignation, which entails a moral evaluation, and envy, which does not—but the contrast between pity and envy is both older and more frequent than the contrast with indignation (Konstan 2006b: 112–13). Imaginative narrative, where the audience will suffer no immediate harm through pitying the possibly undeserving, is the outlier in its freedom to use emotional triggers. Athenian courtroom speakers often ask for pity, but claim to deserve it, as their opponents urge jurors to feel anger and reject pity.[8]

Pity plays a significant role in Latin epic as well, and right from the start. The Latin grammarian Priscus comments that *misereo* was used by the oldest writers, then goes on to quote a line from Ennius' fragmentary *Annales* in which even the enemy takes pity on women weeping at the capture of their city (5.169). It is of course pervasive in Virgil's *Aeneid*. When Euryalus' mother learns of his death, she runs to the battlefield and mournfully addresses her lost son: she reproaches him for leaving her alone and laments she was not able to say a final goodbye or prepare his body for burial, finally offering up her own body to the enemy's weapons (9.481–97; see Hardie 1994 *ad loc.*; Sharrock 2011). Servius, the fourth-century commentator on Virgil, notes that the speech closely follows Cicero's instructions to the orator for arousing pity ("paene omnes partes habet de misericordia commouenda a Cicerone in rhetoricis posita," 9.479).[9] Yet already in the *Iliad*, Andromache complains in her lament over Hector that she was deprived of the final goodbye (*Iliad* 24.743–5; see Fig. 6.1), for the rhetorical tradition often systematizes what was already time-honored practice. Before the speech, Virgil also describes the symptoms of her grief: the warmth leaves her bones, the shuttle and wool fall from her hands, and she wails and tears her hair (*Aeneid* 9.475–80). These last two details are

FIGURE 6.1: Jacques Louis David, *Andromache Mourning Hector* (1783).

conventional features of female grief that the poet expects us to recognize and respond to with pity (Alexiou 2002). Indeed, the Trojans who see and hear her grief begin to wail themselves. The arousal of pity in the internal audience provides a model for how an external audience should respond as well.

The powerful but abrupt ending of the epic where Aeneas kills Turnus has been a locus of recent study about anger (six words indicating anger appear in the last eight lines of the poem).[10] But the scene turns on pity as much as on anger (*Aeneid* 12.932–6). Turnus begs Aeneas to take pity, asking him to think of Turnus' father and his old age, again a strategy used to arouse pity in oratory (see, e.g., Cicero, *Pro Caelio* 79). Turnus also emphasizes similarity (Konstan 2006b: 214–15): Aeneas had such a father himself. Aeneas hesitates, but when he sees that Turnus is wearing the baldric of Pallas, his young friend whom Turnus had killed, pity turns to rage. Recent studies have used Aristotelian and Stoic attitudes toward anger as a way of interpreting whether Aeneas' anger is justified or not.[11] But the complexity of the ending also derives from its relationship to earlier literature, and the passage raises many of the same questions about hostility and evaluation that we saw in the discussion of Greek pity, colored of course by the Romans' history of civil war. Virgil paints Aeneas in the later books of the epic as a Roman Achilles, but diverges from

FIGURE 6.2: Roman silver-gilt drinking cup depicting King Priam of Troy appealing to Achilles for the return of his son Hector's body.

the final book of the *Iliad* where Achilles does remarkably reconcile with the enemy (Barchiesi 2015; see Fig. 6.2). The story of the Danaids, which is depicted on Pallas' baldric, represents a story of murder but also the potential to resist it.[12] For readers schooled in Homer and literary allusion, canonical stories of pity like these would have guided and complicated their response to Aeneas' actions.[13]

The tragic love affair between Aeneas and Dido in *Aeneid* 4 and her abandonment and death also arouse great pity. At the beginning Dido is admirable, an exile like Aeneas who has started an impressive new city. She takes pity on Aeneas, who has encountered numerous troubles since fleeing Troy and has yet to found a new home (*Aeneid* 4.13–14). But the majority of the pity in the remainder of the book is directed towards her. The text encourages a reader to see her as an innocent victim, describing her, for example, as a wounded animal (4.69; see also 4.369–70). The gods take pity on her as well: Juno cannot bear to watch her slow and painful death on the pyre (*longum miserata dolorem*, 4.693) and sends Iris to release her. Even Aeneas takes pity on her in the Underworld for her undeserved fate (6.475–6), not that he blames himself (6.460). In his *Confessions*, Augustine recalls the way he wept over this story when he was young, even though now, at the time of writing, he regrets not crying instead for his own *errores* (1.13.20).[14]

Generic boundaries are important for pity: Herodotus and Thucydides are restrained in depicting pity within their texts and in evoking it, because it is not a common motivator of political action (Lateiner 2005). In a famous passage, Polybius criticizes the historian Phylarchus, particularly in his narrative of the defeat of Mantinea (2.56.7–8):

And being eager to stir the hearts of his readers to pity, and to enlist their sympathies by his story, he introduces women's embraces, and tearing-out of hair, and exposures of breasts; and furthermore the tears and lamentations of men and women, led off into captivity along with their children and aged parents. And this he does again and again throughout his whole history, by way of bringing the terrible scene vividly before his readers.

Phylarchus evidently used the pity-triggers that went back to Homer. Polybius, who argues that history's goals are not those of tragedy, complains (2.56.13):

Phylarchus simply narrates most of such catastrophes and does not even suggest their causes or the nature of these causes, without which it is impossible in any case to feel either legitimate pity or proper anger.

So Polybius objects to the traditional details that arouse pity partly because he is policing the generic boundaries; emotional responses in history should be governed by a judgment that the pity is properly deserved, which in turn requires accurate narrative and analysis of the events. He is himself clearly deeply engaged emotionally on the Achaean side, however, so that his hostility makes him invulnerable to pity; he argues that the Mantineans deserved "more severe and greater vengeance," listing their crimes (particularly murdering the Achaean garrison) and that they suffered only "the plundering of their property and the selling of the free population." Polybius wants the historian to arouse anger towards the Mantineans, not pity (Champion 2004: 125–6; Marincola 2013). He is quite capable of composing pathetic and dramatic narrative himself (Chaniotis 2013c).

In Roman historical texts, too, pity can similarly be aroused by speech and the physical signs of distress. When the Sabine women witness the battle between the Sabines and Romans, they enter the fray and blame themselves for the unrest. Both their disheveled appearance and their speech stop the fighting and silence the men, and even bring about a union of the two cities (Livy 1.13); the echoes of tragedy and epic in the passage are clear.[15] In Tacitus' description of Varus' disastrous defeat in the Teutoburg forest, the fight is long over. But the discovery of the battle site six years later brings fresh horror (*Annales* 1.60). Tacitus puts the devastation vividly before our eyes, re-enacting something of the Romans' struggle through the evidence of the whitened bones lying on the field. The *pathos* of the scene is intensified by the description of Roman heads nailed to barbarian altars and use of sacrificial language. The Romans' unnatural suffering at the hands of the Germans stirs both anger and pity: as they bury the bones, Germanicus' men are described simultaneously as mournful and hostile (*maesti simul infesti*, 1.62; see Grethlein 2013: 133–5).

Pity can also figure in more light-hearted contexts. In a comedy by Terence, a young man weeps at a courtesan's funeral in a way that arouses tremendous pity in the audience. But the young man's father delights at this, since he interprets it to mean that his son will cry even more when his own father dies (*Andria* 110–12). The lovers in Roman comedy and love elegy usually feel pity exclusively for themselves and their failed relationships. This is intended to be funny—their frequent cry *me miserum* reveals an inflated sense of suffering and is a parody of characters in "higher" genres like epic or tragedy.[16] In another manipulation of the epic and tragic paradigm, elegiac lovers also fantasize about their own deaths as a way of testing their mistresses' pity and love for them.

Greek and Romans never theorize disgust as a literary affect. Indeed, Greek has no single word for the emotion, although many scholars treat it as a primary and universal one.¹⁷ Still, Greek has a range of terms that convey revulsion in contexts where purity/impurity and an emotional response akin to physical disgust are involved. The closest is the family of *bdeluros*, whose semantic range extends from moral and social repugnance to physical nausea. The words of this family, however, are mostly excluded from the high genres: they do not appear in epic or tragedy. Demosthenes and Aeschines among the orators use *bdeluros* in passages of abuse, often in close proximity to the vocabulary of shame/shamelessness (*aischunê*) and of impurity (*miaros*), which are also signs of disgust. Someone who experiences intense revulsion can be said to be "in pain" (*lupê, algos*). Medical literature uses *aêdia*, "unpleasantness," for nausea, and the words of this family are used for a semantic range that extends from displeasure to disgust.

Aristotle says that the plot in which a good man goes from good to bad fortune is *miaron*, often translated as "disgusting" (1452b36). The word *aêdia* is not rare in certain rhetorical writers, such as Dionysius of Halicarnassus, but it refers to an audience response always to be avoided, one produced by some kind of excess. Plato indeed regards *bdeluttesthai* as the normal "real life" response to the emotional excess that audiences welcome in epic and tragedy (*Republic* 605e). Greek rhetorical and literary criticism does not explicitly consider that literature may cause a particular, local disgust with a situation or character, although pseudo-Demetrius, quoting Lysias' alleged remark to an old woman's lover that "it was easier to count her teeth than her fingers" (262), comments that Lysias presented the woman "at once most horribly and most laughably."

This absence of theoretical reflection on disgust is not perhaps surprising, both because disgust is not easily distinguished from other forms of dislike, and because so much ancient criticism blurs the distinction between author and character or passages and a whole text. Since nobody would seek to make an audience feel disgusted with a text or performance, it was not easy for ancient theorists to see disgust as a response to aspects of otherwise pleasure-giving works, although Aristotle famously says that people enjoy seeing precise images of what in reality we "see with pain," including corpses (*Poetics* 1448b10). It is still remarkable, however, because some genres of Greek literature freely exploit the primal sources of disgust to arouse an audience response of squeamish amusement. In the low genre of iambic (that is, abusive) poetry, Semonides' tirade against women represents the pig-woman whose house is filthy while she herself, "unwashed, in dirty clothes, grows fat sitting in manure" (7.5–6). Hipponax describes dung-beetles, "more than fifty," drawn by the stink of a latrine (92.10–12 West). Old Comedy exploits both scatology and the most taboo sexual behaviors. The giant dung beetle of *Peace*, which wants "ground" food from a boy prostitute (11–12), combines both. Hermes greets the hero when he reaches Olympus on his beetle with a litany of terms of disgust (*Peace* 182–4)—the dung beetle brings filth to Olympus, where it does not belong. Aristophanes repeatedly accuses Ariphrades of performing cunnilingus (*Knights* 1282–9, *Wasps* 1280–4, *Peace* 883–5). Cleon's monstrous attributes include "the smell of a seal, the unwashed testicles of Lamia, a camel's anus" (and a character in *Wasps* is named Bdelykleon). Any sexual activity by old women is evidently both disgusting and funny.¹⁸

For orators, triggering disgust at an opponent is a valuable technique, especially since the Athenian courts did not impose rules of relevance. It is a conspicuous technique of Aeschines and Demosthenes against each other and of Demosthenes against both Philip of Macedon and Athenian opponents (Fisher 2017; Spatharas 2017). Demosthenes sometimes invites disgust by claiming that he cannot even express how loathsome the topic is: "the rest of those around him are bandits and flatterers and the type who when drunk do dances I shrink from naming to you" (*Olynthiac* 2.19). Pseudo-Andocides (4.22–3) narrates Alcibiades' purchase as a concubine of a woman enslaved from Melos, a city whose destruction he had advocated and carried out, in a way that invites revulsion.

An examination of some cases of Homeric disgust also reveals how characters' emotions do or do not map onto the audience's emotional responses. Odysseus tells Telemachus to kill the maids who had had sexual relations with the suitors with the sword, but Telemachus hangs them instead so that they will not have a "clean death" (*Odysseus* 22.462–4), because they "poured disgrace on my head and on my mother." The language of dirt and contamination indicates that Telemachus feels disgust. Is the external audience supposed to share that disgust? That Odysseus has specified how the women should be killed surely invites us to see Telemachus' command as understandable, but excessive, and so to distance ourselves from his revulsion. The following simile of the maids as birds caught in a snare, and the detail of their twitching feet, seems to invite a limited pity (*Odyssey* 22.468–73): they deserved to die, but not this way.

For Greeks (and universally), rotting corpses are a textbook example of what is disgusting (as in the famous anecdote of Leontius in Plato's *Republic*, 439e–440a).[19] Achilles is afraid that maggots will eat Patroclus' corpse, but his mother promises to keep flies away (*Iliad* 19.23–39). When Achilles in the *Iliad* abuses Hector's corpse, Apollo and Aphrodite miraculously preserve it. Hermes, reassuring Priam that there is a corpse available for ransom, describes vividly what has not happened: the body has not rotted, the maggots are not eating it, and his wounds are closed (*Iliad* 24.411–23). His language clearly evokes the disgust that the body would inspire otherwise. By forcing the audience to imagine with revulsion what Achilles has tried to do, the poet seems to invite moral disgust with Achilles, especially because it is clear that he wants dogs to eat the corpse because he cannot do so himself; cannibalism was disgusting for Greeks. Yet when Apollo complains to the gods of their toleration of Achilles' behavior, although he vigorously appeals to the norms Achilles is violating—he lacks pity and *aidôs*, and his mental state is wild, like a lion's—Apollo does not try to make the gods feel disgust. He threatens *nemesis* of the gods collectively against Achilles. He obviously feels *nemesis* already, and probably disgust. Hera's reply, as the ancient exegetical commentary notes (Scholion bT on 24.22), although she is angry, defends Achilles' honor, not his behavior. The emotional response of an audience must be complicated: Achilles is the protagonist, the focus of audience sympathy. Yet Apollo is clearly right to object to his behavior; somehow the audience, despite their disgust, must avoid being completely alienated from the character.

In Latin literature, disgust (*fastidium*) is almost always bound up with the body. Someone feeling disgust recoils, wanting to distance him- or herself from the source of offence. As in Greek, disgust tends to show up in invective and lower genres, texts in which a speaker tries to alienate someone for behavior that is repellent or taboo (Richlin 1992; Tatum 2007). We also find descriptions of disgust that seem to be focused more on readers than on internal characters, where the aim is to engage the audience through a mix of fascination and revulsion.

A common trigger for disgust is smell, a topic that comes up naturally in epigram and oratory.[20] Both men and women are targets. Rufus has armpits that smell like "rank goat"; that's the reason, Catullus informs him, no girl will sleep with him (poem 69). In a play by the comic playwright Plautus, one of the Menaechmus twins wants to offer his wife's cloak to his mistress as a present, but checks first with the parasite Peniculus to see how it smells. Peniculus agrees to smell only the top, not the bottom, which he says tends to have an odor that "defiles the nose and cannot be washed away" (*nasum sprucatur odore illutili*, *Menaechmi* 167–8). Disgust causes repugnance as well as a fear of being tainted through contact. An epigram by Martial targets Postumus' smell. This time it is a good scent—his kisses are perfumed with myrrh—but this is suspect, too, since it suggests a cover-up (2.12). Causing disgust is inescapable for some of the characters in Martial's poems. Bad breath is particularly offensive, since it almost always signifies oral sex, a common target of ancient invective. In Catullus 97, the speaker says it makes no difference whether you smell Aemilius' mouth or his ass; the latter is in fact cleaner. A man in another one of Martial's epigrams blows on a burning hot tart to cool it; in the process, Martial says, it turns to shit (*merda fuit*, 3.17.6). Disgust caused by smell results in a desire for physical distance, but also reveals the speaker's superiority and cleverness. In expressing their repugnance for certain smells or behaviors, Peniculus and the speakers in Catullus' and Martial's epigrams reveal their powers of discernment and invite the reader to identify with them.[21]

Incest also arouses disgust. Catullus accuses Gellius of sleeping with wife and sister in a series of poems (88–91). He also comments on rumors of an incestuous relationship between Clodius and Clodia (most likely Lesbia, his own mistress); Cicero makes the same insinuations in the *Pro Caelio* (14). The taboo nature of incest ensures the reader's repugnance. Ovid tells several stories of incestuous desire in the *Metamorphoses*, less to expose anyone (his characters are mythical) than to explore perverse desire. Orpheus narrates the story of Myrrha's passion for her father Cinyras (*Metamorphoses* 10.298–355), consummated through the aid of a nurse. He begins by labeling her as a negative example for his readers (10.298–303), though this could of course provoke curiosity more than fear.[22] Book 9 contains the tale of Byblis' incestuous love for her twin brother (*Metamorphoses* 9.439–594), also introduced as a cautionary tale for other girls. When Byblis' brother reads her letter confessing her desire, he becomes angry and violent, even threatening the life of the servant who carried the letter. His physical response makes clear his disgust. Yet an even more violent story of incest, the tale of Procne and Philomela (6.401–674), was often imitated by later writers, suggesting something of the hold this kind of narrative could have.[23]

Corpses cause disgust but also fascination in the Latin tradition. Literature of the Neronian period is particularly rich in this regard.[24] In one example from the *Bellum Civile*, Lucan gives a drawn-out description of Pompey's death and decapitation, replete with gory details about sawing through the neck and removing the brains (8.663–872). By comparison, Virgil had devoted only one and a half lines to describe the decapitation of Priam (*Aeneid* 2.557–78). Pompey's murder has witnesses, including his wife Cornelia who, the narrator tells us, could not help but watch the murder. Yet it is really the reader whom Lucan aims to disgust, as he makes sure that we, too, are spectators at every step of the violation. A second quotation from the *Bellum Civile* captures something possibly more worthy of disgust, one of the lurid rites carried out by the witch Erictho in the graveyard (6.564–9):

> Often, even at a kinsman's funeral, the hideous Thessalian
> bends over well-loved limbs and, while planting kisses, mutilates
> the head and with her teeth she opens up the tight-closed
> mouth and, biting off the tip of tongue which sticks
> to parched throat, pours mumbles into icy lips
> and sends a secret outrage to the Stygian shades.
>
> —trans. S. Braund

Here not only is the body mutilated, but it is simultaneously eroticized, doubling the horror of the scene.[25] Lucan balances the risk of alienating his readers with the belief that at least some of them will not be able to look away.

Invective, both in oratory and in epigram and satire, abounds in its portrayal of the disgusting, often defined through opposition to Roman ideas of moderation and civic duty. So Cicero paints a picture of Marc Antony in the *Philippics* as drunk, neglectful of laws and duties, and running his house like a brothel (see, e.g., 2.5–6). Elsewhere Cicero targets Piso, who is accused of engaging in banquets with Gabinius so wild they resembled the feast of the Lapiths and Centaurs, a *topos* in ancient literature for ill-fated celebrations.[26] Cicero accuses him of not acting like a freeman, of going to parties at Gabinius' house with naked dancing, singing, and cymbals, concluding the passage by reporting that "no one is able say whether Piso drank or vomited or excreted more" (*In Pisonem* 22). Here it is the accumulation of indecent acts and the absolute excess with which Piso pursues them that arouses feelings of scorn and disgust.[27]

We read about another dinner party gone wrong in Horace's *Satires*, though it is considerably tamer and told as if a miniature comedy (*Satires* 2.8). Here it is not so much the food that is excessive, but the host's pretentious lectures about each dish he brings out. When a tapestry falls down and spreads black dust onto the fish course (lines 54–6), it seems like just punishment, and unappetizing enough to bring an end to the dinner. Yet the host carries on until finally the guests run off in disgust; the food has been ruined by the talk, which is compared to the breath of the witch Canidia (*Satires* 2.8.93–6). This example captures many of the effects of disgust we have already seen: the desire to keep one's distance, the fears about contamination, and at the same time, the entertaining and sometimes irresistible qualities of disgust.

In contrast, wonder in classical literature has very little to do with man or the body.[28] A *thauma*, a "wonder," or something "wonderful"—that is, an event, action, or object significantly outside everyday experience—arouses the corresponding emotion, and nothing blocks it. In epic, divine epiphanies usually cause wonder (*thambos*).[29] Wonder blends into related feelings like awe, *sebas*. In Latin, forms of the verb *miror* express wonder, which can also be conveyed by *incredibilis* or *monstrum*; the latter is derived from both *monere*, to warn, and *monstrare*, to show, and signals something that inspires fear as well as awe.[30] The experience of wonder is not entirely passive: often the one who feels it desires to understand more about what they have seen.

For this reason, Plato has Socrates say that "this emotion, wondering, is very characteristic of a philosopher" (*Theatetus* 155d). Wonder for Aristotle, too, lies at the origin of philosophy (*Metaphysics* 1, 982b12–13), and he seems to regard arousing wonder as a desirable literary goal.[31] At *Poetics* 1460a11–14, epic has the advantage over tragedy that it is easier to present wonderful irrationalities. Herodotus defines his purpose as ensuring that "great and wonderful deeds" do not lack glory (1.1.0). An extensive body of ancient literature collected wonders (called by moderns "paradoxography"); the "Marvelous Stories" of Antigonus of Carystus draws from the extant pseudo-Aristotelian "On Marvelous Things Heard" and Callimachus' lost book "Wonders" (Priestley 2013: 75–108). Wonders were central to much ethnography. Since wonder is aroused precisely by what is not frequent in everyday life, it is a particularly literary pleasure. Literature celebrated both natural and artistic wonders; certain works of art, like Myron's cow and the Aphrodite of Cnidus (see Fig. 6.3), became ongoing literary themes.[32]

FIGURE 6.3: Aphrodite of Knidos, Roman copy from the end of first century BCE of a fourth-century BCE Greek original by Praxiteles.

In discussions of literary response, *thauma*-language is often replaced by *ekplêxis*, "amazement," and wonder can be ambivalent or even negative, because it was thought to impede rational judgment. As early as Aristophanes' *Frogs*, Euripides accuses Aeschylus of arousing *ekplêxis* in his audiences, so that they were unable to evaluate his plays critically (*Frogs* 959–63). So in the same passage in which Polybius criticizes Phylarchus for inappropriately arousing pity, he says that the writer of history "should not astound [*ekplêttein*] by wonder-mongering." The treatise *On the Sublime* concerns precisely how to achieve this effect, but simultaneously points to its disturbing side:

> For what is extraordinary brings its auditors not to persuasion, but to entrancement. For the wonderful that brings amazement [*ekplêxis*] is everywhere more powerful than the persuasive or delightful, since the persuasive is mostly in our control, but that, by applying domination and irresistible force, overwhelms every auditor.

The Homeric scholia, although they stress Homer's suspensefulness and immediacy, only occasionally attribute amazement to Homer, as at *Iliad* 24.630 and 15.695 (Nünlist 2009: 144–5; Hillgruber 1994: 93–4). It is, however, always a positive quality when it appears. The ancient commentary (Scholion) on *Iliad* 18.377b, commenting on the formulaic expression "a wonder [*thauma*] to behold," says that Homer's account is more credible because the poet admits that he is introducing "things that are wonderful and cause amazement" (θαυμαστὰ . . . καὶ ἐκπλήττοντα).

Nature is full of *mirabilia*. When Scipio contemplates the cosmos in his dream at the end of Cicero's *De re publica*, he marvels at the movement of the stars and planets (*omnia mihi contemplanti praeclara cetera et mirabilia videbantur*, 16, and *Haec ego admirans*, 19).[33] In a letter to Licinius Sura, Pliny the Younger tells his friend about the remarkable nature of a nearby spring (*huius mira natura*, 4.30.2), which "fills and empties three times a day with a fixed increase and decrease of water." The letter goes on to ask a series of questions about how this is possible; Pliny is not simply amazed, but eager to understand the natural processes at work. Another letter describes Lake Vadimo and its incredible properties (*simul quaedam incredibilia narrantur*, 8.20.3): among other things, it is perfectly circular, has special healing properties, and most spectacular of all, has a number of floating islands which can join together to increase or decrease the size of the lake (Beagon 2007). Here we see not questions but simply the pleasure of sharing something wondrous with others.

The unnatural or the paradoxical can trigger awe. Daedalus and Icarus build wings to escape from the labyrinth in Crete (Ovid, *Metamorphoses* 8.183–235). People below happen to look up and see them in flight, a sight that stops them in their tracks (*obstipuit*, 219); they conclude that the two figures must be gods (220).[34] The Egyptian ritual of the *bugonia* in which bees generate spontaneously out of the carcass of a cow is a special source of mystery and wonder. Virgil describes it in *Georgics* Book 4, a book full of miraculous things, including Aristaeus' descent under water to visit his mother, the nymph Cyrene, and his capture of Proteus, the shape-shifter. But the *bugonia* is particularly astonishing because of its paradoxical nature and the emergence of life from death (4.554–8).[35] While the practice resembles animal sacrifice in certain respects, Virgil combines sacrifice with something almost mystical.[36]

Omens, prophecies, and portents indicating the future show up in all genres of Roman literature.[37] While useful for literary foreshadowing, they nonetheless bring an element of the marvelous to a narrative. In Suetonius' *Life of Caesar*, the fateful decision to cross the Rubicon is confirmed by an apparition in which a remarkable man (*quidam eximia magnitudine et forma*, 32) picks up a trumpet and sounds the battle cry. When Anchises, father of Aeneas, refuses to leave Troy in *Aeneid* 2, the sight of flames on top of his grandson's head (2.682–4) persuades him to go, though he requests one more sign from Jupiter as confirmation. This is granted first with thunder and then a spectacular comet lighting up the sky (2.694–8).[38]

We see a literary dimension to wonder in the Roman novels by Petronius and Apuleius, where marvels are not isolated events: both writers dazzle the reader with an unending stream of fantastical adventures and dangerous encounters. In recounting Trimalchio's feast in the *Satyricon*, Encolpius describes the lavish and decadent dishes of food, inventive storytelling, and bizarre behavior that took place; both narrator and reader experience a mixture of wonder, amusement, and disgust, and in the end Encolpius barely escapes alive.[39] Fellini's film powerfully brings out this aspect of the novel both in this episode and elsewhere, in a sequence images at once surprising, fascinating, and repellent (see Fig. 6.4). *The Golden Ass* includes stories of witches, ghosts, and the tale of Cupid and Psyche, and towards the end in Book 11, the marvelous return of Lucius, transformed into an ass in Book 3, to human form (11.12–13).[40] But the narrators' naivety and gullibility are

FIGURE 6.4: Trimalchio's dinner, in *Satyricon* by Federico Fellini.

themselves cues to the wonder of these stories. Throughout the *Satyricon*, Encolpius wonders, marvels, even chokes in amazement. Lucius is *curiosus*, both curious and meddlesome in a way that points to his puzzlement and desire to know more.[41] Whatever our own more critical distance, these impressionistic narrators enhance our pleasure in reading their wondrous tales.[42]

CHAPTER SEVEN

In Private: The Individual and the Domestic Community

LIN FOXHALL

INTRODUCTION

The close relationships, and usually, physical proximity, of household and family life offer a breeding ground for a range of strong emotional engagements, encounters, and ties in most cultures. The Greek and Roman worlds are no exception, although the emotional relationships of private life are played out in ways specific to those cultures.

Within a household or family, status, gender, and age must have channeled the emotional content of many relationships. Cultural values about how particular kinds of relationships "ought" to work, ideals about how people in particular roles "ought" to feel or behave towards each other, or how certain kinds of people in relation to oneself "ought" to be treated or regarded must all have been important in constructing and shaping the emotional content of relationships, regardless of how they might be performed in reality. As will become evident, these factors certainly shape the expression of emotions in private life. But beyond this, purely personal and idiosyncratic aspects of individuals' relationships colored and charged the emotions which became entangled in the accumulated baggage of day-to-day encounters over time, however hard these are to access.

The routines and conventions of living in a family create situations susceptible to particular kinds of emotions. Love (in the senses of both affection/attachment and sexual desire), anger, hate, jealousy, worry and fear, grief and happiness all come to mind. Occasionally we get glimpses of this. Andocides' hostile account of the chaotic household of Callias portrays it as tumultuous and chaotic, awash with lust and anger (1.124–7):

> Callias married a daughter of Ischomachus; but he had not been living with her a year before he made her mother his mistress. Was ever a man so utterly without shame? He was the priest of the Mother and the Daughter; yet he lived with mother and daughter and kept them both in his house together.
>
> The thought of the Two Goddesses may not have awoken any shame or fear in Callias; but the daughter of Ischomachus thought death better than an existence where such things went on before her very eyes. She tried to hang herself: but was stopped in the act. Then, when she recovered, she ran away from home; the mother drove out the daughter. Finally Callias grew tired of the mother as well, and drove her out in her

turn. She then said she was pregnant by him; but when she gave birth to a son, Callias denied that the child was his. At that, the woman's relatives came to the altar at the Apatouria with the child and a victim for sacrifice, and told Callias to begin the rites. He asked whose child it was. "The child of Callias, son of Hipponicus," they replied. "But I am he." "Yes, and the child is yours." Callias took hold of the altar and swore that the only son he had or had ever had was Hipponicus, and the mother was Glaucon's daughter. If that was not the truth, he prayed that he and his house might perish from the earth—as they surely will.

Now some time afterwards, gentlemen, he fell in love with the abandoned old hag once more and welcomed her back into his house, while he presented the boy, a grown lad by this time, to the Kerykes, asserting that he was his own son.

In contrast, Chrysilla, the badly behaved mother of Callias' wife, was portrayed very differently by Xenophon in his treatise on household management (*Oeconomicus*), as the archetypal virtuous young bride of Ischomachus and a willing partner subordinate to her husband in the ideal household (Harvey 1984; Ogden 1996: 74–5).

These conflicting representations exemplify how selective is the evidence for emotions in the written record. Literary and other formal textual traditions usually supply more information about cultural values and ideals (or their antitheses) than about real behaviors, and it is not always clear how widely some of these values were held. Certain voices, particularly those of women, children, and slaves, are muted. In the example above, we have no idea what Chrysilla or her daughter actually felt or thought. Rarely do formal or literary texts offer much direct or deep insight into emotional feelings and behaviors within, or even between, households, although they can provide broader contexts for understanding other kinds of evidence.

However, emotions can stimulate actions. People have emotional associations and attachments to places and objects. Emotions and their behavioral outcomes can be played out in less formal texts and in the uses of space and material culture in ways that enable us to see more clearly or to infer the feelings that led to these actions, although the evidence is not always watertight or unproblematic.

This chapter will explore the emotions of domestic life through a series of case studies ranging across the Greek and Roman worlds. Although some themes persist throughout the classical tradition, often with variations, over the whole chronological, spatial, and cultural range of classical antiquity, it is impossible to generalize about exactly when and how emotion featured in domestic relationships. The approach adopted will go beyond a focus on specific words for emotions (covered elsewhere in this volume), and beyond the ideals, to focus on examples where we can see (or think we can see) feelings and their outcomes in action.

FAMILIAL AFFECTION

Conjugal and familial affection and concord is celebrated and valued throughout the classical literary tradition. In the Homeric *Odyssey* (6.180–5), Odysseus, washed up on the shore of Scheria, asks Nausicaa, daughter of the king, if she can loan him some clothing and says to her:

> And then, may the gods give you everything that your heart longs for;
> may they grant you a husband and a house and sweet agreement [*homophrosunē*]
> in all things, for nothing is better than this, more steadfast

than when two people, a man and his wife, keep a harmonious [*homophroneonte*] household; a thing that brings much distress to the people that hate them and pleasure to their well-wishers, and for them the best reputation.

Much later, in the late first–early second century CE, the Roman philosopher Plutarch poignantly expressed the ties of familial affection (*Consolation to his Wife*, Moralia 608C) when he wrote to his wife concerning their grief over the death of their young daughter:

[You know] that this child was especially loved [ἀγπητὸν διαφερόντως], because she was the daughter you desired after bearing four sons and because she offered me the opportunity to bestow your name on her . . .

Many other examples of such ideals surrounding loving relationships between family members could be cited, despite the arguments that have sometimes been made that, for example, young children were "less loved" because of high infant mortality (Sigismund Nielsen 1997: 198–204; Golden 1988) or that arranged marriages precluded love relationships (Keuls 1985: 98–100). We should have no doubt that affection was valued as central to domestic life and relationships, though it can be harder to see in practice.

The literary tradition privileges some relationships over others. For example, affection and discord between fathers and sons or fathers and daughters are more fully documented than between mothers and daughters (for Rome, Hallett 1984; Dixon 1988: 210–11; Cantarella 2003). However, underplayed affective relationships can sometimes be traced in other ways. In Greek culture, relationships between mothers and daughters are valorized mythologically in the story of the separation and reunification of Demeter and Kore (Persephone), as presented, for example, in the *Homeric Hymn to Demeter* (Foley 1994). This translates into the celebration of the Thesmophoria in honor of the Two Goddesses (Demeter and Kore) by women in communities all over the Greek world. In many places, women came together and celebrated in family groups, so that daughters separated from their mothers by marriage might sometimes be reunited (Clinton 1996; Foxhall 2013: 145–6).

Ties between closely related women, almost certainly including mothers and daughters, can be picked up in the material cultural record. Loom weights, in the Greek world tools for weaving symbolically and practically associated with women, are regularly marked as personal possessions. These marks include graffiti, stamp seals (usually from rings), impressions of jewelry and other personal objects, and finger marks. When houses were abandoned, women generally seem to have taken most of their loom weights with them, suggesting that though they were not valuable, these were valued. Most of the marks are unique, but sometimes it is possible to see these marked loom weights moving through time and space in ways that suggest that they have been handed down from mothers to daughters. These objects, then, became a material reification of the affective relationships between women of the same family. So, the ideals of the love between mothers and daughters expressed in myth and literature can also be seen on the ground, as objects entangled with those very relationships and with the work of making cloth together as groups of related women (Foxhall 2012).

Examples of loom weights significantly older than the use context in which they were found, appear at a number of sites, including Athens and Corinth (Foxhall 2011: 547; Davidson et al. 1943: 84, no. 56; Davidson 1952: 152). At Metaponto, one of the two loom weights discovered in the excavated Fattoria Fabrizio farmhouse was found on a floor with material of the late fourth–early third century BCE. It may possibly have fallen from a shelf (see Fig. 7.1a). However, the graffito (IN) cannot be later than the early fifth century BCE, and the curved iota may suggest that whoever incised it came from further south in Italy (see Fig. 7.1b; Foxhall 2014). It seems most likely that this object arrived with a woman who brought it with her around two centuries earlier, and was passed down the family who dwelt in this house, almost certainly along female lines.

Affection and love for household members who are not kin also feature in our evidence. Wet nurses and nannies (*titthai*) appear regularly as objects of affection in Greek and Roman texts. Most seem to have been of slave or freed status (Demosthenes 47), although free women in straitened circumstances also took on these roles (Demosthenes 57). Demosthenes 47 is a courtroom speech delivered by a man whose household was invaded, he claims, by aggressive debt collectors while he was out. We first meet the nurse as she is seated at lunch with the wife and children of the family, at the moment when the debt collectors arrive. She had first entered the household when the speaker was a baby, as his wet nurse, and stayed on as nanny to the children. When her owner (the father of the speaker) died, she was manumitted along with another, male slave and the two of them set up house together as a "married" couple, suggesting that they were already in a conjugal relationship before manumission. This couple, now freed, would have had metic (resident alien) status, but were not citizens. It is likely that they were foreign in origin

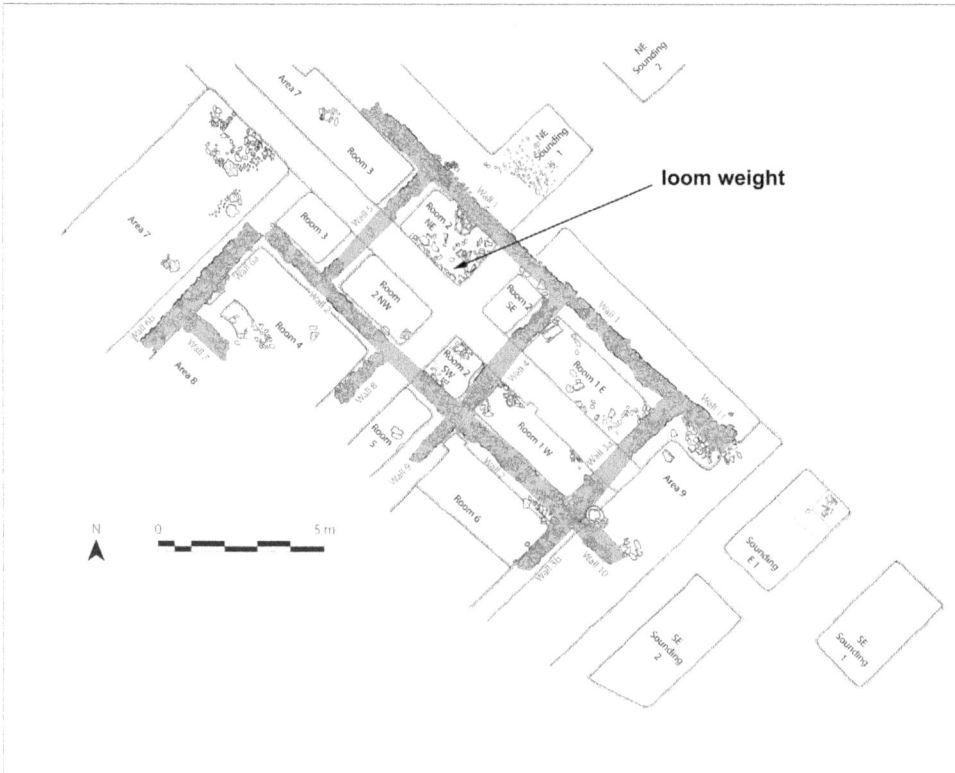

FIGURE 7.1a: Fattoria Fabrizio farmhouse in the Metaponto countryside, fourth–third century BCE.

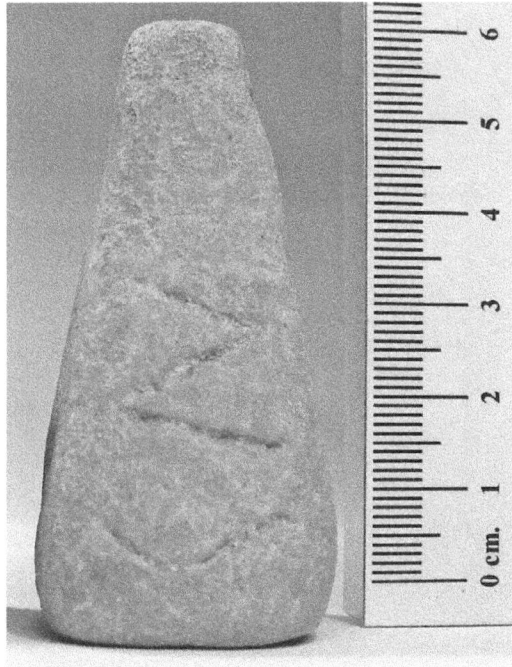

FIGURE 7.1b: Pyramidal loom weight inscribed, late sixth–early fifth century BCE.

and were certainly non-Athenian. When the man of this freed couple died, the nanny, now elderly, came back to live in the household of her former charge, now with a wife and family of his own. In Athens freed slaves normally retained ties to their former owners. It is likely that she had nowhere else to go, and no kin of her own in Athens. However, she was treated as a family member, at least as represented in this speech. Not only was she eating with them, but when she was seriously injured while trying to protect the family valuables, the husband called in his own doctor to treat her.

Non-literary source material supports this picture of affection for nurses and nannies. There are twelve tombs of nurses surviving from fourth-century Athens. Kosmopoulou (2001: 289, 304–5) has shown that the nurses are consistently depicted as wearing the chiton and mantle, like citizen women, suggesting "respectability," and they are generally not represented using "slave" conventions that sometimes appear in this artistic genre (short hair, small stature), even though many were plainly of freed or slave status. Epitaphs identify these women as *titthai* (sing. *titthê*), but their status is not explicitly identified in the inscriptions, though it is sometimes relatively clear from their names. But they are regularly praised as *chrêstê* ("good"), a term not used on Attic grave stelae for women of citizen status (Kosmopoulou 2001: 290–1). This maps nicely onto the representation of the elderly nanny in Demosthenes 47, though we should not assume that all nannies were regarded so affectionately.

The grave monument of Phanostrate (Kosmopoulou 2001: 299–300) (see Fig. 7.2), who is identified in the epitaph as "midwife" (*maia*) and "doctor" (*iatros*), presents another interesting scenario. She too is dressed as a "respectable" Athenian woman, and only the epitaph makes clear her "job." However, it seems likely that Antiphile (also

FIGURE 7.2: Grave stele of Phanostrate, late fourth century BCE.

represented on the stele) erected the monument, and there is no indication that she is a relative of Phanostrate. In fact, it seems more likely that she is not and that the erection of the stele was an act of affection towards an unrelated, and possibly lower-status, woman who lived in Antiphile's household.

These tombs reflect not the status of the women, but the status of the families burying them. All of them, like the old nurse in Demosthenes 47, have been taken in by families other than their own. What has made these women "respectable," and clearly loved, is precisely that they have been absorbed, closely and deeply, into the affective networks of other people's households. What we see in these monuments is the outcome of the emotional response to their loss. So it is not that nursing was an honorable or respectable profession in itself (Brock 1994: 337, 339; Kosmopoulou 2001: 305), but that these individuals became honored and respected by a particular family, who commemorated them as "part of the family."

Roman sources similarly depict nurses as much loved by the families in which they worked. Many of these women, too, were of slave or freed status, working in the homes of much wealthier families. Kampen (1981: 109–10) noted over sixty tombstones for nurses in Rome alone, and there are more documented from other parts of the empire.

One of the letters of Pliny the Younger (3.1) concerns the management of "a little field" that he left to his former nurse to provide an income for her. This must have been quite a generous pension, as it was valued at 100,000 sesterces. In another of his letters (Pliny, *Epistle* 8.16), Pliny represents himself as sentimental and affectionate towards his slaves, freeing them before death if possible and allowing them to leave their possessions to others within the household, and grieving when they die, although it is not at all clear that the slaves would have viewed Pliny's behavior in the same way.

HUSBANDS AND WIVES: LOVE, DESIRE, AND JEALOUSY

Marriages in the Greek and Roman world were arranged by families, and there were constraints on the choice of a marital partner, though to a much lesser extent for men than for women. Most discussions of Greek marriage skirt the topic of love to focus on its legal, political, and economic aspects (Patterson 1998: 108–14; Pomeroy 1997: 33–6; "love" is not in the index of either of these works). Indeed, Odysseus' blessing on meeting Nausicaa, quoted above, expresses precisely this ideal. In contrast, Treggiari's still masterful and comprehensive account of Roman marriage devotes a chapter to love between spouses (Treggiari 1991: 229–61). Foucault (1986: 78–9) saw a significant change in the role of love (and sexual desire) in marriage between classical Greece and the Roman Principate. But this observation may reflect a change in the nature of our source material, and the degree to which love and desire were publicly celebrated as elements of marriage, more than any genuine indication that these emotions were absent from marriage in earlier periods (Stafford 2013: 200–5).

Although the topic of love and desire in marriage does indeed feature more strongly in Latin than in Greek literary texts, Treggiari's discussion draws heavily on the evidence of epitaphs inscribed on tomb monuments. While these inscriptions are formalized and formulaic, expressing conventional and idealized sentiments about the deceased, their virtues, and their relationship to the partner left behind, Treggiari (1991: 246–7) points out that a number of them go beyond the conventional to express their love for the deceased partner in very specific and individual ways:

> Laughter and life I always delighted in, in the company of my dear friends, but such a life after the death of my chaste lady Valeria I did not find; while I could I had an enjoyable life with my holy wife.
> —CIL 8.7156; Treggiari 1991: 246

Curse tablets and magic spells provide another glimpse of marital (and other) emotions, revealing "the unspoken resentments that smouldered beneath the surfaces" (Eidinow 2007: 154). Curses were often written on small lead tablets, sometimes rolled up or folded then pierced with a nail. Many were placed in graves as secondary deposits, that is, after the corpse had already been buried, though some are found in houses and sanctuaries. Like epitaphs, the language of Greek and Latin curses has its own formulae and conventions, but the emotional turmoil of the perpetrator sometimes comes through strongly. The deposition process also suggests real desperation on the part of the person enacting the curse: going to a dark cemetery and digging up a recent grave likely to contain a particularly vengeful spirit in the dead of night must have taken some determination and courage.

The text below is a good example of someone suffering unrequited or unattainable love. It was found in a cemetery east of the agora in Pella. It had been placed in a grave dating to 380–350 BCE, next to the upper part of the right thighbone of the corpse (Eidinow 2007: 452–3; Voutiras 1998).

> Of Thetima and Dionysophon the ritual wedding and marriage I bind by a written spell, as well as [the marriage] of all other women [to him], both widows and maidens, but above all of Thetima; and I entrust [this spell] to Macron and to the *daimones*. And were I ever to unfold and read these words again after digging [the tablet] up, only then should Dionysophon marry, not before. Let him not marry any other woman but me, but let me grow old by the side of Dionysophon and no one else. I implore you have pity for [Phila?] dear *daimones*, [for I am indeed bereft?] of all my dear ones and abandoned. But please keep this [piece of writing] for my sake so that these events do not happen and wretched Thetima perishes miserably. [gap in text] but let me become happy and blessed. [gap in text]

Producing (or commissioning) this tablet and placing it in the grave were surely not undertaken casually but must have been the outcome of a highly charged emotional situation. The strength of feeling in the text and its genuineness are undeniable.

But even with curses there are limits. In a number of instances the curser directs his or her ire at an entire household (e.g., Eidinow 2007: 368 (DTA77), Attic, third century BCE). This is interesting as it recalls in reverse the sentiment expressed from Homer onward that a harmonious household is the best defense against enemies. Correspondingly, there are no clear instances I have been able to find of individuals cursing a close relative or someone indicated as part of the same household (see also a lead tablets from Knidos, Eidinow 2007: 388–9 (DT4), below). The woman in the example from Pella, above, directs her curse not at her husband but at the woman trying to take him away. Many curse tablets consist almost entirely of lists of names, with no indication of who they are or their relationship to the perpetrator, so we cannot be absolutely certain of this habit. But, it was almost certainly not appropriate in the conventions of cursing to direct maledictions at a person *named* as a close family member.

The use of other kinds of love magic, potions, and charms also indicates strong feelings resulting in desperate measures. Both in the literary record and in other kinds of less formal written documents these are stereotypically used by women on men. When love magic is used within the family, it is wives who use it on husbands, as Deianira does, in Sophocles' *Trachiniai*, when she attempts to lure her husband, Heracles, back to her and away from another woman, but accidentally kills him with a poisoned cloak (Wohl 2011: 51–60). But love potions and charms carry their own ambiguity, and the motives of the women who used them were often questioned—did they mean to charm or kill; were they spurred by love, fear of abandonment, or hate (Faraone 1999: 118)? Other versions of the story of Deianira present her murder of Heracles as intentional (Faraone 1999: 110–13). In reality, motives may have varied and could have been mixed. Two lead tablets from an assemblage of thirteen or fourteen found near a statue of Demeter in a sanctuary at Knidos, dating to the second–first century BCE (Eidinow 2007: 387–8 (DT1); Faraone 1999: 113–14; Eidinow 2007: 388–9 (DT4)) may present similar situations:

DT1
Side A

Antigone dedicates to Demeter, Persephone, Pluto and all the gods beside Demeter, both male and female. If I have given a potion to Asclapiadas or conceived in my spirit of doing anything bad to him, or have summoned a woman to the temple, giving her 3 half-*mnai*, so that she might take him from the living, let Antigone come to the temple before Demeter, burning and confess, and may Antigone not find Demeter merciful, but may she be tormented with great suffering. And if anyone say anything against me to Asclapiadas, if [anyone] brings forward [as a witness] against me a woman giving her coppers . . .

Side B

But let me go, innocent of any profanity, both into the baths, and under the same roof, and to the same table [as the person I am cursing].

DT4

Side A

I dedicate to Demeter and Persephone the man who spoke against me . . . that I made poisons for my husband. May he come to the temple of Demeter, burning, along with all his allies/family [people] and publicly confess, and may he not meet with mercy from Demeter and Persephone and the other gods with Demeter. But let me be innocent and free under the same roof, or whenever I have dealings with him in any way. I dedicate also the man who has written [accusations] against me or directed another man to accuse me. Do not let him find Demeter or Persephone or the gods with Demeter merciful, but let him burn and come before Demeter with his allies/family [people].

The first tablet (Eidinow 2007: 387–8 (DT1)) clearly involves an accusation of using love magic. It seems to be halfway between a curse and a judicial oath, where a defendant or a witness in a lawsuit swears to the truth of something before the gods. This example, however, is less formal than other judicial oaths we know, for instance, in Demosthenes 49.4–5, where the speaker gives an account of a woman who swears that the father of the speaker is also the father of her sons. Such oaths were taken very seriously. In this lead tablet, it is not clear that the woman even did the things of which she was accused, what the relationship between Antigone and Asclapiadas was, nor what precisely she felt. However, the final surviving lines of side A suggest that she did not want to be separated from or on bad terms with Asclapiadas.

The second tablet (Eidinow 2007: 388–9 (DT4)) is a proper curse directed at the man believed by the woman who deposited it to have falsely accused her of poisoning her husband. In this case there is no indication that love magic was a factor in the alleged poisoning. The accuser is not named, nor is it clear what relationship, if any, he bears to the instigator of the curse. However, it appears that she expects to encounter him regularly in her everyday life. If he is a relative, he is not named as such: it is possible that he was a relative of her husband, but if the marriage is now dissolved by death (and potentially a lawsuit has arisen from this accusation), it may be that she and her family do not consider him to be "family" at this point.

A fifth-century Athenian law court speech, Antiphon 1 (Wohl 2011; Faraone 1999: 114–16) also presents the outcome of a love potion that went wrong. In this speech, a range of family rivalries and tensions are exposed. The woman on trial was accused of the deliberate murder of her husband, and was his second wife. The son of the victim's first wife is making this speech as the prosecutor, and the woman is being defended by her own sons, the half-brothers of the speaker. The speaker's version of the story is that his father rented out a room in his house to a friend from overseas, who used it to lodge a slave concubine (*pallakê*) with whom he stayed when he was in Athens. According to the speaker, the second wife made friends with the concubine, and convinced her that as they were both being treated badly and their men were straying, they should take steps to entice them back. The concubine had allegedly been threatened with being sold to a brothel (Antiphon 1.14–15). The wife offered to obtain a love potion (*pharmakon*, "drug," "charm"), and when the two men were dining the concubine administered it (Antiphon 1.16–17). The husband died after an agonizing twenty days, while his lodger died instantly. The speaker claims that the second wife masterminded the plot because she intended all along to murder her husband and deceived the concubine that the *pharmakon* was a love potion (Antiphon 1.20). His half-brother mounting the defense seems to have claimed the poisoning was accidental (Antiphon 1.27).

The love charm gone wrong is a recurring theme across the classical literary tradition (Faraone 1999: 110–31). Its persistence suggests that for some women, hanging onto their men, whether husbands, lovers, patrons, or customers, may have driven them to take desperate measures. They may have been motivated by emotions beyond love, including jealousy, fear, and hate, or a combination of these. Equally, men, including the male writers in whose works these ideas were promulgated, undoubtedly overestimated the use of love charms by women through paranoia, fear, or worry that women were trying to hang onto, entice, manipulate, or control them. Wherever the realities may have lain, it is plain that love charms and magic became an emotionally charged theme because they were perceived as an extreme response to conflicting emotions in a personal relationship, frequently within a domestic setting, however often they may or may not have been deployed in reality.

LETTERS: AFFECTION, CONCERN, AND WORRY

It seems "natural" that family members should feel concern over each other's health and wellbeing and express worry or fear when something went wrong. In the classical literary tradition these concerns are most clearly manifest in letters. The tradition of published, "literary" letters is Roman, not Greek. Cicero's letters, particularly those to his close friend Atticus (also connected by marriage), are peppered with references to his family expressing affection and concern for their wellbeing or assuring Atticus that they are well.

> My darling Tullia is demanding your little present and calling on me as surety. I have made up my mind to repudiate sooner than pay up.
> —Cicero, *Letters to Atticus* 1.8.3

> We are expecting Quintus [Cicero's brother, married to Atticus' sister] back any day. Terentia has a bad attack of rheumatism. She is very fond of you and of your sister and mother, and sends her best love, as does my darling little Tullia. Take care of yourself and your affection for me; and be sure of my brotherly affection in return.
> —Cicero, *Letters to Atticus* 1.5.8

Roman literary letters were clearly published with an audience wider than the recipient in mind. It is not surprising that expressions of emotion are conventionalized. Pliny's letters to Calpurnia generally express how much he misses her (Pliny, *Epistle* 6.7; 7.5).

When she was away from home recovering from illness (possibly in the aftermath of a miscarriage), he expresses his worries in his letter to her (Pliny, *Epistle* 4.4.3–5):

> Indeed, I should worry when you are away even if you were well, for there are always anxious moments without news of anyone one loves dearly, and, as things are, I have the thought of your health as well as your absence to alarm me with fluctuating doubts and fears. I am full of forebodings of every imaginable disaster, and like all nervous people dwell most on what I pray fervently will not happen. So do please think of my anxiety and write to me once or even twice a day—I shall worry less while I am reading your letters, but my fears will return as soon as I have finished them.

Many personal, private letters written on papyrus survive in Egypt, dating between the third century BCE and the sixth century CE. Although never intended for publication, these letters are mostly written quite formally and express affection, concern, and other emotions in conventionalized terms. A second-century CE example of a young soldier serving in the Roman army writing home to his mother (Hunt and Edgar 1932: no. 111, 302–5) starts:

> Apollinarius to Taesis, his mother and lady, many greetings. Before all I pray for your health. I myself am well and make supplication for you before the gods of this place.

After explaining that he arrived in Rome safely and where he will be posted he goes on to say:

> I beg you then, mother, look after yourself and do not worry about me; for I have come to a fine place. Please write me a letter about your welfare and that of my brothers and of all your folk. And whenever I find a messenger I will write to you; never will I be slow to write. Many salutations to my brothers and Apollinarius and his children and Caralas and his children. I salute Ptolemaeus and Ptolemais and her children and Heraclous and her children. I have sent you by Euctemon a portrait of myself.

In many of these letters formal and conventionalized language expresses affection that appears to be entirely genuine. In some cases this may be because the letters were written by professional scribes, not by the senders themselves. However, we know that many people wrote their own letters, which suggests that, as in many epistolary traditions before the age of emails and texts, even very personal letters were regularly framed in the formal and conventional language deemed suitable for letters regardless of the depth of emotion felt by the writer.

Occasionally, however, we can literally see the personal touch, as in the birthday party invitation preserved on a wooden tablet (Vindolanda Tablet 291, http://vindolanda.csad.ox.ac.uk/TVII–291, accessed March 17, 2018) written by Claudia Severa to her friend Sulpicia Lepidina:

> [1st hand] Claudia Severa to her Lepidina greetings. On 11 September, sister, for the day of the celebration of my birthday, I give you a warm invitation to make sure that you come to us, to make the day more enjoyable for me by your arrival, if you are present [?]. Give my greetings to your Cerialis. My Aelius and my little son send him [?] their greetings. [2nd hand] I shall expect you, sister. Farewell, sister, my dearest soul, as I hope to prosper, and hail. [Back, 1st hand] To Sulpicia Lepidina, wife of Cerialis, from Severa.

The private letters from Vindolanda show that the conventions of private letter-writing and the sentiments expressed in them were shared across the Roman Empire and were not specific to Egypt. The recipient, Sulpicia Lepidina, was the wife of Flavius Cerialis, a Roman army officer of the equestrian order who served as the prefect of the Ninth Cohort of Batavians at the fort of Vindolanda on Hadrian's Wall in Britain around 97–102/3 CE. The sender, Claudia Severa, was the wife of Aelius Brocchus, the commander of another fort near Vindolanda. This is one of several personal letters between the two women that survive. Although they are not literally sisters, it is clear from the correspondence that they were intimate friends (Vindolanda Tablet 292, http://vindolanda.csad.ox.ac.uk/TVII–292, accessed March 17, 2018). This letter was written by two people. The first part, the greeting and the party invitation, and the address on the back were written by a scribe. However, at the end of the formal invitation, Claudia Severa added an affectionate personal note to her friend in her own handwriting. For two upper-class women living in military camps, probably far from home at the edges of the empire, it is easy to see why they valued their close friendship.

It is not surprising that emotion breaks through letter-writing conventions most strikingly when the writer was distressed, as in the example below.

> Apion to Didymus greeting. The instant you receive this letter of mine put off everything and come to me, for your sister is ill. And when you come, bring the white tunic of hers which is with you. Do not bring the turquoise one, but if you wish to sell it, sell it, or if you wish to let your daughter have it, do so. But do not neglect her in any sort, and do not worry your wife or the children. And when you come, come to Theogonis. I pray for your health.
> —Hunt and Edgar 1932: no. 135, 340–3, third century CE

Here the urgency comes through strongly. It is possible that the request for the white tunic suggests the writer believed the woman was dying. White was the proper color for funerary clothing, so that is why the blue one could be given away or sold.

Sometimes affection and concerns are expressed in ways that we would not expect, revealing qualitatively different attachments. In the example below, a husband writes to his wife expressing affection for his child and his wife, but for his unborn child he expresses interest only if it is a boy.

> Hilarion to his sister [actually, his wife] Alis very many greetings, likewise to my lady Berous and Apollonarion. Know that we are still in Alexandria. Do not be anxious; if they really go home, I will remain in Alexandria. I beg and entreat you, take care of the little one, and as soon as we receive our pay I will send it up to you. If by chance you bear a child, if it is a boy, let it be, if it is a girl, cast it out. You have said to Aphrodisias "Do not forget me." How can I forget you? I beg you then not to be anxious. The 29th year of Caesar, Pauni 23. [Addressed] Deliver to Alis from Hilarion.
> —Hunt and Edgar 1932: no. 105, 294–5, c. 1 BCE

APPEALING TO THE GODS: FEAR AND GRATITUDE

Another way in which we can see concern for the wellbeing of family members expressed is through prayers and gifts to the gods. In the letter below, the writer has asked someone who is almost certainly a family member, probably an uncle or a cousin, for help after a disastrous flood. The first thing he requests is that his kinsman give thanks to the gods for their survival. Such a reaction would have been normal in almost any part of the classical world in any period.

> Petesouchus son of Marres, cultivator at Kerkesephis, to Marres son of Petosiris [line missing] . . . and to his brother greeting. Know that our plain has been flooded and we have not so much as food for our cattle. Please therefore first of all to give thanks to the gods and secondly to save many lives by seeking out in the neighbourhood of your village five arourae of land for our maintenance, in order that we may thence obtain food for ourselves. If you do this, you will oblige me for all time. Goodbye . . .
> —Hunt and Edgar 1932: no. 102, 290–1, *c.* late second century BCE

Sometimes votives (objects left in sanctuaries indicating personal engagement or communications with the gods) can provide evidence of worry, concern, or gratitude on the part of the donor, although usually we do not know which, or the individual circumstances that prompted the gift. One example of this is the fourth-century BCE lists of clothing and textiles dedicated and deposited in the Temple of Artemis at Brauron in Attica (Linders 1972; Cleland 2005). The votive textiles themselves do not survive, but inventories inscribed on stone describe the items in some detail and give the names of the donors, although not the reasons for their dedication. All of the donors are women, but they were not necessarily depositing their own clothing. There are examples of many different kinds of garments, belts, hairnets, and headbands, including items of men's and children's clothing. Some garments are described as unfinished and there also seem to be dedications of loom warps, the "lengthwise" threads ready to set up for weaving (Cleland 2005: 24, lines 137–8), as well as unspun (?) wool and thread (wool: Cleland 2005: 16, 134, line 54; linen thread: Cleland 2005: 33, 143, line 245). Some items are described as "ragged," though whether this is because they were deposited as worn-out garments or had deteriorated because they had been in the sanctuary for a long time is impossible to determine. This dedicatory habit also appears elsewhere. For example, model textiles, clothing, and loom warps in the Sanctuary of Artemis Orthia near Sparta feature among the thousands of lead figurines (Dawkins 1929; Foxhall and Stears 1999: Fig. 5) (see Fig. 7.3).

Although it has been suggested that some of these dedications were thank-offerings for safe and successful childbirth (Lee 2015: 213), the wide range of offerings suggests that many different motivations may have stimulated these gifts. The dedication of items of men's and children's clothing seems most likely to have accompanied a request to the goddess for the recovery, safety, or wellbeing of a loved one, in most cases a close relative, or a thank-offering for the fulfillment of such deliverance. There is no reason why some of the women's clothing could not have been dedicated for the same reasons, on behalf of closely related women. And, of course, there are many possible personal motivations which we cannot know. The balance of probability is that a number of these dedications were actions undertaken as the outcome of worry, concern, or fear for a close family member. Some, indeed, may have been dedicated on behalf of people who had died. Euripides (*Iphigenia among the Taurians* 1462–7) mentions a shrine in the sanctuary at Brauron to Iphigeneia where the clothing of women who had died in childbirth was dedicated, but that clearly could not account for all of the clothing dedications listed in the inventories. As in the case of letters, discussed above, we are seeing the outcome of emotion channeled through an established behavioral, in this case ritual, convention.

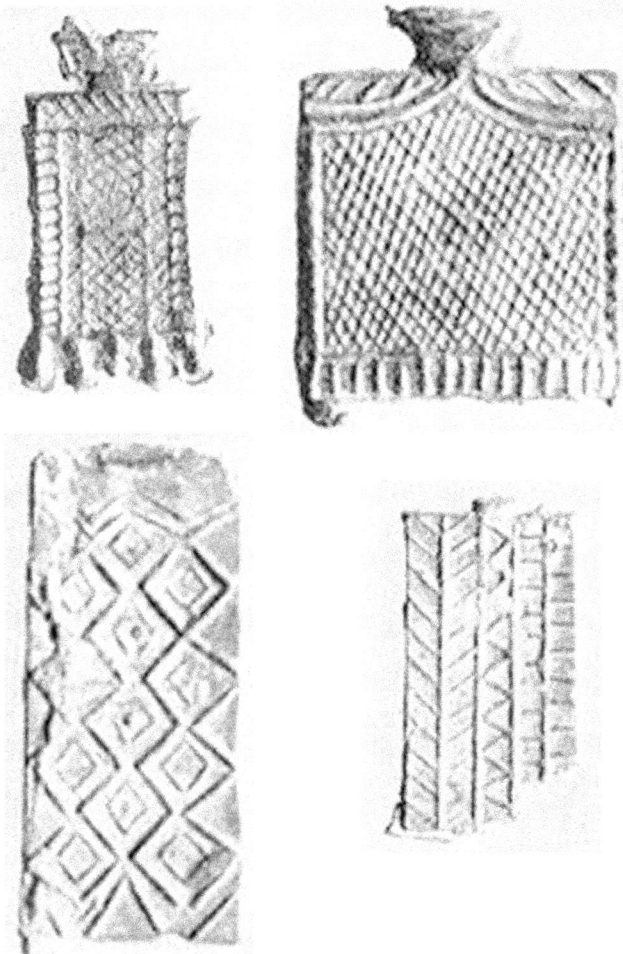

FIGURE 7.3: Model textiles in lead from the Sanctuary of Artemis Orthia, Sparta.

GRIEF AND CONDOLENCE

The commemoration of close and much-loved family members is an obvious setting for expressions of grief, especially in the case of those whose deaths were felt to be untimely. Greek traditions of funerary monuments generally focus less on young children than Roman ones, though there are some interesting exceptions. The famous stele of Ampharete (see Fig. 7.4), where the image appears to be a mother and child, is revealed by the inscription to commemorate the death of a grandmother and her grandchild. A number of Roman tombstones, often erected by parents of freed status, mark the tragic deaths of young children and celebrate their sweetness and the achievements of their short lives (Rawson 1997: 198–204; Sigismund Nielsen 1997).

Expressions of grief in literary sources on the deaths of children seem heartfelt and genuine (e.g., Cicero on the death of his adult daughter Tullia, *Letters to Atticus* 12),

FIGURE 7.4: Grave stele of Ampharete holding her grandchild.

but there is also a theme running through these expressions that such grief should be kept under control. Plutarch's *Consolation to his Wife*, cited above, is a good example (Plutarch, *Consolation* 2): "Only, O wife, at this sad moment, keep yourself, and me, calm. I know that I can get the measure of what has happened, but if I see you grieving to excess, that will hurt me more than the loss." Similar sentiments also appear in one of Pliny's letters (*Epistle* 4.2), where he derides Regulus for an excessive display of grief on the death of his son, "mourning with wild extravagance," and killing all of the boy's exotic pets and setting them around his funeral pyre (cf. Pliny, *Epistle* 8.16.5; Seneca, *Epistle* 63.1).

It is interesting to compare the contemplation and expression of grief on the death of a loved one in literary letters and similar texts with genuine letters of condolence on papyrus from Roman Egypt. Thirteen examples of such letters dating from the second to the sixth–seventh centuries CE survive (Chapa 1998: 17–18). Generally these letters seem to be written in situations when the writer is unable to be with the bereaved recipient, usually a close relative, in person (Chapa 1998: 30–2). Like other personal letters on papyrus, as discussed above, these letters, although expressing genuine and heartfelt emotions of sadness, loss, and worry for the bereaved, do so within conventionalized forms of expression (Chapa 1998: 49). As in the literary letters, excessive mourning and shows of grief are discouraged and the bereaved is encouraged to bear the loss "nobly" (*gennaiôs*):

> To her brother Neilos from Tasoucharion. I was distressed when I heard of the death of Taonnōphrios [his wife]. Bear up nobly, brother, for the sake of your children.
> —Chapa 1993: 66–7, no. 3; second–third century CE; BGU III 801 (P.Berol. inv. 8636), lines 1–7

The private letters, however, regularly express a degree of fatalism, that death is inevitable, unstoppable, and comes to us all (Chapa 1998: 34–5), that is absent for the most part in literary texts.

> Serenus to Antonia his mother. Fare well. When I heard, lady, about the death of the doctor, I was distressed. But that is the human condition, and indeed we also pursue this same path.
> —Chapa 1998: 108–9, no. 7, third century CE; (P.Ross. Georg. III 2, lines 1–4)

In Plutarch's *Consolation to his Wife*, we have an interesting convergence of literary text and private letter. Plutarch has adopted the structure, language, and some of the conventions of these private letters for this treatise, deliberately blurring the boundaries between private emotions and philosophical (and literary) deliberation. The contextual setting of the treatise is identical to the private letters: Plutarch is supposedly writing while away from home having heard of the death of their young daughter. Like Serenus, he greets his wife "fare well" (*eu prattein*). The normal greeting for opening letters was *chairein*, a word used for both "hello" and "goodbye" in ancient Greek, but carrying the underlying connotation, "be happy." It is understandable why this was not always felt to be appropriate for sympathy letters, hence the use in some cases of an alternative greeting, with the connotation of "bear up" (Chapa 1998: 24–5).

Plutarch does not include the fatalistic sentiments common in the papyrus letters that death is part of being human, nothing can be done, and we are all heading that way, perhaps because they conflicted with his philosophical views on the immortality of the soul. However, similarly to some of the papyrus letters (Chapa 1998: 37–8), Plutarch does take comfort that, in death, his little daughter will escape the sufferings of life, although Plutarch's take on this common sentiment is more philosophical and less fatalistic than the private letters.

> She has come to painlessness; she does not need to cause us pain. What ill have we from her, if she now knows no pain? Depravation of even great blessings loses its painfulness when the need is there no more.
> —Plutarch, *Consolation* 611 (9)

Compare Eudaimon writing to Hermodorus on the death of his daughter, expressing a more brutal sentiment: "Blessed is she who has escaped this wretched and toilsome life before its disasters arrive" (Chapa 1998: 118, no. 8, third–fourth century CE; SBXVIII 13946 (P.Vindob. inv. G 2713 +21703 + 23127)). Significantly, in this letter the writer also says to the recipient that he knows the bereaved father will bear it like a man, but he should encourage his wife not to indulge in excessive mourning, a core theme of Plutarch's treatise (cf. Seneca, *Epistle* 63.13). What these similarities suggest is that Plutarch was engaging with contemporary real and popular forms of expressing grief on the death of a loved one. Whether or not the treatise was an elaboration on a "real" letter is difficult to say, and does not really matter. Its perspective expresses his philosophical beliefs, but in form and to some extent content it echoes private expressions of grief.

FAMILY DISPUTES AND SIBLING RIVALRY: ANGER AND HATE

Tensions and quarrels within families entwined with feelings of anger and rivalry are sometimes portrayed in literary sources. Examples include marital disputes, the generational tensions between fathers and sons satirized in Aristophanes' *Clouds*, or the dispute over the patrimonial inheritance between Hesiod and his brother Perses memorialized in the *Works and Days*. While such sources enable us to see that such difficulties in family relationships regularly existed, it is much harder to see emotions in action in these kinds of situations. Cicero's letters to Atticus document in almost soap-opera detail the marital troubles between Cicero's brother Quintus and Atticus' sister Pomponia and the subsequent tensions between in-laws (Dixon 1997: 155–8), but the actual emotional content of these interactions is beyond our reach, especially the feelings of Pomponia. One of the key concerns for Cicero and probably Atticus, however, appears to be whether the couple had the "right kind" of emotional relationship and feelings of affection for each other.

Private letters are again a helpful source, occasionally giving us glimpses of the feelings of those emmeshed in such conflicts. The sender of the letter below, who was actually writing to his older brother, was clearly very angry with him (Hunt and Edgar 1932: no. 100, 288–9, *c.* 152 BCE).

> Apollonius to Ptolemaeus his father greeting. I swear by Sarapis that if I had not a little compunction, you would never have seen my face again; for you utter nothing but lies and your gods likewise, for they have plunged us into a deep mire in which we may die, and when you have a vision that we are to be rescued, then we sink outright . . .

In contrast, none of our surviving Greek (Athenian and mostly fourth century BCE) courtroom speeches features a direct conflict between full brothers over the division of an inheritance. There are many inheritance disputes, but generally these are between more distant relatives, usually in the absence of direct male heirs. This corpus of speeches has wider importance, as the versions we have surviving are "literary" texts written down for posterity and used as exemplars for teaching rhetoric right through the classical, Hellenistic, and Roman periods into late antiquity. It seems highly unlikely that brothers never took each other to court in classical Athens over dividing the family property, which we know from other sources could be a stressful process. What is interesting is that if speeches had been written by prominent orators for such cases, they were not included in our surviving corpus. This could be for many reasons. But one might be the reluctance, noted above, to present family discord, conflict (including domestic violence), and hatred openly and publicly. Part of what lay behind this could be the widespread ideal that feelings such as hatred and rivalry ought not to be part of the emotional life of families, even though sometimes they genuinely were.

Archaeological evidence may sometimes indicate family disputes over inheritance. Most ancient Greek houses were not continuously occupied for more than two or three generations. While sometimes brothers were content not to divide the estate and to continue sharing a house (Lysias 32.4), there are cases where single houses have clearly been modified to form two separate dwelling units.

A particularly carefully excavated and well-published example of private housing in the Athenian Agora is found in the so-called Industrial District (Young 1951). These houses had two phases, one in the fifth century and another in the fourth century after the construction of the Great Drain, which entailed a significant change in the street plan. The occupation and structural histories of these houses are complex, and they were frequently modified. A brief consideration of two of them, Houses A and B, gives some idea of this (see Fig. 7.5).

House B was probably built early in the fifth century BCE, and had already been there fifteen or twenty years when house A was built in the mid-fifth century BCE. House B lasted to the later fifth century BCE, perhaps to the building of the Great Drain at the very end of the century. House A's first phase of occupation was relatively short; it is not clear exactly how long from the published evidence but probably under fifty years. Then in the early fourth century BCE, House A expanded into House B's space—this arrangement lasted through the century, but during this period the space was reorganized several times and at one point House B was divided into two houses, after quite a chunk of it had already been incorporated into House A.

In a large and prosperous city such as Athens there are many possible reasons why houses might be modified. However, in Athens, only citizens could own houses, although of course others might rent them. Domestic dwellings were also regularly used as "business" space, for shops, crafts, and manufacturing of various kinds. Although some of these modifications might have been made when houses were bought and sold, the continual rearrangement of space between these two houses might suggest that the properties were owned by related families. The most usual reason for the division of a single house into two was probably division of the domestic space between two sons on

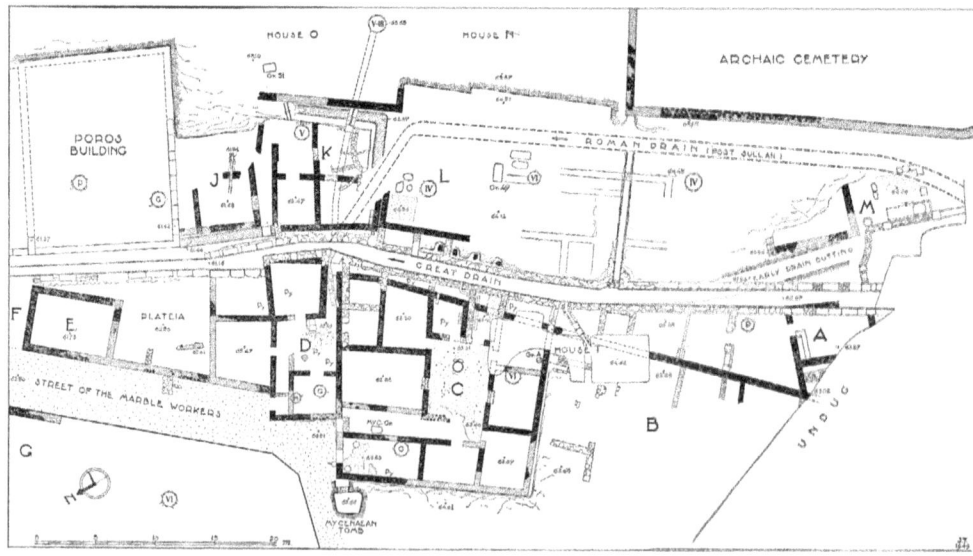

FIGURE 7.5: Houses in the Athenian agora (Young 1951: 189, Fig. 7).

the death of a parent. Of course, we have no idea in any archaeological example how amicable or not the process was. But it is easy to see from the physical traces how and why the transfer of real property from one generation to another could have been stressful even in the happiest families, given the degree of conceptual, emotional, and physical effort involved in the rearrangement of space.

Similarly, the abandonment of a house might signal the "planning blight" that occurs when heirs cannot agree on what to do with the family house. The Umbro Greek house, a rural "farmhouse" in southern Calabria, has two phases of occupation lasting about 100 years between the final quarter of the fifth century BCE to the later part of the fourth century BCE (Foxhall and Yoon 2016: Fig. 4). At the end of the first phase, the building was abandoned for long enough that the tiled roof entirely collapsed, which must have taken at least ten to twenty years (see Fig. 7.6a). Some of the complete roof tiles were removed (probably for reuse elsewhere) either before or after the collapse of the roof, but a number of them were left in situ on the floor, and in the second phase a new earth floor was laid directly over them. In this later phase the building seems to have served as a storehouse and animal shelter, not as a domestic dwelling (see Fig. 7.6b). Of course, there are many reasons why houses might be abandoned, but certainly one of the most common reasons in more recent centuries was the dilemma of what to do with the family house when the heirs disagreed on the division of the property (Forbes 2007: 232). In this archaeological example, that is one possible scenario.

FIGURE 7.6a: The Umbro Greek site, a classical rural "farmhouse" near Bova Marina, Calabria. Primary phase with roof tiles lying on floor.

FIGURE 7.6b: The Umbro Greek site, a classical rural "farmhouse" near Bova Marina, Calabria. Secondary phase divided into probable animal stalls.

CONCLUSION

Domestic life is always something of a black box to the outsider; it is almost impossible to know the full details of what goes on in the intimate spaces of others' personal and private relationships. Most of our source material for ancient Greece and Rome reflects that reluctance to open the shutters on private lives. Consequently, our sources virtually never present "real" feelings and emotions directly, but they do show us other very interesting things. One is ideals, the culturally accepted values about how particular relationships ought to work and how individuals ought to feel, regardless of whether those ideals are realized in any particular situation. For classical antiquity we do not always know how fully all the cultural values projected in elite sources were accepted across the full socio-economic spectrum, but it is clear that some were quite deeply embedded.

Beyond the ideals themselves, there is also the question of the language of emotion. Halliwell (2017) has explored the complexities of the asymmetry between ancient writers and their audiences. He has explored how writers themselves understood the relationship between the emotions they wished to convey to an audience and how they might in different ways manipulate, simulate, or imagine feelings to create the right language to inspire an emotional response in their audience. Although Halliwell is interested in how language mediates and structures the transmission of emotion from author to audience in literature, analogous issues arise with the language of private, non-literary documents. As we have seen, the language of private letters and curses is not freeform, but to a considerable extent feelings are channeled through accepted forms of expression. Nonetheless, writers of these documents sometimes stretch conventional forms and language to express personal feelings, although in many cases it is impossible to access the feelings (if any) behind the formulae. This is very different from the way conventions were used in public documents, where the emotional content of some words and expressions completely dissolves as they become established as polite formulae for use in official letters (Dickey 2016: 244–9).

A second thing they show is the gaps. There are some highly emotional situations that probably occurred regularly in ancient family life where there is no direct documentation, and that absence is striking. As discussed above, we know that brothers did sometimes fall out over the division of family property (Hesiod, *Works and Days*), yet we rarely find full brothers, or indeed sons and mothers, in direct conflict in our non-literary sources.

Another example is domestic violence against women, and its acceptability within limits, which is documented in literary sources. Zeus threatens his jealous wife Hera in a tense moment (Homer, *Iliad* 1.536–89). Similarly, the bitch-wife in Semonides' misogynistic poem (fr. 7.15–16) enrages a husband to violence: "A man could not stop her either with threats nor if angered he knocked out her teeth with a stone." We might have expected to hear women expressing fear or anger, or seeking retaliation or relief from such treatment among the curse tablets or letters, or even in votives, but their voices are silent. The same could be said about violence against slaves or children. This suggests that there were some aspects of life which, even if they generated strong emotional feelings for individuals or groups, were out of bounds for the explicit expression of even very private emotions, at least in any material form that we might recover. These were at least marginally acceptable practices, and it is striking that even though they must have been emotionally distressing, they were not challenged even in the realm of the supernatural. Whether this was because such behaviors were so embedded in the moral order of social relationships that they could not be challenged, or because of the apparent reluctance to express hostility, anger, or other negative emotions directly against close relatives, spouses, or social superiors is difficult to determine.

Finally, the third thing they show us, closely related to the first and second, is what people believe others think they *ought* to feel in response to a specific event, situation, or relationship, whether or not that is what any person stuck in in the middle of it actually feels. This leads to the interesting question of whether people come to feel specific emotions in particular ways in any given circumstance because prevailing cultural values and expectations suggest there is a "proper" selection of emotions to feel, just as there are more and less "correct" behaviors for dealing with specific situations. For the most part, the private emotions in domestic settings that are visible to us are channeled through more or less conventional forms of expression: letters, votives, prayers, and even curses all provide good examples of this, where the language both shapes and is partially shaped by the feelings of the writer. The big question is the extent to which these conventional expressions of feeling might come to embody as well as express the content of many people's feelings about their close familial and personal relationships. To understand this would be also to understand the degree of access that we might, or might not, have to the emotional life of domestic settings.

CHAPTER EIGHT

In Public: Collectivities and Polities

ANGELOS CHANIOTIS AND CATHERINE STEEL

THE GREEK WORLD

Greek public life, a world of emotions

Disgust is a basic emotion whose study reveals significant aspects of a culture (Lateiner and Spatharas 2017b). However, disgust certainly is not the first emotion that comes to mind when one thinks of emotions in public life. But consider an incident that took place in Tarsus, a Greek city in south-west Turkey, during Augustus' reign (late first century BCE). The city was dominated by the demagogue Boethus. When the philosopher Athenodorus returned from Rome to his hometown, he used the authority given to him by Augustus to send Boethus and some of his followers into exile. Thereupon, Boethus' partisans

> . . . wrote against him on the walls, "Deeds are for the young, counsels for the middle-aged, but farts for the old men." When Athenodorus took the inscription as a joke, he ordered the addition of "thunders for old men." But then someone who despised all decency and had a loose belly came in the night to his house and profusely bespattered the door and the wall. When Athenodorus brought accusations in the assembly against that faction, he said: "One may recognize the city's illness and disaffection in many ways, and in particular from its excrement."
>
> —Strabo 14.5.14

In Tarsus, smells replaced political arguments; instead of appealing to the judgment of their fellow citizens, the opponents of Athenodorus invoked the emotion of disgust; political discourse became a scatological discourse.

* * *

Life in any community unavoidably and continually confronts its members with the full range of emotions: affection or hatred for a leader, grief for death and sorrow for a failure, indignation for injustice and pride for success, fear in the face of danger and envy aroused by inequality, gratitude for a benefactor and joy in conviviality, hope for an enterprise and pity for a catastrophe, and so on. There is hardly any communal activity that is not connected with emotions, either because it offers an opportunity for the expression and display of emotions or because it is shaped by emotions.

Emotions, especially collective emotions, can be observed in Greek public life in a variety of situations. The following examples are only suggestive: the remarks of a Corinthian orator in Thucydides on the emotional disposition of the Athenians (1.70); the arousal of anger, envy, and contempt by orators in the assembly (Chaniotis 2013a and 2013b; van Nijf 2013) or the court (Rubinstein 2004 and 2013; Sanders 2012, 2014: 79–99; Fisher 2017), or by comic poets in the theater (Sanders 2014: 100–29); collective fear in the face of a foreign invasion, collective grief after a defeat, and collective joy and pride after a victory; hatred, envy, and indignation in the context of civil wars; collective pride among the audience of epideictic encomia; hatred, wrath, fear, and hope in reconciliation agreements (see below); the prescription of emotions by authorities: hatred against enemies in oaths, joy in public celebrations for victories of monarchs, and grief during the funeral of members of the elite,[1] and so on. Instead of compiling a list of such situations, we shall focus on selected aspects in the study of collective emotions.

Collective emotions

In specific situations groups of people share the same emotions (Redl 1942; Neckel 1999; Ciompi and Endert 2011; Scheve and Salmela 2014; see Fig. 8.1): for example, the fear that inhabitants of a city felt during an earthquake or a siege; the emotions aroused by a

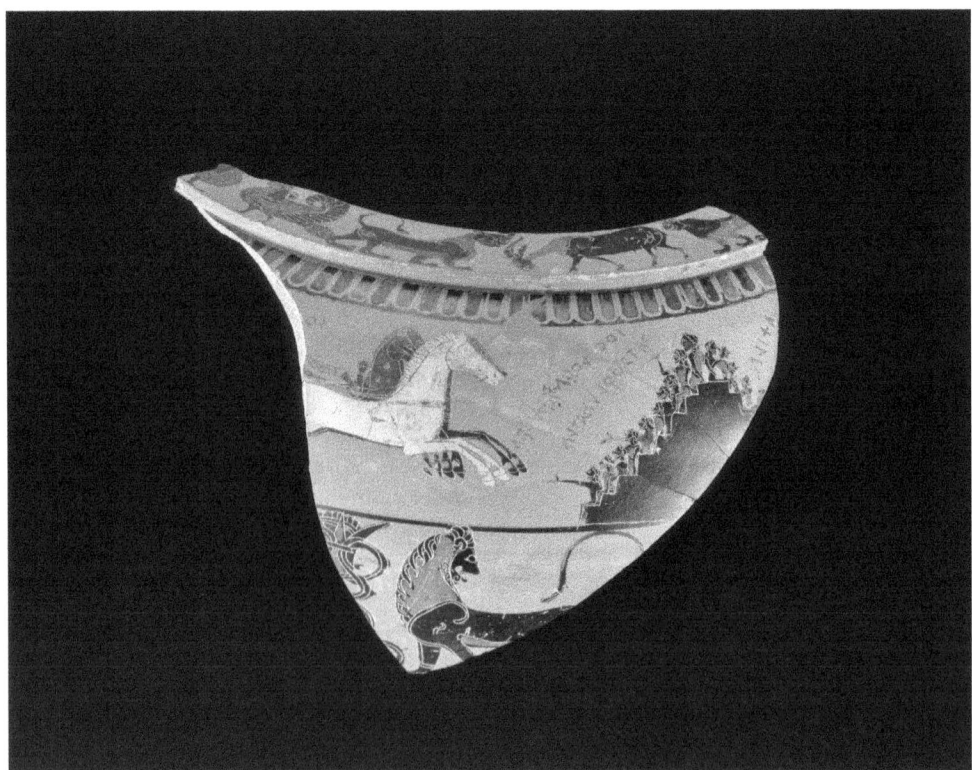

FIGURE 8.1: Funeral games for Patroclus: Attic bf. dinos by Sophilos, 570–560 BCE.

speaker in a court of law among the jurors—indignation, envy, and contempt for the opponent, gratitude or pity for the defendant (Rubinstein 2004 and 2013; Sanders 2012 and 2014: 79–99; Fisher 2017); emotions aroused, felt and displayed during a meeting of the popular assembly (Chaniotis 2013a, 2013b; van Nijf 2013); emotions of soldiers before battle—fear of defeat, death, and humiliation, hope for victory, loyalty, and affection towards the soldiers placed next to them, hatred and contempt for the enemy, trust in the commanding officer; the emotions felt by the audience of a theatrical performance—especially fear and pity, according to Aristotle's famous definition of tragedy (Aristotle, *Poetics* 6.2, 1449b23–28). Such collective feelings are sometimes attributed to a group by an external observer, such as a historian.[2]

An ancient historian can best study the collective feelings of groups that were defined according to clear criteria, for instance, communities of citizens and worshipers, soldiers serving in the same unit, jurors, participants in ceremonies and rituals, the members of voluntary associations, conspirators, and so on. When such groups "adhere to the same norms of emotional expression and value—or devalue—the same or related emotions" (Rosenwein 2006: 2), they constitute "emotional communities" (in the plural). By contrast, "emotional community" (in the singular) is the shared emotional response in a certain situation—a funeral, the announcement of good news, and so on (Chaniotis 2016). This shared emotional response, enhanced through interventions by recognizable agents, may create a feeling of togetherness.

Recognizing emotions in public life

In 371 BCE the Spartans suffered at Leuctra a great defeat. Xenophon describes how the news arrived in Sparta:

> The messenger sent to Sparta to announce the disaster arrived on the last day of the festival of the *Gymnopaidiai*, during the performance of the men's chorus. When the ephors [chief magistrates] heard about the disaster, they were greatly grieved, as, naturally, one would expect them to be. However, they did not order the chorus to leave the theater but instead they allowed them to finish the competition. Then they revealed the names of the dead to the relatives of each one of them. They ordered the women not to cry out but to bear their suffering in silence. On the next day, one could see the relatives of those who were killed going around with bright and happy faces, while you would have hardly seen on the street any of those whose relatives had been reported as still alive, and these few were making their way with gloomy expressions and downcast faces.[3]

This passage exemplifies the complexity of the study of emotions in public life. We observe the intervention by authorities and the effort to prescribe emotional display. We observe how the same event stirred up different emotions in the same community: the general sorrow for the defeat was combined with pride in the case of the relatives of the war dead, with shame in the case of the relatives of the survivors. But we also recognize the potential discrepancy between display of emotion and true feeling. And finally, we recognize the problem of our source's reliability. Xenophon's report was determined by his admiration for Spartan customs. His text is not the objective report of an uninvolved observer, but an evaluation of a community's value system. Xenophon turned a military defeat into a moral victory, exactly as he had done in the case of an earlier Spartan defeat, at Lechaion in 390 BCE (*Hellenica* 4.5.10).[4]

We encounter a selective representation of emotional responses in public life also when we study documentary sources, such as inscriptions (Chaniotis 2014). For instance, the author of an honorific decree for the benefactor Protogenes in the Pontic city of Olbia (c. 200 BCE) chose to highlight the fear of the population, when the largest part of the city was not fortified and an attack was expected, in order to stress the magnitude of Protogenes' service and justify the honors:

> Because of this, the people convened in an assembly in deep despair, as they saw before them the danger that lay ahead and the terrors in store, and called on all who were able-bodied to help and not to watch with indifference their native city being subjected by the enemy, after it had been preserved for many years.[5]

The author of this decree referred to collective fear in order to elicit gratitude for the benefactor; he deployed collective gratitude in order to eliminate the collective envy that is expected towards a wealthy man despite his generosity (Chaniotis 2013a). In most cases, our sources for emotions in public life are selective reports written by members of the propertied and educated classes.

Fortunately, there are exceptions. For instance, inscriptions on sling bullets addressed to the targets reveal the feelings of soldiers before the battle (mainly fourth to second century BCE): "get this," "all yours," "it rains [bullets]," "blood," "ouch," "get pregnant [with this]" (Chaniotis 2005: 95). Black humor helped the soldiers overcome the anxiety of battle by verbally reassuring them and showing contempt for the enemy. Oracular inquiries reveal the collective anxieties of a community. When the authorities of Dodona addressed the local oracle asking "if it is because of the impurity of a man that the god brings the bad weather" (Lhôte 2006: no. 14), their inquiry reflected anxiety, fear, and suspicion. Similarly, the dedication of war booty in sanctuaries, the minting of coins commemorating victories, and the establishment of commemorative anniversaries after the liberation of cities are reliable sources for public feelings. Also, when normative texts such as decrees, laws, and statutes seek to solve problems, they respond to the anxieties and desires of larger groups.

Two case studies: ostracism and amnesty

In the sixth month of the official Athenian year the citizens were asked during an assembly whether they wanted to hold an "ostracism." If the majority was in favor, a vote was held two months later. The citizens were asked to write on a potsherd—*ostrakon*—the name of an Athenian who should be exiled for a period of ten years (see Fig. 8.2). If at least 6,000 votes were cast, then the citizen whose name appeared in the relative majority of the ostraka was sent into exile. Between 487 and 416 BCE, thirteen statesmen and members of wealthy and influential families fell victim to ostracism. Thousands of ostraka have been discovered during excavations in Athens (Forsdyke 2005).

This institution was justified by an emotion: the fear that a citizen might threaten democracy or that he might betray his city. But to judge from the comments and images that were inscribed on some of the ostraka, fear was not the only emotion in play.[6] These graffiti suggest hatred and indignation: "get this!"; "the traitor"; "Menon of Gargettos, the king of the idiots"; "this ostrakon says that of all the accursed *prytaneis*, Xanthippus, son of Arrhiphron, does most wrong." The drawing of a Persian archer on an ostrakon against Callias (c. 471 BCE) alludes to his sympathies for the Persians and the fear of treason.

FIGURE 8.2: Ostrakon inscribed with name of the Athenian politician Themistocles, fifth century BCE.

Such ostraka are the result of the collective action of hundreds of emotional men who wished to inflict pain on an influential man because of fear, envy, anger, indignation, or contempt. The expression of emotions that took place during the ostracism was ritualized, and therefore monitored and regulated (Kosmin 2015). Ostracism was a process of decision-making in which cognition—the close screening of the behavior of public figures and the rational observation of potential threats—was closely combined with emotion. Usually, political considerations determined the outcome of ostracism; sometimes ostraka were prepared in advance in order to be distributed among the followers of one statesman and opponents of another. Whether a citizen's vote was determined by rational considerations or emotions depended on social factors and the general political climate at a given moment. It is said that an illiterate man once asked Aristides, without knowing him, to write the name "Aristides" on an ostrakon. When Aristides, known by the nickname "the just," asked the man what harm Aristides had done him, the man answered that he did not even know him; but he could not stand that everybody called him "the just." Doing justice to his nickname, Aristides wrote his name on the sherd (Plutarch, *Life of Aristides* 7.5–6). The very existence of this institution made Athenian statesmen and members of elite families cautious. Ultimately, it did not save Athens from the bad influence of demagogues.

Greek popular morality expected the victims of wrongdoing and their relatives to continually remember the injustice that they had suffered and to do everything in their power to inflict pain on their opponents. Amnesty agreements, of which several are known from the fifth century BCE onwards,[7] are directly opposed to this code. By forbidding the "memory of bad things" (*mnêsikakein*) and banning "anger because of bad memories" (*mnêsicholein*), they intervened in memory and feeling. To ask a citizen to refrain from revenge and the prosecution of those who had committed injustice meant to ask him not only to control affect but also to neglect the duty to avenge the death of relatives. Amnesty required citizens to give priority to the advantage of the living (concord) over the right of the dead (revenge) (Chaniotis 2013d).

A reconciliation agreement in Athens in 403/2 BCE put an end to the rule of an oligarchic regime and allowed the democrats to return to the city (Carawan 2013, with earlier bibliography). Democracy was fully restored, and general immunity was imposed. Only a few men who were directly involved in the oligarchic rule were exempted. Yet this did not stop democrats from prosecuting citizens for their involvement in political crimes during the oligarchic rule, only a few years later. Lysias' speeches against Eratosthenes (12) and Agoratus (13) are excellent sources for the emotional background of these cases (Carawan 2013: 115–95). Lysias describes in great detail his own sufferings and those of the Athenian people, urging the jurors to remember, to be angry, and to act in accordance with their anger, to show neither pity nor forgiveness, and to condemn the defendants (Lysias 12.79–80 and 96; 13.44, 48, and 95). Lysias' speeches were effective because of their appeal to memory and emotion. The request for amnesty of the descendants of tyrants in Eresus in the late fourth century BCE failed for a similar reason. With vivid images of cruelty, the opponents of amnesty reminded the popular assembly the people's suffering under the tyrants (Ellis-Evans 2012; Chaniotis 2013d: 59–60).

The Greeks were aware of the precarious state of amnesty agreements because of the strong feeling of anger and hatred. For this reason, they attempted to impose a hierarchy of norms: concord should be valued more than revenge. In order to strengthen amnesty agreements, the Greeks introduced rituals that were expected to weaken hatred and strengthen concord: oath ceremonies, the cult of Concord, rituals of "selective memory," processions and festivals that promoted new forms of solidarity within the community (Chaniotis 2013d).

The reconciliation in Nacone in Sicily is a case in point. When a civil war divided the citizens in the third century BCE, amnesty forbade the prosecution of past acts of violence; but would it eliminate the hatred? The Naconians decided to take a radical measure: they brought the former enemies together into new, artificial families (Dössel 2003: 235–47; Gray 2015: 37–41). Each of the two factions presented a list of thirty members of the other. Casting lots, they formed new families consisting of two enemies plus three neutral citizens. Hatred was expelled by means of the ritualized commemoration of reconciliation with an annual sacrifice to Concord.

Group dynamics and decision-making

The historian Polybius describes the emotions of the Achaeans who attended the federal assembly shortly after a defeat in 219 BCE (Polybius 4.14.1–8):

> Both the whole body jointly and each individual citizen separately were bitterly disposed toward Aratus as having indisputably caused the aforementioned disaster. So, when his political opponents accused him and produced clear proofs of his responsibility, the assembly became still more indignant and exasperated against him [ἠγανάκτει καὶ παρωξύνετο τὸ πλῆθος] ... However, as soon as Aratus rose to speak and reminded them of his previous political conduct and his achievements, defending himself against the accusations, arguing that he was not responsible for what had occurred, asking for their pardon if he had possibly overseen something in the battle, and saying that they should view facts without bitterness but considering human nature, the feelings of the

assembly changed so fast and with such indulgence [μεγαλοψύχως] that they remained for long displeased [δυσαρεστῆσαι] with those of his opponents who had joined in the attack on him and followed Aratus' advice for all affairs in the immediate future.

Polybius' narrative exemplifies three important aspects of emotions in public life: the interconnection between emotion and memory; how emotions influence decisions; and how group dynamics change emotions (Redl 1942). Of course, this narrative, too, is the result of selection and composition. With words such as "jointly" (κοινῇ), "everything" (πάντα), and "the assembly" (τὸ πλῆθος, three times), the historian creates the impression that the assembly was an undifferentiated group sharing the same feelings. Only the mention of opponents (ἀντιπολιτευόμενοι) reminds the reader that there were very different opinions and subgroups. Polybius was not an eyewitness of that assembly; Aratus' memoirs are his most likely source. If we are to believe Aratus that during that single meeting the indignation of the overwhelming majority was turned into gratitude and affections for past services, understanding and compassion for human shortcomings, and ultimately to trust and support, this change must have occurred not only because of Aratus' speech but also because of the audience's response: shouts against Aratus at the beginning and against his opponents at the end. Many sources attest to how shouts and acclamations during gatherings of the people contributed to the emotional atmosphere.[8]

The impact of group dynamics is illustrated by a famous episode during Paul's stay in Ephesus around 55 CE. A silversmith who made silver shrines of Artemis recognized a threat to his business from the spread of Christianity and instigated protests by the local guild of silversmiths. People rushed together to the theater, in a spontaneous meeting of the assembly. "Some were shouting one thing, some another; and most of them did not know why they had come together." When a Jew attempted to address the assembly, the people shouted in unison for hours "Great is Artemis of the Ephesians" (*Acts* 19.23–41). The acclamations transformed a confused and divided group into an emotional community. The expression of the collective feeling of an organized group became a compulsive force for all.

The development of emotions in public life: hope as a case study

Fear and hope are more closely connected with judgment, appraisal, and memory than other emotions. The expectation of a positive or a negative outcome in the future is based on past experiences. Although hope is a trans-historical and universal emotion, the way it is presented in public discourse is instructive for an important aspect of the study of emotions in public life: the historical development of the expression, representation, and display of feelings.

When mentioned in grave epigrams *elpis* aims to increase grief and empathy: the unexpected, usually premature, death of an individual deceives the hopes or expectations of the relatives, the deceased person, and the entire community.[9] From private funerary epigraphy, the *topos* of the deceived expectations was taken over by the authors of civic decrees in the Hellenistic and Imperial periods. They used it to honor both deceased benefactors and the offspring of elite families. The decree for an individual called Dados in the Black Sea city of Olbia (*c.* 200 CE) states that "he was being praised by all and he was expected to fulfill all the liturgies, in accordance with the status of his family, but he was mercilessly snatched away when all-conquering fate came upon him."[10] Such decrees are more than expressions of grief; they are a strategy of communication between people and elite: the death of a benefactor was assimilated to the death of a family member creating the fiction of the orphaned people. The public demonstration of the people's grief and gratitude encouraged other members of the elite to follow the benefactor's model. The fiction of an intimate relation between the people and the elite was also expressed through the honorary titles of "the son of the people," "the daughter of the people," and so on. These titles created the illusion of a big family, in which the benefactors had to fulfill the role of a caring daughter, son, father, or mother.[11] The *topos* of deceived hope contributed to the construction of the image of the city as a family, in which the city could have the same legitimate expectations of the wealthy elite as parents of their children. This strategy occurred in the context of asymmetrical relations, in which the civic communities were dependent on the elite and its benefactions. The sources of communal hope were no longer the citizens but the notables.

From the reign of Augustus onwards, *elpis* is continually invoked in documents concerning the relations between cities or provinces and the emperor. It refers to the expectations a subordinate community has of a higher authority; these were beyond the control of citizen communities and depended on the goodwill and abilities of the emperor and his administration. *Elpis* indicated subordination, loyalty, and trust.[12]

This change in the use of *elpis* in the epigraphic material is connected with deep changes in society and communal organization—the rise of monarchy and the dependence on benefactors—but also in religion. In religious texts *elpis* appears in contexts that underline the fact that divine power defies human reasoning, by making possible things that no mortal could have hoped for.[13] Christianity brought a further transformation of hope by making *elpis* a synonym of unconditional faith.[14]

THE ROMAN WORLD

Oratory and the emotions

Any examination of the role of emotion in Roman public life must deal, first and foremost, with oratory and its pervasive position in Roman education, law, and politics. The earliest rhetorical treatises in Latin show relatively little interest in the persuasive force of the emotions as a separate topic; their theory, derived ultimately from Hermagoras' stasis theory on the identification of "issues" as adapted to a Roman forensic environment, is chiefly concerned with establishing a typology of arguments and with the effective structuring of speeches.[15] Emotion features chiefly in discussion of the peroration of a speech, in which an appeal to the jurors' pity might feature.[16] It is only with the rhetorical treatises from Cicero's maturity, written in the 50s and 40s BCE, that we find a theory of emotional persuasion set out. This is in sharp contrast to what we can hypothesize about oratorical practice at Rome, where episodes of intense emotion are recorded from the middle of the second century BCE, more or less contemporaneously with the earliest substantial amounts of evidence about any aspect of oratory at Rome.

In *De oratore* (*On the Ideal Orator*) Cicero (see Fig. 8.3) draws on the Aristotelian triad of *logos*, *ethos*, and *pathos* to critique the formulaic approach of the handbooks and demand instead an oratory which draws on a broad education and extensive experience and understanding of the forensic environment to blend rational argument, the speaker's persona and emotional appeal into a persuasive whole (Wisse 1989; Fantham 2004: 161–85). The discussion of *pathos* is found in the second book of the treatise, 2.185–211; the extended and pivotal treatment of the trial of Norbanus falls within it (197–204), emphasizing the importance of *pathos* to oratorical theory and successful oratorical

FIGURE 8.3: Marcus Tullius Cicero (106–43 BCE). Portrait from Villa Quintilii, Appian Way.

practice. The topic is handled by Antonius, the work's deuteragonist, and is presented as part of his treatment of *inuentio*. He identifies (206) nine emotions which the orator might need to arouse: these are *amor* (love), *odium* (hatred), *iracundia* (anger), *inuidia* (hostility), *misericordia* (pity), *spes* (hope), *laetitia* (happiness), *timor* (fear), and *molestia* (distress).[17] Slightly earlier, he acknowledges that this process of stirring up emotion is much more straightforward if the audience is already inclining towards the desired emotion; however, oratory can provoke the right emotion even in someone who is resistant to it. The Aristotelian triad also aligns with the idea that a speech has three tasks to fulfill, which Cicero first articulates in *De oratore* (2.114–28, esp. 115): to instruct (*docere*), to conciliate (*delectare*), and to move (*mouere*). Instruction involves argument, conciliation the speaker's character, and movement emotion.

The role of emotion is further embedded into rhetorical theory through its alignment with theories of style and the relationship that is posited between different styles and different oratorical tasks. Thus the simple style is appropriate for instruction (*docere*), the middle style for winning over and pleasing the audience (*delectare*), and the high style moves hearers' feelings (*mouere*). In this respect, there are some points of continuity with the earlier treatises. The discussion of style in the fourth book of *Ad Herennium* does not invoke emotion in its characterization of each of the three styles (and their faulty manifestations), but it does acknowledge that some figures of speech are linked to emotional effects. Thus effective use of *apostrophe* (4.22) can generate *indignatio* and *dolor*, and *licentia* (4.49) is presented as a figure whose use can prevent the audience from feeling *iracundia* or *molestia*.

In *Orator*, Cicero returns to questions of style to argue his conviction that the perfect orator must be capable of using all three styles.[18] To navigate between the different styles the orator should rely on the concept of *decorum*, what is appropriate; that, rather than *a priori* convictions about the superiority of one style over another, is the orator's guide. Thus emotion is an integral part of oratory, but only in those situations where it is appropriate to the topic and audience: "he, then, will be eloquent, who can fit his speech to whatever is appropriate."[19] It becomes apparent during the work that the deployment of *ethos* to win over the audience also has some emotional content, albeit of a more moderate kind.[20] *Brutus*' catalog purposely avoids grand theories of speech in favor of the diversity of actual practice, yet effective deployment of emotion is among the characteristics to which Cicero draws attention. So, for example, in the course of discussing his contemporary M. Calidius, one of the great forensic talents of the period (Cicero, *Brutus* 274–8), Cicero suggests that Calidius, despite his skill in exposition and pleasing manner of speaking, lacked *tertia illa laus* (*Brutus* 276), that is the capacity to move and rouse his audience's feelings.

The structure of Quintilian's oratorical handbook is based on the five parts of rhetoric, but the importance he places on emotion within oratory is evident from the ways in which he adapts the structure to make room for the discussion of the emotions. This occurs most extensively during the treatment of the parts of a speech (which Quintilian handles under *inuentio*), where the peroration of a speech is discussed largely as an opportunity to create emotional effects, a discussion which takes up much of book 6. Much of what Quintilian says can be compared with Cicero's analysis: the importance of emotion, particularly pity (6.1.23–5, 6.2.1); the dangers if it used inexpertly (6.1.44–5); and the necessity for the orator to feel the emotion which he is trying to arouse (6.2.26–36). But there are a number of developments and expansions. Quintilian uses the triad of *logos*, *ethos*, and *pathos*, but the blurring of a distinction between the latter two is well advanced: in his analysis (6.8–25), both are types of *adfectus*. He offers a variety of definitions which distinguish between the two, testimony to active debate around this area of rhetorical theory as well as to a degree of confusion: thus *ethos* is like comedy whereas *pathos* is like tragedy (6.2.20), or *ethos* is permanent where *pathos* is temporary (6.2.10). He offers as his own view (6.2.12) a distinction based either on intensity, *pathos* being the stronger feeling, or one which sets the calming function of *ethos* against the disturbance created by *pathos*. Earlier in the work (3.5.2), when introducing the three functions of the orator as one structuring device in the study of rhetoric, he notes some also simply offer a twofold distinction between *res* (facts) and *adfectus* (emotions); in this view, both *delectare* and *docere* are primarily emotional tasks. Quintilian also acknowledges that emotion is a force throughout a speech (6.2.1–7): "Proofs may make the jurors think our case is the stronger one, but emotions will also make them want this to be the case."[21]

How in practice did the Roman orator use emotion? Before turning to Cicero's speeches, let us consider two episodes, much retold, from the second and early first century BCE, whose impact depends as much on the record of the audience's response as on the orator's words and actions: that is, these stories—in contrast to the texts of Cicero's speeches—show us an orator interacting with his audience through the effective use of emotionally based persuasion.

In 149 BCE Servius Sulpicius Galba faced prosecution for extortion after he had been governor of Hispania Ulterior in 151–150. The case was notorious, the accused's guilt evident. Yet he escaped penalty, apparently because he managed to rouse the audience's pity by displaying young relatives to them and evoking their vulnerability were he to be convicted:

So Rutilius criticized Galba because he had almost pulled up on his shoulders his relative Gaius Sulpicius Galus' son, his ward Quintus, to move the people to tears through the reminder and memory of his outstanding father; and because he had entrusted his two small sons to the protection of the people and had said that, like a soldier making his will without scales or tablets, he appointed the Roman people guardians of their bereft state.[22]

Galba escaped, to the consternation of his enemies; the establishment of a standing court to try extortion cases may have been a response to this episode, particularly as Galba's emotional manipulation appears to have taken place in order to persuade the people not to establish a court to try him, rather than at a trial.

Around a half-century later, Marcus Antonius, the grandfather of the triumvir, whose appearance as a character in *De oratore* is discussed above, defended Manius Aquillius, probably on extortion charges (Alexander no. 84). His defense became notorious for the way in which he used Aquillius' body as character evidence:

I recall the authority and weight that Marcus Antonius' speech at the trial of Manius Aquilius was considered to possess; in accordance with his courage as a speaker, as well as his wisdom, when he had almost finished arguing the case he personally grabbed Aquillius and placed him where everyone could see and tore his tunic off his chest, so that the Roman people and the jurors might see the scars which he had received on the front of his body; at the same time he said a lot about the wound which Aquillius had received in the head from the enemy's leader, and carried along those who were going to deliver the verdict so stirringly that they became afraid that a man whom chance had rescued from the enemy's missiles, since he had not spared himself, would seem to have been preserved not for the reputation of the Roman people but for the cruelty of the courts.[23]

These were both cases in which the defendant was acquitted because he or his advocate managed to elicit a beneficial emotional response from the audience. In the case of Galba, the emotion is identified as *misericordia*: "he stirred up the people's pity."[24] This pity is fundamentally domestic, and is provoked by people other than Galba himself: it is pity for children left vulnerable through the disappearance of their natural protector, expressed in such a way as to emphasize the shared experience between Galba and other male citizens who served in Rome's armies and whose role as protectors of their children should pass to the state in the case of their deaths. The presence of emotion is signified not only by the presence of Galba's dependents but also by his tears, which were within Roman political contexts entirely acceptable as a marker of heightened personal vulnerability.[25] This aspect of Galba's defense also lies behind the description of it in *De oratore* (1.228) as *tragoediae*, "tragic devices": here, as elsewhere, drama was an important source both for oratorical technique and for the tools with which oratorical performance was analyzed.[26] In the case of Aquillius, the fundamental emotion was also pity, but its sources and operation were arguably more complex. In Cicero's treatment of the episode in the Verrines, he does not identify the precise emotion Antonius sought to create. When he returned to the episode in *De oratore* (2.194–9) it is discussed by the character Antonius, who uses this reflection on a case from earlier in his career to argue that the orator must himself feel the emotion which he is trying to stir up in his audience: "I did not try to stir up pity in others before I myself fell prey to pity." He contributed tears as well as words to the defense, and was also helped by the tears of Marius, present in court, whom Antonius used to broaden the threat to Aquillius into one shared by all military leaders, including the greatest military hero of the day. Aquillius evokes pity on his own account, as an old man, physically weak and facing an overwhelming penalty if convicted, but he is also to be pitied because he is suffering now as a direct result of his services to the *res publica*: the gap between what should have been the response to his heroism and what in fact could be the response, were he to be convicted, is pitiable. Finally, both cases were subject to criticism because of the role that emotion played. Galba's acquittal was obviously an outrage; in *De oratore*, it is introduced precisely in order to be criticized. But Antonius' tactics on behalf of Aquillius could also, it seems, be criticized. In the *Verrines*, Cicero brings Aquillius into his argument as an example of the persuasive power of military service, which causes him anxiety because he sees that Verres' defense is trying the same method to ensure his acquittal, relying on Verres' military success in Sicily to outweigh all his crimes. Cicero does not say that Aquillius was guilty. But he implies that his acquittal was the result of the successful deployment of stereotyped emotions stirred up by the contemplation of military courage and achievement, which work whether or not the military hero is virtuous in other respects as well.

These two examples of emotional oratory were forensic, and trials in the standing *quaestiones* (law courts), which dealt with offenses relating to the *res publica*, and in front of the Roman people were the most important location for emotionally charged oratory. Cicero himself became notorious for his appeals to pity in such circumstances, as a result of which he would take the last position, in cases where a team of advocates spoke for the defense, so that the defense as a whole could conclude with his appeal to the jurors' pity. In *Orator* (130–3) he claims that his prominence in this aspect of oratory is less a matter of talent than of his capacity to feel genuine grief (*dolor*) at the plight of his clients. He notes in this passage an occasion on which he delivered his peroration holding a baby and another when he deployed the defendant's young son: the former case cannot be easily identified, though the latter may well be *Pro Flacco*. Other good examples from Cicero's surviving speeches of perorations which seek the jurors' pity through appeal not only to the situation which the defendant would face if convicted but also the implications for their families are the defenses of Caelius and Fonteius, where the family members are respectively a father, and a mother and a sister; in Fonteius' case, the fact that his sister was a Vestal Virgin allows Cicero to ramp up the emotional appeal even further, since her religious duties transform her grief from a purely personal into a civic matter: "take care that the eternal fire which Fonteia preserves through her watchful nights of toil is not said to be extinguished by the tears of your priestess."[27] Realism is evident, though, in the adage "nothing dries more quickly than a tear": the technique could be overplayed and when it was unsuccessful, the result could be unhelpful amusement rather than useful emotion.[28] "Just as this emotion, when powerful, is by far the most effective, so it falls flat when it does not work; a weak performer would have done better to leave it to the jurors' silent reflections."[29]

Judging by our surviving evidence, pity was the most consistently used emotion in forensic oratory, though the huge bias towards defense oratory among our surviving texts (because Cicero was unwilling to prosecute) must be a factor in this result. Even within Cicero's forensic oratory there was scope for the deployment of anger, particularly in those cases where his defense relied on identifying the "real" perpetrator. So in the defense of Roscius the jurors are supposed to feel anger at Magnus and Capito, the relatives of the defendant who, Cicero claims, have plotted to deprive him of his inheritance, and perhaps also envy of Chrysogonus, the freedman of Sulla with whom

Magnus and Capito were plotting. Similarly, the charges against Cluentius are dissipated by Cicero by a combination of relentless argument and the hostile characterization of his homicidal relatives: Cluentius himself is a colorless figure, and the appeal to pity draws such force as it has less from our sympathy for him as from the emotions of horror at Sassia's and Oppianicus' behavior and pity for their other victims. In deploying these tactics, Cicero, and we can assume other orators, drew on the epideictic mode of oratory to praise and, more commonly, blame the people whom they discussed.[30] And, insofar as Cicero's defense speeches often identify an alternative villain on whom guilt can be pinned, there is no clear dividing line between the use of emotion in them and in the only surviving forensic prosecution, Cicero's *In Verrem*. In that collection of speeches, Verres is set up as the object of the jurors' *indignatio*, both for his personal failings and for his dereliction of duty; pity, conversely, is to be felt for the Sicilian victims of his cruel and illegal behavior, culminating in the long description of judicial executions in the fifth speech of the *Second Actio*.[31]

Forensic oratory was not, however, the only acceptable location for emotion at Rome. Funeral orations were an established aspect of mourning rituals. And deliberative oratory, both that delivered in front of the people at *contiones* and senatorial oratory, could deploy emotional appeals. There are many points of contact with forensic oratory in terms of the treatment of individuals, particularly hostile treatment: thus Catiline (see Fig. 8.4), Clodius, and Antonius all face extended attacks on their character and behavior which use a similar blend of personal and public failings to that which we find in the presentation of Verres. Pity is, however, less important. This is not surprising: deliberative oratory is designed to provoke (or prevent) action: action against someone is best stimulated by anger, and action which requires Roman leadership is to be based on admiration—thus the positive characterizations of Pompeius in *Pro lege Manilia* and Caesar in *De provinciis*

FIGURE 8.4: Cicero denounces Catiline. Fresco by Cesare Maccari.

consularibus. The culmination of this strand of oratory, via Cicero's *Pro Marcello*, can be seen in Pliny's *Panegyricus*, where Trajan's embodiment of the virtues of leadership and government provoke the listeners' sustained *admiratio*. Insofar as Cicero deploys pity in his deliberative oratory, it is for the victims of those against whom he desires action, such as the Romans who have suffered at Mithridates' hands, or those whom Catiline threatens with his destructive schemes.

There are, however, some sources of emotional appeal which are found more prominently in deliberative than in forensic oratory. Two in particular can be highlighted: the *res publica*, and the gods. These topics are important in speeches to the Senate and in those to the people at *contiones*, and attempts to distinguish between the expectations of the two sets of audience have not yielded any decisive findings; the topic deserves more study, but the answer is likely to be as much about the function of conventions of performance as the differing attitudes between the citizen body as a whole and senators. That is, contional oratory was more consistently elevated and substantial, whereas contributions in the Senate had a greater range, from the brief and mundane to the highly charged. Cicero's surviving contional oratory is, to a great extent, the oratory of crisis, where threats to the city and *res publica* must urgently be met; his contributions in the Senate cover a broader range.[32] The placing of *res publica* and the gods in oratorical contexts is driven by the emotional response towards them that the audience is assumed to have. A good example of this nexus is the end of Cicero's speech of thanks to the people immediately after his return from exile:

> And let this concern, citizens, be ever fixed in my soul: to seem both to you, who for me are the holders of the immortal gods' power and spirit, and to your descendants and to all nations, entirely worthy of this state which has demonstrated, through every one of its votes, that unless it received me back, it could not retain its own worth.[33]

Roman orators had no hesitation in deploying emotion to secure their ends: this is apparent from the earliest records of speech at Rome, and took place with the entire cooperation of the audience, who accepted that emotion was a legitimate technique and rewarded its effective use. The absence of mechanisms to police what was said beyond the reaction of the audience facilitated this aspect of oratory: the presiding officer in the *iudicia publica* did not have the scope to declare material inadmissible and senators were not, it seems, liable to interruption.[34] In forensic oratory, effective use of emotion centered on manipulating the jurors' attitudes towards individuals, and thus relied heavily on pity and on *indignatio*; emotion underpins the importance of invective in Roman forensic emotion. In deliberative oratory, the audience's decisions about the future are shaped by their emotional attachment to their community, as represented by the Roman *res publica* and by the city of Rome itself; and take place with the involvement of the gods, towards whom reverence and fear should be felt.

CONCLUSION

Our sources for the study of public life always have an emotional background: they are the product of emotions; they aim to arouse emotions; they describe feelings; or they use emotions in order to explain individual or group decisions and actions. Literary texts, inscriptions, and papyri are the product of intentions, selection, and composition. In them, emotions are described to explain actions or to increase the dramatic impact of a text. Historians who ignore emotions miss an important part of the sources' context.

They also miss an important factor in the understanding of Greek and Roman political life and decision-making.

An otherwise unknown Greek historian of the last civil wars of the Roman Republic, Philippus of Pergamon, explained in the preface of his work, inscribed on the base of his statue in Epidaurus, why he had written his history:

> With my pious hand I delivered to the Greeks the historical narrative of the most recent deeds—all sorts of sufferings and a continual mutual slaughter having taken place in our days in Asia and Europe, in the tribes of Libya and in the cities of the islanders. I did this, so that they may learn also through us, how many evils are brought forth by courting the mob and by love of profit, by civil strife and by the breaking of trust, and thus, by observing the sufferings of others, they may live their lives in the right way.
>
> —Goukowski 1995

Philippus places emotions, directly and indirectly, in the foreground of his political history: pain and suffering, hatred and lack of trust, desire for profit and power. Not unlike Aristotle's ideal tragic poet, he aimed to arouse fear and pity and by doing so to purge his audience of the passions that cause suffering. The value of studying emotions in public life has not changed much since Philippus' times.

NOTES ON CONTRIBUTORS

Douglas Cairns (FRSE, FBA, MAE) is Professor of Classics in the University of Edinburgh. He is author of *Aidōs: The Psychology and Ethics of Honour and Shame in Ancient Greek Literature* (1993), *Bacchylides: Five Epinician Odes* (2010), and *Sophocles: Antigone* (2016). Recent edited volumes include *Emotions between Greece and Rome* (2015, with Laurel Fulkerson), *Greek Laughter and Tears* (2017, with Margaret Alexiou), *Emotions in the Classical World* (2017, with Damien Nelis), *Seneca's Tragic Passions* (2017, with Damien Nelis), and *The Edinburgh History of Distributed Cognition* (vol. 1, 2018, with Miranda Anderson and Mark Sprevak). He currently holds a European Research Council Advanced Grant (Honour in Classical Greece, 2018–22) and an Anneliese Maier Research Award from the Alexander von Humboldt Foundation (2018–23).

Ruth R. Caston is Associate Professor of Classical Studies at the University of Michigan, where she has been teaching since 2005. Her work is mainly in Latin literature, especially elegy, satire, and comedy. In addition to a number of articles in these areas, she has a book on jealousy in Roman love elegy (2012), a co-edited collection (with Robert Kaster) on positive emotions titled *Hope, Joy, and Affection in the Classical World* (2016), and is currently writing a book on all six plays of Terence for Oxford University Press.

Angelos Chaniotis is Professor of Ancient History and Classics at the Institute for Advanced Study, Princeton. His books include *War in the Hellenistic World: A Social and Cultural History* (2005) and *Age of Conquests: The Greek World from Alexander to Hadrian* (2018). He is the editor of many volumes, including *Unveiling Emotions: Sources and Methods for the Study of Emotions in the Greek World* (2012) and *After Sunset: Perceptions and Histories of the Night in the Graeco-Roman World* (2018). Professor Chaniotis directed the European Research Council project 'The Social and Cultural Construction of Emotions: the Greek Paradigm' (Oxford, 2009–13) and co-curated the exhibition 'A World of Emotions: Ancient Greece 700 BC–200 AD' (New York, 2017).

Lin Foxhall (MBE (Hon.)) is Rathbone Professor of Ancient History and Classical Archaeology and Dean of the School of Histories, Languages and Cultures at the University of Liverpool. Previously she was Professor of Greek Archaeology and History at the University of Leicester, and Head of the School of Archaeology and Ancient History. She has held posts at St Hilda's College, Oxford, and University College London, and Visiting Professorships in Germany, Denmark, and the USA. She studied at Bryn Mawr College, the University of Pennsylvania and the University of Liverpool, where she obtained her doctorate.

George Kazantzidis (DPhil Oxon, 2011) is Assistant Professor of Latin Literature at the University of Patras, Greece. His research interests lie in the history of mental illness and the history of emotions in classical antiquity. He has recently published articles on the concept of disgust in Hippocratic medicine and on the topic of insanity in ancient paradoxography. A volume on hope (*elpis, spes*) in antiquity (co-edited with Dimos Spatharas) is forthcoming in 2018 (in the subseries *Ancient Emotions*, hosted by *Trends in Classics*, De Gruyter), as are two further edited volumes: *Morbid Laughter: Exploring the Comic Dimensions of Disease in Classical Antiquity* (Illinois Classical Studies, co-edited with Natalia Tsoumpra) and *Medicine and Paradoxography in the Classical World* (De Gruyter). Dr Kazantzidis is currently working on a book provisionally entitled *Paradoxography in Greek and Roman Antiquity: Medical Science, Horror, and the Sublime*.

David Konstan is Professor of Classics at New York University. Among his publications are *Roman Comedy* (1983), *Greek Comedy and Ideology*(1995), *Pity Transformed* (2001), *The Emotions of the Ancient Greeks: Studies in Aristotle and Classical Literature* (2006), and *Beauty: The Fortunes of an Ancient Greek Idea* (2014). He is a co-editor of *Women in Roman Republican Drama* (2015), and has translated Seneca's two tragedies on Hercules into English verse (2017). Professor Konstan is a Fellow of the American Academy of Arts and Sciences and an Honorary Fellow of the Australian Academy of the Humanities; he is a past president of the American Philological Association (now the Society for Classical Studies).

F. S. Naiden is Professor of History at the University of North Carolina at Chapel Hill, where he specializes in Greek history, especially Greek religion, law, and warfare, with attention to parallels with the Near East. He concentrates on the Archaic and Classical Periods; the early and middle Roman Republic is a secondary interest. Professor Naiden's interest in the history of ancient religious emotions arises from his two monographs: *Ancient Supplication*, which deals with both Greece and Rome; and *Smoke Signals for the Gods: Ancient Greek Sacrifice from the Archaic through Roman Periods*. His next book, *Soldier, Priest, and God*, a biography of Alexander the Great, will appear in autumn 2018.

Viktoria Räuchle is Assistant Professor of Classical Archaeology at the Ludwig-Maximilians-Universität München, and specializes in the visual culture of ancient Greece and Rome. Her monograph *Die Mütter Athens und ihre Kinder: Verhaltens- und Gefühlsideale in klassischer Zeit* (2016) deals with the visual representation of maternal emotions in classical Athens. Dr. Räuchle's interest in the history of emotions is also reflected in the organization of the conference *Pathos and Polis: The Pragmatics of Emotion in Ancient Greece* (publication in preparation). In her current research project, she is exploring visual strategies for expressing and eliciting emotions in Pompeian wall painting.

Eleonora Rocconi is Associate Professor of Classics in the Department of Musicology and Cultural Heritage at the University of Pavia (Italy). She is editor-in-chief of *Greek and Roman Musical Studies*, the first specialist periodical in the fields of ancient Greek and Roman music, and co-editor of the *Blackwell Companion to Ancient Greek and Roman Music* (forthcoming). Her research interests focus on ancient Greek music (especially technical terminology related to music and dance, ancient rhythmics, and musical aesthetics) and on ancient Greek theatre, especially comedy.

Ruth Scodel, educated at UC Berkeley and Harvard, is D. R. Shackleton Bailey Collegiate Professor of Greek and Latin at the University of Michigan. Her books include *Credible Impossibilities: Conventions and Strategies of Verisimilitude in Homer and Greek Tragedy* (1999), *Listening to Homer* (2002), *Epic Facework: Self-presentation and Social Interaction* *in Homer* (2008), *Whither Quo Vadis? Sienkiewicz's Novel in Film and Television* (2009, with Anja Bettenworth), and *An Introduction to Greek Tragedy* (2010).

Catherine Steel is Professor of Classics at the University of Glasgow. Her research deals with Roman oratory, particularly Cicero, and Roman political history. She held a European Research Council grant (2012–17) to work on the fragments of Republican oratory (see www.frro.gla.ac.uk). Key publications include *The Cambridge Companion to Cicero* (2013) and *The End of the Roman Republic 146 to 44 BC: Conquest and Crisis* (2013).

NOTES

Introduction

1. For a taste of the debate, see the special section of the journal *Emotion Review* 4 (2012): 337–93.
2. For the original list of six basic emotions, and its relation to recognition of facial expression, see Ekman and Friesen 1971. Contempt was added to the original six in Ekman and Friesen 1986. For a recent iteration of Ekman's list, with additional elements, see Ekman and Cordaro 2011. See also Ekman 1980, and cf. Ekman [1972] 1982; also Ekman's edition of Darwin 1998 (esp. 445–8). Cf. Eibl-Eibesfeldt 1989: 425–547 *passim*. For criticism, see Russell 1994, 1995; Nelson and Russell 2013; with responses in Ekman 1994, 1999b.
3. The responses of the participants in Shaver et al. 1987 (see esp. p. 1068) fail to establish surprise as one of the "best examples" of the category "emotion." Cf. Fehr and Russell 1984: 469; Clore and Ortony 1988: 388; Russell 1991: 44.
4. See Rosch 1978; Lakoff 1987. For prototype approaches to emotion categories, see Fehr and Russell 1984; Shaver et al. 1987; Russell 1991; Roberts 2003 (esp. p. 20: "it is better to think of what folks call emotions as not fracturing into several natural kinds, but as belonging to one category, albeit one that is fuzzy on the edges and held together in part by family resemblances").
5. Prinz 2004b: 3. Cf. his p. 244: to believe that "bodily changes, propositional attitudes, action dispositions are essential parts or preconditions for emotions" is to "pack in too much." Here, Prinz is reacting primarily to dimensional appraisal theories of emotion, as associated especially with Magda Arnold, Nico Frijda, and Klaus Scherer, and discussed in (e.g.) *Emotion Review* 5 (2013): 119–91. Prinz (after James and Lange) argues instead for a simpler theory of emotions as "embodied appraisals," perceptions of bodily change that register and prepare the organism to respond to features of the world.
6. For recent reviews of the progress and scope of research in this area, see Frevert 2009, 2011; Plamper 2010, 2012, 2015; Hitzer 2011; Matt 2011; Rosenwein 2011; Matt and Stearns 2014; Schnell 2015. Cf. Stearns and Stearns 1985. For ancient Greece, see Chaniotis 2012c, esp. 11–36.
7. For example, the claims that all languages have a word for "feel," even if it is a word meaning "liver" or "insides" and that "no language fails to distinguish between THINKING and FEELING" (Wierzbicka 1999: 276–7). Both the claim that "feel" is a univocal semantic primitive (1999: 15) and the sense in which the semantics of English "feel" are identically rendered in a language which allegedly represents the same concept using terms meaning "liver" or "insides" require, at least, more substantial justification
8. As in the case of the "component process model" developed by the Geneva school under Klaus Scherer: see the interview with Scherer in Lombardo and Mulligan 2008. For the development of appraisal theories, see (e.g.) Arnold 1960; Frijda 1986; Lazarus 1991.
9. On this feature as a plausible link that unities "affect program responses" and "higher cognitive emotions," see Griffiths 1997: 242–3.

10. Fortenbaugh 1975; a second edition appeared in 2002.
11. Monographs: e.g. Harris 2001; Konstan 2001; Graver 2002; Zaborowski 2002; Kaster 2005; Sternberg 2006; Konstan 2006; Graver 2007; Konstan 2010; Caston 2012; Munteanu 2012; Fulkerson 2013; Sanders 2014. Edited collections: e.g. Braund and Gill 1997; Braund and Most 2003; Konstan and Rutter 2003; Sternberg 2005; Fitzgerald 2008; Munteanu 2011; Sanders et al. 2013; Caston and Kaster 2016; Lateiner and Spatharas 2017b. See also the monographs by the philosophers Bernard Williams (1993) and Martha Nussbaum (1994, 2001).
12. See Konstan 2006 on Aristotle, 2015 and 2017b on Seneca. On the Stoics, see also (in primis) Graver 2007; on the Epicureans, see Annas 1989; Fowler 1997; Procopé 1998; Armstrong 2008. On emotion in Hellenistic ethics and psychology, see also Annas 1992; Nussbaum 1994; Sihvola and Engberg-Pedersen 1998; Gill 2010. Cf. Fitzgerald 2008. For contemporary cognitivist approaches, see, e.g., Nussbaum 2001; Solomon 2003, 2006.
13. See esp. Konstan 2001 on pity and 2010 on forgiveness.
14. See, e.g. (on emotion, moral and social norms, and the emotional scripts of ordinary social interaction), Harris 2001; Kaster 2005; Sanders 2014. On the affective character of ancient Greek moral, social, and legal norms, see also Cairns 1993, 2003a, 2003b, 2015. Cf., e.g., Graver 2017 on the norms, scripts, and display rules that conditioned Cicero's grief over the death of his daughter.
15. On the intimate relationship between emotions and social norms, see esp. Elster 1999. On the emotional character of moral norms, see, e.g., Prinz 2007; De Sousa 2008; Bagnoli 2011. On emotions, values, and legal norms, see Deigh 2008 and the January 2016 issue of *Emotion Review* 8, no. 1: 3–61.
16. To use the term introduced by Rosenwein 2006; see also Chaniotis 2011.
17. See Cairns 2014a, esp. 103–9; cf. Cairns 2017a: 53–78, with references in n. 69; Munteanu 2017.
18. See Tooby and Cosmides [2001] 2010; Carroll 2006; Zunshine 2006; Boyd 2009, esp. 188–208; Dutton 2009: 109–26; Smith 2011, esp. 109–11; Oatley 2011: 32–3, 37–8, 45, 55–79, 100–1, 105–6, 108–32, and esp. 156–75 (with reference to empirical studies in support of the notion that fiction builds capacity in other-understanding and empathy; cf. Oatley 2012, esp. 121–6, 159–62, 184–8).
19. See further Colombetti 2009.
20. See F. Cairns 2005; Nelis 2015; Battistella and Nelis 2017; cf. Scodel and Caston, this volume.
21. See the various chapters in Cairns and Nelis 2017.
22. See esp. Oatley 2011, 2012.
23. For recent discussions, see Cairns 2017a; Halliwell 2017.
24. See Halliwell 2017, and cf. Damon 2017: 183–4 on Thucydides 7.29–30.
25. See now the bibliography on "cognitive Classics" created by Felix Budelmann and Katharine Earnshaw at https://cognitiveclassics.blogs.sas.ac.uk/cognitive-classics-bibliography/ (accessed August 10, 2017).
26. See Cairns 2017a; Halliwell 2017.
27. Cf. esp. Chaniotis 2012c: 24–7, with the input of other contributors at 2012d: 37–150, 177–355, 389–430.
28. Kotsifou 2012a, 2012b, 2012c.
29. Chaniotis 2012a; Salvo 2012.
30. Chaniotis 2012a, 2012b; Martzavou 2012a, 2012b; Chaniotis 2015.
31. See Chaniotis 2012c: 18, 27; Masséglia 2012a: 137–9, 2012c.
32. See especially the recent contributions of Masséglia 2012c, 2013; Bobou 2013.

33. Sittl 1890; Neumann 1965. On body language in general (chiefly in literary sources), see Maier-Eichhorn 1989; Bremmer and Roodenburg 1991; Lateiner 1995; Aldrete 1999; Boegehold 1999; Lobe 1999; Ricottili 2000; Fögen 2001; Llewellyn-Jones 2003; Corbeill 2004; D. L. Cairns 2005. Among works on emotion expression in particular, one might single out Halliwell 2008 (on Greek laughter), Beard 2014 (on Roman); on tears, see the chapters in Fögen 2009. On both laughter and tears in ancient and Byzantine Greek cultures, see now Alexiou and Cairns 2017.

34. As well as the works cited in n. 33, note also, e.g., Davies 1985, 1994, 1997, 2002, 2005; McNiven 2000a (and his unpublished 1982 dissertation). For Roman art, Brilliant 1963 remains valuable. See also Kenner 1960 on laughter and tears in Greek art. One area in which the emotionality of ancient visual culture has been more systematically explored is that of grief and mourning: see, e.g. (on Greek art), Shapiro 1991; Huber 2001; Oakley 2004. This belongs with a long-standing tradition of studies of (especially Greek) lamentation (see Alexiou [1974] 2002; Holst-Warhaft 1992; Schauer 2002; Dué 2002, 2006; Suter 2008) and funerary customs more generally (e.g. Vermeule 1979; Garland 1985; Loraux [1990] 1998; Seaford 1994; Engels 1998; Derderian 2001).

35. See Chaniotis 2011, 2012a.

36. Cf., e.g., Masséglia 2012b.

37. See, e.g., Masséglia 2012a, 2012b; Bourbou 2013.

38. Cf. the works cited in nn. 33–4 above on body language, and cf. (on objects) Mueller 2016.

39. See Cairns 2013a, 2013b, 2014, 2016a, 2016b, 2016c, 2017a, 2017b. See also Cánovas 2011 on the arrows of love. Latinists have focused less closely on emotion, but for the general approach, see Short 2012, 2013, 2014.

40. See Cairns 2013a, 2017a on shudders (*phrikê*) and 2016a on clouds and garments.

41. For an account of ancient Greek emotion based on the discussion in the *Rhetoric*, see Konstan 2006b. See also Fortenbaugh [1975] 2002; Cooper 1996; Leighton 1996.

42. See Charles 2008, with the response by Caston 2008, for stronger and weaker interpretations of what this means.

43. E.g. *Parts of Animals* 2.4, 650b33–651a17, 4.11, 692a22–5, *On the Generation of Animals* 3.1, 749b33, *Politics* 7.7, 1327b23–36; cf. the post-Aristotelian *Problems* 2.26, 869a5–6, 8.20, 889a15–25, 10.60, 898a4–8, 15.16, 910a38–b8, 20.2, 923a9–12, 27.3, 947b23–948a12, 30.1, 954a31–4.

44. See Heath 2017 for a new approach to the apparent inconsistencies between *Poetics* 13 and 14 on this point.

45. See Epicurus, *Epistle* 3.127; for discussion, see Annas 1989; Fowler 1997; Procopé 1998; Armstrong 2008.

46. I cite Philodemus' work from the widely used edition of Indelli 1988, but have benefited greatly from advance sight of the outstanding new text, translation, and commentary by Armstrong and McOsker 2018. I am very grateful to both for allowing me access to their work.

47. See Long and Sedley 1987, §65 A 3–4 (Stobaeus), B (Andronicus), E (Stobaeus); Cicero, *Tusculan Disputations* 4.11; Graver 2007: 53–9.

48. See Long and Sedley 1987, §65 A 1 (Stobaeus), J (Galen on Chrysippus); cf. Plutarch, *On Moral Virtue* 441C–D; Seneca, *On Anger* 1.7; Graver 2007: 61–2, 67–8.

49. See Long and Sedley 1987, §65 G = Plutarch, *On Moral Virtue* 446F–447A; Graver 2007: 71.

50. Graver argues (against Sorabji 2000: 66–9 and passim) that this is original Stoic doctrine, and not something that derives solely from Seneca. For these "pre-emotions," cf. Konstan 2017b, and in this volume.

51. Gellius, *Attic Nights* 19.1.17–18 = Epictetus fr. 9 = Long and Sedley 1987, §65 Y; cf. Seneca, *On Anger* 2.2.2.
52. For the issue of whether non-virtuous people can (in effect) have *eupatheiai*, i.e. emotions that involve true beliefs about what is valuable (Cicero, *Tusculan Disputations* 3.77–8), see Brennan 1998: 51; Graver 2007: 6, 53 (on Seneca, *Moral Epistles* 23.4–6, the *potential* joy of the ordinary person), 59–60.
53. See Nussbaum 2001: 28, 87.

Chapter 1

1. Cf. [Hippoc.] *Coan Prognoses* 473, 5.690 L.
2. Singer 1992: 142; cf. Beardslee 1918: 35–6; Simon 1978: 215; Gundert 2000: 35; van der Eijk 2005: 125–6; Holmes 2010a: 190–1.
3. For some useful discussions, see Ackrill 1963; Robinson 1983; Shields 1988; Frede 1992; and van der Eijk 2000.
4. See Pearson 2014; cf. Introduction, this volume, pp. 10–11. On the body–mind relationship and the separability of the mind in Aristotle, see Barnes 1971–2; Heinaman 1990; Kahn 1992: 375–9; van der Eijk 2000: 69–70; and Miller 2012.
5. See Lyons 1980: 34.
6. See Konstan 2003; cf. Fortenbaugh 1970.
7. For the association between *phusikos* and physician, see Lloyd 2003: 177.
8. Cf. Grosz 1994: xi.
9. Frede 1992: 94. Cf. Shields 2007.
10. For detailed discussions, see Jouanna 2007 and Bartos 2015.
11. Frede 1992: 97.
12. See van der Eijk 2005: 45–73; cf. Hankinson 1998.
13. See the seminal studies in the 1970s by Ekman 1973; Ekman and Friesen 1971, 1975; cf. Ekman and Friesen 1986; Ekman 1999a. For an overview, see Reisenzein 2015: 29–32.
14. See Thumiger 2016b. Later in the text (ch. 15 = 6.388 L.), fear and anger (caused by the brain's corruption with bile) are also mentioned; see Jouanna 2013: 99. Finally, whereas surprise is not highlighted as an independent emotion, the adverb "suddenly" (ἐξαίφνης/ἐξαπίνης) is used by the author to qualify emotional experience in general; see, e.g., the "sudden fear" in ch. 10, 6.378–80 L.
15. On the association between *aêdia* ("unpleasantness") and disgust in the Hippocratic corpus, see Kazantzidis 2017.
16. On "higher cognitive emotions" as opposed to instinctual emotional responses, see Griffiths 1997: 77–99 and 100–22.
17. Miller 1997: 10; cf. Lateiner and Spatharas 2017b.
18. For a discussion of these complicated terms, see Gundert 2000: 21–2, and van der Eijk 2005: 126–7. Cf. Miller 1948 and Pigeaud 1981: 33–41; 1987: 47–63. The fact that the Hippocratic treatise deploys an extremely rich vocabulary for human cognition makes it all the more problematic that the latter's relation to emotion is left without discussion.
19. See Gundert 2000: 29, n. 97.
20. On the ongoing debate as to whether emotions can be elicited non-cognitively, see the discussions in Zajonc 1980, 1984; Leventhal and Scherer 1987; Storbeck and Clore 2007.
21. See Overwien 2014: 215; cf. Pigeaud 1981: 43.
22. The "action" of the body is indicated in the Greek text with the phrase τοῦ σώματος τῇ πρήξει. Similar wording (πρήξεσι παντὸς τοῦ σώματος) occurs also in [Hippoc.] *On Regimen*

4.86 [6.640 L.], in a passage which argues that when we are awake all psychic activity is subordinated to an "acting" body; for a discussion, see Harris 2009: 243–5, and Bartos 2015: 175, 201–5; cf. Hulskamp 2016.
23. Cf. James 1884: 193–4.
24. See, e.g., the skepticism in Konstan 2006b: 25–6; cf. Nussbaum 2001: 37, n. 34. For the idea that even instinctual physiological reactions (such as turning pale at the sudden sight of a snake) can be mediated by unconscious appraisal processes, see Siemer and Reisenzein 2007; cf. Reisenzein 2009.
25. Compare how (pathological) bodily occurrences are also described as occurring unexpectedly, e.g. in *Aphorisms* 7.40 (4.588 L.); *Epidemics* 5.106 (5.258 L.); *Coan Prognoses* 470 (5.688 L.); see Ciani 1987.
26. See Aristotle, *Metaphysics* 980a24–31, with Sears 1993: 24, and Baltussen 2015: 30. Cf. [Hippoc.] *On Flesh* 16 (8.604 L.) with Gundert 2000: 20.
27. See van der Eijk 2005: 127.
28. See van der Eijk 2000: 66–7; cf. van der Eijk 1997b: 257, n. 99; Charles 2007.
29. Prinz 2004a: 58.
30. See Öhman et al. (2001); Prinz 2002: 140; 2004a: 74–5; Robinson 2010: 652–3.
31. Colombetti 2014: 111–12.
32. In much the same way as a person would behave when affected emotionally. See, e.g., the description of fear in *On the Diseases of Girls* 1 (8.468 L.); cf. Lami 2007: 46–9.
33. See, e.g., [Hippoc.] *On Affections* 52; cf. Mattern 2016 on the psychological meaning of *lupê* in Galen (second century CE).
34. As in, e.g., Euripides, *Hippolytus* 188.
35. E.g. in Aeschylus, *Libation Bearers* 463.
36. See, e.g., [Hippoc.] *Epidemics* 2.4.5; *Epidemics* 4.1.51. The same medical "narrowing" of meaning applies to the Hippocratic use of *phrikê* ("shivering," "shuddering"); cf. Cairns 2013; 2017a.
37. On mind, body, and metaphor in the discussions of ancient emotions, see Cairns 2016b.
38. See esp. Holmes 2010b: 121–47.
39. See the seminal discussion by Kudlien 1973; cf. Langholf 1990: 48, and Padel 1992: 24 on the metaphorical associations of "blackness" when applied to bodily fluids.
40. This shift is witnessed for the first time in Archilochus; see Nelson-Hawkins 2016.
41. See Langholf 1990: 38; cf. Cairns 2003a; 2016b: 14–15.
42. See Clarke 1992: 92–3, and Hanson 2003: 185–6.
43. See *Epid.* 7.10 (5.380 L.).
44. See Pigeaud 1981: 446. On the interchangeable meanings of *kardiê* and *thumos* as "mental organs," see Jahn 1987: 9–17. Although *thumos* is rich in metaphorical associations (see Cairns 2014b), we should note the general Hippocratic tendency to avoid (and modify the meaning of) traditional terms indicating psychological concepts. Thumiger 2017: 400 notes, for instance, that while *phrenes* is extremely common in classical poetry as a term for intellectual activity, in Hippocratic discussions of mental life it is not so prominent and it appears mostly as a bodily organ that is affected by physical illness.
45. See Gundert 2000: 21–2 and 29.
46. See Gundert 2000: 29, n. 97.
47. The patient's psychological support is addressed independently only in later medical texts, during the first and second centuries CE. See Porter 2016; cf. Letts 2016.
48. See, e.g., *Coan Prognoses* 4 (5.588 L.); cf. [Aristotle] *Problems* 30.1, 954b35.

49. See Jouanna 2013: 101.
50. Cf. *Epidemics* 3.3.17 (3.142 L.), which mentions sudden fits of crying as an indication of emotional imbalance.
51. On the different views regarding the location of the mind in early Greek medicine (the main three proposing the brain, the blood, and the heart), see Manuli and Vegetti (1977); Hankinson 1991; Singer 1992; Gundert 2000.
52. For the patient's marginalized voice in Hippocratic medicine, see especially Petridou and Thumiger 2016b. Cf. Letts 2016; Thumiger 2016a; and Webster 2016.
53. On the vocabulary of insanity in the Hippocratics, see Thumiger 2013.
54. See Lloyd 1991: 362.
55. On this text, see Jouanna 2007.
56. That would bring us closer to Aristotle's emphasis on "mental pictures" (*phantasia*) while we experience an emotion. See Striker 1996: 291, and Pearson 2014: 166; cf. Konstan 2006b: 101.
57. See Flashar 1966: 32–5. Cf. Müri 1953.
58. Cf. [Aristotle] *Problems* 30.1, 954b 16–18. See Horwitz and Wakefield 2007: 58, and Radden 2009: 183–4.
59. See Pigeaud 1981: 124; cf. Thumiger 2013: 63.
60. Jouanna 2012: 235.
61. See King 2013: 265.
62. See Thumiger 2016a: 212.
63. See Sassi 2001.
64. See the evidence collected in Parker 2012: 108–11.
65. *On Ancient Medicine* 10; *Epidemics* 1.2.9; 3.2.6; 3.2.11; *Aphorisms* 6.23; *On the Diseases of Women* 2.182.
66. See Horden 1999: 300.
67. See Thumiger 2016a: 124.
68. See, e.g., [Hippoc.] *On Diseases* 2.72 (7.110 L.) on a disease called *phrontis*; the word is used in ancient Greek to indicate "mental preoccupation." See Langholf 1990: 54; cf. *Epidemics* 6.5.5 (5.316 L.) with Gundert 2000: 25, n. 69.
69. See especially the case of Parmeniscus in *Epidemics* 7.89 [5.446 L.], who is suffering from alternating fits of joy (*euthumiê*) and depression (*athumiai*). See Montiglio 2000: 232, and Thumiger 2016a: 122.
70. See Gundert 2000: 25; cf. Entralgo 1970: 341–2.
71. See Pormann 2008: 27.
72. Rufus of Ephesus, fr.69 (Pormann 2008: 70–1).
73. Holmes 2013a: 18.
74. See Holmes 2010a. Cf. Frede 1986.
75. Holmes 2013a: 21.
76. On the issue of medical authority in the Hippocratic corpus, see Holmes 2013b.
77. On the suppression of the doctor's emotions in the Hippocratic corpus (conceived as a strategy that is complementary to what Holmes 2013b calls the physician's "disembodied authority"), see Kazantzidis 2017; cf. Kosak 2005.

Chapter 2

1. For a review of these and other versions, see Grossardt 2001.
2. Appraisals as at Scherer, Schorr, and Johnstone 2001. For an older bibliography on appraisal, see Cairns 1993: 5, nn. 7, 8. Before the advent of appraisal theory, emotional

responses were taken to be immediate and intuitive, as they are again, to an extent, in the embodied appraisal theory of Prinz 2004b.
3. Konstan 2006b, chs 4, 10, and the essays at Chaniotis 2012d: 175–291. See also Nussbaum 1978: 146–58.
4. Old Testament sacrificial joy was fundamental to J. Wellhausen's influential monograph (1878).
5. So also the Isis Aretalogies, as at Martzavou 2012b: 283.
6. *IG* iv² 1.121–2. Laughter: nos 8, 9, 19. Disparaging laughter *vel sim.*: 3, 4. Naiveté: 9. Grief: 10 (only because master's property broken accidentally by a slave). Shame: 19 (*aischunê*, because of laughter).
7. *Nemesis*: Fontenrose 1968. Curse: Larson 1995: 135, on Phyllis (Lucian, *Salt* 40). Shame: Plutarch,. *Greek Questions* 293C–F (Charilla); Pausanias 4.4.2, 4.31.3 with Strabo 8.1.9 (rape victims at Limnai). Grief: Larsen 1995: 140, on Erigone (Callimachus fr. 178, ed. Pfeifer).
8. Odyssean *xenia*, often linked to supplication: Naiden 2009: 116–17. Later examples: Naiden 2009: 144–6. Supplication plays, in the sense that a long act of supplication is underway at the start, or takes up at least 200 lines: Aeschylus, *Eumenides, Supliant.*; Sophocles, *Oedipus at Colonus*; Euripides, *Andromache, Heraclidae, Heracles, Orestes, Suppliants*. A *xenia* play: Euripides, *Alcestis*.
9. Altar: Aeschylus, *Suppliants* 345. Social respect: *Odyssey* 14.37–8 with Cairns 1993: 108–9.
10. Naiden 2009: 122–5, to which add Seneca, *Controversiae* 10.1.1.
11. Tacitus, *Annals* 3. 36; *Digest* 47. 10. 38. pr., 48. 19. 28. 7 (cf. 28. 5. 92. pr.). Cf. Ovid, *Metamorphoses* 13.408–14.
12. Vernant and Detienne 1979, recently critiqued on several grounds, as at Naiden 2015, but not on this one. The emotion of sacrificial guilt, accepted by Vernant and Detienne, but derived from Burkert 1983, is now often rejected, notably by McClymond 2008. Background for these theories: Naiden and Rives 2015.
13. Plutarch, *Quaestiones convivales (Table Talk)*, 632C; this paragraph is adapted from Naiden 2015: 117.
14. Thucydides 2.38, Plato, *Republic* 364b–c, 364e–365a.
15. *Homeric Hymn* 26.12, *Orphic Hymns* 45.7, 66.11; as a consequence of peace, Aristophanes, *Peace* 1015.
16. Chantraine 1968, s.v. γάνυμαι, γηθέω.
17. Mommsen, *CIL* I² p. 290, emending Festus p. 165, ed. Mueller. Wissowa 1912, however, does not divide Roman festivals in this way, and neither did Lindsay 1930.
18. Greek examples: Naiden 2015: 52–6. Roman: Hahn 2007: 239–45.
19. Sacrifice and curse: Aeschines 1.23, 2.158, Demosthenes 24.20; Demosthenes 19.70, 23.97. Seeing only the human side of this equation or transfer: Chaniotis 2006b: 237, on regulations of the Andanian Mysteries.
20. Sokolowski 1955, no. 16.17–27.
21. *Pensées* 4.250.
22. Observed, and then had to analyze: Artemidorus, *Oneirocriticon* 2.33, dividing gods into those which were self-evident, and those which had to be discerned, a common formula, but here applied even to gods seen in dreams.
23. For the distinctive element of shock and disorientation, see Keltner and Haidt 2003: 303–4. Shuddering fear: Cairns 2013: 79–80.
24. Other such cases: Pfister 1924, col. 318; and not only to humankind but to natural elements *P.Oxy.* 1380.159–60.

25. *Il.* 1.9 *cholos*, 1.75 *mênis*, 21.468 *aidôs*, 4.507 *nemesis*, 23.274 *eleos*, 15.524 *tharsos*; *charis* vel. sim. is never used of Apollo, but he feels it for Hector. *Phobos* of Aphrodite: 5.352. Friendliness: Ares, 15.11; Hera, 4.151; Zeus, 16.433, 18.118; all gods, 24.67. Hate or *echthra*: Hades, 9.159. *Misos*: Zeus, 17.272. Only *zêlos* (zeal) and *praotês* (gentleness) are missing.
26. For the contrast, see Konstan 2003b. The same distinction appears briefly at Lloyd-Jones 1983: 69–70. In Latin, divine *phthonos* was *invidia*: see Kaster 2005: 185.
27. Apuleius, *Metamorphoses* 11.23. Another view of initiations, seeing them as sources of community akin to festivals: Chaniotis 2011.
28. Plutarch, *Theseus* 35.5; Pausanias 1.15.3, 1.32.5.
29. Frontinus 1.11.8; [Aurelius Victor] *De viris illustribus* 16; Cicero, *On the Nature of the Gods* 2.6; Dionysius of Halicarnassus 13.1–2 adds a second epiphany of the twins in the Roman forum.
30. Ister *FGrH* 334 F 50–52; scene 24 as at Settis et al. 1988.
31. Speculation and debate: Meineck and Konstan 2014, especially Tritle 2014: 91, diagnosing Epizelus. Awareness of the religious aspect of episodes like that of Epizelus, but without any perspective informed by religious history: Hanson 1989: 192–3.
32. Maslow 1964, although he supposed that peak experiences of a religious type befell seers and prophets, not worshipers *in extremis*.
33. *Hieros Logos* 4.50 (i.e., *Oration* 50). A simple or typical case: 2.18.
34. Macrobius, *Satires* 1.23.3, as at Versnel (1987: 47), drawing the same distinction among types of epiphanies.
35. Two neglected terms: see Aubriot-Sevin 1992: 273–5, noting the difference between *hilaskesthai* and both *euchesthai* and *arasthai*.
36. *Sebas* towards guests and parents: Aeschylus, *Eumenides* 269–72. Relevant passages, and treatment of the necessary distance as a sign of fear: Jäkel 1972, 1975, 1979.
37. Kaster 2005 (ch. 1), but without these contrasts.
38. Personifications of some similar emotions without cult: *deos*, *atê* (delusion/disaster, not quite an emotion, but certainly a psychological experience and one that is often associated with emotions of regret), *pavor*, *invidia*. The altar of *eleos* (Pausanias 1.17.1) was likely not a place of cult; see Wycherley 1954. Neither these nor the emotions given cult status have ever been studied as a group, rather than separately, but see, e.g., the characteristically Victorian attempt to historicize the development of cults and personifications in Farnell 1896 (v. 5, ch. 11). The only recent general treatment: Clark 2007.
39. Hesiod, *Works and Days* 195–200.
40. Pausanias 1.17.1; Eustathius on *Iliad* 22.451, another location; Hesychius s.v. αἰδοῦς βωμός, a third. Sparta: Pausanias 3.20.10.
41. Pliny, *Natural History* 11.251.
42. *Iliad* 9.502–9; Euripides fr. 436, ed. Kannicht (from *Hippolytus Veiled*), *Medea* 439–40.
43. Euripides, *Hippolyyus* 78–81. Cf. Plato, *Protagoras* 320c–322d, where *aidôs* is a quality bestowed on mankind by Zeus, but not a goddess, and is later in the sophist's speech replaced by prudence, or *sôphrosunê*. The same pair of nouns: Plato, *Charmides* 157d. Konstan (2006b: 119) observes that *phthonos* eventually replaced *nemesis*, another change.
44. Although no such two-part prayer is extant. The ethical and psychological relation between the two: Cairns 1993: 51–4, anticipated by Redfield 1975: 113–19.
45. Theognis 1.280; Plato, *Cratylus* 401a, *Theatetus* 175e, *Laws* 3.684e, 9.876c; Aeschines 3.66; Callicmachus, *Hymn to Artemis* 64, *Hymn to Delos* 107.
46. The denial at Euripides, *Hippolytus* 536–42, is tendentious; see Pausanias 1.30.1, *IG* i³ 1382. Other locations: Waser 1909, col. 489–93.

47. I.e., the *erastês* ("lover") and the *erômenos* ("beloved"); Pausanias 130.1 (Athens) and 6.23.3–5 (Elis).
48. Athenaeus 13.561d. Spartan pre-battle sacrifice: 13.561d.
49. Sicyon: *SIG* 1122. Closed: Plutarch, *Cleomenes* 8–9.
50. Thus Wilamowitz-Moellendorff (1931–2: 1.274–5) supposed that Phobos was an old war god, and that the personifications associated with Phobos, such as Homeric Deimos, developed later; cf. Farnell 1896 (v. 5, ch. 11). Further history: Patera 2012.
51. *Iliad* 11.37, Hesiod, *Scutum* 144 ; Hesychius s.v. γοργώ. Phobos as a ghost: Dieterich 1891: 86.
52. I.e., the temple of *vetus Spes*, in contrast to the temple built by A. Atilius Calatinus; see Latte 1929 and Wissowa 1912: 273–4.
53. Tib. 1.1.9, *CIL* VI 2043.2.10, as at Wissowa 1912, 326–30.
54. Apollonius Rhodius 2.715. No particulars for Harmonia at Thebes, save for Plato, *Phaedo* 95a.
55. Pudicitia was only for *matronae univirae* (i.e. women married only once): Radke 1959.
56. Hesiod, *Theogony* 935. Speculation on this odd pair: West 1966 ad loc.
57. Pliny, *Natural History* 35.157. The complications arising from allowing both old and new divine images: Platt 2011: 83–5.
58. Distress: *Hieros Logos* 1.62, 69, 2.38, 2.57 (i.e., Oration 47, 48). Respite: 1.57, 4.9. Joy: 1.78, as a cure for his sick nurse. Contentment: 2.23. Gratitude: 2.11.
59. Other interpretations do not take this cognitive approach, including Martazavou 2012: 194–5, a "construction of anxiety and hope"; faith-healing at Edelstein 1945: 1.142–5; construction of false hope in response to despair at Wilamowitz-Moellendorff 1886: 37.
60. Military views as at n. 31 above, to which add Chaniotis 2005: 145, on Hellenistic epiphanies attaining "the dimensions of a massive delusion."
61. Or, to paraphrase Cairns and Fulkerson (2015: 9), these emotions are known through cultural and historical reconstruction, and not directly, through apprehension of psychological or physiological universals.

Chapter 3

1. Among the ever-growing bibliography on the topic of music and emotions, see the following collections of papers (most of which will be quoted below): Juslin and Sloboda 2010; Cochrane, Fantini, and Scherer 2013. More specifically on Greece: Restani 2001.
2. Component process theories, for instance, assume that we should identify emotion categories, such as the aesthetic, the utilitarian, and the epistemic (Scherer and Coutinho 2013: 124–8).
3. Iamblichus, *On the Pythagorean Life* 112; Philodemus, *On Music* 4, col. 42.39–45 Delattre; Sextus Empiricus, *Against the Mathematicians* 6.8; Cicero, *On His Policies* fr. 2 Orelli [4.992] *apud* Boethius *On Music* 1.1; Quintilian, *Institutes of Oratory* 1.10.32.
4. The Dorian is usually described as a melody which induced courage and bravery (as at Plato, *Republic* 399a–c). In different versions of the tale (Galen, *On the Doctrines of Plato and Hippocrates* 5.6.21; Martianus Capella, *On the Marriage of Philology and Mercury* 9.926), the protagonist is Damon of Oa, the philosopher identified by some scholars as the main source of Plato's theorizing on the moral effects of music (but *contra* see Wallace 2015, esp. 153–5).
5. On music's appeal on animals, see also Plato, *Statesman* 268b.
6. According to modern aesthetics, there are three quite distinct ways in which a work of art can be related to its subject matter or content: representing, expressing, and merely

copying it (Scruton 1997: 118–19). Recent studies (especially Halliwell 2002) have shown how broad and variegated the meanings and philosophical implications of ancient *mimêsis* could be, and how the different connotations of this term—the oldest concept in Western aesthetics—might have all been implied in its ancient occurrences.

7. The same consequentiality among these three items is outlined in Aristotle, *Rhetoric* 1388b31–6 (trans. Freese 1926): "Let us now describe the nature of the characters of men according to their emotions, habits, ages, and fortunes. By the emotions I mean anger, desire, and the like, of which we have already spoken; by habits virtues and vices, of which also we have previously spoken, as well as the kind of things men individually and deliberately choose and practise."

8. On this long passage of the *Politics*, see Barker 2005: 99–111, and Destrée 2017.

9. I follow here Susemihl's emendation of the text ("even when there are no words, owing to rhythms and melodies themselves," instead of "even when they are not accompanied by rhythms and melodies," which Barker refers to in the footnote, cf. 175, n. 10), suggested by Aristotle's reference to Olympus, the mythical composer for solo *aulos*, in the previous sentence.

10. In modern aesthetics, the so-called *arousal theory* explains music's expressiveness as its propensity to evoke the corresponding emotion in the listener (Davies 2010).

11. For an interpretation of the passage of the *Politics* quoted above as a passage which, in a similar vein, musical motions contain likenesses of the same motion they excite, see Simpson 1998: 272.

12. Cf. Aristoxenus, *Rhythmic Elements* 2, p. 2.5–8 Pearson: "we also explained in the preceding passage that it is to do with durations [*chronoi*, lit. "times"] and the perception of them, but this must be said again now, for it is in a way the first principle of knowledge concerned with rhythms"; trans. Barker 1989.

13. At this purpose, Kivy talks about *Enhanced Formalism* (Kivy 2002: 87). On Kivy's denial of the possibility that music displays emotions, see Kivy 1989, 1999.

14. On the importance of the performance experience in acquiring virtuous habits, both in Plato and Aristotle, see Jones 2012: 161–4. More specifically on the importance of music in building character, see Brüllmann 2013.

15. The sequence of books 1–8 of the *Politics* in the manuscripts is an achievement of late antiquity: the last part of the Aristotelian text is the earliest part of the whole *Politics*, most probably earlier than the composition of the *Poetics* (Düring 1966).

16. Also Damon (quoted at n. 4) is credited with having claimed that music arises from a movement of the soul (Athenaeus, *Sophists at Dinner* 628c); moreover, Galen associated him with music therapy (see *On the Doctrines of Plato and Hippocrates* 5.453, DK 37 A 8).

17. Earlier evidence which rejects the notion of musical emotional and ethical power is the so-called Hibeh Papyrus on music (mid-third century BCE), quoted in Barker 1984: 183–5. On emotions in Hellenistic philosophy, see Sihvola and Engberg-Pedersen 1998.

18. Nowadays, neurosciences have proved the neural separability of vocal from facial emotions: the two modes of expression seem in fact to be subserved by independent neural systems (Peretz 2010).

19. Aristotle, *Rhetoric* 1378a19–b22, the point of departure of Konstan's discussion, who describes the Aristotelian work as "the most sophisticated and detailed analyses of the emotions to come down to us from classical antiquity" (Konstan 2006b: 41).

20. For a survey on the topic, see Allen 1978: 83–8 (who holds a contrary view), Nougaret 1986 and Adamik 2013.

21. Cf. *Institutes of Oratory* 11.3.62: "the voice, which is the intermediary between ourselves and our hearers, will then produce precisely the same emotion in the judge that we have put into it." In his treatise (esp. 11.3.17), Quintilian heavily relies on Aristotle's *Rhetoric*, reproducing exactly the same distinctions between volume, tone, and rhythm of the voice.
22. By contrast, Cicero had regarded theatrical actors as paradigms of inspiration in order to obtain the desired pathemic vocality (see *On the Ideal Orator* 3.102–3 and 3.217–21).
23. An inscription describes the pantomime dancer as an "actor of tragic rhythmical movement" (Delphi III 1. 551). But pantomimic performances had precedents in other contexts too: see the suggestive tableau of the mythical love of Dionysus and Ariadne, accompanied by music, described in Xenophon, *Symposium* 9.2–7.
24. The mimetic power of *choreia* had been clearly stated since Plato, according to whom "what is involved in choric performance is imitations [*mimêmata*] of characters, appearing in actions and eventualities of all kinds which each performer goes through by means of habits and imitations" (*Laws* 655d, trans. Barker 1984).
25. On the relationship between pantomime and rhetoric, see Schlapbach 2008.

Chapter 4

1. I owe this insight to my teacher, Moses Hadas.
2. Green 1991: 33: "We have no surviving fifth-century representation of tragic actors acting, or even of chorusmen performing in the orchestra shown as chorusmen in the literal way that comic chorusmen are." Green goes on to remark (1991: 40), "We have noticed that comedy, with its frequent rupture of 'dramatic illusion', was seen literally, as men dressed up being funny. Tragedy, on the other hand, constantly maintained the illusion, and in fact could not risk breaking it. At one level, the figures seen in the theatre recreated myth-history and they were to that degree 'real'. When the vase-painter showed them, he therefore showed them as real."
3. So, too, Strepsiades manifests a righteous dudgeon toward Socrates and his ilk for their ostensible subversion of traditional values in the *Clouds*; in the end, he burns down Socrates' school.
4. We may compare the conclusion to Aeschylus' *Eumenides*, the final play in his trilogy, *Oresteia*; conceivably this too is part of the reason why Dionysus ends up preferring Aeschylus over Euripides in the *Frogs*. *Euphrosunê* or "good cheer" was associated with festivities, for example at symposia, as illustrated in an elegiac fragment by the archaic poet and thinker Xenophanes (fragment 1).
5. Kaster 2005: 23 observes that slaves were universally regarded as shameless in Rome.
6. Cf. Staley 2010: 95: "The vividness of tragedy's images may arouse our emotions, but these are only preliminary and involuntary; we can in the end judge their truth value." Thus, "if the emotional pull we feel in response to vivid events is not really emotion in the full Stoic sense of that word, then it cannot really be harmful" (2010: 74). Staley concludes that "Seneca purposely takes tragedy beyond fear to the production of horror, to something that both Longinus and Aristotle would see as monstrous tragedy" (2010: 108).
7. Compare Diogenes of Halicarnassus' distinction between two types of response to a literary work (*On Thucydides* 4.3): one type involves an irrational kind of sensation and emotion, which all are capable of experiencing (τῶν τε δι'αἰσθήσεως ἀλόγου καὶ τοῖς πάθεσι καταλαμβανομένων); the other involves the reasoned judgment of the expert orator. According to Dionysius, all art aims at stimulating the former response. Viidebaum 2015: 167–70 adduces Dionysius' own response to Isocrates' speeches, the effect of which he compares to that of music (*Demosthenes* 22.1).

Chapter 5

1. Single emotions: McNiven 2000b (fear in ancient Greece); Huber 2001 (Greek grief and mourning); Oakley 2004 (grief and sadness on lekythoi); Sojc 2004 (sadness on Classical grave reliefs); Räuchle 2017 (maternal emotions in classical Athens). On gestures and body language: Kenner 1960 (laughing and weeping in Greek art); Brilliant 1963 (gesture and rank in Roman art); Neumann 1965 (gestures in Greek art); Franzoni 2006 (*pathos* and *êthos* in Greek art); Catoni 2008 (*schêmata* in Greek art); Maderna 2009 (dangerous passions in Greek and Roman art); Masséglia 2015 (body language in Hellenistic art); Davies 2017 (proxemics in Roman art).
2. On extreme violence in the fifth century BCE, see Fischer and Moraw 2005; Seidensticker and Vöhler 2006; Muth 2008; Zimmermann 2009.
3. Exceptions: Franzoni 2006; Catoni 2008; Masséglia 2012a; Masséglia 2015; Räuchle 2017; Chaniotis et al. 2017.
4. Cf. Schnell 2007, esp. 177–80; see also Chaniotis 2012c: 14: "In direct communication, we have other media to increase the accuracy of the expression of feelings, such as facial expressions, raising or lowering the voice, and body-language . . . mimic and gestures are also represented in art. This information is, however, filtered and sometimes subject to conventions of representation."
5. Group of centaur biting Lapith, *c.* 460 BCE, Archaeological Museum, Olympia: Ridgway 1965: 49; Maderna 2009: 10, Fig. 2.
6. Roman marble copy from Hellenistic original around 150–120 BCE, Loggia dei Lanzi, Florence: Mylonopoulos 2017: 81, Fig. 7.
7. Prioux 2011: 137; see also Franzoni 2006: 63–8. On *sôphrosunê* in general, see North 1966. On *sôphrosunê* and emotion control, see Harris 2001: 80–7. On female *sôphrosunê*, see North 1977; Räuchle 2017: 28–30, 139–40.
8. Neumann 1965: 106: "Während die 'Momentangebärden' affekthaft und durch ausfahrende Gesten gekennzeichnet sind, sind die 'Zustandsgebärden' überwiegend von kontemplativ-nachdenklichem Charakter. Sie geben Kunde von der spezifischen Verfassung der Gestalt, von der mehr oder weniger dauerhaften inneren Zuständlichkeit." ("While the *Momentangebärden* are emotional and marked by outward gestures, the *Zustandsgebärden* are predominantly contemplative and thoughtful in character. They give information about the specific consitution of the figure, of the more or less permanent inner state.")
9. Red-figure lekythos, *c.* 420 BCE, Metropolitan Museum, New York 17.230.35: BAPD 214280; Reeder 1995: 356–7, no. 113.
10. Cairns 2016b: 7. On personifications between allegory and belief, see Stafford 2000: 1–44.
11. Alcman fr. 58 (trans. Campbell 1988: 435): Ἀφροδίτα μὲν οὐκ ἔστι, μάργος δ᾽ Ἔρως οἷα <παῖς> παίσδει, / ἄκρ᾽ ἐπ᾽ ἄνθη καβαίνων, ἅ μή μοι θίγης, τῷ κυπαιρίσκῳ.
12. *IG* I³ 1290: Ἀμφαρέτη. | τέκνον ἐμῆς θυγατρὸς τόδ᾽ ἔχω φίλον, ὅμπερ ὅτε αὐγάς: / ὄμμασιν ἠ|ελίο ζῶντες ἐδερκόμεθα, / ἔχον ἐμοῖς γόνασιν καὶ νῦν φθίμενον φθιμένη ᾽χω.
13. Euripides, *Suppliants* 815–17 (trans. E. P. Coleridge): δόθ᾽, ὡς περιπτυχαῖσι δὴ / χέρας προσαρμόσασ᾽ ἐμοῖς / ἐν ἀγκῶσι τέκνα θῶμαι.
14. See Räuchle 2017: 210–18. Funerary plate with inscription labeling the woman embracing the head of the deceased as the mother (*mêtêr*): black figure pinax, *c.* 500 BCE, Louvre, Paris MNB 1905: BAPD 463; Neils and Oakley 2003: 165, Fig. 3. Older man and woman touching the deceased youth's head, likely to be identified as father and mother: white lekythos, 410–390 BCE, Antikensammlung Berlin F 2684: BAPD 217904; Oakley 2004:

84, Fig. 54. Old nurse standing at the top of the bier and bidding farewell to the untimely deceased woman: red figure loutrophoros, 475–450 BCE, National Museum, Athens 1170: BAPD 205750; Huber 2001: 127.

15. White lekythos, c. 430 BCE, National Museum, Athens 19355: BAPD 214321; Oakley 2004: 163.
16. Originally used in the nuptial rites, the loutrophoros became a grave marker for those who died unmarried and childless: see Sabetai 2008.
17. Sarcophagus, c. 120–130 CE, Museo Nazionale, Agrigento: Amedick 1991: 121 cat. no. 2.
18. Plutarch, *Consolation to his Wife* 609a: (trans. De Lacy and Einarson 1959: 587) οὐ γὰρ 'ἐν βακχεύμασι' δεῖ μόνον τὴν σώφρονα μένειν ἀδιάφθορον, ἀλλὰ μηδὲν οἴεσθαι ἧττον τὸν ἐν πένθεσι σάλον καὶ τὸ κίνημα τοῦ πάθους ἐγκρατείας δεῖσθαι διαμαχομένης οὐ πρὸς τὸ φιλόστοργον, ὡς οἱ πολλοὶ νομίζουσιν, ἀλλὰ πρὸς τὸ ἀκόλαστον τῆς ψυχῆς.
19. E.g. Homer, *Iliad* 18.22: "The black cloud of sorrow enwrapped Achilles" (τὸν δ' ἄχεος νεφέλη ἐκάλυψε μέλαινα); 8.124: "Then was the soul of Hector clouded with dread sorrow" ("Εκτορα δ' αἰνὸν ἄχος πύκασε φρένας); Euripides, *Heracles* 1140: "Alas! a cloud of lamentation envelops me" (αἰαῖ□στεναγμῶν γάρ με περιβάλλει νέφος). For further examples, see Cairns 2016a: esp. 34–6; cf. Cairns 2009, esp. 51: "The grief itself is the cloud or the concealing garment of which the literal garment is the external visual symbol."
20. Euripides, *Iphigenia at Aulis* 1547–50 (trans. Kovacs 2002: 335): ὡς δ' ἐσεῖδεν Ἀγαμέμνων ἄναξ | ἐπὶ σφαγὰς στείχουσαν εἰς ἄλσος κόρην, | ἀνεστέναξε, κἄμπαλιν στρέψας κάρα | δάκρυε, πρόσθεν ὀμμάτων πέπλον προθείς. Cf. Cairns 2011b: 19.
21. Quintilian 2.13.12–13 (trans. Russell 2001: 345): "Quid? non in oratione operienda sunt quaedam, sive ostendi non debent sive exprimi pro dignitate non possunt? Ut fecit Timanthes, opinor, Cythnius in ea tabula qua Coloten Teium vicit. Nam cum in Iphigeniae immolatione pinxisset tristem Calchantem, tristiorem Ulixem, addidisset Menelao quem summum poterat ars efficere maerorem: consumptis adfectibus non reperiens quo digne modo patris vultum posset exprimere, velavit eius caput et suo cuique animo dedit aestimandum."
22. Wall painting from the "House of the Tragic Poet" in Pompei, 62–79 CE, Museo Archeologico Nazionale di Napoli 9112: Lorenz 2008: 392, Fig. 200; Chaniotis et al. 2017: 115, no. 31.
23. Iphigenia does not "stand at the altar awaiting her doom," as Pliny describes ("qua stante ad aras peritura," *Naturalis Historia* 35.73), but is carried by two male figures and raises her arms in a gesture of heightened emotionality. As noted above, this gesture is ambiguous and could in the present context either denote panic or supplication.
24. Cf. Cairns 2009: 47–8: "The gesture of veiling, then, is a characteristic and powerful marker of grief, one that will have been familiar to Greek audiences not only from epic, tragedy and the visual arts, but from their own experience."
25. On visual representations of the episode, see Mangold 2000: 80–102, 184–96; Ritter 2005. On the various versions of the episode in literature, see Mangold 2000: 81–2. On the conflicting emotions of Menelaus in this episode, see Kaltsas 2017: 101–2.
26. Athenian red-figure krater, c. 450 BCE, Louvre Paris G 424: BAPD 214486; Ritter 2005: 276, Fig. 6.
27. Athenian red-figure lekythos, c. 460–450 BCE, State Hermitage Museum St Petersburg b 4524: BAPD 215792; Ritter 2005: 272, Fig. 4a–b. For other examples of Eros with *phialê*, see Ritter 2005: 270–6.
28. Euripides, *Hippolytus* 525–7 (trans. Kovacs 1995: 175): Ἔρως Ἔρως, ὁ κατ' ὀμμάτων στάζων πόθον, εἰσάγων γλυκεῖαν ψυχᾷ χάριν οὓς ἐπιστρατεύσῃ . . .

29. Athenian red-figure loutrophoros, *c*. 420 BCE, Ashmolean Museum Oxford 1966.888: BAPD 34; Reeder 1995: 169, no. 25.
30. Euripides, *Hippolytus* 528–9 (trans. Kovacs 1995: 175): μή μοί ποτε σὺν κακῷ φανείης μηδ' ἄρρυθμος ἔλθοις.
31. Wall paintings from the "House of Punished Love" in Pompei, first century CE, Museo Archeologico Nazionale di Napoli 9249. 9257: Lorenz 2008: 153, Fig. 48, 266, Fig. 125.
32. For visual representations of the punishment of Eros, see Curtius 1930; Delivorrias 1984: no. 1252–4; Hermary and Cassimatis 1986: no. 417–26; Blanc and Gury 1986: no. 77–84. For the poetic tradition regarding a statue of "Eros in chains," see *Anthologia Graeca* 16.195–9.
33. *Anthologia Graeca* 16.199 (trans. Paton 1943: 257–7): καὶ κλαῖε καὶ στέναζε, συσφίγχθεὶς χεροῖν / τένοντας, ὦ 'πίβουλε· τοῖά τοι πρέπει. / οὐκ ἔσθ' ὁ λύσων· μὴ 'λεείν' ὑπόβλεπε. / αὐτὸς γὰρ ἄλλων ἐκ μὲν ὀμμάτων δάκρυ / ἔθλιψας, ἐν δὲ πικρὰ καρδίᾳ βέλη / πήξας ἀφύκτων ἰὸν ἔσταξας πόθων, / Ἔρως· τὰ θνητῶν δ' ἐστί σοι γέλως ἄχη. / πέπονθας, οἷ' ἔρεξας. ἐσθλὸν ἡ δίκη.
34. Grave stele, *c*. 350 BCE, Athens Kerameikos Museum P688: Clairmont 1993: 4, no. 4.415. Inscription (*IG* II^{3}11891): Κοράλλιον Ἀγάθωνος γυνή.
35. Gestures that can be interpreted as explicitly emotional, e.g. the touching of another person's shoulder or chin, are mostly performed by women; see Meyer 1999: 122–9; on the gender-specific display of emotion, see below.
36. On the handshake in general, see Neumann 1965: 49–59. On Greek funerary art, see Davies 1985; Pemberton 1989; Meyer 1999; Räuchle 2017: 235–7.
37. Cf. Alexandridis 2000: 17–18; Larsson Lovén 2010: 214; Davies 2012: 29.
38. The differences in composition and style create a curious and paradoxical effect: the Greek *dexiôsis* scenes purport to reproduce reality, though they do not, whereas representations of the *dextrarum iunctio* often have a certain unrealistic touch even though the gesture formed an integral part in the actual wedding ritual.
39. Funerary altar, first century CE, Museo Nazionale Romano 124514: Larsson Lovén 2010: 212, Fig. 22.
40. Aristotle, *Nicomachean Ethics* 1157b27–32 (trans. Rackham 1926): ἔοικε δ' ἡ μὲν φίλησις πάθει, ἡ δὲ φιλία ἕξει. ἡ γὰρ φίλησις οὐχ ἧττον πρὸς τὰ ἄψυχά ἐστιν, ἀντιφιλοῦσι δὲ μετὰ προαιρέσεως, ἡ δὲ προαίρεσις ἀφ' ἕξεως. Considered as a *hexis*, then, (conjugal) *philia* depends upon a specific emotional attitude towards the other person (i.e. spouse) and a certain choice to act accordingly, thus comprising both rational and emotional components; cf. Ward 1996: 160.
41. This interrelation between *pathos* and *hexis* is also apparent in ancient physiognomic treatises: while they are generally more interested in *hexis* than in *pathos*, they derive many of their judgements on permanent character traits from facial expressions of acute emotions; e.g. Aristotle, *Physiognomics* 805a29–b9; cf. D. L. Cairns 2005: 127, n. 18 with further references.
42. On the "Greater Dedication," see Schober 1936; Hölscher 1985; Pirson 2002; Marszal 2000; Kunze 2002, 40–51; Winkler-Horaçek 2011. The nicknames were coined to distinguish the votive from the "Lesser Attalid Dedication," which stood on the Athenian Acropolis and was significantly smaller in scale. The highly controversial discussion regarding the original context, dating, and reconstruction of the Lesser Dedication cannot be considered here. For a thorough discussion, see Engel 2015.
43. "Ludovisi Gaul," Roman marble copy from Hellenistic original *c*. 220 BCE, Museo Nazionale Romano 144: Kunze 2002: tab. 5, Figs 9–10.

44. Aristotle, *Rhetoric* 2.8, 1385b13–16 (trans. Konstan 2006b: 204): ἔστω δὴ ἔλεος λύπη τις ἐπὶ φαινομένῳ κακῷ φθαρτικῷ ἢ λυπηρῷ τοῦ ἀναξίου τυγχάνειν, ὃ κἂν αὐτὸς προσδοκήσειεν ἂν παθεῖν ἢ τῶν αὐτοῦ τινα, καὶ τοῦτο ὅταν πλησίον φαίνηται.
45. Moreover, even Aristotle allows for a basic emotional reaction to another person's suffering. In his *Poetics* (13, 1453a2–6) he states that the suffering of a profoundly bad person may not be able to trigger *eleos* or *phobos* but *to philanthrôpon*, an emotional response to another's misfortune that is indifferent to desert, "an instinctive sensitivity to the suffering of others" (Konstan 2006b: 217).
46. "Gerade in der Antike haben wir vielfach mit einem neugierigen aber kühlen, genießenden Blick zu rechnen, dem die möglichst präzise und konkrete Schilderung von Gewalt in erster Linie Anlass zu ästhetischem Vergnügen gewesen zu sein scheint" ("In antiquity, we often have to reckon with a curious but cool, appreciative look, to which the most precise and concrete portrayal of violence seems to have been primarily a cause of aesthetic pleasure," Giuliani 2004: 20).

Chapter 6

1. On emotion and cultural variation, see Lutz 1988; Mesquita and Frijda 1992; Wierzbicka 1999; and Schweder and Haidt 2000.
2. There are surveys of interpretations in Halliwell 1998: 350–6; Holzhausen 2000: 7–33, 2009: 618–23.
3. Philodemus apparently responded to the discussion of catharsis in Aristotle's *On Poets*; see Janko 2011: 512–21.
4. On anger in Juvenal, esp. *Satires* 1 and 2, see Anderson 1964; Braund 1996; and now Keane 2015, demonstrating the much broader range of emotion in Juvenal than anger alone.
5. According to Cicero, they also made for a more pleasurable read: see *Ad Fam.* 5.12: "at viri saepe excellentis ancipites variique casus habent admirationem exspectationem, laetitiam molestiam, spem timorem; si vero exitu notabili concluduntur, expletur animus iucundissima lectionis voluptate." The Greek novel particularly presented conflicting emotions: see Fusillo 1999.
6. The "scale of affection" comes from Kakridis 1949: 152–64.
7. Whether *eleos* and *oiktos* meaningfully differ is disputed (Burkert 1955: 42–8; Casadio 1970–2; Scott 1979; Kim 2000: 58, n.49).
8. For anger, see Rubenstein 2004; Stevens 1944 on pre-emptive arguments against pity; on the close connection between pity and innocence, Konstan 2000. On the Roman side, Cicero, *Brutus* 23.90–1 cites the story of Galba, who saved himself from a serious charge, though obviously guilty, by an appeal to pity.
9. Cicero gives sixteen topics for arousing pity in *De inventione* 106–9.
10. See esp. Putnam 1995; Gill 1997; Galinsky 1998.
11. The debate over Aeneas' actions goes back to Servius (see *ad* 12.940).
12. On Pallas' baldric, see Putnam 1998: ch. 6.
13. See Bonner 2011: 212–13 on the importance of Homer in Roman education.
14. On Augustine as reader of Virgilian *pathos*, see MacCormack 1998: 89–131.
15. See Eckstein 2014 on differences between Polybius and Livy in the arousal of emotion.
16. The phrase appears in the first poem of all three major elegists: Prop. 1.1.1, Tib. 1.1.55–6, Ov. *Am.* 1.1.12.

17. Disgust has been extensively discussed in psychology, often from an evolutionary perspective (Plutchik 1980; Olatunji et al. 2004; Paul Rozin has published widely on disgust). In recent philosophy there is a rich debate about whether disgust should be a basis for legislation, with Miller 1997 on one side and Nussbaum 2004 on the other. On ancient disgust, see now Lateiner and Spatharas 2017b.
18. Olatunji et al. 2004 includes the connection between humor and disgust as a puzzle for future research.
19. Menninghaus 2003: 1: "Every book about disgust is not least a book about the rotting corpse."
20. On smell in Roman culture and literature, see Butler and Purves 2014; Bradley 2015.
21. See Kaster 2005: 105–21, where he distinguishes between a more reflexive aversion, or *per se fastidium*, and *fastidium*, which involves status and "deliberate ranking."
22. See Nagle 1983 for a comparison of the Byblis and Myrrha stories.
23. On the Tereus, Procne, and Philomela episode, see Oliensis 2009 and Gildenhard and Zissos 2007; the latter covers the story's reception in later literature as well.
24. See Dinter 2012 on this theme in Lucan and Most 1992 in Neronian literature generally; both examine "dismemberment" not just as theme, but as stylistic device.
25. See Gordon 1987; Masters 1992: ch. 6; and Finiello 2005.
26. For representations of this story elsewhere in Latin literature, see Horace, *Odes* 1.18, and Ovid, *Metamorphoses* 12.210–579.
27. On *fastidium* and satiety, see Kaster 2005: 106–8.
28. Though we find exceptions in Book 7 of Pliny the Elder's *Natural History*, on the marvels of different peoples and unusual births; see also Pythagoras' *miracula animalium* in *Metamorphoses* 15.
29. See Clausen 2002: 28 on the contrast between Odysseus' lack of emotion at *Odyssey* 7.78 and Aeneas at *Aeneid* 1.407–9.
30. On monsters and monstrosity in antiquity, see Felton 2012 and most recently Lowe 2015.
31. There is a rich tradition about wonder in Western philosophy; Descartes calls it the first passion in *The Passions of the Soul* (1645), 53, but worries that too much wonder inhibits reason, 76. Both Hobbes and Spinoza critique Descartes.
32. On the cow, see Squire 2010; for Aphrodite, Havelock 2007.
33. In a sign of how overwhelming this is, Scipio needs to be corrected several times for fixing his gaze back down at earth (chs 17 and 19).
34. Note that neither Daedalus nor Icarus marvels at the sky, on which see Feldherr 2010: 129–30.
35. There is an earlier description of the *bugonia* at *Georgics* 4.281–314; on differences between the two, see, e.g., Schiesaro 1997; Gale 2000.
36. On wonder and the marvelous in Augustan literature, see Hardie 2009.
37. See Rüpke 2007; Santangelo 2013.
38. This comet prefigures the one seen after the death of Caesar, which was interpreted as a sign of his apotheosis. See Green 2014 on Caesar's comet.
39. Encolpius is amazed from the moment he first sees Trimalchio (*miraremur*, 27; *admiratio saturi*, 28; *miratus sum*, 30; *nobis mirantibus*, 35, etc.). On the abundance of disgust in both Petronius and Apuleius, see Lateiner 2017.
40. The Cupid and Psyche episode is often considered an early example of fairy tale: see, e.g., Swahn 1955; Brewer 2003.
41. On *curiosus and curiositas* in Apuleius, see De Filippo 1990; Schlam 1992: ch. 5; Leigh 2013.

Chapter 8

1. Prescribed hatred: *IC* I.ix.1 (Dreros, late third century BCE). Joy: *IEphesos* 1448; *SEG* XXIII 206. Grief: *IG* V.1.1427; *SEG* XXVIII 953.
2. See Tamiolaki 2013 (Xenophon); Visvardi 2015: 34–93 (Thucydides).
3. Xenophon, *Hellenica* 6.4.15–16 (translated by R. B. Strassler and J. Marincola, slightly modified).
4. On both passages see Tamiolaki 2013: 40–1.
5. *IPE* I^2 32 B lines 22–7; Chaniotis 2013e: 209–12.
6. Ostraka with textual and pictorial graffiti: Brenne 2002: 80–166.
7. Dössel 2003; Bencivenni 2003: 39–103; Chaniotis 2013d; Gray 2015: 35–107, 159–291. A new text: *IG* XII.4.132 (reconciliation in Telos, *c*. 300 BCE).
8. E.g. Plutarch, *Alcibiades* 10.1; *Phocion* 9; Dio, *Oration* 7.22–6, 29–30, 59; Kuhn 2012.
9. *IG* II^2 11477; *I.Thespiai* 1247; *I.Beroia* 404; *I.Tomis* 384, 459; *I.Kallatis* 148; *TAM* V.1.550; *SEG* VIII 269; *SEG* XXIII 433; *SEG* XXXV 630; *CEG* II 630; *GV* 759, 949, 1576, 1989, 2081.
10. *IOSPE* I^2 52 lines 5–10. Other examples: *IOSPE* I^2 46 lines 4–7; 51 lines 9–11.
11. Honorary titles: van Nijf 2013: 383–7. The fiction of the orphaned family: Jones 1999; Chaniotis 2006b: 223–6.
12. Augustus: *GIBM* 894 and *SEG* LVI 1233. Caligula: *I.Assos* 26. Geta: *IG* II^2 1077. Cf. *IG* VII 2711 lines 68–9, 99–101, 107–9; Reynolds 1982: no. 25.
13. E.g. *IGUR* 148; *SEG* XXXVIII 1236.
14. *IGLS* IV 1427, 1460/1461, 1732; V 2546; *SEG* VII 875.
15. In the case of Cicero's *De inuentione*, this focus is driven by the work's topic, the first part of a projected and presumably abandoned complete treatment of rhetoric; the *Rhetorica ad Herennium* addresses all five parts of rhetoric, though it is evident from the relative scale of the different parts that *inuentio* was regarded as the major topic of study by the school of rhetorical instruction represented by these two works. See further Kennedy 1972; Corbeill 2002; Gaines 2007; Calboli 2009.
16. *Rhetorica ad Herennium* 2.50; Cicero, *De inuentione* 1.106–9.
17. Compare 185, at the start of this section of the treatise: there Antonius identifies twelve emotions that the orator might wish his audience to feel. Anger is absent, and the additions are the desire for someone's safety (*saluum uelle*), greed (*cupire*), disgust (*abhorrere*), and the desire to inflict punishment (*poenum uelle*). On the two lists, see Leeman, Pinkster, and Rabbie 1989 *ad loc*.
18. For a summary of the contemporary stylistic debate between the Atticists and Asianists which appears to be heavily implicated in Cicero's aims for *Orator*, see Wisse 1995; O'Sullivan 1997.
19. *Orator* 123, "is erit ergo eloquens, qui ad id quodcumque decebit poterit accommodare orationem".
20. E.g. *Orator* 129 (*benevolentia*); see further Vickers 1988: 74–5.
21. "Probationes enim efficiant sane ut causam nostram meliorem esse iudices putent, adfectus praestant ut etiam uelint."

---

42. A number of chapters in de Jong, Nünlist, and Bowie 2004 on authors of the second sophistic touch on the issue of narrators and wonder; see esp. Whitmarsh 2004: 433–5 on Philostratus.

22. Cicero, *De oratore* 1.228. On the trial (Alexander no. 1) and Galba's actions, Flaig 2003: 119–20; Hall 2014: 8–10.
23. Cicero, *Verrine* 2.5.3; cf. *De oratore* 2.194–9; Quintilian 2.5.17.
24. Cicero, *De oratore* 1.227, *populi misericordiam concitasset*.
25. On tears within Roman oratory, see Hall 2014: 99–128.
26. On drama and Roman oratory, see Axer 1980; Hughes 1997; Harries 2005; Batstone 2009. This chapter has deliberately excluded humor from this consideration of emotion within Roman rhetoric; key ancient sources are Cicero, *De oratore* 2.216-90 and Quintilian 6.3.
27. *For Marcus Fonteius* 47–8, "prospicite ne ille ignis aeternus nocturnis Fonteiae laboribus uigiliisque seruatus sacerdotis uestrae lacrimis extinctus esse dicatur."
28. *Nihil citius lacrima arescit uel sim.*, Cicero *De inuentione* 1.109; *De partitione oratoria* 57; *Rhetorica ad Herennium* 2.50; Quintilian 6.1.27. A neat example of a failed attempt to arouse pity is an anecdote Cicero tells in *Pro Cluentio* (58–9) of the advocate Cannutius' attempt to arouse pity for his client Fabricius through repeated imperatives *respicite*, "look towards"; when he did so himself, he found Fabricius had slunk off in despair at his advocate's incompetence.
29. Quintilian 6.1.44: ". . . nam ut est longe uehementissimus hic cum inualuit adfectus, ita si nil efficit tepet; quem melius infirmus actor tacitis iudicum cogitationibus reliquisset."
30. Compare the attack on Gaius Antonius by the orator Caelius, of which Quintilian preserves a quotation (4.2.123–4), in which Antonius is both incompetent and personally vicious.
31. On Cicero's use of emotion in his attack on Verres, see Kaster 2005: 20–1.
32. Mack 1937; on the oratory of crisis, see Hall 2013.
33. "Atque haec cura, Quirites, erit infixa animo meo sempiterna, ut cum uobis, qui apud me deorum immortalium uim et numen tenetis, tum posteris uestris cunctisque gentibus dignissimus ea ciuitate uidear quae suam dignitatem non posse se tenere, nisi me reciperasset, cunctis suffragiis iudicauit."
34. The *contio* is perhaps a slightly different case, as the presiding magistrate was, in some interpretations, responsible for any violence that might arise as a result of the meeting; but even in such cases the magistrate's duty was to dissolve the meeting, not moderate the words of speakers.

REFERENCES

Ackrill, J. L. (1963), "Aristotle's Definition of Psyche," *Proceedings of the Aristotelian Society* 73: 119–33.
Adamik, B. (2013), "Zur Problematik der Akzentqualität im klassischen Latein," *SPFB(klas)* 18: 3–22.
Aldrete, G. (1999), *Gestures and Acclamations in Ancient Rome*, Baltimore, MD: Johns Hopkins University Press.
Alexander, M. C. (1990), *Trials in the Late Roman Republic, 149 B.C. to 50 B.C.*, Toronto: Toronto University Press.
Alexandridis, A. (2000), "Exklusiv oder bürgernah? Die Frauen des römischen Kaiserhauses im Bild," in C. Kunst and U. Riemer (eds), *Grenzen der Macht: Zur Rolle der römischen Kaiserfrauen*, 9–28, Stuttgart: Steiner.
Alexiou, M. ([1974] 2002), *The Ritual Lament in Greek Tradition*, 2nd edition, revised by D. Yatromanolakis and P. Roilos, Lanham, MD: Rowman and Littlefield.
Alexiou, M. and D. L. Cairns, eds (2017), *Greek Laughter and Tears: Antiquity and After*, Edinburgh: Edinburgh University Press.
Allen, W. S. (1978), *Vox Latina: A Guide to the Pronunciation of Classical Latin*, 2nd edition, Cambridge: Cambridge University Press.
Amedick, R. (1991), *Vita Privata: Die Sarkophage mit Darstellungen aus dem Menschenleben*, ASR 1.4, Berlin: Mann.
Anderson, W. S. (1964), *Anger in Juvenal and Seneca*, Berkeley and Los Angeles: University of California Press.
Angier, T. (2010), *Technē in Aristotle's Ethics: Crafting the Moral Life*, New York: Continuum.
Annas, J. (1989), "Epicurean Emotions," *Greek, Roman, and Byzantine Studies* 30: 145–64.
Annas, J. (1992), *Hellenistic Philosophy of Mind*, Berkeley and Los Angeles: University of California Press.
Armstrong, D. (2008), "'Be angry and sin not': Philodemus versus the Stoics on Natural Bites and Natural Emotions," in J. T. Fitzgerald (ed.), *Passions and Moral Progress in Graeco-Roman Thought*, 79–121, London: Routledge.
Armstrong, D. and M. McOsker, eds (2018), *Philodemus, On Anger*, Atlanta, GA: Society for Biblical Literature.
Arnold, M. (1960), *Emotion and Personality*, New York: Columbia University Press.
Athanassaki, L. (2012), "Recreating the Emotional Experience of Contest and Victory Celebrations: Spectators and Celebrants in Pindar's Epinicians," in X. Riu and J. Pòrtulas (eds), *Approaches to Archaic Greek Poetry*, 173–219, Chieti: Dipartimento di Scienze dell'Antichità.
Aubriot-Sevin, D. (1992), *Prière et conceptions religieuses en Grèce ancienne jusqu' à la fin du Ve siècle av. J.-C.*, Lyons: Maison de l'Orient Méditerranéen.
Axer, J. (1980), *The Style and Composition of Cicero's Speech* Pro Roscio Comoedo: *Origin and Function*, Warsaw: Wydawnictwa Uniwersytetu Warszawskiego.
Bagnoli, C., ed. (2011), *Morality and the Emotions*, Oxford: Oxford University Press.

Balot, R. (2014), *Courage in the Democratic Polis: Ideology and Critique in Classical Athens*, Oxford: Oxford University Press.

Baltussen, H. (2015), "Ancient Philosophers on the Sense of Smell," in M. Bradley (ed.), *Smell and the Ancient Senses*, 30–45, London and New York: Routledge.

Barchiesi, A. (2015), *Homeric Effects in Vergil's Narrative*, translated by I. Marchesi and M. Fox, Princeton, NJ: Princeton University Press.

Barker, A. (1984), *Greek Musical Writings I: The Musician and his Art*, Cambridge: Cambridge University Press.

Barker, A. (1989), *Greek Musical Writings II: Harmonic and Acoustic Theory*, Cambridge: Cambridge University Press.

Barker, A. (2005), *Psicomusicologia nella Grecia antica*, Naples: Guida Editore.

Barnes, J. (1971–2), "Aristotle's Concept of Mind," *Proceedings of the Aristotelian Society* 72: 101–14.

Bartos, H. (2015), *Philosophy and Dietetics in the Hippocratic* On Regimen: *A Delicate Balance of Health*, Leiden: Brill.

Batstone, W. (2009), "The Drama of Rhetoric at Rome," in E. Gunderson (ed.), *The Cambridge Companion to Ancient Rhetoric*, 212–27, Cambridge: Cambridge University Press.

Battistella, C. and D. P. Nelis, "Some Thoughts on the Anger of Seneca's Medea," in D. L. Cairns and D. P. Nelis (eds), *Emotions in the Classical World: Methods, Approaches, and Directions*, 245–56, Stuttgart: Steiner.

Beagon, M. (2007), "Situating Nature's Wonders in Pliny's *Natural History*," *Bulletin of the Institute of Classical Studies* 50: 19–40.

Beard, M. (2014), *Laughter in Ancient Rome: On Joking, Tickling, and Cracking Up*, Berkeley and Los Angeles: University of California Press.

Beardslee, J. W. (1918), *The Use of Phusis in Fifth-Century Greek Literature*, Chicago: University of Chicago Press.

Bencivenni, A. (2003), *Progetti di riforme costituzionali nelle epigrafi greche dei secoli IV–II a.C.*, Bologna: Lo Scarabeo.

Betts, R. (1998), "The Sceptics and the Emotions," in J. Sihvola and T. Engberg-Pedersen (eds), *The Emotions in Hellenistic Philosophy*, 197–218, Dordrecht: Kluwer.

Biles, Z. (2011), *Aristophanes and the Poetics of Competition*, Cambridge: Cambridge University Press.

Blanc, N. and F. Gury (1986), "Eros/Amor, Cupido," *Lexicon Iconographicum Mythologiae Classicae*, 3, 966–1049, Heidelberg: Heidelberger Akademie der Wissenschaften.

Bobou, O. (2013), "Emotionality in Greek Art," in A. Chaniotis and P. Ducrey (eds), *Unveiling Emotions II. Emotions in Greece and Rome: Texts, Images, Material Culture*, 273–311, Stuttgart: Steiner.

Boegehold, A. L. (1999), *When a Gesture was Expected*, Princeton, NJ: Princeton University Press.

Bonner, S. F. ([1977] 2011), *Education in Ancient Rome*, London: Routledge.

Bostanov, V. and B. Kotchoubey (2004), "Recognition of Affective Prosody: Continuous Wavelet Measures of Event-related Brain Potentials to Emotional Exclamations," *Psychophysiology* 41, no. 2: 259–68.

Bourbou, C. (2013), "The Imprint of Emotions Surrounding the Death of Children in Antiquity," in A. Chaniotis and P. Ducrey (eds.), *Unveiling Emotions II. Emotions in Greece and Rome: Texts, Images, Material Culture*, 331–50, Stuttgart: Steiner.

Boyd, B. (2009), *On the Origin of Stories: Evolution, Cognition, and Fiction*, Cambridge MA: Harvard University Press.

Boyd, B., J. Carroll, and J. Gottschall, eds (2010), *Evolution, Literature, and Film: A Reader*, New York: Columbia University Press.
Bradley, M., ed. (2015), *Smell and the Ancient Senses: The Senses in Antiquity*, London: Routledge.
Braund, S. M. (1996), *Juvenal: Satires Book 1*, Cambridge: Cambridge University Press.
Braund, S. M. and C. Gill (1997), *The Passions in Roman Thought and Literature*, Cambridge: Cambridge University Press.
Braund, S. M. and G. W. Most, eds (2003), *Ancient Anger: Perspectives from Homer to Galen*, Cambridge: Cambridge University Press.
Bremmer, J. N. and H. Roodenberg, eds (1991), *A Cultural History of Gesture: From Antiquity to the Present Day*, London: Polity.
Brennan, T. (1998), "The Old Stoic Theory of Emotions," in J. Sihvola and T. Engberg-Pedersen (eds), *The Emotions in Hellenistic Philosophy*, 27–70, Dordrecht: Kluwer.
Brenne, S. (2002), "Die Ostraka (487–ca. 416 v. Chr.) als Testimonien," in P. Siewert (ed.), *Ostrakismos-Testimonien I. Die Zeugnisse antiker Autoren, der Inschriften und Ostraka über das athenische Scherbengericht aus vorhellenistischer Zeit (487–322 v. Chr.)*, 31–166, Stuttgart: Steiner.
Brewer, D. (2003), "The Interpretation of Fairy Tales," in H. E. Davidson and A. Chaudhri (eds), *A Companion to the Fairy Tale*, 15–38, Rochester, NY: D.S. Brewer.
Brilliant, R. (1963), *Gesture and Rank in Roman Art: The Use of Gestures to Denote Status in Roman Sculpture and Coinage*, New Haven: Connecticut Academy of Arts and Sciences.
Brock, R. (1994), "The Labour of Women in Classical Athens," *Classical Quarterly* 44: 336–46.
Brüllmann, P. (2013), "Music Builds Character: Aristotle, *Politics* VIII 5, 1340a14-b5," *Apeiron* 46, no. 4: 345–73.
Bruun, H. (1999), "Sudden Death as an Apoplectic Sign in the Hippocratic Corpus," *Classica et Mediaevalia* 50: 5–24.
Burkert, W. (1955), *Zum altgriechischen Mitleidsbegriff*, PhD dissertation, University of Erlangen.
Burkert, W. (1983), *Homo Necans: Interpetationen der altgriechischer Opferriten und Mythen, Religionsgeschictliche und Vorsuchen und Vorarbeiten*, 32, Berlin: De Gruyter.
Bury, R. G., ed. (1926), *Plato, Vol. X: Laws, Books 1–6*, Cambridge, MA, and London: Harvard University Press.
Butler, H. E. (1920), *The Institutio Oratoria of Quintilian*, 4 vols, Cambridge, MA, and London: Harvard University Press.
Butler, S. and A. Purves (2014), *Synaesthesia and the Ancient Senses*, New York: Routledge.
Cairns, D. L. (1993), *Aidōs: The Psychology and Ethics of Honour and Shame in Ancient Greek Literature*, Oxford: Oxford University Press.
Cairns, D. L. (2002), "The Meaning of the Veil in Ancient Greek Culture," in L. Llewellyn-Jones and S. Blundell (eds), *Women's Dress in the Ancient Greek World*, 73–93, London: Duckworth.
Cairns, D. L. (2003a), "Ethics, Ethology, Terminology: Iliadic Anger and the Cross-Cultural Study of Emotion," in S. M. Braund and G. W. Most (eds), *Ancient Anger: Perspectives from Homer to Galen*, 11–49, Cambridge: Cambridge University Press.
Cairns, D. L. (2003b), "The Politics of Envy: Envy and Equality in Ancient Greece," in D. Konstan and K. Rutter (eds), *Envy, Spite, and Jealousy: The Rivalrous Emotions in Ancient Greece*, 235–52, Edinburgh: Edinburgh University Press.
Cairns, D. L. (2004), "Pity in the Classical World (Review of Konstan 2001)," *Hermathena* 176: 59–74.

Cairns, D. L (2005), "Bullish Looks and Sidelong Glances: Social Interaction and the Eyes in Ancient Greek Culture," in D. L. Cairns (ed.), *Body Language in the Greek and Roman Worlds*, 123–55, Swansea: Classical Press of Wales.

Cairns, D. L. (2008), "Look Both Ways: Studying Emotion in Ancient Greek," *Critical Quarterly* 50, no. 4: 43–62.

Cairns, D. L. (2009), "Weeping and Veiling: Grief, Display, and Concealment in Ancient Greek Culture," in T. Fögen (ed.), *Tears in the Graeco-Roman World*, 37–57, Berlin: De Gruyter.

Cairns, D. L. (2011a), "Looks of Love and Loathing: Cultural Models of Vision and Emotion in Ancient Greek Culture," *Mètis* 9: 37–50.

Cairns, D. L. (2011b), "Veiling Grief on the Tragic Stage," in D. L. Munteanu (ed.), *Emotion, Genre, and Gender in Classical Antiquity*, 15–33, London: Bloomsbury.

Cairns, D. L. (2013), "A Short History of Shudders," in A. Chaniotis and P. Ducrey (eds), *Unveiling Emotions II. Emotions in Greece and Rome: Texts, Images, and Material Culture*, 85–107, Stuttgart: Steiner.

Cairns, D. L. (2014a), "Exemplarity and Narrative in the Greek Tradition," in D. L. Cairns and R. Scodel (eds), *Defining Greek Narrative*, 103–36, Edinburgh: Edinburgh University Press.

Cairns, D. L. (2014b), "*Psyche, Thymos,* and Metaphor in Homer and Plato," *Les Études Platoniciennes* 11 http://etudesplatoniciennes.revues.org/566 (accessed March 17, 2018).

Cairns, D. L. (2015), "Revenge, Punishment, and Justice in Athenian Homicide Law," *Journal of Value Enquiry* 49: 645–65

Cairns, D. L. (2016a), "Clothed in Shamelessness, Shrouded in Grief: The Role of 'Garment' Metaphors in Ancient Greek Concepts of Emotion," in G. Fanfani, M. Harlow, and M.-L. Nosch (eds), *Spinning Fates and the Song of the Loom: The Use of Textiles, Clothing and Cloth Production as Metaphor, Symbol, and Narrative*, 25–41, Oxford: Oxbow.

Cairns, D. L. (2016b), "Mind, Body, and Metaphor in Ancient Greek Concepts of Emotion," *L'Atelier du Centre de recherche historique* 16, http://acrh.revues.org/7416 (accessed March 17, 2018).

Cairns, D. L. (2016c), "Metaphors for Hope in Archaic and Classical Greek Poetry," in R. Caston and R. A. Kaster (eds), *Hope, Joy and Affection in the Classical World*, 13–44, Oxford: Oxford Classical Press.

Cairns, D. L. (2017a), "Horror, Pity, and the Visual in Ancient Greek Aesthetics," in D. L. Cairns and D. Nelis (eds), *Emotions in the Classical World: Methods, Approaches, and Directions*, 53–77, Stuttgart: Steiner.

Cairns, D. L. (2017b), "Mind, Metaphor, and Emotion in Euripides (*Hippolytus*) and Seneca (*Phaedra*)," in D. L. Cairns and D. P. Nelis (eds), *Seneca's Tragic Passions*, 247–67, Rome: = *Maia* 69.2.

Cairns, D. L. and L. Fulkerson, eds (2015a), *Emotions between Greece and Rome*. London: Institute of Classical Studies.

Cairns, D. L. and L. Fulkerson (2015b), "Introduction," in D. Cairns and L. Fulkerson (eds), *Emotions Between Greece and Rome*, BICS Supplement 125, 1–22, London: Institute of Classical Studies.

Cairns, D. L. and D. P. Nelis, eds (2017), *Emotions in the Classical World: Methods, Approaches, and Directions*. Stuttgart: Steiner.

Cairns, F. (2005), "Lavinia's Blush (Virgil *Aeneid* 12.64–70)," in D. L. Cairns (ed.), *Body Language in the Greek and Roman Worlds*, 195–213, Swansea: Classical Press of Wales.

Calboli, G. (2009), "Introduzione alla Inventione," in B. Santalucia (ed.), *La repressione criminale nella Roma repubblicana fra norma e persuasione*, 185–221, Pavia: IUSS.

Campbell, D. A., ed. (1988), *Greek Lyric II: Anacreon, Anacreonta, Choral Lyric from Olympus to Alcman*, Loeb Classical Library, Cambridge, MA: Harvard University Press.

Cánovas, C. P. (2011), "The Genesis of the Arrows of Love: Diachronic Conceptual Integration in Greek Mythology," *American Journal of Philology* 132: 553–79.

Cantarella, E. (2003), "Fathers and Sons in Rome," *Classical World* 96: 281–98.

Carawan, E. (2013), *The Athenian Amnesty and Reconstructing the Law*, Oxford: Oxford University Press.

Carroll, J. (2006), "The Human Revolution and the Adaptive Function of Literature," *Philosophy and Literature* 30: 33–49.

Casadio, V. (1970–2), "L'eleos nel' epica," *Museum Criticum* 5–7: 54–9.

Caston, R. R. (2012), *The Elegiac Passion: Jealousy in Roman Love Elegy*, New York: Oxford University Press.

Caston, R. R. and R. A. Kaster, eds (2016), *Hope, Joy, and Affection in the Classical World*, New York: Oxford University Press.

Caston, V. (2008), "Commentary on Charles," *Proceedings of the Boston Area Colloquium in Ancient Philosophy* 24: 30–47.

Catoni, M. L. (2008), *La comunicazione non verbale nella Grecia antica: Gli schemata nella danza, nell'arte, nella vita*, Turin: Bollati Boringhieri.

Champion, C. (2004), *Cultural Politics in Polybius' Histories*, Berkeley and Los Angeles: University of California Press.

Chaniotis, A. (2005), *War in the Hellenistic World: A Social and Cultural History*, Malden, MA/ Oxford: Wiley-Blackwell.

Chaniotis, A. (2006a), "Familiensache: Demonstration von Zusammengehörigkeit im altgriechischen Grabritual," in R. Reichmann (ed.), *Der Odem des Menschen ist eine Leuchte des Herrn: Aharon Agus Zum Gedenken*, 205–9, Heidelberg: Winter.

Chaniotis, A. (2006b), "Rituals between Norms and Emotions: Rituals as Shared Experience and Memory," in E. Stavrianopoulou (ed.), *Rituals and Communication in the Graeco-Roman World*, 211–38, Liège: Centre international d'étude de la religion grecque antique.

Chaniotis, A. (2011), "Emotional Community through Ritual: Initiates, Citizens, and Pilgrims as Emotional Communities in the Greek World," in A. Chaniotis (ed.), *Ritual Dynamics in the Ancient Mediterranean: Agency, Emotion, Gender, Representation*, 263–90, Stuttgart: Steiner.

Chaniotis, A. (2012a), "Constructing the Fear of the Gods: Epigraphic Evidence from Greece and Asia Minor," in A. Chaniotis (ed.), *Unveiling Emotions: Sources and Methods for the Study of Emotions in the Greek World*, 205–34, Stuttgart: Steiner.

Chaniotis, A. (2012b), "Moving Stones: The Study of Emotions in Greek Inscriptions," in A. Chaniotis (ed.), *Unveiling Emotions: Sources and Methods for the Study of Emotions in the Greek World*, 91–130, Stuttgart: Steiner.

Chaniotis, A. (2012c), "Unveiling Emotions in the Greek World: Introduction," in A. Chaniotis (ed), *Unveiling Emotions: Sources and Methods for the Study of Emotions in the Greek World*, 11–36, Stuttgart: Steiner.

Chaniotis, A., ed. (2012d), *Unveiling Emotions: Sources and Methods for the Study of Emotions in the Greek World*, Stuttgart: Franz Steiner Verlag.

Chaniotis, A. (2013a), "Affective Epigraphy: Emotions in Public Inscriptions of the Hellenistic Age," *Mediterraneo Antico* 16, no. 2: 745–60.

Chaniotis, A. (2013b), "Emotional Language in Hellenistic Decrees and Hellenistic Histories," in M. Mari and J. Thornton (eds), *Parole in movimento: linguaggio politico e lessico storiografico nel mondo ellenistico; atti del convegno internazionale, Roma, 21–23 febbraio 2011*, 339–52, Pisa: F. Serra.

Chaniotis, A. (2013c), "Empathy, Emotional Display, Theatricality, and Illusion in Hellenistic Historiography," in A. Chaniotis and P. Ducrey (eds), *Unveiling Emotions II. Emotions in Greece and Rome: Texts, Images, Material Culture*, 53–84, Stuttgart: Steiner.

Chaniotis, A. (2013d), "Normen stärker als Emotionen? Der kulturhistorische Kontext der griechischen Amnestie," in K. Harter-Uibopuu and F. Mitthof (eds), *Vergeben und Vergessen? Amnestie in der Antike. Akten des ersten Wiener Kolloquiums zur Antiken Rechtsgeschichte, Wien, 27.–28.10.2008*, 47–70, Vienna: Holzhausen.

Chaniotis, A. (2013e), "*Paradoxon, Enargeia*, Empathy: Hellenistic Decrees and Hellenistic Oratory," in C. Kremmydas and K. Tempest (eds), *Hellenistic Oratory: Continuity and Change*, 201–16, Oxford: Oxford University Press.

Chaniotis, A. (2014), "Mnemopoetik: die epigraphische Konstruktion von Erinnerung in den griechischen Poleis," in O. Dahly, T. Hölscher, S. Muth, and R. Schneider (eds), *Medien der Geschichte: Antikes Griechenland und Rom*, 132–169, Berlin: De Gruyter.

Chaniotis, A. (2015), "Affective Diplomacy: Emotional Scripts between Greek Communities and Roman Authorities," in D. L. Cairns and L. Fulkerson (eds.), *Emotions Between Greece and Rome*, 87–103, London: Institute of Classical Studies.

Chaniotis, A. (2016), "Displaying Emotional Community: The Epigraphic Evidence," in E. Sanders and M. Johncock (eds), *Emotion and Persuasion in Classical Antiquity*, 93–111, Stuttgart: Steiner.

Chaniotis, A. (2017), "The Life of Statues: Emotion and Agency," in D. L. Cairns and D. P. Nelis (eds), *Emotions in the Classical World: Methods, Approaches, and Directions*, 143–58, Stuttgart: Steiner.

Chaniotis, A. and P. Ducrey, eds (2013), *Unveiling Emotions II. Emotions in Greece and Rome: Texts, Images, Material Culture*, Stuttgart: Steiner.

Chaniotis, A., N. Kaltsas, and I. Mylonopoulos, eds (2017), *A World of Emotions: Ancient Greece, 700 BC–200 AD*, New York: Onassis Foundation.

Chantraine, P. (1968), *Dictionnaire étymologique de la langue grecque. Histoire des mots*, Paris: Klincksieck.

Chapa, J. (1998), *Letters of Condolence in Greek Papyri*, Florence: Edizioni Gonnelli.

Charles, D. (2007), "Aristotle on Desire in Action," in D. Frede and B. Reis (eds), *Body and Soul in Ancient Philosophy*, 291–308, Berlin and New York: De Gruyter.

Charles, D. (2008), "Aristotle's Psychological Theory," *Proceedings of the Boston Area Colloquium in Ancient Philosophy* 24: 1–29.

Ciompi, L. and E. Endert (2011), *Gefühle machen Geschichte: Die Wirkung kollektiver Emotionen, von Hitler bis Obama*, Göttingen: Vandenhoeck and Ruprecht.

Clairmont, C. W. (1993), *Classical Attic Tombstones*, Kilchberg: Akanthus.

Clark, A. (2007), *Divine Qualities: Cult and Community in Republican Rome*, Oxford: Oxford University Press.

Clarke, M. J. (1999), *Flesh and Spirit in the Songs of Homer: A Study of Words and Myths*, Oxford: Oxford University Press.

Clausen, W. (2002), *Virgil's* Aeneid: *Decorum, Allusion, and Ideology*, Munich: K.G. Saur.

Cleland, L. (2005), *The Brauron Clothing Catalogues: Text, Analysis, Glossary and Translation*, Oxford: BAR.

Clinton, K. (1996), "The Thesmophorion in Central Athens and the Celebration of the Thesmophoria in Attica," in R. Hägg (ed.), *The Role of Religion in the Early Greek Polis*, 111–25, Stockholm: Swedish Institute at Athens.

Clore, G. L. and A. Ortony (1988), "The Semantics of the Affective Lexicon," in V. Hamilton, G. H. Bower, and N. H. Frijda (eds), *Cognitive Perspectives on Emotion and Motivation*, 367–97, Norwell, MA: Springer.

Cochrane, T., B. Fantini, and K. R. Scherer (2013), *The Emotional Power of Music*, Oxford: Oxford University Press.

Coleridge, E. P. (1938), *Euripides: The Suppliants*, New York: Random House.

Colombetti, G. (2009), "What Language Does to Feelings," *Journal of Consciousness Studies* 16, no. 9: 4–26.

Colombetti, G. (2014), *The Feeling Body: Affective Science Meets the Enactive Mind*, Cambridge, MA: MIT Press.

Conze, A. (1893), *Die attischen Grabreliefs I*, Berlin: Spemann.

Cooper, J. M. (1996), "An Aristotelian Theory of the Emotions," in A. O. Rorty (ed.), *Essays on Aristotle's Rhetoric*, 238–57, Berkeley and Los Angeles: University of California Press.

Corbeill, A. (2002), "Rhetorical Education in Cicero's Youth," in J. May (ed,), *Brill's Companion to Cicero: Rhetoric and Oratory*, 23–48, Leiden: Brill.

Corbeill, A. (2004), *Nature Embodied: Gesture in Ancient Rome*, Princeton, NJ: Princeton University Press.

Curtius, L. (1930), "Poenitentia," in [no editor given], *Festschrift für James Loeb: zum sechzigsten Geburtstag gewidmet von seinen archäologischen Freunden in Deutschland und Amerika*, Munich: Bruckmann.

Daehner, J. and K. Lapatin, eds (2015), *Power and Pathos: Bronze Sculpture of the Hellenistic World*, Los Angeles: J. Paul Getty Museum.

Damasio, A. R. (1994), *Descartes' Error: Emotion, Reason, and the Human Brain*, New York: Putnam.

Damon, C. (2017), "Emotions as a Historiographical Dilemma," in D. L. Cairns and D. P. Nelis (eds), *Emotions in the Classical World: Methods, Approaches, and Directions*, 177–94, Stuttgart: Steiner.

Darwin, C. (1998), *The Expression of the Emotions in Man and Animals*, 3rd edition, London: Harper Collins.

Davidson, G. R. (1952), *Corinth XII: The Minor Objects*, Princeton, NJ: American School of Classical Studies at Athens.

Davidson, G. R., D. B. Thompson, and H. A. Thompson (1943), *Small Objects from the Pnyx: I. Hesperia*, Supplements 7, Princeton, NJ: American School of Classical Studies at Athens.

Davies, G. (1985), "The Significance of the Handshake Motif in Classical Funerary Art," *American Journal of Archaeology* 89, no. 4: 627–40.

Davies, G. M. (1994), "The Language of Gesture in Greek Art: Gender and Status on Grave Stelai," *Apollo* 140, no. 389: 6–11.

Davies, G. M. (1997), "Gender and Body Language in Roman Art," in T. Cornell and K. Lomas (eds), *Gender and Ethnicity in Ancient Italy*, 97–107, London: Accordia.

Davies, G. M. (2002), "Clothes as Sign: The Case of the Large and Small Herculaneum Women," in L. Llewellyn-Jones (ed.), *Women's Dress in the Ancient Greek World*, 227–42, London and Swansea: Duckworth/Classical Press of Wales.

Davies, G. M. (2005), "On Being Seated: Gender and Body Language in Hellenistic and Roman Art," in D. L. Cairns (ed.), *Body Language in the Greek and Roman Worlds*, 215–38, Swansea: Classical Press of Wales.

Davies, G. M. (2012), "The Face of the Social Climber," in S. Bell and T. Ramsby (eds), *Free at Last! The Impact of Freed Slaves on the Roman Empire*, London: Bristol Classical Press.

Davies, G. M. (2017), "Touching Behaviour: Proxemics in Roman Art," in D. L. Cairns and D. Nelis (eds), *Emotions in the Classical World: Methods, Approaches, and Directions*, 159–76, Stuttgart: Steiner.

Davies, S. (2010), "Emotions Expressed and Aroused by Music: Philosophical Perspectives," in P. N. Juslin and J. A. Sloboda (eds), *Handbook of Music and Emotion: Theory, Research, Applications*, 15–43, Oxford: Oxford University Press.

Dawkins, R. M., ed. (1929), *The Sanctuary of Artemis Orthia at Sparta*, London: Society for the Promotion of Hellenic Studies.

De Filippo, J. (1990), "*Curiositas* and the Platonism of Apuleius' *Golden Ass*," *American Journal of Philology* 111: 471–92.

Deigh, J. (2008), *Emotions, Values, and the Law*, New York: Oxford University Press.

De Jong, I. J. F., R. Nünlist, and A. Bowie, eds (2004), *Narrators, Narratees, and Narratives in Ancient Greek Literature*, Leiden: Brill.

De Lacy, P. H. and B. Einarson (1959), *Plutarch: Moralia, Vol. VII*, Loeb Classical Library, Cambridge: Harvard University Press.

Delivorrias, A. (1984), "Aphrodite," in *Lexicon Iconographicum Mythologiae Classicae*, 2, 2–151, Heidelberg: Heidelberger Akademie der Wissenschaften.

Derderian, K. (2001), *Leaving Words to Remember: Greek Mourning and the Advent of Literacy*, Leiden: Brill.

De Romilly, J. (1971), "La vengeance comme explication historique dans l'oeuvre d'Hérodote," *Revue des études grecques* 84: 314–47.

De Sousa, R. (2008), "Really, What Else is There? Emotions, Value, and Morality," *Critical Quarterly* 50, no. 4: 12–23.

Destrée, P. (2017), "Aristotle on Music for Leisure," in A. D'Angour and T. Philips (eds), *Music, Texts, and Culture in Ancient Greece*, Oxford: Oxford University Press.

Dickey, E. (2016), "Emotional Language and Formulae of Persuasion in Greek Papyrus Letters," in E. Sanders and M. Johncock (eds), *Emotion and Persuasion in Classical Antiquity*, 237–62, Stuttgart: Steiner.

Diddle Uzzi, J. (2005), *Children in the Visual Arts of Imperial Rome*, Cambridge: Cambridge University Press.

Dieterich, A. (1891), *Abraxas: Studien zur Religionsgeschichte des späteren Altertums*, Leipzig: Teubner.

Dimas, S. (1998), *Untersuchungen zur Themenwahl und Bildgestaltung auf römischen Kindersarkophagen*, Münster: Scriptorium.

Dinter, M. T. (2012), *Anatomizing Civil War: Studies in Lucan's Epic Technique*, Ann Arbor: University of Michigan Press.

Dixon, S. (1988), *The Roman Mother*, London: Croom Helm.

Dixon, S. (1997), "Conflict in the Roman Family," in B. Rawson and P. Weaver (eds), *The Roman Family in Italy: Status, Sentiment, Space*, 149–67, Oxford: Oxford University Press.

Dixon, T. (2003), *From Passions to Emotions: The Creation of a Secular Psychological Category*, Cambridge: Cambridge University Press.

Dixon, T. (2012), "'Emotion': The History of a Keyword in Crisis," *Emotion Review* 4: 338–44.

Dössel, A. (2003), *Die Beilegung innerstaatlicher Konflikte in den griechischen Poleis vom 5.–3. Jahrhundert v. Chr.*, Frankfurt: Lang.

Dué, C. (2002), *Homeric Variations on a Lament by Briseis*, Lanham, MD: Rowman and Littlefield.

Dué, C. (2006), *The Captive Woman's Lament in Greek Tragedy*, Austin: University of Texas Press.

Düring, I. (1966), *Aristoteles: Darstellung und Interpretation seines Denkens*, Heidelberg: Winter.
Dutton, D. (2009), *The Art Instinct: Beauty, Pleasure, and Human Evolution*, Oxford: Oxford University Press.
Eckstein, A. M. (2014), "Livy, Polybius, and the Greek East (Books 31–45)," in B. Mineo (ed.), *A Companion to Livy*, 407–22, Chichester: Wiley-Blackwell.
Edelstein, L. and E. (1945), *Asclepius: The Testimonies*, Baltimore, MD: Johns Hopkins University Press.
Eibl-Eibesfeldt, I. (1989), *Human Ethology*, New York: Aldine de Gruyter.
Eidinow, E. (2007), *Oracles, Curses, and Risk among the Ancient Greeks*, Oxford: Oxford University Press.
Ekman, P. (1973), *Darwin and Facial Expression: A Century of Research in Review*, New York: Academic Press.
Ekman, P. (1980), *Face of Man: Universal Expression in a New Guinea Village*, San Francisco: Garland.
Ekman, P. (1994), "Strong Evidence for Universals in Facial Expressions: A Reply to Russell's Mistaken Critique," *Psychological Bulletin* 115: 268–87.
Ekman, P. (1999a), "Basic Emotions," in T. Dalgleish and M. Power (eds), *Handbook of Cognition and Emotion*, 45–60, Chichester: Wiley.
Ekman, P. (1999b), "Facial Expressions," in T. Dalgleish and M. Power (eds), *Handbook of Cognition and Emotion*, 301–20, Chichester: Wiley.
Ekman P., ed. ([1972] 1982), *Emotion in the Human Face*, 2nd edition, Cambridge: Cambridge University Press (first published, New York: Pergamon).
Ekman, P. and D. Cordaro (2011), "What is Meant by Calling Emotions Basic?" *Emotion Review* 3: 364–70.
Ekman, P. and W. V. Friesen (1971), "Constants across Cultures in the Face and Emotion," *Journal of Personality and Social Psychology* 17: 124–9.
Ekman, P. and W. V. Friesen, (1975), *Unmaking the Face: A Guide to Recognizing Emotions from Facial Clues*, Englewood Cliffs, NJ: Prentice-Hall.
Ekman, P. and W. V. Friesen (1986), "A New Pan-cultural Facial Expression of Emotion," *Motivation and Emotion* 10: 159–68.
Ellis-Evans, A. (2012), "The Tyrants Dossier from Eresos," *Chiron* 42: 183–212.
Elsner, J. (2007), *Roman Eyes: Visuality and Subjectivity in Art and Text*, Princeton, NJ: Princeton University Press.
Elster, J. (1999), *Alchemies of the Mind: Rationality and the Emotions*, Cambridge: Cambridge University Press.
Engel, H. (2015), "Feindbilder im Hellenismus: Untersuchungen der Figuren des 'Kleinen Attalischen Weihgeschenks'," in C. Klose, L. C. Bossert, and W. Leveritt (eds.), *Fresh Perspectives on Graeco-Roman Visual Culture* Cambridge, 35–57, http://dx.doi.org/10.18452/17865 (accessed July 25, 2018).
Engels, J. (1998), *Funerum sepulchrorumque magnificentia: Begräbnis- und Grabluxusgesetze in der griechisch-römischen Welt mit einigen Ausblicken auf Einschränkungen des funeralen und sepulkralen Luxus im Mittelalter und in der Neuzeit*, Stuttgart: Steiner.
Entralgo, P. L. (1970), *La medicina Hipocrática*, Barcelona: Salvat.
Fantham, E. (2004), *The Roman World of Cicero's De Oratore*, Oxford: Oxford University Press.
Faraone, C. A. (1999), *Ancient Greek Love Magic*, Cambridge, MA: Harvard University Press.
Farnell, L. (1896–1909), *Cults of the Greek States*, Oxford: Oxford University Press.
Fehr, B. and J. A. Russell (1984), "Concept of Emotion Viewed from a Prototype Perspective," *Journal of Experimental Psychology: General* 113: 464–86.

Feldherr, A. (2010), *Playing Gods: Ovid's* Metamorphoses *and the Politics of Fiction*, Princeton, NJ: Princeton University Press.

Felton, D. (2012), "Rejecting and Embracing the Monstrous in Ancient Greece and Rome," in A. S. Mittman and P. J. Dendle (eds), *The Ashgate Research Companion to Monsters and the Monstrous*, 103–31, Farnham: Ashgate.

Finiello, C. (2005), "Der Bürgerkrieg: Reine Männersache? Keine Männersache! Erictho und die Frauengestalten im Bellum Civile Lucans," in C. Walde (ed.), *Lucan im 21. Jarhundert*, 155–85, Munich and Leipzig: Saur.

Fischer, G. and S. Moraw, eds (2005), *Die andere Seite der Klassik: Gewalt im 5. und 4. Jahrhundert v. Chr.*, Stuttgart: Steiner.

Fisher, N. (2017), "Demosthenes and the Use of Disgust," in D. Lateiner and D. Spatharas (eds), *Disgust: An Ancient Emotion*, 103–24, Oxford: Oxford University Press.

Fitzgerald, J. T., ed. (2008), *Passions and Moral Progress in Graeco-Roman Thought*, London: Routledge.

Flaig, E. (2003), *Ritualisierte Politik: Zeichen, Gesten und Herrschaft im Alten Rom*, Göttingen: Vandenhoeck and Ruprecht.

Flashar, H. (1966), *Melancholie und Melancholiker in den medizinischen Theorien der Antike*, Berlin: De Gruyter.

Fögen, T. (2001), "Ancient Theorizing on Non-Verbal Communication," in R. M. Brend, A. Lommel, and A. Melby (eds), *Speaking and Comprehending: Papers of the 27th Forum of the Linguistic Association of Canada and the United States*, LACUS Forum 27: 203–16.

Fögen, T., ed. (2009), *Tears in the Graeco-Roman World*, Berlin: De Gruyter.

Foley, H., ed. (1994), *The Homeric Hymn to Demeter: Translation, Commentary and Interpretive Essays*, Princeton, NJ: Princeton University Press.

Fontenrose, J. (1968), "The Hero as Athlete," *Classical Antiquity* 1: 73–104.

Forbes, H. (2007), *Meaning and Identity in a Greek Landscape*, Cambridge: Cambridge University Press.

Forsdyke, S. (2005), *Exile, Ostracism, and Democracy: The Politics of Expulsion in Ancient Greece*, Princeton, NJ: Princeton University Press.

Fortenbaugh, W. W. (1970), "Aristotle's *Rhetoric* on Emotions," *Archiv für Geschichte der Philosophie* 52: 40–70.

Fortenbaugh, W. W. (1975), *Aristotle on Emotion*, London: Duckworth.

Fortenbaugh, W. W. (2002), *Aristotle on Emotion*, 2nd edition, London: Duckworth.

Fortenbaugh, W.W. (2012), "Apollonius on Theophrastus on Aristoxenus," in C.A. Huffman (ed.), *Aristoxenus of Tarentum: Discussion*, 155–75, New Brunswick, NJ: Transaction Publishers.

Foucault, M. (1986), *The History of Sexuality III: The Care of the Self*, translated by R. Hurley, London: Allen Lane/Penguin. Originally published in 1984 as *Histoire de sexualité III: Le souci de soi*, Paris: Editions Gallimard.

Fowler, D. P. (1997), "Epicurean anger," in S. M. Braund and C. Gill (eds), *The Passions in Roman Thought and Literature*, 16–35, Cambridge: Cambridge University Press.

Foxhall, L. (2011), "Loom Weights," in J. C. Carter and A. Prieto (eds), *Archaeological Field Survey: Bradano to Basento. The Chora of Metaponto 3*, 539–54, Austin: University of Texas Press.

Foxhall, L. (2012), "Family Time: Temporality, Materiality and Women's Networks in Ancient Greece," in J. Marincola, L. Llewellyn-Jones, and C. Maciver (eds), *Greek Notions of the Past in the Archaic and Classical Eras: History without Historians*, 183–206, Edinburgh: Edinburgh University Press.

Foxhall, L. (2013), *Studying Gender in Classical Antiquity*, Cambridge: Cambridge University Press.

Foxhall, L. (2014), "Loom Weights," in E. Lanza Catti, K. Swift, and J. C. Carter (eds), *A Greek Farmhouse at Ponte Fabrizio: The Chora of Metaponto 5*, 351–2, Austin: University of Texas Press.

Foxhall, L. and K. Stears (1999), "Redressing the Balance: Dedications of Clothing to Artemis and the Order of Life Stages," in M. Donald and L. Hurcombe (eds), *Gender and Material Culture in Historical Perspective*, 1–22, London: Macmillan.

Foxhall, L. and D. Yoon (2016), "Carving out a Territory: Rhegion, Locri and the Households and Communities of the Classical Countryside," *World Archaeology* 48, no. 3: 431–48.

Franzoni, C. (2006), *Tirannia dello sguardo: corpo, gesto, espressione nell'arte greca*, Turin: Enaudi.

Frede, M. (1986), "Philosophy and Medicine in Antiquity," in A. Donagan, A. Perovich, and M. Wedin (eds), *Human Nature and Natural Knowledge: Essays Presented to Marjorie Grene on the Occasion of her 75th Birthday*, 211–32, Dordrecht: Kluwer.

Frede, M. (1992), "On Aristotle's Conception of the Soul," in M. C. Nussbaum and A. O. Rorty (eds), *Essays on Aristotle's De Anima*, 93–106, Oxford: Oxford University Press.

Freese, J. H., ed. (1926), *Aristotle: Rhetoric*, Loeb Classical Library, Cambridge, MA, and London: Harvard University Press.

Frevert, U. (2009), "Was haben Gefühle in der Geschichte zu suchen?" *Geschichte und Gesellschaft* 35: 183–209.

Frevert, U., ed. (2011), *Emotions in History – Lost and Found*, Budapest: Central European University Press.

Frevert, U. and A. Schmidt (2011), "Geschichte, Emotionen und die Macht der Bilder," *Geschichte und Gesellschaft* 37, no. 1: 5–25.

Frijda, N. H. (1986), *The Emotions*, Cambridge: Cambridge University Press.

Frijda, N. H. and W. G. Parrott (2011), "Basic Emotions or Ur-emotions?" *Emotion Review* 3: 406–15.

Fulkerson, L. (2013), *No Regrets: Remorse in Classical Antiquity*, Oxford: Oxford University Press.

Fusillo, M. (1999), "The Conflict of Emotions: A Topos in the Greek Erotic Novel," in S. Swain (ed.), *Oxford Readings in the Greek Novel*, 60–82, Oxford: Oxford University Press. (Translation of "Le conflit des émotions : un topos du roman érotique grec," *Museum Helveticum* 47 (1990): 201–21.)

Gabrielsson, A. (2010), "The Role of Structure in the Musical Expression of Emotions," in P. N. Juslin and J. A. Sloboda (eds), *Handbook of Music and Emotion: Theory, Research, Applications*, 367–400, Oxford: Oxford University Press.

Gaines, R. (2007), "Roman Rhetorical Handbooks," in W. Dominik and J. Hall (eds), *A Companion to Roman Rhetoric*, 163–80, Malden, MA: Blackwell.

Gale, M. (2000), *Virgil on the Nature of Things: The Georgics, Lucretius, and the Didactic Tradition*, Cambridge: Cambridge University Press.

Galinsky, K. (1988), "The Anger of Aeneas," *American Journal of Philology* 109: 321–48.

Garland, R. (1985), *The Greek Way of Death*, London: Duckworth.

Gildenhard, I. and A. Zissos (2007), "Barbarian Variations: Tereus, Procne and Philomela in Ovid (*Met.* 6.412–674) and Beyond," *Dictynna* 4, https://journals.openedition.org/dictynna/150 (accessed March 17, 2018).

Gill, C. (1997), "Passion as Madness in Roman Poetry," in S. M. Braund and C. Gill (eds), *The Passions in Roman Thought and Literature*, 213–41, Cambridge: Cambridge University Press.

Gill, C. (1998), "Did Galen Understand Platonic and Stoic Thinking on Emotions?" in J. Sihvola and T. Engberg-Pedersen (eds), *The Emotions in Hellenistic Philosophy*, 138–48, Dordrecht: Kluwer.

Gill, C. (2010), "Stoicism and Epicureanism," in P. Goldie (ed.), *The Oxford Handbook of Philosophy of Emotion*, 143–65, Oxford, Oxford University Press.

Giuliani, L. (2004), "Die Not des Sterbens als ästhetisches Phänomen. Zur Mitleidlosigkeit des antiken Betrachters," *Pegasus. Berliner Beiträge zum Nachleben der Antike* 6: 9–22.

Golden, M. (1988), "Did the Ancients Care When their Children Died?" *Greece & Rome* 35: 152–63.

Gordon, R. (1987), "Lucan's Erictho," in M. Whitby, P. Hardie, and M. Whitby (eds), *Homo Viator: Classical Essays for John Bramble*, 231–42, Bristol: Bristol Classical Press.

Gostoli, A. (1995), "L'armonia frigia nei progetti politico-pedagogici di Platone e Aristotele," in B. Gentili and F. Perusino (eds), *Mousiké. Metrica, ritmica e musica in memoria di Giovanni Comotti*, 133–44, Pisa and Rome: Istituti Editoriali e Poligrafici Internazionali.

Goukowski, P. (1995), "Philippe de Pergame et l'histoire des guerres civiles," in C. Brixhe (ed.), *Hellenika Symmeikta II*, 39–53, Paris: de Boccard.

Graver, M. (2002), *Cicero on the Emotions: Tusculan Disputations 3 and 4*, Chicago: University of Chicago Press.

Graver, M. (2007), *Stoicism and Emotion*, Chicago: University of Chicago Press.

Graver, M. (2017), "The Performance of Grief: Cicero, Stoicism, and the Public Eye," in D. L. Cairns and D. P. Nelis (eds), *Emotions in the Classical World: Methods, Approaches, and Directions*, 195–206, Stuttgart: Steiner.

Gray, B. (2015), *Stasis and Stability: Exile, the Polis, and Political Thought, c. 404–146 BC*, Oxford: Oxford University Press.

Green, J. R. (1991), "On Seeing and Depicting the Theatre in Classical Athens," *Greek, Roman, and Byzantine Studies* 32: 15–50.

Green, S. J. (2014), *Disclosure and Discretion in Roman Astrology: Manilius and his Augustan Contemporaries*, Oxford: Oxford University Press.

Grethlein, J. (2013), *Experience and Teleology in Ancient Historiography: "Futures Past" from Herodotus to Augustine*, Cambridge: Cambridge University Press.

Griffiths, P. E. (1997), *What Emotions Really Are: The Problem of Psychological Categories*, Chicago: University of Chicago Press.

Gross, D. (2006), *The Secret History of Emotion: From Aristotle's Rhetoric to Modern Brain Science*, Chicago: University of Chicago Press.

Grossardt, P. (2001), *Die Erzählung von Meleagros: Zur literarischen Entwicklung der kalydonischen Kultlegende*, Leiden: Brill.

Grosz, E. (1994), *Volatile Bodies: Toward a Corporeal Feminism*, Bloomington: Indiana University Press.

Gummere, R. M., ed. (1925), *Seneca: Moral Letters to Lucilius (Epistulae orales ad Lucilium)*, Loeb Classical Library, Cambridge, MA, and London: Harvard University Press.

Gundert, B. (2000), "Soma and Psyche in Hippocratic medicine," in J. P. Wright and P. Potter (eds), *Psyche and Soma: Physicians and Metaphysicians on the Mind–Body Problem from Antiquity to Enlightenment*, 13–36, Oxford: Oxford University Press.

Habinek, T. (1990), "Sacrifice, Society and Vergil's Ox-Born Bees," in M. Griffith and D. Mastronarde (eds), *Cabinet of the Muses: Essays in Classical and Comparative Literature in Honor of Thomas G. Rosenmeyer*, 209–23, Atlanta, GA: Scholars Press.

Hahn, F. (2007), "Performing the Sacred: Prayers and Hymns," in J. Rüpke (ed.), *A Companion to Roman Religion*, 235–49, London: Routledge.

Hall, J. (2013), "Saviour of the Republic and Father of the Fatherland: Cicero and Political Crisis," in C. Steel (ed.), *The Cambridge Companion to Cicero*, 215–29, Cambridge: Cambridge University Press.

Hall, J. (2014), *Cicero's Use of Judicial Theater*, Ann Arbor: University of Michigan Press.
Hallett, J. (1984), *Fathers and Daughters in Roman Society*, Princeton, NJ: Princeton University Press.
Halliwell, S. (1998), *Aristotle's Poetics*, 2nd edition, London: Duckworth.
Halliwell, S. (2002), *The Aesthetics of Mimesis: Ancient Texts and Modern Problems*, Princeton, NJ: Princeton University Press.
Halliwell, S. (2008), *Greek Laughter: A Study of Cultural Psychology from Homer to Early Christianity*, Cambridge: Cambridge University Press.
Halliwell, S. (2011), *Between Ecstasy and Truth: Interpretations of Greek Poetics from Homer to Longinus*, Oxford: Oxford University Press.
Halliwell, S. (2017), "The Poetics of Emotional Expression: Some Problems of Ancient Theory," in D. Cairns and D. Nelis (eds), *Emotions in the Classical World: Methods, Approaches and Directions*, 105–23, Stuttgart: Steiner.
Hankinson, R. J. (1991), "Greek Medical Models of the Mind," in S. Everson (ed.), *Psychology*, 194–217, Cambridge: Cambridge University Press.
Hankinson, R. J. (1998), "Magic, Religion and Science: Divine and Human in the Hippocratic Corpus," *Apeiron* 31: 1–34.
Hanson, A. E. (2003), "'Your Mother Nursed you with Bile': Anger in Babies and Small Children," in S. Braund and G. W. Most (eds), *The Ancient Anger: Perspectives from Homer to Galen*, 182–207, Cambridge: Cambridge University Press.
Hanson, V. D. (1989), *The Western Way of War: Infantry Battle in Classical Greece*, Berkeley and Los Angeles: University of California Press.
Hardie, P., ed. (1994), *Virgil: Aeneid Book IX*, Cambridge: Cambridge University Press.
Hardie, P., ed. (2009), *Paradox and the Marvellous in Augustan Literature and Culture*, Oxford: Oxford University Press.
Harmon, A. M., ed. (1936), *Lucian: The Passing of Peregrinus. The Runaways. Toxaris or Friendship. The Dance. Lexiphanes. The Eunuch. Astrology. The Mistaken Critic. The Parliament of the Gods. The Tyrannicide. Disowned*, Loeb Classical Library, Cambridge, MA, and London: Harvard University Press.
Harries, B. (2007), "Acting the Part: Techniques of the Comic Stage in Cicero's Early Speeches," in J. Booth (ed.), *Cicero on the Attack: Invective and Subversion in the Orations and Beyond*, 129–47, Swansea: Classical Press of Wales.
Harris, W. V. (2001), *Restraining Rage: The Ideology of Anger Control in Classical Antiquity*, Cambridge, MA: Harvard University Press.
Harris, W. V. (2009), *Dreams and Experience in Classical Antiquity*, Cambridge, MA, and London: Harvard University Press.
Hartmann, E. (2002), *Heirat, Hetärentum und Konkubinat im klassischen Athen*, Frankfurt: Campus.
Harvey, F. D. (1984), "The Wicked Wife of Ischomachus," *Echoes du Monde Classique/Classical Views* 28: 68–70.
Hatfield, E., J. T. Cacioppo, and R. L. Rapson (1994), *Emotional Contagion*, New York: Cambridge University Press.
Hau, L. I. (2016), *Moral History from Herodotus to Diodorus Siculus*, Edinburgh: Edinburgh University Press.
Havelock, C. M. (2007), *The Aphrodite of Knidos and her Successors: A Historical Review of the Female Nude in Greek Art*, Ann Arbor: University of Michigan Press.
Havelock, E. A. (1963), *Preface to Plato*, Cambridge, MA, and London: Harvard University Press.

Heath, M. (2013), *Ancient Philosophical Poetics*, Cambridge: Cambridge University Press.
Heath, M. F. (2017), "Aristotle on the Best Kind of Tragic Plot: Re-Reading *Poetics* 13–14," in R. Polansky and W. Wians (eds), *Reading Aristotle: Exposition and Argument*, 334–51, Leiden: Brill.
Heinaman, R. (1990), "Aristotle and the Mind–Body Problem," *Phronesis* 35: 83–102.
Hermary, A. and H. Cassimatis (1986), "Eros," in *Lexicon Iconographicum Mythologiae Classicae* 3, 933–42, Heidelberg: Heidelberger Akademie der Wissenschaften.
Hillgruber, M. (1994), *Die Pseudoplutarchische Schrift* de Homero, Stuttgart: Teubner.
Hitzer, B. (2011), "Emotionsgeschichte—ein Anfang mit Folgen," *H- Soz-Kult*, 23 November 2011, http:// hsozkult.geschichte.hu-berlin.de/forum/2011-11-001 (accessed March 17, 2018).
Hoffleit, H. B. and P. A. Clement (1969), *Plutarch: Moralia, Vol. VIII*, Loeb Classical Library, Cambridge, MA: Harvard University Press.
Holmes, B. (2010a), "Body, Soul, and Medical Analogy in Plato," in K. Basil and J. Euben (eds), *When Worlds Elide: Classics, Politics, Culture*, 345–85, Lanham, MD: Rowman and Littlefield.
Holmes, B. (2010b), *The Symptom and the Subject: The Emergence of the Physical Body in Ancient Greece*, Princeton, NJ, and Oxford: Princeton University Press.
Holmes, B. (2013a), "Causality, Agency, and the Limits of Medicine," *Apeiron* 46: 302–26.
Holmes, B. (2013b), "In Strange Lands: Disembodied Authority and the Role of the Physician in the Hippocratic Corpus and Beyond," in M. Asper (ed.), *Writing Science: Medical and Mathematical Authorship in Ancient Greece*, 431–72, Berlin: De Gruyter.
Hölscher, T. (1985), "Die Geschlagenen und Ausgelieferten in der Kunst des Hellenismus," *Antike Kunst*, 28: 120–136.
Holst-Warhaft, G. (1992), *Dangerous Voices: Women's Laments and Greek Literature*, London: Routledge.
Holzhausen, J. (2000), *Paideia oder Paidiá: Aristoteles und Aristophanes zur Wirkung der griechischen Tragödie*, Stuttgart: Steiner.
Horden, P. (1999), "Pain in Hippocratic Medicine," in J. R. Hinnells and R. Porter (eds), *Religion, Health and Suffering*, 295–315, London and New York: Routledge.
Horwitz, A. V. and J. C. Wakefield (2007), *The Loss of Sadness: How Psychiatry Transformed Normal Sorrow into Depressive Disorder*, Oxford and New York: Oxford University Press.
Huber, I. (2001), *Die Ikonographie der Trauer in der griechischen Kunst*, Mannheim and Möhnesee: Bibliopolis.
Hughes, J. (1997), "*Inter tribunal et scaenam*: Comedy and Rhetoric in Rome," in W. Dominik (ed.), *Roman Eloquence: Rhetoric in Society and Literature*, 182–97, London: Routledge.
Hulskamp, M. (2016), "*On Regimen* and the Question of Medical Dreams in the Hippocratic Corpus," in L. Dean-Jones and R. Rosen (eds), *Ancient Concepts of the Hippocratic*, 258–72, Leiden: Brill.
Hume, D. ([1739–40] 1906), *A Treatise of Human Nature*, edited by L.A. Selby-Bigge, Oxford: Oxford University Press.
Hunt, A. S. and C. C. Edgar, eds (1932), *Select Papyri I. Private Documents*, Loeb Classical Library, Cambridge, MA, and London: Harvard University Press.
Indelli, G. ed. (1988), *Filodemo, L'ira*, La Scuola di Epicuro Vol. V, Naples: Bibliopolis.
Jahn, T. (1987), *Zum Wortfeld "Seele-Geist" in der Sprache Homers*, Munich: Beck.
Jäkel, S. (1972), "Φόβος und σέβας im frühen Griechischen," *Archiv für Begriffsgeschichte* 16: 141–65.
Jäkel, S. (1975), "Φόβος und σέβας πάθος und μάθος im Drama des Aischylos," *Eirene* 13: 43–76.
Jäkel, S. (1979), "Φόβος und σέβας bei Sophokles," *Arktos* 13: 31–41.
James, W. (1884), "What is an Emotion?" *Mind* 9: 188–205.

James, W. (1890), *The Principles of Psychology*, New York: Macmillan.
Janko, R. (1984), *Aristotle on Comedy: Towards a Reconstruction of Poetics II*, Berkeley and Los Angeles: University of California Press.
Janko, R. (2011), *Philodemus: On Poems 3–4 with the Fragments of Aristotle On Poets*, Oxford: Oxford University Press.
Jones, C. P. (1999), "Interrupted Funerals," *Proceedings of the American Philosophical Society* 143: 588–600.
Jones, E. M. (2012), "Allocating Musical Pleasure: Performance, Pleasure, and Value in Aristotle's *Politics*," in I. Sluiter and R. M. Rosen (eds), *Aesthetic Value in Classical Antiquity*, 159–82, Leiden: Brill.
Jones, W. H. S., ed. (1923a), *Hippocrates, Vol. I*, Cambridge, MA, and London: Harvard University Press.
Jones, W. H. S., ed. (1923b), *Hippocrates, Vol. II*, Cambridge, MA, and London: Harvard University Press.
Jones, W. H. S., ed. (1931), *Hippocrates, Vol. IV*, Cambridge, MA, and London: Harvard University Press.
Jouanna, J. (1983), *Hippocrate: Maladies II*, Paris: Les Belles Lettres.
Jouanna, J. (2007), "La theorie de la sensation, de la pensée et de l'âme dans le traite hippocratique du *Régime*: ses rapports avec Empédocle et le *Timée* de Platon," *AION: Annali dell'Istituto Universitario Orientale di Napoli. Sezione filologico-letteraria* 29: 9–38.
Jouanna, J. (2012), *Greek Medicine From Hippocrates to Galen*, translated by N. Allies, Leiden: Brill.
Jouanna, J. (2013), "The Typology and Aetiology of Madness," in W. V. Harris (ed.), *Mental Disorders in the Classical World*, 97–118, Leiden: Brill.
Juslin, P. N. and J.A. Sloboda, eds (2010), *Handbook of Music and Emotion: Theory, Research, Applications*, Oxford: Oxford University Press.
Kahn, C. (1992), "Aristotle on Thinking," in M. C. Nussbaum and A. Oksenberg Rorty (eds), *Essays on Aristotle's De Anima*, 359–80, Oxford: Oxford University Press.
Kakridis, J. T. (1949), *Homeric Researches*, Lund: Gleerup.
Kaltsas, N. (2017), "Conflicting Emotions," in A. Chaniotis, N. Kaltsas, and I. Mylonopoulos (eds), *A World of Emotions: Ancient Greece, 700 BC–200 AD*, 101–11, New York: Onassis Foundation.
Kampen, N. (1981), *Image and Status: Roman Working Women in Ostia*, Berlin: Mann.
Kaster, R. (2005), *Emotion, Restraint and Community in Ancient Rome*, New York: Oxford University Press.
Kazantzidis, G. (2017), "Empathy and the Limits of Disgust in the Hippocratic Corpus," in D. Lateiner and D. Spatharas (eds), *The Ancient Emotion of Disgust*, 45–68, Oxford: Oxford University Press.
Keane, C. (2015), *Juvenal and the Satiric Emotions*, Oxford: Oxford University Press.
Keltner D. and J. Haidt (2003), "Approaching Awe, a Moral, Spiritual and Aesthetic Emotion," *Cognition and Emotion* 17: 297–314.
Kennedy, G. (1972), *The Art of Rhetoric in the Roman World 300 B.C.–A.D. 300*, Princeton, NJ: Princeton University Press
Kenner, H. (1960), *Weinen und Lachen in der griechischen Kunst*, Abhandlungen der Österreichischen Akademie der Wissenschaften. Philosophisch-historische Klasse, 234 (2), Vienna: Rohrer.
Keuls, E. (1985), *The Reign of the Phallus: Sexual Politics in Ancient Athens*, Berkeley and Los Angeles: University of California Press.

Kim, J. (2000), *The Pity of Achilles: Oral Style and the Unity of the* Iliad, Lanham, MD: Rowman and Littlefield.

King, H. (1993), *Hippocrates' Woman: Reading the Female Body in Ancient Greece*, New York and London: Routledge.

King, H. (2013), "Fear of Flute Girls, Fear of Falling," in W. V. Harris (ed.), *Mental Disorders in the Classical World*, 265–82, Leiden: Brill.

Kivy, P. (1989), *Sound Sentiment*, Philadelphia, PA: Temple University Press.

Kivy, P. (1999), "Feeling the Musical Emotions," *British Journal of Aesthetics* 39: 1–13.

Kivy, P. (2002), *Introduction to a Philosophy of Music*, Oxford: Oxford University Press.

Knox, B. M. W. (1964), *The Heroic Temper: Studies in Sophoclean Tragedy*, Berkeley and Los Angeles: University of California Press.

Konstan, D (1997), *Friendship in the Classical World*, Cambridge: Cambridge University Press.

Konstan, D. (2000), "Pity and the Law in Greek Theory and Practice," *Dike* 4: 124–45.

Konstan, D. (2001), *Pity Transformed*, London: Duckworth.

Konstan, D. (2003a), "Aristotle on Anger and the Emotions: The Strategies of Status," in S. Braund and G. W. Most (eds), *The Ancient Anger: Perspectives from Homer to Galen*, 99–120, Cambridge: Cambridge University Press.

Konstan, D. (2003b), "Nemesis and Phthonos," in G. Bakewell and J. Sickinger (eds), *Gestures: Essays in Ancient History, Literature and Philosophy Presented to Alan J. Boegehold*, 74–87, Oxford: Blackwell.

Konstan, D. (2006a), "The Concept of 'Emotion' from Plato to Cicero," *Méthexis* 19: 139–51.

Konstan, D. (2006b), *The Emotions of the Ancient Greeks: Studies in Aristotle and Classical Literature*, Toronto: University of Toronto Press.

Konstan, D. (2008), "In Defense of Croesus, or Suspense as an Aesthetic Emotion," *Aisthe* 3: 1–15, http://www.aisthe.ifcs.ufrj.br/vol%20II/KONSTAN.pdf (accessed March 17, 2018); reprinted in F. Santoro, T. Ribeiro, and H. Cairus (eds), *Pathos: A Poética das Emoções: Acts of the II Simpósio Internacional OUSIA de Estudos Clássicos*, Rio de Janeiro: Arquimedes Editora, 2009.

Konstan, D. (2010), *Before Forgiveness: The Origins of a Moral Idea*, New York: Cambridge University Press.

Konstan, D. (2017a), "Ancient Views on Emotion," in A. Chaniotis, N. Kaltsas, and I. Mylonopoulos (eds), *A World of Emotions: Ancient Greece, 700 BC–200 AD*, 39–49, New York: Onassis Foundation.

Konstan, D. (2017b), "Reason vs. Emotion in Seneca," in D. L. Cairns and D. P. Nelis (eds), *Emotions in the Classical World: Methods, Approaches, and Directions*, 231–43, Stuttgart: Steiner.

Konstan, D. and K. Rutter, eds (2003), *Envy, Spite, and Jealousy: The Rivalrous Emotions in Ancient Greece*, Edinburgh: Edinburgh University Press.

Korte, G. (1874), *Über Personificationen psychologischer Affekte in der späteren Vasenmalerei*, Berlin: Vahlen.

Kosak, J. C. (2005), "A Crying Shame: Pitying the Sick in the Hippocratic Corpus and Greek Tragedy," in R. H. Sternberg (ed.), *Pity and Power in Ancient Athens*, 253–76, Cambridge: Cambridge University Press.

Kosmin, P. (2015), "A Phenomenology of Democracy: Ostracism as Political Ritual," *Classical Antiquity* 34: 121–62.

Kosmopoulou, A. (2001), "'Working Women': Female Professionals on Classical Attic Gravestones", *Annual of the British School at Athens* 96: 281–319.

Kotsifou, C. (2012a), "A Glimpse into the World of Petitions: The Case of Aurelia Artemis and her Orphaned Children," in A. Chaniotis (ed.), *Unveiling Emotions: Sources and Methods for the Study of Emotions in the Greek World*, 317–27, Stuttgart: Steiner.

Kotsifou, C. (2012b), "'Being unable to come to you and lament and weep with you': Grief and Condolence Letters on Papyrus," in A. Chaniotis (ed.), *Unveiling Emotions: Sources and Methods for the Study of Emotions in the Greek World*, 389–412, Stuttgart: Steiner.

Kotsifou, C. (2012c), "Emotions and Papyri: Insights into the Theatre of Human Experience," in A. Chaniotis (ed.), *Unveiling Emotions: Sources and Methods for the Study of Emotions in the Greek World*, 39–90, Stuttgart: Steiner.

Kovacs, D. (2002), *Euripides: Bacchae—Iphigenia at Aulis—Rhesus*, Loeb Classical Library, Cambridge, MA, and London: Harvard University Press.

Kovacs, D., ed. (1994), *Euripides: Cyclops—Alcestis—Medea*, Loeb Classical Library, Cambridge, MA, and London: Harvard University Press.

Kovacs, D., ed. (1995), *Euripides: The Children of Heracles—Hippolytos—Andromache—Hecuba*, Loeb Classical Library, Cambridge, MA, and London: Harvard University Press.

Kowalzig, B. (2007), *Singing for the Gods: Performances of Myth and Ritual in Archaic and Classical Greece*, Oxford: Oxford University Press.

Kudlien, F. (1973), "Schwärzliche Organe im frühgriechischen Denken," *Medizinhistorisches Journal* 8: 53–8.

Kuhn, C. (2012), "Emotionality in the Political Culture of the Graeco-Roman East: The Role of Acclamations," in A. Chaniotis (ed.), *Unveiling Emotions: Sources and Methods for the Study of Emotions in the Greek World*, 295–316, Stuttgart: Steiner.

Kunze, C. (2002), *Zum Greifen nah: Stilphänomene in der Hellenistischen Skulptur und ihre inhaltliche Interpretation*, Munich: Biering and Brinkmann.

Lakoff, G. (1987), *Women, Fire, and Dangerous Things: What Categories Reveal about the Mind*, Chicago: University of Chicago Press.

Lami, A. (2007), "[Ippocrate], *Sui disturbi virginali*: testo, traduzione e commento," *Galenos* 1: 15–59.

Langholf, V. (1990), *Medical Theories in Hippocrates: Early Texts and the "Epidemics,"* Berlin: De Gruyter.

Larson, J. (1995), *Greek Heroine Cults*, Madison: University of Wisconsin Press.

Larsson-Lovén, L. (2010), "Coniugal Concordia: Marriage and Marital Ideals on Roman Funerary Monuments," in L. Larsson-Lovén and A. Strömberg (eds), *Ancient Marriage in Myth and Reality*, 204–20, Newcastle: Cambridge Scholars Publishing.

Lateiner, D. (1995), *Sardonic Smile: Nonverbal Behavior in Homeric Epic*, Ann Arbor: University of Michigan Press.

Lateiner, D. (2005), "The Pitiers and the Pitied in Herodotus and Thucydides," in R. Sternberg (ed.), *Pity And Power in Ancient Athens*, 67–97, New York: Cambridge University Press.

Lateiner, D. (2017), "Evoking Disgust in the Latin Novels of Petronius and Apuleius," in D. Lateiner and D. Spatharas (eds), *The Ancient Emotion of Disgust*, 203–33, Oxford: Oxford University Press.

Lateiner, D. and D. Spatharas (2017a), "Introduction: Ancient and Modern Modes of Understanding and Manipulating Disgust," in D. Lateiner and D. Spatharas (eds), *The Ancient Emotion of Disgust*, 1–44, Oxford: Oxford University Press.

Lateiner, D. and D. Spatharas, eds (2017b), *The Ancient Emotion of Disgust*, Oxford: Oxford University Press.

Latte, K. (1929), "Spes," in *Paulys Realencyclopädie zur classischen Altertumswissenschaft*, Supp. 3a.2.1634–5, Stuttgart: Metzler.

Lazarus, R. S. (1991), *Emotion and Adaptation*, New York: Guilford.
Lee, M. (2015), *Body, Dress and Identity in Ancient Greece*, Cambridge: Cambridge University Press.
Leeman, A., H. Pinkster, and E. Rabbie, eds (1989), *M. Tullius Cicero De Oratore libri III: Kommentar, Bd. 3, Buch II, 99–290*, Heidelberg: Winter.
Leigh, M. (2013), *From Polypragmon to Curiosus: Ancient Concepts of Curious and Meddlesome Behaviour*, Oxford: Oxford University Press.
Leighton, S. R. (1996), "Aristotle and the Emotions," in A. O. Rorty (ed.), *Essays on Aristotle's Rhetoric*, 206–37, Berkeley and Los Angeles: University of California Press.
Letts, M. (2016), "Questioning the Patient, Questioning Hippocrates: Rufus of Ephesus and the Pursuit of Knowledge," in G. Petridou and C. Thumiger (eds), *Homo Patiens: Approaches to the Patient in the Ancient World*, 81–106, Leiden: Brill.
Levene, D. S. (1997), "Pity, Fear, and the Historical Audience: Tacitus on the Fall of Vitellius," in S. M. Braund and C. Gill (eds), *The Passions in Roman Thought and Literature*, 128–49, Cambridge: Cambridge University Press.
Leventhal, H. and K. R. Scherer (1987), "The Relationship of Emotion and Cognition: A Functional Approach to a Semantic Controversy," *Cognition and Emotion* 1: 3–28.
Lewis, S. (2002), *The Athenian Woman: An Iconographic Handbook*, London: Routledge.
Lhôte, É. (2006), *Les lamelles oraculaires de Dodone*, Geneva: Droz.
Linders, T. (1972), *Studies in the Treasure Records of Artemis Brauronia*, Stockholm: Swedish Institute at Athens.
Lindsay, W. M. (1930), *Festus: De verborum significatu*, Paris: Les Belles Lettres.
Llewellyn-Jones, L. (2003), *Aphrodite's Tortoise: The Veiled Woman of Ancient Greece*, Swansea: Classical Press of Wales.
Lloyd, G. E. R. (1991), *Methods and Problems in Greek Science*, Cambridge: Cambridge University Press.
Lloyd, G. E. R. (2003), *In the Grip of Disease: Studies in the Greek Imagination*, Oxford: Oxford University Press.
Lloyd, G. E. R. (2007), *Cognitive Variations: Reflections on the Unity and Diversity of the Human Mind*, Oxford: Oxford University Press.
Lloyd-Jones, H. (1983), *The Justice of Zeus*, 2nd edition, Berkeley and Los Angeles: University of California Press.
Lobe, M. (1999), *De Gebärden in Vergils Aeneis: zur Bedeutung und Funktion von Körpersprache im romischen Epik*, Frankfurt: Lang.
Lombardo, P. and K. Mulligan (2008), "The Geneva School of Emotions: An Interview with Klaus Scherer," *Critical Quarterly* 50, no. 4: 26–39.
Long, A. A. and D. N. Sedley (1987), *The Hellenistic Philosophers*, 2 volumes, Cambridge: Cambridge University Press.
Lonsdale, S. H. (1993), *Dance and Ritual Play in Greek Religion*, Baltimore, MD: Johns Hopkins University Press.
Loraux, N. ([1990] 1998), *Mothers in Mourning*, Ithaca, NY: Cornell University Press.
Lorenz, K. (2008), *Bilder Machen Räume: Mythenbilder in pompeianischen Häusern*, Berlin: De Gruyter.
Lowe, D. (2015), *Monsters and Monstrosity in Augustan Literature*, Ann Arbor: University of Michigan Press.
Lutz, C. A. (1988), *Unnatural Emotions: Everyday Sentiments on a Micronesian Atoll and their Challenge to Western Theory*, Chicago: University of Chicago Press.
Lyons, W. (1980), *Emotion*, Cambridge: Cambridge University Press.

Mack, D. (1937), *Senatsreden und Volksreden bei Cicero*, Würzburg: Triltsch.
Maderna, C. (2009), "Von der Ordnung der Mimik: Bedrohliche Leidenschaften in der antiken Bildkunst," *Städel-Jahrbuch* 20: 7–54.
Maier-Eichhorn, U. (1989), *Die Gestikulation in Quintilians Rhetorik*, Frankfurt: Lang.
Mangold, M. (2000), *Kassandra in Athen: Die Eroberung Trojas auf attischen Vasenbildern*, Berlin: Reimer.
Manuli, P. and M. Veggetti (1977), *Cuore, sangue, cervello: biologia e antropologia nel pensiero antico*, Milan: Episteme.
Marincola, J. (2003), "Beyond Pity and Fear: The Emotions of History," *Ancient Society* 33: 285–315.
Marincola, J. (2013), "Polybius, Phylarchus, and 'Tragic History': A Reconsideration," in B. Gibson and T. Harrison (eds), *Polybius and his World: Essays in Memory of F. W. Walbank*, 73–90, Oxford: Oxford University Press.
Marszal, J. R. (2000), "Ubiquitous Barbarians: Representations of the Gauls at Pergamon and Elsewhere," in N. T. de Grummond and B. S. Ridgway (eds), *From Pergamum to Sperlonga: Sculpture and Context*, 191–234, Berkeley and Los Angeles: University of California Press.
Martzavou, P. (2012a), "Dream, Narrative, and the Construction of Hope in the 'Healing Miracles' of Epidauros," in A. Chaniotis (ed.), *Unveiling Emotions: Sources and Methods for the Study of Emotions in the Greek World*, 177–204, Stuttgart: Steiner.
Martzavou, P. (2012b), "Isis Aretalogies, Initiations, and Emotions: The Isis Aretalogies as a Source for the Study of Emotions," in A. Chaniotis (ed.), *Unveiling Emotions: Sources and Methods for the Study of Emotions in the Greek World*, 267–92, Stuttgart: Steiner.
Maslow, A. (1964), *Religions, Values and Peak-Experiences*, Columbus: Ohio State University Press.
Masséglia, J. (2012a), "Emotions and Archaeological Sources: A Methodological Introduction," in A. Chaniotis (ed.), *Unveiling Emotions: Sources and Methods for the Study of Emotions in the Greek World*, 131–50, Stuttgart: Steiner.
Masséglia, J. (2012b), "Make or Break Decisions: The Archaeology of Allegiance in Ephesos," in A. Chaniotis (ed.), *Unveiling Emotions: Sources and Methods for the Study of Emotions in the Greek World*, 329–55, Stuttgart: Steiner.
Masséglia, J. (2012c), "'Reasons to be Cheerful': Conflicting Emotions in the Drunken Old Women of Munich and Rome," in A. Chaniotis (ed.), *Unveiling Emotions: Sources and Methods for the Study of Emotions in the Greek World*, 413–30, Stuttgart: Steiner.
Masséglia, J. (2013), "Feeling Low: Social Status and Emotional Display in Hellenistic Art," in A. Chaniotis and P. Ducrey (eds), *Unveiling Emotions II. Emotions in Greece and Rome: Texts, Images, Material Culture*, 313–30, Stuttgart: Steiner.
Masséglia, J. (2015), *Body Language in Hellenistic Art and Society*, Oxford: Oxford University Press.
Masters, J. (1992), *Poetry and Civil War in Lucan's Bellum Civile*, Cambridge: Cambridge University Press.
Matt, S. J. (2011), "Current Emotion Research in History: Or, Doing History from the Inside Out," *Emotion Review* 3: 117–24.
Matt, S. J. and P. N. Stearns, eds (2014), *Doing Emotions History*, Urbana, Chicago, and Springfield: University of Illinois Press.
Mattern, S. (2016), "Galen's Anxious Patiens: *Lypē* as Anxiety Disorder," in G. Petridou and C. Thumiger (eds), *Homo Patiens: Approaches to the Patient in the Ancient World*, 203–23, Leiden: Brill.
May, J. M. and J. Wisse (2001), *On the Ideal Orator (De oratore)*, New York: Oxford University Press.

Mayhew, R. (2011), *Aristotle: Problems Books 1–19*, Loeb Classical Library, Cambridge, MA, and London: Harvard University Press.

McCarthy, K. (2000), *Slaves, Masters and the Art of Authority in Plautine Comedy*, Princeton, NJ: Princeton University Press.

McClymond, K. (2008), *Beyond Sacred Violence: A Comparative Study of Sacrifice*, Baltimore, MD: Johns Hopkins University Press.

MacCormack, S. (1998), *Shadows of Poetry: Vergil in the Mind of Augustine*, The Transformation of the Classical Heritage, vol. XXVI Berkeley and Los Angeles: University of California Press.

McNiven, T. (1982), "Gestures in Attic Vase-painting: Use and Meaning 550–450 BC," unpublished PhD dissertation, University of Michigan.

McNiven, T. (2000a), "Behaving like an Other: Gender-specific Gestures in Athenian Vase Painting," in B. Cohen (ed.), *Not the Classical Ideal: Athens and the Construction of the Other in Greek Art*, 71–97, Leiden: Brill.

McNiven, T. (2000b), "Fear and Gender in Greek Art," in A. E. Rautman (ed.), *Reading the Body: Representations and Remains in the Archaeological Record*, 124–31, Philadelphia: University of Pennsylvania Museum.

Meineck, P. and D. Konstan, eds (2014), *Combat Trauma and the Ancient Greeks*, New York: Palgrave Macmillan.

Menninghaus, W. (2003), *Disgust: The History and Theory of a Strong Sensation*, translated by H. Eidland and J. Gelb, Albany, NY: SUNY Press.

Mesquita, B. and N. H. Frijda (1992), "Cultural Variations in Emotions: A Review," *Psychological Bulletin* 112: 179–204.

Meyer, M. (1999), "Gesten der Zusammengehörigkeit und Zuwendung: Zum Sinngehalt attischer Grabreliefs in klassischer Zeit," *Thetis* 5: 115–32.

Miller, F. D. (2012), "Aristotle on the Separability of the Mind," in C. Shields (ed.), *The Oxford Handbook of Aristotle*, 306–39, Oxford: Oxford University Press.

Miller, H. W. (1948), "A Medical Theory of Cognition," *Transactions of the American Philological Association* 79: 168–83.

Miller, W. I. (1997), *The Anatomy of Disgust*, Cambridge, MA, and London: Harvard University Press.

Montiglio, S. (2000), *Silence in the Land of Logos*, Princeton, NJ: Princeton University Press.

Most, G. W. (1992), "Disiecta Membra Poetae: The Rhetoric of Dismemberment in Neronian Literature," in R. Hexter and D. Selden (eds), *Innovations of Antiquity*, 319–419, New York: Routledge.

Mueller, M. (2016), *Objects as Actors: Props and the Poetics of Performance in Greek Tragedy*, Chicago: University of Chicago Press.

Mulvaney, J. and P. De Angelis (2010), *Dear Mrs. Kennedy: The World Shares Its Grief, Letters November 1963*, New York: St. Martin's Press.

Munteanu, D. L. (2012), *Tragic Pathos: Pity and Fear in Greek Philosophy and Tragedy*, Cambridge: Cambridge University Press.

Munteanu, D. L. (2017), "Grief: The Power and Shortcomings of Greek Tragic Consolation," in D. L. Cairns and D. P. Nelis (eds), *Emotions in the Classical World: Methods, Approaches, and Directions*, 79–103, Stuttgart: Steiner.

Munteanu, D. L., ed. (2011), *Emotion, Genre, and Gender in Classical Antiquity*, London: Bloomsbury.

Müri, W. (1953), "Melancholie und schwarze Galle," *Museum Helveticum* 10: 21–38.

Muth, S. (2008), *Gewalt im Bild: Das Phänomen der medialen Gewalt im Athen des 6. und 5. Jahrhunderts v. Chr*, Berlin: De Gruyter.

Mylonopoulos, I. (2017), "Emotions in Ancient Greek Art," in A. Chaniotis, N. Kaltsas, and I. Mylonopoulos (eds), *A World of Emotions: Ancient Greece, 700 BC–200 AD*, 73–84, New York: Onassis Foundation.

Nagle, B. R. (1983), "Byblis and Myrrha: Two Incest Narratives in the *Metamorphoses*," *Classical Journal* 78: 301–15.

Naiden, F. S. (2009), *Ancient Supplication*, Oxford: Oxford University Press.

Naiden, F. S. (2015), *Smoke Signals for the Gods: Greek Sacrifice from the Archaic through Roman Periods*, Oxford: Oxford University Press.

Naiden, F. S. and J. Rives (2015), "Sacrifice," *Oxford Bibliographies Online*, Oxford: Oxford University Press.

Neckel, S. (1999), "Blanker Neid, blinde Wut? Sozialstruktur und kollektive Gefühle," *Leviathan* 27, no. 2: 145–65.

Neils, J. and J. H. Oakley, eds (2003), *Coming of Age in Ancient Greece: Images of Childhood from the Classical Past*, New Haven, CT: Yale University Press.

Nelis, D. P. (2015), "Juno, Sea-storm, and Emotion in Virgil, *Aeneid* 1.1–156: Homeric and Epicurean Contexts," in D. L. Cairns and L. Fulkerson (eds), *Emotions between Greece and Rome*, 149–62, London: Institute of Classical Studies.

Nelson, N. L. and J. A. Russell (2013), "Universality Revisited," *Emotion Review* 5: 8–15.

Nelson-Hawkins, J. (2016), "Anger, Bile, and the Patient's Body in the Archilochean Tradition," in L. Swift and C. Carey (eds), *Greek Iambus and Elegy: New Approaches*, 310–39, Oxford: Oxford University Press.

Neumann, G. (1965), *Gesten und Gebärden in der griechischen Kunst*, Berlin: De Gruyter.

North, H. F. (1966), *Sophrosyne: Self-Knowledge and Self-Restraint*, Ithaca, NY: Cornell University Press.

North, H. F. (1977), "The Mare, the Vixen, and the Bee: Sophrosyne as the Virtue of Women in Antiquity," *Illinois Classical Studies* 2: 35–48.

Nougaret, L. (1986), *Traité de métrique latine classique*, 2nd edition, Paris: Klincksieck.

Nünlist, R. (2009), *The Ancient Critic at Work: Terms and Concepts of Literary Criticism in Greek Scholia*, Cambridge: Cambridge University Press.

Nussbaum, M. C. (1978), *Aristotle's De motu animalium*, Princeton, NJ: Princeton University Press.

Nussbaum, M. C. (1994), *The Therapy of Desire: Theory and Practice in Hellenistic Ethics*, Princeton, NJ: Princeton University Press.

Nussbaum, M. C. (2001), *Upheavals of Thought: The Intelligence of Emotions*, Cambridge: Cambridge University Press.

Nussbaum, M. C. (2004), *Hiding From Humanity: Disgust, Shame, and the Law*, Princeton, NJ: Princeton University Press.

Oakley, J. H. (2004), *Picturing Death in Classical Athens: The Evidence of the White Lekythoi*, New York: Cambridge University Press.

Oatley, K. (2011), *Such Stuff as Dreams: The Psychology of Fiction*, Oxford and Malden, MA: Wiley-Blackwell.

Oatley, K. (2012), *The Passionate Muse: Exploring Emotion in Stories*, Oxford: Oxford University Press.

Ogden, D. (1996), *Greek Bastardy in the Classical and Hellenistic Periods*, Oxford: Oxford University Press.

Öhman, A., A. Flykt, and F. Esteves (2001), "Emotion Drives Attention: Detecting the Snake in the Grass," *Journal of Experimental Psychology: General* 130: 466–78.

Olatunji, B. O., J. Haidt, D. McKay, and B. David (2008), "Core, Animal Reminder, and Contamination Disgust: Three Kinds of Disgust with Distinct Personality, Behavioral, Physiological, and Clinical Correlates," *Journal of Research in Personality* 42, no. 5: 1243–59.

Oliensis, E. (2009), *Freud's Rome: Psychoanalysis and Latin Poetry*, Cambridge and New York: Cambridge University Press.

O'Sullivan, N. (1997), "Caecilius, the 'Canons' of Writers and the Origins of Atticism," in W. Dominik (ed.), *Roman Eloquence: Rhetoric in Society and Literature*, 32–49, London: Routledge.

Overwien, O. (2014), *Hippocratis De humoribus*, Berlin: De Gruyter.

Padel, R. (1992), *In and Out of the Mind: Greek Images of the Tragic Self*, Princeton, NJ: Princeton University Press.

Pagliara, A. (2000), "Musica e politica nella speculazione platonica: considerazioni intorno all'*ethos* del modo frigio," in A. C. Cassio, D. Musti, and L. E. Rossi (eds), *Synaulia: Cultura musicale in Grecia e contatti mediterranei*, 157–216, Naples: Istituto Universitario Orientale.

Parker, H. (2012), "Women and Medicine," in S. L. James and S. Dillon (eds), *A Companion to Women in the Ancient World*, 107–24, Malden, MA, and Oxford: Wiley-Blackwell.

Patera, M. (2013), "Reflections on the Discourse of Fear in Greek Sources," in A. Chaniotis and P. Ducrey (eds), *Unveiling Emotions* II. *Emotions in Greece and Rome: Texts, Images, Material Culture*, 109–34, Stuttgart: Steiner.

Paton, W. R., ed. (1943), *The Greek Anthology in Five Volumes*, Loeb Classical Library, Cambridge, MA, and London: Harvard University Press.

Patterson, C. (1998), *The Family in Greek History*, Cambridge, MA, and London: Harvard University Press.

Pearson, G. (2014), "Aristotle and the Cognitive Component of Emotions," *Oxford Studies in Ancient Philosophy* 46: 165–212.

Pelosi, F. (2010), *Plato on Music, Soul and Body*, Cambridge: Cambridge University Press.

Pemberton, E. G. (1989), "The Dexiosis on Attic Gravestones," *Mediterranean Archaeology* 2: 45–50.

Peponi, A.-E. (2012), *Frontiers of Pleasure: Models of Aesthetic Response in Archaic and Classical Greek Thought*, Oxford: Oxford University Press.

Peretz, I. (2010), "Towards a Neurobiology of Musical Emotions," in P. N. Juslin and J. A. Sloboda (eds), *Handbook of Music and Emotion: Theory, Research, Applications*, 99–126, Oxford: Oxford University Press.

Perry, E. E. (2002), "Rhetoric, Literary Criticism, and the Roman Aesthetics of Artistic Imitation," in E. K. Gazda (ed.), *The Ancient Art of Emulation: Studies in Artistic Originality and Tradition from the Present to Classical Antiquity*, 153–71, Ann Arbor: University of Michigan Press.

Petridou, G. and C. Thumiger (2016), "Towards a History of the Ancient Patient's View," in G. Petridou and C. Thumiger (eds), *Homo Patiens: Approaches to the Patient in the Ancient World*, 1–22, Leiden: Brill.

Pfister, F. (1924), "Epiphanie," in *Paulys Realencyclopädie zur classischen Altertumswissenschaft*, Supp. 4, 277–323, Stuttgart: Metzler.

Pigeaud, J. (1981), *La maladie de l'âme*, Paris: Les Belles Lettres.

Pigeaud, J. (1987), *Folie et cures de la folie chez les médecins de l'antiquité Gréco-Romaine*, Paris: Les Belles Lettres.

Pirson, F. (2002), "Vom Kämpfen und Sterben der Kelten in der antiken Kunst," in H.-U. Cain (ed.), *Die Religion der Kelten: fromm, fremd, barbarisch. Eine Sonderausstellung der Universität Leipzig*, 71–81, Mainz: von Zabern.

Plamper, J. (2010), "The History of Emotions: An Interview with William Reddy, Barbara Rosenwein, and Peter Stearns," *History and Theory* 49: 237–65.
Plamper, J. (2012), *Geschichte und Gefühl: Grundlagen der Emotionsgeschichte*, Munich: Siedler.
Plamper, J. (2015), *The History of Emotions: An Introduction*, Oxford: Oxford University Press.
Platt, V. (2011), *Facing the Gods: Epiphany and Representation in Graeco-Roman Art, Literature, and Religion*, Cambridge: Cambridge University Press.
Plutchik, R. (1980), "A General Psychoevolutionary Theory of Emotion," in R. Plutchik and H. Kellerman (eds), *Emotion: Theory, Research, and Experience; Vol. 1: Theories of Emotion*, 3–33, New York: Academic.
Pomeroy, S. B. (1997), *Families in Classical and Hellenistic Greece*, Oxford: Oxford University Press.
Pormann, P. E., ed. (2008), *Rufus: On Melancholy*, Tübingen: Mohr Siebeck.
Porter, A. J. (2016), "Compassion in Soranus' *Gynecology* and Caelius Aurelianus' *On Chronic Diseases*," in G. Petridou and C. Thumiger (eds), *Homo Patiens: Approaches to the Patient in the Ancient World*, 285–303, Leiden: Brill.
Price, A. W. (2010), "Emotions in Plato and Aristotle," in P. Goldie (ed.), *The Oxford Handbook of Philosophy of Emotion*, 121–43, Oxford: Oxford University Press.
Priestley, J. (2013), *Herodotus and Hellenistic Culture*, Oxford: Oxford University Press.
Prinz, J. J. (2002), "Consciousness, Computation and Emotion," in S. C. Moore and M. Oaksford (eds), *Emotional Brain: From Brain to Behaviour*, 137–55, Amsterdam and Philadelphia: John Benjamins.
Prinz, J. J. (2004a), "Embodied Emotions," in R. C. Solomon (ed.), *Thinking About Feeling*, 44–60, Oxford: Oxford University Press.
Prinz, J. J. (2004b), *Gut Reactions: A Perceptual Theory of Emotions*, Oxford: Oxford University Press.
Prinz, J. J. (2007), *The Emotional Construction of Morals*, Oxford: Oxford University Press.
Prioux, É. (2011), "Emotions in Ekphrasis and Art Criticism," in D. L. Munteanu (ed.), *Emotion, Genre, and Gender in Classical Antiquity*, 135–74, London: Bloomsbury.
Procopé, J. F. (1998), "Epicureans on Anger," in J. Sihvola and T. Engberg-Pedersen (eds), *The Emotions in Hellenistic Philosophy*, 171–96, Dordrecht: Kluwer.
Provenza, A. (2012), "Aristoxenus and Music Therapy: Fr. 26 Wehrli within the Tradition on Music and Catharsis," in C. A. Huffman (ed.), *Aristoxenus of Tarentum: Discussion*, 91–128, New Brunswick, NJ: Transaction.
Putnam, M. C. J. (1995), "Anger, Blindness and Insight in Virgil's *Aeneid*," *Apeiron* 23: 7–40.
Putnam, M. C. J. (1998), *Virgil's Epic Designs: Ekphrasis in the Aeneid*, New Haven, CT: Yale University Press.
Rackham, H., ed. (1926), *Aristotle: The Nicomachean Ethics*, Loeb Classical Library, Cambridge, MA, and London: Harvard University Press.
Radden, J. (2009), *Moody Minds Distempered: Essays on Melancholy and Depression*, Oxford: Oxford University Press.
Radke, G. (1959), "Pudicitia," in *Paulys Realencyclopädie zur classischen Altertumswissenschaft*, 23.2.1942–5, Stuttgart: Metzler.
Räuchle, V. (2017), *Die Mütter Athens und ihre Kinder: Verhaltens- und Gefühlsideale in klassischer Zeit*, Berlin: Reimer.
Rawson, B. (1997), "The Iconography of Roman Childhood," in B. Rawson and P. Weaver (eds), *The Roman Family in Italy: Status, Sentiment, Space*, 205–32, Oxford: Oxford University Press.

Redfield, J. (1975), *Nature and Culture in the Iliad: The Tragedy of Hector*, Chicago: University of Chicago Press.

Redl, F. (1942), "Group Emotion and Leadership," *Psychiatry: Journal for the Study of Interpersonal Processes* 5: 573–96.

Reeder, E. D., ed. (1995), *Pandora: Women in Classical Greece*, Baltimore, MD: Walters Art Gallery.

Reisenzein, R. (2009), "Emotional Experience in the Computational Belief-Desire Theory of Emotion," *Emotion Review* 1: 214–22.

Reisenzein, R. (2015), "A Short History of Psychological Perspectives of Emotion," in R. A. Calvo, S. D'Mello, J. Gratch, and A. Kappas (eds), *The Oxford Handbook of Affective Computing*, 21–37, Oxford: Oxford University Press.

Restani, D. (2001), "Musica ed emozioni nella Grecia antica: alcuni testi e percorsi," in C. Assenza and B. Passannanti (eds), *Musica, storia, cultura ed educazione*, 63–75, Milan: Franco Angeli.

Reynolds, J. (1982), *Aphrodisias and Rome*, London: Society for the Promotion of Roman Studies.

Richlin, A. (1992), *The Garden of Priapus: Sexuality and Aggression in Roman Humor*, Oxford: Oxford University Press.

Ricottilli, L. (2000), *Gesto e parola nell'Eneide*, Bologna: Pàtron.

Ridgway, B. S. (1965), "Wounded Figures in Greek Sculpture," *Archaeology* 18: 47–54.

Ritter, S. (2005), "Eros und Gewalt: Menelaos und Helena in der attischen Vasenmalerei des 5. Jhs. v. Chr.," in G. Fischer and S. Moraw (eds), *Die andere Seite der Klassik: Gewalt im 5. und 4. Jahrhundert v. Chr.*, 265–85, Stuttgart: Steiner.

Roberts, R. C. (2003), *Emotions: An Essay in Aid of Moral Psychology*, Cambridge: Cambridge University Press.

Robinson, H. M. (1983), "Aristotelian Dualism," *Oxford Studies in Ancient Philosophy* 1: 123–44.

Robinson, J. (2005), *Deeper than Reason: Emotion and its Role in Literature, Music and Art*, Oxford: Oxford University Press.

Robinson, J. (2010), "Emotional Responses to Music: What are They? How Do They Work? And Are They Relevant to Aesthetic Appreciation?" in P. Goldie (ed.), *The Oxford Handbook of Philosophy of Emotion*, 651–80, Oxford: Oxford University Press.

Rocconi, E. (2014), "Effetti speciali sonori e mimetismo musicale nelle fonti greche," *Annali della Scuola Normale Superiore di Pisa, Classe di Lettere e Filosofia* 5: 703–19.

Rocconi, E. (2015), "Music and Dance in Greece and Rome," in P. Destrée and P. Murray (eds), *A Companion to Ancient Aesthetics*, 81–93, Hoboken, NJ: Wiley-Blackwell.

Rorty, A. O., ed. (1992), *Essays on Aristotle's Poetics*, Princeton, NJ: Princeton University Press.

Rosch, E. (1978), "Principles of Categorization," in E. Rosch and B. B. Lloyd (eds), *Cognition and Categorization*, 27–48, Hillsdale, NJ: Erlbaum.

Rosenwein, B. (2006), *Emotional Communities in the Early Middle Ages*, Ithaca, NY: Cornell University Press.

Rosenwein, B. H. (2011), "Problems and Methods in the History of Emotions," in *Passions in Context* 1, www.passionsincontext.de/uploads/media/01_Rosenwein.pdf (accessed March 17, 2018).

Roueché, C. (1984), "Acclamations in the Later Roman Empire: New Evidence from Aphrodisias," *Journal of Roman Studies* 74: 181–99.

Rozin, P., J. Haidt, and C. R. McCauley (2009), "Disgust," in D. Sander and K. Scherer (eds), *Oxford Companion to Affective Sciences*, 121–2, Oxford: Oxford University Press.

Rubenstein, L. (2004), "Stirring up Dicastic Anger," in D. L. Cairns and R. A. Knox (eds), *Law, Rhetoric, and Comedy in Classical Athens: Essays in Honour of Douglas M. MacDowell*, 187–203, Swansea: Classical Press of Wales.

Rubinstein, L. (2013), "Evoking Anger through Pity: Portraits of the Vulnerable and Defenceless in Attic Oratory," in A. Chaniotis and P. Ducrey (eds), *Unveiling Emotions II. Emotions in Greece and Rome: Texts, Images, Material Culture*, 135–65, Stuttgart: Steiner.

Rüpke, J. (2007), *The Religion of the Romans*, Cambridge: Polity Press.

Russell, D. A., ed. (2001), *Quintilian: The Orator's Education, Books 1–2*, Loeb Classical Library, Cambridge, MA, and London: Harvard University Press.

Russell, J. A. (1991), "In Defense of a Prototype Approach to Emotion Concepts," *Journal of Personality and Social Psychology* 60: 37–47.

Russell, J. A. (1994), "Is There Universal Recognition of Emotion from Facial Expression? A Review of Cross-cultural Studies," *Psychological Bulletin* 115: 102–41.

Russell, J. A. (1995), "Facial Expressions of Emotion: What Lies behind Minimal Universality?" *Psychological Bulletin* 118: 379–91.

Russell, J. A. (2012), "Introduction to Special Section: On Defining Emotion," *Emotion Review* 4: 337.

Sabetai, V. (2008), "Women's Ritual Roles in the Cycle of Life," in N. Kaltsas and H. A. Shapiro (eds), *Worshiping Women: Ritual and Reality in Classical Athens*, 289–97, New York: Alexander S. Onassis Public Benefit Foundation.

Salvo, I. (2012), "Sweet Revenge: Emotional Factors in 'Prayers for Justice'," in A. Chaniotis (ed.), *Unveiling Emotions: Sources and Methods for the Study of Emotions in the Greek World*, 235–66, Stuttgart: Steiner.

Salvo, I. (2016), "Emotion, Persuasion and Gender in Greek Erotic Curses," in E. Sanders and M. Johncock (eds), *Emotion and Persuasion in Classical Antiquity*, 263–79, Stuttgart: Steiner.

Sanders, E. (2012), "'He Is a Liar, a Bounder, and a Cad': The Arousal of Hostile Emotions in Attic Forensic Oratory," in A. Chaniotis (ed.), *Unveiling Emotions: Sources and Methods for the Study of Emotions in the Greek World*, 359–87, Stuttgart: Steiner.

Sanders, E. (2014), *Envy and Jealousy in Classical Athens: A Socio-Psychological Approach*, Oxford: Oxford University Press.

Sanders, E., C. Thumiger, C. Carey, and N. J. Lowe, eds (2013), *Erôs in Ancient Greece*, Oxford: Oxford University Press.

Santangelo, F. (2013), *Divination, Prediction and the End of the Roman Republic*, Cambridge: Cambridge University Press

Sassi, M. M. (2001), *The Science of Man in Ancient Greece*, translated by P. Tucker, Chicago and London: University of Chicago Press.

Schauer, M. (2002), *Tragisches Klagen: Form und Funktion der Klagedarstellung bei Aischylus, Sophokles und Euripides*, Munich: Narr.

Scherer, K. R. (2005), "What Are Emotions? And How Can They Be Measured?" *Social Science Information* 44, no. 4: 693-727.

Scherer, K. R. and E. Coutinho (2013), "How Music Creates Emotion: A Multifactorial Process Approach," in T. Cochrane, B. Fantini, and K. R. Scherer (eds), *The Emotional Power of Music: Multidisciplinary Perspective on Musical Arousal, Expression, and Social Control*, Oxford: Oxford University Press, 121–45.

Scherer, K. R., A. Schorr, and T. Johnstone, eds (2001), *Appraisal Processes in Emotion: Theory, Method, Research*, Oxford: Oxford University Press.

Scheve, C. von and M. Salmela, eds (2014), *Collective Emotions*, Oxford: Oxford University Press.

Schiesaro, A. (1997), "The Boundaries of Knowledge in Virgil's *Georgics*," in T. Habinek and A. Schiesaro (eds), *The Roman Cultural Revolution*, 63–89, Cambridge: Cambridge University Press.

Schlam, C. C. (1992), *The Metamorphoses of Apuleius: On Making an Ass of Oneself*, Chapel Hill: University of North Carolina Press.

Schlapbach, K. (2008), "Lucian's *On Dancing* and the Models for a Discourse on Pantomime," in E. Hall and R. Wyles (eds), *New Directions in Ancient Pantomime*, 314–37, Oxford: Oxford University Press.

Schnell, R. (2007), "Historische Emotionsforschung: Eine mediävistische Standortbestimmung," *Frühmittelalterliche Studien* 38: 173–276.

Schnell, R. (2015), *Haben Gefühle eine Geschichte? Aporien einer History of Emotions*, Göttingen: Vandenhoeck and Ruprecht.

Schober, A. (1936), "Epigonos von Pergamon und die frühpergamenische Kunst," *Jahrbuch des Deutschen Archäologischen Instituts* 53: 126–49.

Schopenhauer, A. (1995), *On the Basis of Morality*, translated by E. F. J. Payne, Providence, RI: Berghahn.

Schweder, R. A. and J. Haidt (2000), "The Cultural Psychology of the Emotions," in M. Lewis and J. M. Haviland-Jones (eds), *Handbook of Emotions*, 397–414, New York: Guilford Press.

Scott, M. (1979), "Pity and Pathos in the *Iliad*," *Acta Classica* 22: 1–14.

Scruton, R. (1997), *The Aesthetics of Music*, Oxford: Oxford University Press.

Seaford, R. (1994), *Reciprocity and Ritual: Homer and Tragedy in the Developing City-State*, Oxford: Oxford University Press.

Sears, E. (1993), "Sensory Perception and its Metaphors in the Time of Richard of Fournival," in W. F. Bynum and R. Porter (eds), *Medicine and the Five Senses*, 17–39, Cambridge: Cambridge University Press.

Seidensticker, B. and M. Vöhler, eds (2006), *Gewalt und Ästhetik: Zur Gewalt und Ihrer Darstellung in der griechischen Klassik*, Berlin: De Gruyter.

Seltman, C. T. (1923–5), "Eros: In Early Attic Legend and Art," *Annual of the British School at Athens* 26: 88–105.

Settis, S., A. La Regina, and G. Agosti (1988), *La Colonna Traiana*, Turin: Einaudi.

Shapiro, H. A. (1991), "The Iconography of Mourning in Athenian Art," *American Journal of Archaeology* 95: 629–56.

Sharrock, A. (2011), "Womanly Wailing? Euryalus' Mother and Gendered Reading," *EuGeSta* 1: 55–77.

Shaver, P., J. Schwarz, D. Kirson, and C. O'Connor (1987), "Emotion and Emotion Knowledge: Further Explanations of a Prototype Approach," *Journal of Personality and Social Psychology* 52: 1061–86.

Shields, C. (1988), "Soul and Body in Aristotle," *Oxford Studies in Ancient Philosophy* 6: 103–37.

Shields, C. (2007), "The Priority of Soul in Aristotle's *De anima*: Mistaking Categories?" in D. Frede and B. Reis (eds), *Body and Soul in Ancient Philosophy*, 267–90, Berlin and New York: De Gruyter.

Siemer, M. and R. Reisenzein (2007), "Appraisals and Emotions: Can you Have the One without the Other?" *Emotion* 7: 26–9.

Sifakis, G. M. (1971), *Parabasis and Animal Choruses: A Contribution to the History of Attic Comedy*, London: Athlone.

Sigismund Nielsen, H. (1997), "Interpreting Epithets in Roman Epitaphs," in B. Rawson and P. Weaver (eds), *The Roman Family in Italy: Status, Sentiment, Space*, 169–204, Oxford: Oxford University Press.

Sihvola, J. and T. Engberg-Pedersen, eds (1998), *The Emotions in Hellenistic Philosophy*, Dordrecht: Kluwer.

Simon, B. (1978), *Mind and Madness in Ancient Greece: The Classical Roots of Modern Psychiatry*, Ithaca, NY: Cornell University Press.
Simpson, P. L. P. (1998), *A Philosophical Commentary on the Politics of Aristotle*, Chapel Hill and London: University of North Carolina Press.
Singer, P. (1992), "Some Hippocratic Mind–Body Problems," in A. López Férez (ed.), *Actas del VIIe Colloque International Hippocratique*, 131–43, Madrid: Universidad Nacional de Educación a Distancia.
Sittl, C. (1890), *Die Gebärden der Griechen und Römer*, Leipzig: Teubner.
Smith, M. (2011), "Empathy, Expansionism, and the Extended Mind," in A. Coplan and P. Goldie (eds), *Empathy: Philosophical and Psychological Perspectives*, 99–117, Oxford: Oxford University Press.
Sojc, N. (2005), *Trauer auf Attischen Grabreliefs: Frauendarstellungen zwischen Ideal und Wirklichkeit*, Berlin: Reimer.
Sokolowski, F. (1955), *Lois sacrées de l'Asie Mineure*, Paris: de Boccard.
Solomon, R. C. (2003), *Not Passion's Slave: Emotions and Choice*, Oxford: Oxford University Press.
Solomon, R. C. (2006), *True to Our Feelings: What Our Emotions Are Really Telling Us*, Oxford: Oxford University Press.
Sorabji, R. (2001), *Emotion and Peace of Mind: From Stoic Agitation to Christian Temptation*, Oxford: Oxford University Press.
Spatharas, D. (2017), "Sex, Politics, and Disgust in Aeschines' *Against Timarchus*," in D. Lateiner and D. Spatharas (eds), *The Ancient Emotion of Disgust*, 125–39, Oxford: Oxford University Press.
Squire, M. (2010), "Making Myron's Cow Moo? Ecphrastic Epigram and the Poetics of Simulation," *American Journal of Philology* 131: 589–634.
Stafford, E. (2013), "From the Gymnasium to the Wedding: Eros in Athenian Art and Cult," in E. Sanders, C. Thumiger, C. Carey, and N. J. Lowe (eds), *Erôs in Ancient Greece*, 175–208, Oxford: Oxford University Press.
Staley, G. A. (2010), *Seneca and the Idea of Tragedy*, Oxford: Oxford University Press.
Stearns, P. N. (1989), *Jealousy: The Evolution of an Emotion in American History*, New York: Oxford University Press.
Stearns, P. N. (1994) *American Cool: Constructing a Twentieth-Century Emotional Style*, New York: NYU Press.
Stearns, P. N. and C. Z. Stearns (1985), "Emotionology: Clarifying the History of Emotions and Emotional Standards," *American Historical Review* 90: 813–30.
Stearns, P. N. and C. Z. Stearns (1986), *Anger: The Struggle for Emotional Control in American History*, Chicago: University of Chicago Press.
Sternberg, R. H. (2006), *Tragedy Offstage: Suffering and Sympathy in Ancient Athens*, Austin: University of Texas Press.
Sternberg, R. H., ed. (2005), *Pity and Power in Ancient Athens*, Cambridge: Cambridge University Press.
Stevens, E. (1944), "Some Attic Commonplaces of Pity," *American Journal of Philology* 65: 1–24.
Stewart, A. (1995), "Rape?," in E. D. Reeder (ed.), *Pandora: Women in Classical Greece*, 74–90, Baltimore, MD: Walters Art Gallery.
Stewart, A. (1997), *Art, Desire, and the Body in Ancient Greece*, Cambridge: Cambridge University Press.
Stewart, A. (2004), *Attalos, Athens, and the Acropolis: The Pergamene "Little Barbarians" and their Roman and Renaissance Legacy*, Cambridge: Cambridge University Press.

Storbeck, J. and G. L. Clore (2007), "On the Interdependence of Cognition and Emotion," *Cognition and Emotion* 21: 1212–37.
Striker, G. (1996), "Emotions in Context: Aristotle's Treatment of the Passions in the *Rhetoric* and His Moral Psychology," in A. Oksenberg Rorty (ed.), *Essays on Aristotle's* Rhetoric, 286–302, Berkeley and Los Angeles: University of California Press.
Suter, A., ed. (2008a), *Lament: Studies in the Ancient Mediterranean and Beyond*, Oxford: Oxford University Press.
Suter, A. (2008b), "Male Lament in Greek Tragedy," in A. Suter (ed.), *Lament: Studies in the Ancient Mediterranean and Beyond*, 245–88, Oxford: Oxford University Press.
Swahn, J.-Ö. (1955), *The Tale of Cupid and Psyche*, Lund: Gleerup.
Tamiolaki, M. (2013), "Emotions and Historical Representation in Xenophon's *Hellenika*," in A. Chaniotis and P. Ducrey (eds), *Unveiling Emotions II. Emotions in Greece and Rome: Texts, Images, Material Culture*, 15–51, Stuttgart: Steiner.
Tarnopolsky, C. H. (2010), *Prudes, Perverts, and Tyrants: Plato's* Gorgias *and the Politics of Shame*, Princeton, NJ: Princeton University Press.
Tatum, W. J. (2007), "Social Commentary and Political Invective," in M. B. Skinner (ed.), *A Companion to Catullus*, 333–53, Malden, MA, and Oxford: Blackwell.
Taylor, M. W. (1992), *The Tyrant Slayers: The Heroic Image in Fifth Century B.C. Athenian Art and Politics*, Salem, NH: Ayer.
Telò, M. (2016), *Aristophanes and the Cloak of Comedy: From Affect to the Canon*, Chicago: University of Chicago Press.
Thumiger, C. (2013), "Early Medical Vocabulary of Insanity," in W. V. Harris (ed.), *Mental Disorders in the Classical World*, 61–96, Leiden: Brill.
Thumiger, C. (2016a), "Fear, Hope and the Definition of Hippocratic Medicine," in W. V. Harris (ed.), *Popular Medicine in Graeco-Roman Antiquity: Explorations*, 198–214, Leiden: Brill.
Thumiger, C. (2016b), "Grief and Cheerfulness in Early Greek Medical Writings," in P. R. Bosman (ed.), *Ancient Routes to Happiness*, 95–116, Pretoria: Classical Association of South Africa.
Thumiger, C. (2016c), "Patient Function and Physician Function in the Hippocratic Cases," in G. Petridou and C. Thumiger (eds), *Homo Patiens: Approaches to the Patient in the Ancient World*, 107–37, Leiden: Brill.
Thumiger, C. (2017), *A History of the Mind and Mental Health in Classical Greek Medical Thought*, Cambridge: Cambridge University Press.
Tooby, J. and L. Cosmides ([2001] 2010), "Does Beauty Build Adapted Minds? Towards an Evolutionary Theory of Aesthetics, Fiction, and the Arts," in B. Boyd, J. Carroll, and J. Gottschall (eds), *Evolution, Literature, and Film: A Reader*, 174–83, New York: Columbia University Press
Toynbee, J. M. C. (1971), *Death and Burial in the Roman World*, London: Thames and Hudson.
Treggiari, S. (1991), *Roman Marriage*, Oxford: Oxford University Press.
Tritle, L. (2014), "Ravished Minds in the Ancient World," in P. Meineck and D. Konstan (eds), *Combat Trauma and the Ancient Greeks*, 87–103, New York: Palgrave Macmillan.
Van der Eijk, P. J. (1997a), "The Matter of the Mind: Aristotle on the Biology of 'Psychic' Processes and the Bodily Aspects of Thinking," in W. Kullmann and S. Föllinger (eds), *Aristotelische Biologie: Intentionen, Methoden, Ergebnisse*, 221–58, Stuttgart: Steiner.
Van der Eijk, P. J. (1997b), "Towards a Rhetoric of Ancient Scientific Discourse: Some Formal Characteristics of Greek Medical and Philosophical Texts (Hippocratic Corpus, Aristotle)," in E. J. Bakker (ed.), *Grammar as Interpretation: Greek Literature in its Linguistic Contexts*, 77–129, Leiden: Brill.

Van der Eijk, P. J. (2000), "Aristotle's Psycho-physical Account of the Soul–Body Relationship," in J. P. Wright and P. Potter (eds), *Psyche and Soma: Physicians and Metaphysicians on the Mind–Body Problem from Antiquity to Enlightenment*, 57–77, Oxford: Oxford University Press.

Van der Eijk, P. J. (2005), *Medicine and Philosophy in Classical Antiquity: Doctors and Philosophers on Nature, Soul, Health and Disease*, Cambridge: Cambridge University Press.

Van Nijf, O. M. (2013), "Affective Politics: The Emotional Regime in the Imperial City," in A. Chaniotis and P. Ducrey (eds), *Unveiling Emotions II. Emotions in Greece and Rome: Texts, Images, Material Culture*, 351–68, Stuttgart: Steiner.

Vermeule, E. T. (1979), *Aspects of Death in Early Greek Art and Poetry*, Berkeley and Los Angeles: University of California Press.

Vernant, J.-P. and M. Detienne, eds (1979), *La Cuisine du sacrifice en pays grec*, Paris: Gallimard.

Versnel, H. (1987), "What Did Ancient Man See When He Saw a God? Reflections on Greek and Roman Epiphanies," in D. van der Plas (ed.), *Effigies Dei: Essays on the History of Religion*, 42–56, Leiden: Brill.

Viidebaum, L. (2015), "Creating the Rhetorical Tradition: The Reception of Lysias and Isokrates from Plato to Dionysios of Halikarnassos," unpublished PhD dissertation, Cambridge University.

Vindolanda Tablets Online, http://vindolanda.csad.ox.ac.uk/ (accessed March 17, 2018) (incorporates Bowman, A. and D. Thomas (1983), *Vindolanda: The Latin Writing Tablets*, London: Society for the Promotion of Roman Studies; and Bowman, A. and D. Thomas (1994), *The Vindolanda Writing Tablets*, London: British Museum Press).

Visvardi, E. (2015), *Emotion in Action: Thucydides and the Tragic Chorus*, Leiden: Brill.

Voutiras, E. (1998), *ΔΙΟΝΥΣΟΦΩΝΤΟΣ ΓΑΜΟΙ: Marital Life and Marriage in Fourth-Century Pella*, Amsterdam: Gieben.

Wagner-Hasel, B. (2006), "Die Reglementierung von Traueraufwand und die Tradierung des Nachruhms der Toten in Griechenland," in T. Späth and B. Wagner-Hasel (eds), *Frauenwelten in der Antike: Geschlechterordnung und weibliche Lebenspraxis*, 81–102, Stuttgart: J. B. Metzler.

Wallace, R. W. (2015), *Reconstructing Damon: Music, Wisdom Teaching, and Politics in Perikles' Athens*, Oxford: Oxford University Press.

Ward, J. K. (1996), "Aristotle on Philia: The Beginning of a Feminist Ideal of Friendship?," in J. K. Ward (ed.), *Feminism and Ancient Philosophy*, 155–71, New York: Routledge.

Waser, O. (1909), "Eros," in *Paulys Realencyclopädie zur classischen Altertumswissenschaft*, 6.484–542, Stuttgart: Metzler.

Watson, W. (2012), *The Lost Second Book of Aristotle's "Poetics,"* Chicago: University of Chicago Press.

Webb, R. (1997), "Imagination and the Arousal of the Emotions," in S. M. Braund and C. Gill (eds), *The Passions in Roman Thought and Literature*, 112–27, Cambridge: Cambridge University Press.

Webb, R. (2009), *Ekphrasis, Imagination, and Persuasion in Ancient Rhetorical Theory and Practice*, Farnham and Burlington, VT: Ashgate.

Webster, C. (2016), "Voice Pathologies and the Hippocratic 'Triangle'," in G. Petridou and C. Thumiger (eds), *Homo Patiens: Approaches to the Patient in the Ancient World*, 166–99, Leiden: Brill.

Wellhausen, J. (1878), *Prolegomena zur Geschichte Israels*, Berlin: Reimer.

Wenning, R. (1978), *Die Galateranatheme Attalos I: Eine Untersuchung zum Bestand und zur Nachwirkung pergamenischer Skulptur*, Pergamenische Forschungen 4, Berlin: De Gruyter.

Whitmarsh, T. (2004), "Philostratus," in I. J. F. de Jong, R. Nünlist, and A. Bowie (eds), *Narrators, Narratees, and Narratives in Ancient Greek Literature*, 423–39, Leiden: Brill.

Wierzbicka, A. (1999), *Emotions across Languages and Cultures: Diversity and Universals*, Cambridge: Cambridge University Press.

Wilamowitz-Moellendorff, U. von (1886), *Isyllos von Epidaurus*, Berlin: Weidmann.

Wilamowitz-Moellendorff, U. von (1931–2), *Der Glaube der Hellenen*, 2 vols, Berlin: Weidmann.

Winkler-Horaçek, L. (2011), "Sieger und Besiegte: Die großen Schlachtenanatheme der Attaliden," in R. Grüßinger, V. Kästner, and A. Scholl (eds), *Pergamon: Panorama der antiken Metropole*, 139–43, Berlin: Imhof.

Wisse, J. (1989), *Ethos and Pathos: From Aristotle to Cicero*, Amsterdam: Hakkert

Wisse, J. (1995), "Greeks, Romans and the Rise of Atticism," in J. Abbenes, S. Slings, and I. Sluiter (eds), *Greek Literary Theory after Aristotle: A Collection of Papers in Honour of D. M. Schenkeveld*, 65–82, Amsterdam: Vrije University Press.

Wissowa, G. (1912), *Religion und Kultus der Römer*, 2nd edition, Munich: Beck.

Wohl, V. (2011), "A Tragic Case of Poisoning: Intention between Tragedy and the Law," *Transactions of the American Philological Association* 140: 33–70.

Wycherley, R. (1954), "The Altar of *Eleos*," *Classical Quarterly* 4: 143–50.

Young, R. S. (1951), "An Industrial District of Ancient Athens," *Hesperia* 20: 135–288.

Zajonc, R. (1980), "Feeling and Thinking: Preferences need no Inferences," *American Psychologist* 35: 151–75.

Zajonc, R. (1984), "On the Primacy of Affect," *American Psychologist* 39: 117–24.

Zanker, P. (1975), "Grabreliefs römischer Freigelassener," *Jahrbuch des Deutschen Archäologischen Instituts* 90: 267–315.

Zanobi, A. (2014), *Seneca's Tragedies and the Aesthetics of Pantomime*, London and New York: Bloomsbury.

Zimmermann, M., ed. (2009), *Extreme Formen von Gewalt in Bild und Text des Altertums*, Munich: Utz.

Zunshine, L. (2006), *Why We Read Fiction: Theory of Mind and the Novel*, Columbus: Ohio State University Press.

INDEX

Italic numbers are used for illustrations.

Acharnians (Aristophanes) 73
Achilles 9
Ad Herennium 155
adfectus (emotions) 58, 156
Aeneid (Virgil) 114–16, 123
Aeschylus 66, 67, 69–70
affect program responses 2–3, 20
affection, concern and worry, in letters 134–6
Agamemnon (Aeschylus) 70
Agamemnon (Seneca) 79
Aidôs (goddess) 41
aidôs (shame) 5–6, 37, 39, 87–8, 113
aisthanesthai (feeling) 25, 26
Ajax (Sophocles) 66, 68
Althaea 35
amazement 122
amnesty agreements 151–2
Amor 88, 98, 99, 100
    See also Erôs (god)
ancient historians 13–15
Andocides 125–6
Andromache (Euripides) 68
anger
    Aristotle on 19, 22, 67, 73
    definition of 19, 67, 111
    divine 37, 38, 39
    in drama 67–8, 73, 74–5, 78–9
    as emotional therapy 25
    Epicurean ideas of 12
    in family life 141
    humors and 24
    metaphors for 9
    in oratory 158–9
    and pain 18
    as religious emotion 35
Annales (Ennius) 114
Anterôs (god) 42, *42*
Anthologia Graeca 100
Antingone (Sophocles) 68, 70
Antiphon 133–4
anxiety disorders 30
Aphorisms (Hippocrates) 29, 31

Aphrodite 39
Apollo 35, 36, 39, 40, 43
appraisal theory of emotions 35–6
Apuleius 39, 123
Aristides the Just 151
Aristides, Aelius 36–7, 40, 44–5
Aristides Quintilianus 57–8
Aristophanes 69, 71, 72–3, 118, 122
Aristotle
    on anger 19, 22, 67, 73
    on catharsis 56–7, 70–1, 110
    on comedy 71
    on disgust 118
    on emotions 10–11, 36, 110–11
    on envy 68–9
    on love 103
    on music 51–2, 53–4, 56
    on *nemesis* 68
    on pity and fear 64, 65, 66–7, 69, 105, 114
    on self-control 113
    on slaves 75
    on soul and body 18
    on tragedy 70–1
    on the voice 59
    on wonder 121
Aristoxenus of Tarentum 55, 57
Asclepius 36–7, 40, 44
asê (dizziness/disgust) 24, 30
ataraxia (psychological stability) 12
Athena 40
audience emotional responses 7
    to drama 64–5, 66–7, 70, 71, 72, 77, 78
    to literature 110, 113–14, 118, 119, 122
    in rhetorical theory 10
awe, of the divine 39, 40

Bacchants (Euripides) 67
Bacchylides 35, 36
basic emotions 2–3, 20
battles, responses to 40, 117
Bellum Civile (Lucan) 120–1

blindness 40
bodies, disgust at 118, 119–20
body and emotions 10, 12, 18, 19–33
body language in art 7–8, 84–8, *85*, *87*
brain and emotions 19–20, 21, 26–7, 28
Brothers (Terence) 75
Brutus (Cicero) 156

Cairns, Douglas 5–6, 36
Casina (Plautus) 75
categories of emotion 2–5, 12, 13, 45
catharsis, Aristotle on 56–7, 70–1, 110
Catoni, Maria Luisa 84
Catullus 111, 119, 120
Celsus 32
Chaniotis, Angelos 8, 37, 90
characters, emotions of in drama 65–71, 72–3, 82
children
    deaths of 92, *92*, 127, 138–9, *139*
    images of 88, 89, *139*
cholê (bile) 24
cholos (anger) 24
Cicero
    on *decorum* 93
    on disgusting acts 121
    on emotions 58
    on incest 120
    letters of affection 134, 141
    on *mirabilia* (marvels) 123
    on oratory 154–60, *155*
collective emotions 148–9, 150
Colombetti, Giovanna 22
combat trauma 40
comedy 63, 71–7
communal solidarity 38
concordia 100
Concordia (goddess) 43, *43*
conflicting emotions 111
Consolation to his Wife (Plutarch) 92, 139, 140
contional oratory 159–60
conversion disorder 40
corpses, disgust at 119, 120–1
cults 36, 37, 41, 43–4
cures, evidence of emotion in 36–7
curse tablets 36, 103, 131–3

dance 60–1
Davies, Glenys 7–8
De anima (Aristotle) 10–11, 18, 19
De oratore (Cicero) 154–7

De re publica (Cicero) 123
De rerum natura (Lucretius) 12
decorum and restraint 93, 110–11
delight 37, 40
Demosthenes 114, 118–19, 128
depression 30–1
despondency 17, 30–1
dexiôsis (handshake) 100–2, *101*
dextrarum iunctio (handshake) 102, *102*
diaphragm and emotions 20, 21–2, 25
Dioscuri 40
Diseases of Women (Hippocrates) 28, 30
disgust 20, 24, 30, 117–21, 147
distributed cognition 22
Dixon, Thomas 2
domestic violence 145
drama 63–81
    Greek tragedy 63–71
    New Comedy 74–7
    Old Comedy 63, 71–4, 118
    Roman tragedy 78–81
drama studies 6–7
dramatic festivals 64, 71
dusanios (hard to please/easily annoyed/ grumpy) 30, 31
dusthumiê (despondency) 17, 30–1
Dying Gaul 104–6

Ekman, Paul 2
ekplêxis (amazement) 122
Electra (Euripides) 69, 70
Elpis (goddess) 44
emotion codes 84, 90
emotion, definitions and categorization of 2–5, 10, 12, 13
    anger 19, 67, 111
    love 69, 76
    pity 65–6, 105
    religious emotions 35–6
emotion research in Classics 5–9
emotional communities 6
emotional disturbances 26–7
emotive qualities of art 103–7
enargeia (vividness) 14
Encomium of Helen (Gorgias) 9
Ennius 114
envy, in drama 68–9, 71
epics 112
Epicureans 11–12
Epidaurus 36
Epidemics (Hippocrates) 17, 24, 26, 28, 29, 30–1

epigrams 89, 100, 119–20, 153
epilepsy 19
epiphanic emotions 36, 39–41, 44–5
epitaphs 129, 131
    See also funerary monuments
Erôs (god) 41–3, *42*, 88, 96–8, *97–8*
erotic desire in visual arts 96–8, *97–9*, 100
erotic passion in drama 69–70, 74
erotic pursuit in art 87, *87*
Eudemian Ethics (Aristotle) 11
Eunuch (Terence) 76
eupatheiai (good emotions) 13
euphêmia (good conduct) 38
Euripides
    on *aidôs* (shame) 41
    on anger 67–8
    on envy 68
    on fear 67
    on grief and mourning 90
    on love 69, 96, 97
    on pity 66
    on shrine of Iphigeneia 137
    tragedies of 63
euthumiê (happiness) 24
excitement 106–7
expressions 3, 84, *85*, 86

facial expressions 3, 84, *85*, 86
familial affection 126–31
family disputes 141–3
fear
    appealing to the gods 136–7
    of the divine 37
    in drama 64, 67
    medical understanding 17, 18, 20, 21
    in public life 150
    rituals and 37
feeling 25, 26
fellowship 37
festivals of drama 64, 71
festivals, religious 37–8
fevers, symptoms of 17
forensic oratory 158–60
Fortenbaugh, William 5
Foucault, Michel 131
Franzoni, Claudio 86, 88
Frede, Michael 19
frescoes 93–4, *94*, 98, *99*, 100
friendship 69, 73, 74
Frogs (Aristophanes) 69, 72–3, 122
funerary monuments
    dexiôsis (handshake) on 101–2, *101–2*
    grief on 89, 138, *139*
    hope on 153–4
    of nurses, nannies etc 129–31, *130*
funerary rituals 38, *49*, 90–2, *91–2*, 95–6
Furies, role in tragedy 79

Galen 30, 31
gender
    in displays of love 102–3
    in grief and mourning *49*, 90–6, *91–2*
Georgics (Virgil) 123
gestures in art 84, 86–8
Giuliani, Luca 105, 106
gloominess 30, 31
gnômê (mind) 28–9
Golden Ass (Apuleius) 123
good conduct 38
good emotions 13
Gorgias 9, 109, 110
Greater Attalid Dedication 103–6, *104*
Greek music 47–58, *49–52*
    community responses 48
    effects of 53–6
    mimesis of emotion 50–3
    mousikê (poetic performance) 47–8
    textual sources for 48, 50–1
    as therapy 56–8
Greek public life 147–54
Greek tragedy 63–71
Green, Richard 72
grief
    in drama 70
    and mourning in art *49*, 89, 90–6, *91–2*, 138, *139*
    in private life 138–41
    in public life 149
    regulation of mourning 38
Griffiths, Paul 2
Gross, Daniel 3
group dynamics and decision making 152–3
guest friendship 37

Halliwell, S. 144
handshakes 101–2, *101–2*
happiness 24
Harmonia (goddess) 44
Harmonic Elements (Aristoxenus) 55
harmony in music 50–1
health, emotions in 19–25
heart and emotions 12, 20, 24–5
Hecuba (Euripides) 66
hêdonai (pleasures) 37

Helen (Euripides) 70
Helen (Gorgias) 109, 110
Heracles (Euripides) 69, 70
Hercules Mad (Seneca) 79
Herodotus 14, 15, 40, 116, 121
Hesiod 35, 36, 41
Hippocrates 17, *18*, 19–33
Hippolytus (Euripides) 96, 97
Hipponax 118
history and the classics 1–15
    ancient historians 13–15
    emotion research 5–9
    emotions, definitions of 2–5
    theories of emotion 9–13
Holmes, Brooke 23–4, 33
Hölscher, Tonio 105
Homer
    on amazement 122–3
    on anger 35
    on disgust 119
    on epiphanies 40
    on familial affection 126–7
    on gods and cults 37, 39, 41
    on laughter 112
    on mixed emotions 111
    on pity 14, 113–14
Homeric Hymns 39, 127
honor and shame 5–6
hope 44, 153–4
Horace 121
houses and inheritance 142–3, *142–4*
humors in medicine 20, 21, 23–5, 26–7, 28, 31

iambic poetry 118
Iamblichus of Chalcis 48, 57
Iliad (Homer)
    amazement in 122–3
    anger in 35
    disgust in 119
    epiphanies in 40
    gods and cults in 39, 41
    laughter in 112
    mixed emotions in 111
    pity in 113–14
ill-will 37
imagination 6
imperial cults 37
In Verrem (Cicero) 159
incest, disgust at 120
inheritance disputes 141–3, *142–4*
initiations, religious 39

insanity 26–7, 28
Institutes of Oratory (Quintilian) 59, 60
instrumental music 55–6
intelligence 20, 22, 25, 27
Internal Affections (Hippocrates) 24
invective and disgust 121
invidia (ill-will) 37
Ion (Euripides) 68
Ion (Plato) 109, 110
Iphigenia among the Taurians (Euripides) 137
Iphigenia in Aulis (Euripides) 63, 67
Iris 40

James, William 1
jealousy, in drama 68, 75–6
Jouanna, Jacques 29
joy 13, 36, 37, 38, 73–4
Jupiter 37, 40
Juvenal 111

Kampen, N. 130
katharsis (purgation) 56–7, 70–1, 110
Knights (Aristophanes) 71
Konstan, David 6
Kosmopoulou, A. 129

Lake Regillis, battle of 40
language and music 59–60
language of emotion 144–5
laughter 71–2
Laws (Plato) 10, 50, 52
letters 134–7, 139–41
Letters to Atticus (Cicero) 134, 141
Libanius 61
Life of Caesar (Suetonius) 123
liking 100, 101–2, *101*, 103
literature 109–24
    disgust 117–21
    emotions in 109–12
    pity 14, 113–17
    theory of emotions 112–13
    wonder 121–4
literature studies 6–7, 8
Livy 117
Lloyd, Geoffrey 2
loom weights 127–8, *129*
love
    definition of 69, 76
    in drama 69, 74, 76–7
    in family life 126–31
    gods of 41–3

in marriage 131–4
in visual arts 96–103
love magic 132–4
Lucan 120–1
Lucian 60–1
Lucretius 12
Ludovisi Gaul 104–6, *104*
lupê (pain) 18, 23, *23*, 31
Lysias 152
Lysistrata (Aristophanes) 73

Marathon, battle of 40
Marcus Antonius (orator) 157–8
marriage 100–2, 131–4
Martial 120
marvels 123
masks, use of in comedy 72, 74, 77
Medea (Euripides) 67, 68
Medea (Seneca) 79
medical and scientific understanding 17–33
    health, emotions in 19–25
    symptoms, emotions as 25–32
medical uses of music 56–7
melancholikos (black-bilious) 28–9
melancholy 28–9, 31, 32–3
Meleager 35, 36
melody in music 53–5
Menander 74–5, *75*–6
menstruation 30, 31
mental disorders 26–7
Metamorphoses (Ovid) 120
metaphors 8–9
midwives 129–30, *130*
military epiphanies 40
mime 64
mimesis of music 51–4
mind 28–9
mirabilia (marvels) 123
misericordia (sympathy) 14, 66, 105, 157
modesty of women 87–8
mood 27–8
moral and social norms and emotions 6–7
motherhood 89, *139*
mothers and daughters, relationships between 127–8
motus animi 5
mourning. *See* grief
mousikê (poetic performance), definition of 47–8
music and dance 47–61
    dance 60–1

    Greek antiquity 47–58
    Roman antiquity 58–61

nannies 128–9
Nemesis (goddess) 41, 42, 88
nemesis (rightful indignation) 37, 68
Neumann, Gerhard 86
New Comedy 63, 74–7
Nicomachean Ethics (Aristotle) 11, 103
non-verbal behavior 7–8
nurses 92, *92*, 128–31

Odyssey (Homer) 37, 112, 113–14, 119, 126–7
Oedipus (Seneca) 79
offerings to the gods 44
Ogden, Daniel 68
Old Comedy 63, 71–4, 118
omens, prophecies and portents 123
On Anger (Philodemus) 12
On Anger (Seneca) 78
On Breaths (Hippocrates) 23
On Dance (Lucian) 60–1
On Enthusiasm (Theophrastus) 57
On Humors (Hippocrates) 20–1
On Music (Aristides Quintilianus) 57–8
On Regimen (Hippocrates) 26, 27, 32
On the Ideal Orator (Cicero) 58
On the Nature of Things (*De rerum natura*) (Lucretius) 12
On the Sacred Disease (Hippocrates) 19, 21, 24, 25, 26, 28
On the Soul (*De anima*) (Aristotle) 10–11, 18, 19
On the Sublime 1, 14, 122
Orator (Cicero) 158
oratory 59–60, 154–60
Orestes (Euripides) 67, 69, 70
ostracism in Athens 150–1, *151*
Ovid 120

pain 18, 23, *23*, 31
paintings 93–4, *94*, 98, *99*, 100
Panegyricus (Pliny the Younger) 160
pantomime and music 60
paradoxical and unnatural events 123
parents in comedy 75
pathê of the soul 5, 10, 12–13, 18
pathos (emotion) 4, 38, 65, 88, 104, 154–5, 156
pax deorum 37–8
Peace (Aristophanes) 73, 118

Persians (Aeschylus) 70
personification of emotions 36, 41–4, 88–9
Petronius 123–4
Phaedo (Plato) 111
Phaedrus (Plato) 9, 96
Philebus (Plato) 9
philia (liking) 100, 101–2, *101*, 103
Philippics (Cicero) 121
Philippus of Pergamon 161
Philoctetes (Sophocles) 66, 69, 70
Philodemus 12
phobias 29–30
phobos (fear). *See* fear
Phobos (god) 43, 44
Phoenician Women (Euripides) 69
Phoenician Women (Seneca) 79
phrikê (shivering in excitement) 106–7
phronêsis (intelligence) 20, 22, 25, 27
Phylarchus 14
Pietas (goddess) 44
Pisistratus 40
pity
   in art 105
   definition of 65–6, 105
   in drama 64–6, 69
   in literature 14, 113–17
   in oratory 157–60
Plato
   on audience response 109, 110, 118
   on conflicts of emotion 111
   on desire 96
   on music 48, 50, 52–3
   on pleasure 37
   on self-control 70, 113
   on wonder 121
   works on emotions 9–10
Plautus 63, 75, 119–20
pleasure 37
Pliny the Elder 41, 44, 93
Pliny the Younger 123, 131, 134–5, 139, 160
Plutarch 37, 39, 92, 106, 127, 139, 140
pneuma (a mixture of fire and air) 12
Poetics (Aristotle) 11, 51–2, 64, 66, 71, 121
Politics (Aristotle) 53–4, 56
Polybius 14, 116–17, 152–3
Porphyry of Tyre 57
Postumius, Aulus 40
postures in art 86
pre-emotions 13, 78
Prinz, Jesse 3, 22
Prioux, Évelyne 86
Priscus 114

private life 125–45
   familial affection 126–31
   family disputes 141–3
   gods, appeals to 136–7
   grief and condolence 138–41
   husbands and wives, emotions of 131–4
   letters of affection 134–6
Pro Caelio (Cicero) 120
Problems (ps. Aristotle) 54, 55
Prometheus Bound (Aeschylus) 66
Prorrhetic (Hippocrates) 26
prothesis scenes 49, 90–1
pseudo-Andocides 119
pseudo-Aristotle 54, 55
pseudo-Demetrius 118
psychagogic power of music 48, 55
psychological conditions 23–4, 28–32
psychological stability 12
psychotherapy and music 57–8
public life 147–61
   Greek world 147–54
   Roman world 154–60
Pudicitia (goddess) 44
Pythagoras 48
Pythagoreans 57

Quintilian 59, 60, 74, 93–4, 156

reason and emotions 11, 78
regulation of emotions 86, 112–13
religion and spirituality 35–45
   epiphanic emotions 39–41
   objects and personifications 41–4
   ritual emotions 37–8
religious appeals 136–7
Republic (Plato) 9–10, 53, 113
research in Classics on emotions 5–9
revenge 13–14
rhetoric and emotions 10, 14, 110–11, 155
Rhetoric (Aristotle) 10, 59, 65, 110–11, 114
rhythm in music 50–1, 53–5
ritual emotions 35–6, 37–8
Roman music 58–61
Roman public life 154–60
Roman tragedy 63–4, 78–81
romantic passion in comedy 76
Rufus of Ephesus 32–3
Russell, James A. 2

Sacred Tales (Aristides) 40, 44–5
sacrifices 37–8
Samia (Menander) 74–5

Sanders, Ed 68, 71
Satires (Horace) 121
Satires (Juvenal) 111
satyr plays 64
Satyricon (Petronius) 123–4
scales in music 52–3
schêmata (form/shape/appearance etc) 84, 86
scientific understanding. *See* medical and scientific understanding
sculptures 84, *85*, 86, 103–6, *104*
    See also funerary monuments
self-control of emotions 86, 112–13
Self-Tormentor (Terence) 75
Semonides 118, 145
senatorial oratory 159–60
Seneca 13, 61, 63–4, 72, 78–9, 81
servants 75, 91–2, *92*, 128–9, 131
Servius Sulpicius Galba (consul 144 BCE) 156–7
Seven against Thebes (Aeschylus) 67
shame 5–6, 37, 39, 70, 87–8, 113
shamelessness in comedy 73, 75
Shorn Girl (Menander) 75–6
Singer, Peter 17
slaves 75, 91–2, *92*, 128–9, 131
smells, disgust at 118, 119–20, 147
Sophocles 66, 68, 69, 70, 132
soul
    and emotions 9, 19, 26, 27–8, 33
    pathê of 5, 10, 12–13, 18
speech, power of 110
Spes (goddess of hope) 44
statues 8, 40
Stewart, Andrew 105
Stoics 11, 12–13
Strabo 147
Suetonius 123
suffering "other" in art 103–7, *104*
Suppliants (Aeschylus) 67
Suppliants (Euripides) 90
supplication and fear 37
sympathy 14, 66, 105, 157
symptoms of illness 17, 19, 25–32

Tacitus 14, 117
Terence 63, 75, 76, 117
terpsis (delight) 37, 40
terror 14, 23
Teutoburg forest, battle of 117
textiles and women 127–8, *129*, 137
Theophrastus 57
theories of emotion 9–13, 112

therapeutic effect of music 57–8
Thesmophoriazusae (Aristophanes) 73
Thetis 39
Thucydides 13, 14, 37, 110, 116
thumoeides (spirit, passion) 9
thusia (pleasure) 37
Thyestes (Seneca) 79
Timaeus (Plato) 10
Timanthes 93
tombs. *See* funerary monuments
Trachiniae (Sophocles) 70, 132
Tractatus Coislianus 71
tragedy
    Greek 63–71
    Roman 63–4, 78–81
Trajan's column 40
Treggiari, S. 131
tristes 37–8
tromos (terror) 14, 23

unnatural and paradoxical events 123

Valerius Maximus 93
veils, uses in art 87–8, *92*, 93–5
vengeance 13–14
Verrines (Cicero) 158
Vindolanda letters 135–6
violence against women 145
Virgil 114–16, 123
virtues 11, 13
visual arts 83–108
    affects and attitudes: love 96–103
    embodied emotions 84–9
    emotive images: suffering "other" 103–7
    gender and status: grief and mourning 90–6
visual culture 7–8
Vitellius 14
vividness 14
voice and emotions 59–60
votive textiles 137, *138*

Wagner-Hasel, Beate 93
war, epiphanies during 40
Wasps (Aristophanes) 73
wet nurses 128–9
Wierzbicka, Anna 4–5
women
    diseases of 28–9, 30–1
    disgust of 118, 119
    domestic violence 145
    and drama 64

in drama 67–8, 70
friendships of 135–6
and love 103, 131–4
modesty of 87–8
mother and daughter relationships 127–8
and mourning 38, 90–3
servants and other household members 128–31
and textiles 137

votive textiles of 137
Women of Trachis (Sophocles) 68
wonder 121–4
worship of emotions 41

xenia (guest-friendship) 37
Xenophon 126, 149

Zeus 37, 39

www.ingramcontent.com/pod-product-compliance
Ingram Content Group UK Ltd.
Pitfield, Milton Keynes, MK11 3LW, UK
UKHW060306251125
465390UK00013B/583